Welcome To My Nightmare

Fifty Years of Alice Cooper

Martin Popoff

Welcome To My Nightmare

Fifty Years of Alice Cooper

Martin Popoff

WP
WYMER
PUBLISHING
Bedford, England

First published in Great Britain in 2018
by Wymer Publishing
www.wymerpublishing.co.uk
Tel: 01234 326691
Wymer Publishing is a trading name of Wymer (UK) Ltd

Typeset by The Andys.
Printed and bound in England by Gomer Press.

A catalogue record for this book is available from the British Library.

Cover design by The Andys.
Hardback edition, front cover photo © Alan Perry (Milton Keynes Bowl, 3rd June 2006)
Paperback edition, front cover photo © Bill Baran (Molson Amphitheatre, Toronto, 13th July 2012)

Inner page photo credits:
P9: Notting Hill, London, 1971 © Geoff A Howard / Alamy Stock Photo; P14: The Earwigs, USA, 1964 (unknown); P16: The Earwigs, 1965 (unknown); P24: USA, 1968 © Pictorial Press Ltd / Alamy Stock Photo; P30: USA, 1969 (unknown); P32: USA, 1969 (unknown); P46: circa 1970 (unknown); P50: USA, November 1971 © Trinity Mirror / Mirrorpix / Alamy Stock Photo; P62: USA, 1972 © Marka / Alamy Stock Photo; P64-65: circa 1972 (unknown); P66: Munich beer festival, 16th November 1972) © Keystone Pictures USA / Alamy Stock Photo; P67: circa 1972 (unknown); P72: with Salvador Dali, 1973 (unknown); P73: Arriving in London ahead of his tour, 15th March 1974. © Trinity Mirror / Mirrorpix / Alamy Stock Photo; P74-76: circa 1974 (unknown); P77: No More Mr Nice Guy promo shot, 1973 © UtCon Collection / Alamy Stock Photo; P78: circa 1974 (unknown); P83-86: circa 1974 (unknown); P96: Grammy Awards, Los Angeles with Stevie Wonder, 1974 (unknown); P97: London Airport, 15th March 1974 © Trinity Mirror / Mirrorpix / Alamy Stock Photo; P99: circa 1974 (unknown); P103: USA, 1974 © Pictorial Press Ltd / Alamy Stock Photo; P104: 17th May 1975, Assembly Center, Tulsa, Oklahoma © Richard Galbraith; P108: circa 1975 © Pictorial Press Ltd / Alamy Stock Photo; P110: Empire Theatre, Liverpool, 14th September 1975 © Alan Perry; P112: 17th May 1975, Assembly Center, Tulsa, Oklahoma © Richard Galbraith; P116: Empire Theatre, Liverpool, 14th September 1975 © Alan Perry; P118: Empire Theatre, Liverpool, 14th September 1975 © Alan Perry; P120: France, 1975 © Philippe Gras / Alamy Stock Photo; P121: Riverside Park, New York City, 12th August 75 © Lewton Cole / Alamy Stock Photo; P129: (unknown); P133: 14th April 1979, Norman Center, Norman, Oklahoma © Richard Galbraith; P135-6: 14th April 1979, Norman Center, Norman, Oklahoma © Richard Galbraith; P143-6: Hammersmith Odeon, 14th February 1982 © Alan Perry; P148: (unknown); P152, 154, 156 & 159: Molson Amphitheatre, Toronto, 13th July 2012 © Trevor Shaikin; P165: Molson Amphitheatre, Toronto, 13th July 2012; P168: Chicago, Illinois, 20th July 1991 © Gene Ambo / MediaPunch; P173: Freddy's Dead: The Final Nightmare, 1991© New Line Cinema/courtesy; P183: Cincinnati Gardens, Cincinnati, Ohio, 13th January 1988 © Rod Dysinger; P187-8: © Bill Baran; P192: Molson Amphitheatre, Toronto, 13th July 2012 © Bill Baran; P194: British Comedy Awards 2003, BBC Television Centre, London, 10th December 2003 © Allstar Picture Library / Alamy Stock Photo; P196: Molson Amphitheatre, Toronto, 13th July 2012 © Bill Baran; P198: (top) Molson Amphitheatre, Toronto, 13th July 2012 © Bill Baran, (bottom) Alice receiving the 2,243rd Star on the Hollywood Walk Fame in Los Angeles, 2nd December 2003 © Tsuni / USA / Alamy Stock Photo; P199: Celebrity hole-in-one golf tournament, Ojai, California, 1st July 2002 © Zuma Press, Inc. / Alamy Stock Photo; P202-6, 208 & 210: Milton Keynes Bowl, 3rd June 2006 © Alan Perry; P212: © Trevor Shaikin; P216, 218 & 220: Molson Amphitheatre, Toronto, 13th July 2012 © Bill Baran; P225: Alice with his wife, Sheryl Goddard at 2013 Toronto International Film Festival at Roy Thomson Hall) © Splash News / Alamy Stock Photo; P227: Rose Smith, Neal Smith, Sheryl Goddard, Alice Cooper at the premiere of Super Duper Alice Cooper during the 2014 Tribeca Film Festival, at Chelsea Bow-Tie Cinemas, New York City) © Splash News / Alamy Stock Photo.

INTRO

So here we are, people, and it's hard to believe — a half century of Alice Cooper living his nine lives constantly in front of ours, in the peripheral vision, a cultural touchstone whether you wanted to devote the eyeballs or not. That's really how I look at good ol' Alice now, as a force of nature who has been there always, basically my whole conscious life, from childhood through to many times interviewing him and meeting him and being confronted with a new record, Alice at middle age, Alice in old age, Alice relentlessly participating in American life.

And that last bit? I've thought hard about this. I actually can't think of anybody who has packed more living into 70 years in any field of endeavour, ever. You want sports? Alice played baseball, softball, ran through the desert, became a massive golfer of quantity and quality. Girls? Alice partook of every rock star fantasy, but also had a long-time glamorous girlfriend, then met a sweetheart in Sheryl and they've been together since the mid-'70s, rock's best success at marriage. Even though they had their dramas too where she actually lit out for a spell — again, tick another life box.

Medical drama? Alice almost died as child, had asthma, almost killed himself with booze twice (and who knows what the cocaine and crack did to his insides), and still walks, stalks and most definitely talks amongst us. And what of living that blessed and blitzed-out life? Where's that on this form? Okay, check. He was the best at beer, did a heckuva job at hard booze, could snort with the best of them and was a mad scientist with crack. And just to annoy us all, he functioned at a high-energy burn rate through 80% of it, maybe 90%, doing the work of two or three rock 'n' rollers everyday.

Career? Alice was the leader (let's face it), in a high school band, a garage band that made sides, a psych band that made albums for Frank Zappa, and the world's first big shock rock band, huge in the early '70s (but never as big as they always boast). Then he mounted a legendary tour of huge elaborate fun as a solo artist, did a Bowie for a few years (with ballads), became a new wave artist, a successful hair metal goofball, and then has tried out another four, five personas and directions since.

Further on career, toured all the time, everywhere. On loads of TV and in quite a few movies. Worked with Dali, knew all the old Hollywood greats from multiple generations before him. *Muppets,*

Hollywood Squares, the talk shows, and let's not even get into radio and print.

Back to personal, two great kids (and Dash an' him do cars, like Alice needs another hobby), a deep spiritual and church life, great parents and in-laws. Lived—and not just dabbled—in Los Angeles, Phoenix, Detroit, Connecticut, Chicago and New York City. And like I say, snapped to the MO I maintain as "How the heck can anybody pack more in to 70 years?" hit some of these places multiple times and really experienced them.

Knew people? Pfft. More than anybody. Plus how many interviews, meet and greets, restaurant meals, parties? Get all the way out of town. Which he did. Alice has seen high quality vacationing too. Major establishment, stand-up guy, incredibly charitable with his time and money, and at the same time, was more than once the most incendiary figure sucking up all the oxygen in America (and even efficiently hated in LA at the beginning as just too freaky, if you can believe it).

The loopy thing is that I'm positive I'm leaving out lots (you'll find them as you read the book). But I'm glad he did it, and I'm glad he's been this distant buddy in my life—actually Dennis Dunaway even more so, like more than an acquaintance—through so many phases.

If I may venture my favourite two memories — One is filmy, almost dream-stated. But I can picture the shot in my head, snake, on stage, shot from below, white leotard… I used to think this was in *Time,* which we got at the house as kids, but folks now tell me it was *Newsweek.* I was about ten, already into rock, but to have this monster invade the establishment like this was impactful. And no one looked as white-knuckle edgy and frightening at the time. Plus they backed it up with music I thought was pretty heavy at that age, and then turns out, Alice wasn't a heavy metal act until Kane.

That point bears a little side-trip: in the '70s, I only liked heavy metal, but Alice, using his usual charms, had me on the Alice train. It only takes a trawl from *Pretties for You* through *Muscle of Love* to realise I'd been duped—but I like it. Part B of memory one however, which lined up with Alice in *Newsweek* (?) was the whole visual horror of *Killer* and *Billion Dollar Babies.* And, yes, even *School's Out* and *Muscle of Love,* the first like a threat to an institution that gave me structure and an extended family, the second… it just seemed like a package made for drug trafficking.

Strong memory number two is the anticipation and then viewing of the *Welcome to My Nightmare* album come to life on TV. Growing up in the interior of BC, there were no big cities so not a lot of direct exposure to rock stuff (granted I was 11). You got your fix through the record stores and going to L&J Bookstore downtown Trail and buying *Creem, Circus* and *Hit Parader.* For TV, there was pretty much *Don Kirshner's Rock Concert* and *The Midnight Special,* but here comes Alice with a real show (Kiss of course did it later too).

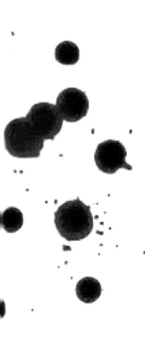

As well, it's hard to believe, but do the math: by a slim margin, *Welcome to My Nightmare* was Alice's heaviest album yet. Stupid but true. It's easy to remember only the title track, "Some Folks" and "Only Women Bleed," but there were actual properly recorded heavy guitars here. I gotta say, Ezrin gets too much credit. The classic Alice albums from *Love It to Death* through *Muscle of Love* generally sound like crap, thin and mid-rangey, no warmth, no power.

Granted, I keep forgetting this is the early '70s. Still, Sabbath, Deep Purple and most successfully Uriah Heep had some good sounding records. Plus it was even easier to dial in the medium rock that—let's face it—was the Alice Cooper group's stock and trade. And then as I often maintain, after *Montrose* and *Dark Side of the Moon* in 1973, no one had an excuse for bad fidelity any more. To Ezrin's credit, *Welcome to My Nightmare* is a good sounding record, but someone's gotta call him out on the early ones because no one ever seems to bring that up. So I just did: they are badly produced, from the point of view of sonic range anyway. I dunno, call it engineering if you want, because I know Bob did a million other things to help.

Okay, enough. I'll have plenty of space to pontificate in the mini-intros to come throughout the book. But I do want to comment on the structure of the book. This timeline with quotes thing, I've done this like a dozen times now and I still don't have a solid sense if readers like it a lot, like it a little or don't like it. So I continue forward blind on that. But I do like it for certain things, especially, looping back, for a life so packed full, which means lots of digressions.

Plus this allows us to keep tabs on the other important figures in Alice's life (his musical life—this is mostly a book about music and even more pointedly, focussing on the records). So I hope you find this a satisfying read. Like I say, I've used this for bands like Ozzy, Mötley, Maiden, Purple (twice) and Yes, along with a massive early history of heavy metal (ending in 1971!), another on hair metal, two books on the New Wave of British Heavy Metal and an 800-page trilogy on thrash (all is explained at martinpopoff.com).

I like it because in the end, it makes for a natural and easy read, given its sort of multiple forced paragraph breaks, as it were. What I don't like is that my own conversational and opinion flow is taken out of regular circulation, and that's the reason for the recurring mini intros, which I think serve as segues, regular check-ins from the author to see if you're doing okay. On that front, you might have seen already in the contents how I break up the chunks of time. I thought long and hard about this. I went with spans for everything except the '70s, which I broke down one year at a time, given the bustle of activity that takes place during that decade.

Quick point on how the sequence of dates work: January 1968 goes before any event in January where I know the actual day. Similarly, with year: 1968 goes before January 1968. Plus you'll get the hang of where early, mid and late go, plus the seasons. I think I've been consistent here, although I may have cheated a little if I wanted the actual stuff discussed to line up more sensibly, i.e. for the sake of the narrative.

So that's it. Like I say, I have built in spots to say more later so we can leave it at this for now. A quick flip of the book, and it becomes obvious what you get, and that's hard fact snapped to a temporal grid with buckets of oral history, dialogue, to back up or elaborate on the event or point at hand, to give it some humanity and substantiation.

Although, ha ha, one final thing, the Alice Cooper camp are one of the best, first examples of fake news as applied to a rock band, the generating of rumours and exaggeration from the inside, or the allowing of imaginations to run wild with no refutation. So many of these stories told by the guys are told quite differently by the next guy who was there, that at times, I just wanted to throw up my hands (witness "the chicken incident").

So suffice to say, any given ardent Alice expert is gonna spot things and say, "That's not how that happened." But I gotta tell ya, I'm all too aware of, say, the different crowd size numbers or the different dollar amounts or the different sequence of events over those days and months, but I've taken the stance of letting the guy tell his story. Some things, sure, I've qualified and even given you a couple or three sides, but often, I'm just letting one guy… lie, and as I could tell, given my excellent bullshit detector, sometimes quite knowingly and aggressively, sometimes just forgetting, sometimes just adding 10% like a good salesman would.

Frig, this went long. Sorry. Let's stop. It's a bloody big book. On with the show.

Martin Popoff
martinp@inforamp.net

1940 – 1959

Given that we are just starting this journey and you've just heard from me at length, I'm not going to say much here, in this first intro by major year grouping. Suffice to say Alice finds himself bumping and scraping his way through a childhood that serves as a microcosm for his future life as busy as any human being's ever, bar none, redundancy intended.

His colourful parents, salt of the earth, nonetheless live on the edge of getting by and they move around for the sake of Alice's health. He and his sisters' soak in American culture, participate in the world and generally have a childhood stuffed with American apple pie but also a modicum of drama. All of this will serve Alice well as he throws himself into American cultural life while simultaneously throwing American cultural life into his life's work.

December 14, 1942. Richard Allen "Dick" Wagner is born, in Oelwein, Iowa.

December 9, 1946. Dennis Dunaway is born in Cottage Grove, Oregon.

September 23, 1947. Neal Smith is born in Akron, Ohio.

November 10, 1947. Glen Buxton is born in Akron, Ohio.

February 4, 1948. Vincent "Alice Cooper" Damon Furnier (middle name being a nod to writer Damon Runyon) is born at the Saratoga Community Hospital (a.k.a. "the butcher shop") in northeast Detroit, Michigan, to parents Ether and Ella Mae. The Furniers would soon move to Los Angeles to try help with Vincent's infantile asthma, shortly after which they would be back in east Detroit, a multi-cultural area of Italians, Poles and Irish, where Alice's dad was "an honest used car salesman."

March 25, 1949. Producer-to-be Robert Alan "Bob" Ezrin is born, in Toronto, Canada.

1951. The Furniers move to Phoenix, again, the idea being that the dry heat would be good for Vincent. Alice was regularly using an inhaler for his blocked bronchial tubes. Alice's father also had battled asthma. The Dunaways also leave Oregon and move to Phoenix.

1953. The Furniers move back to Detroit again for a few years. When he wasn't playing baseball or going to the movies, Alice would gather up a few friends would play-act as Davy Crockett, all the rage in the mid-'50s. Abbott and Costello, Dean Martin and Jerry Lewis were also favourites, as well as a scary radio show called *Lights Out*.

Alice Cooper:
When I was a kid, when I was seven years old, eight years old in Detroit, my parents would drop me off at the movies every Saturday and it was *The Creature from the Black Lagoon, It Came from Outer Space,* and *The Thing.* They dropped me off at the movies in the morning and they'd pick us up when the sun was going down. There was nothing cooler than horror movies on Saturday, and that just stayed with me. When *The Twilight Zone* came out I went… if you really look at *The Twilight Zone*, it was a 30-minute story with a bizarre little ironic ending in it, and I started thinking why couldn't that be a song? Why couldn't a song do that?

September 14, 1955. Little Richard records "Tutti Frutti," which features a fairly extreme vocal, although the song is piano-centric. Little Richard's first album wouldn't arrive until 1957. Elvis includes his version of "Tutti Frutti" on his January 31, 1956 self-titled debut album.

1956. Screamin' Jay Hawkins issues "I Put a Spell on You." Soon after, Alan Freed paid Hawkins $300 to emerge from a coffin on stage and thereafter the act incorporated horror or "shock rock" tropes like rubber snakes and his trademark smoking skull, prompting the tag "the black Vincent Price." Hawkins therefore is very much is an antecedent to Alice Cooper and even King Diamond and Marilyn Manson.

Neal Smith:
Talk about outrageous costumes. He came right out of the voodoo world almost. He had the snakes and all the Cajun stuff going on. He had great rhythms andtremendous stage presence. I hate to say it, being the owner of Kachina on the *Killer* album, but he was the first one that I know of that has a snake onstage. He would wear a snake on the stage. For what he did back in the day, he was probably as outrageous in his time as Alice Cooper was and still is in that style of music. Definitely one of the pioneers.

Gavin Baddeley (author):
Screamin' Jay Hawkins is a very significant figure in a number of respects. He's been called the goth father, the forefather of goth, because he's the first guy who introduced us to this really macabre element to all his stage shows. Obviously you can always go further back, but he's the first high-profile guy who starts coming out of coffins with a skull called Henry and singing about cannibalism and voodoo and so forth.

He's also been identified as the forefather of shock rock, and I think there's a large element of truth there. It's easy to underestimate how shocking some of this stuff was in the 1950s. The song which he's best known for, "I Put a Spell on You," originally was supposed to be a much more soft and seductive number and they just couldn't get it right. So in the end they ended up getting absolutely plastered while recording this and rolling about on the floor singing this song, which had now turned into this really sinister black magic evocation. Well that's one interpretation and it's the one I favour. Again the story goes that when he recorded it, he actually had to listen to the record again in order to re-learn the song because he couldn't remember what in the hell he'd done.

But also the other factor, which is happily less relevant now, is that he was a black performer. And so alongside "I Put a Spell on You" with the voodoo elements, which again some people might refer to as racist— I'm not sure they were—he's also singing song about the Mau Mau. The Mau Mau were this quasi-mystical revolutionary movement in Kenya active in the 1950s, secret society, who in trying to throw off the British colonial yolk committed quite a lot of atrocities. So a guy singing about this stuff would, you know, push a few buttons among frightened white Americans, and certainly frightened white British people.

Screamin' Jay Hawkins never really received the material benefits from his career that he probably should have, but he has influenced a hell of a lot of artists. "I Put a Spell on You" has been covered by so many bands, including Marilyn Manson. Everybody remembers the skull in the coffin, but there's also things like "Constipation Blues." And later in his career he took to wheeling a toilet out onstage, which is certainly an indication of being willing to go the extra mile to grab people's attention.

September 9, 1956. Elvis Presley appears for the first time on *The Ed Sullivan Show*.

Alice Cooper:
I was seven, eight years old when I first saw Elvis on *Ed Sullivan*, and I went oh, that's cool. Of course I dug Elvis. I was at that age where rock 'n' roll was just starting. Little Richard, great. Little Richard was unbelievable. Chuck Berry, still the best lyricist to this day. Anybody that would make up a word like botheration; if he didn't have a word, he would just make one up. Don't give me no botheration. I said oh, you can do that. All those guys were very theatrical. More theatrical than bands today, even, which is a little confusing to me. It seems like in the '70s when we started, there was an Elton John that was Elton John. He was a character unto himself. Bowie was a character unto himself. Alice was a character. And now it seems like bands want to blend in rather than stand out, so it's very bizarre. So yeah those bands did influence us, but not as much as the Beatles.

Spring 1958. The Furniers move for a short time to Los Angeles. Even though Alice's grandfather, Thurman, was an evangelist, his parents are not yet full embracers of the Christian faith, although in LA, they start going to church. Alice's father, Ether, would get work in LA at the Jet Propulsion Laboratory, brought into the fold by Alice's flamboyant "Rat Packer" uncle Lefty Ronson. Alice's other uncle on his dad's side owned a pool hall in Detroit, plus boxed and played a little guitar.

1960 - 1964

Summing up ruthlessly, one might say that the two most important events in shaping Alice—and in one case, literally scarring him—are his near death experience of almost dying from burst insides and the emergence of The Beatles, on the radio and on *Ed Sullivan*.

Along with that, young wise-cracking Vincent Furnier, meets his future band mates, and before this period of high school years is out, they've put on a show as a fake band and then at the very end of 1964, as a real band. Both ends of that duality bear some significance, given that what will become the Alice Cooper group is both a theatrical thing and a musical thing.

February 1961. The Buxtons leave the rust belt and move to Phoenix. Coincidentally, this month also represents the opening in the local JC building of Jack Curtis' VIP club, where the future Alice Cooper band boys would hone their act. With a capacity of about 400, Curtis tended to pack 700 kids in the place.

April 1961. Alice's father Ether Furnier is ordained as a minister.

May 1961. The Furniers move from LA back to Phoenix, Alice's father taking a job with Goodyear Aerospace where he continues to work with top-secret military technology. Soon he will put this career path behind him and become a pastor, working with the local Apache community. Alice's life revolved around baseball and church, which he attended three days a week.

July 4, 1961. Young Vincent Furnier almost dies when it's discovered that his appendix had burst, sealed over, and seeped poison into his system gradually, gravely infecting most of his organs. After throwing up green for two days he's admitted to hospital with acute peritonitis. Doctors, who didn't think Alice would survive, immediately drain three quarts of infected fluid from him while they quickly consider how to save his failing organs.

Cooper would be in hospital for three months, amusing himself every evening by watching the six o'clock dust storm out of his south-facing window, as well as commandeering the first TV remote control he'd ever encountered. Already a light 80 pounds going in, Alice eventually emerges from hospital for more convalescence at 68 pounds and losing his hair as well. Sports was out of the question, driving Alice nuts, as he ate a regular regimen of steak and beats to get iron back into his blood. A year later, doctors open Alice up again and remove his appendix.

August 25, 1962. Bobby "Boris" Pickett & The Crypt-Kickers merges horror and (lite) rock with perennial Halloween favourite "Monster Mash." Two weeks later it is banned by the BBC as offensive.

September 1962. Vincent, 14 years old, enrols at Cortez High School where he excelled at long-distance running. Meanwhile, the Buxtons move house, resulting in Glen enrolling in Cortez as well. Alice is getting well enough to try his hand at long-distance running, which he and Dennis do together to great success, writing song parodies together as they trot through the desert.

Dennis Dunaway:
Glen was just a natural born rebel. The very first time I went over to his house he was sleeping late because it wasn't a school morning and I thought, "Man, its afternoon and he's still asleep." His mom just pointed to his room. So I go in and I open the door and it's all dark except for this one little orange light and there's just a

foot sticking out from under the blanket. This was in Arizona so you hardly ever saw a dark room during the day, but he had tin foil on his windows. He had been partying the night before and that's how it always was.

March 22, 1963. Beatles' first album, *Please Please Me* is issued, featuring the likes of "Twist and Shout" and "I Saw Her Standing There."

September 16, 1963. The Beatles "She Loves You" is issued as a single in the US. Alice remembers this as the first Beatles song he had ever heard, on the radio while up a ladder painting the house with his mother. The Coopers had just bought their first house in a new development where the houses were an astronomical $10,000 but $9000 if you painted it yourself. Soon from the radio came "I Saw Her Standing There" and more Beatles as they painted. Alice calls up Dennis the next day after seeing a picture of the Beatles in the paper and the two discuss.

Alice Cooper:
When the Beatles happened I was 15; the Rolling Stones, how great is that? The Kinks. We're starting to see hair now coming down to the shoulders and I was just at that age going, "Absolutely, that's exactly what I want to do."

Michael Bruce:
I walked into high school one day, and they were playing "She Loves You" and I was mesmerized. I hadn't heard anything about the Beatles and I heard them playing that record. I had been taking a little piano and I had been playing a little acoustic guitar as a folk singer. When I heard that, I just decided, that's what I'm gonna do (laughs). So I went out and got an electric guitar and locked myself away, basically inside my place every night and learned all the Beatles songs I could. I learned how to write from listening to them as well.

January 11, 1964. The Whiskey A Go Go opens in West Hollywood, at 8901 Sunset Strip.

February 9, 1964. The Beatles perform on CBS' *The Ed Sullivan Show,* playing five songs. The monumental rock 'n' roll event may not have directly invented heavy metal, but it sure inspired scores of future hard rock musicians—and musicians of many ilk, among the shows estimated 73 million viewers—to pick up a guitar and play.

Spring 1964. Vincent Furnier, Dennis Dunaway, Glen Buxton, along with school chums John Speer and John Tatum, perform as The Earwigs at the Letterman Talent Show at their school, Cortez High School in Phoenix, Arizona. The band simply mimed to the Beatles, but they are but in a hard by the rock 'n' roll bug. As Alice says, nobody talked about baseball anymore; it was all about the Beatles. John Speer quickly started learning how to play drums, Dennis picked up the bass, and Alice, inspired by "Love Me Do," learned harmonica.

May 11, 1964. The Beach Boys issue "I Get Around" as a single. To this day it's Alice Cooper's favourite song.

Summer 1964. Dennis works on his grandfather's farm near Creswell, Oregon to raise enough money to buy his first bass guitar.

Early October 1964. The Earwigs perform their first shows with real instruments, at lunch hour at Cortez High School.

October 23, 1964. The band play their first real gig, the Pit and the Pendulum dance at the guys' high school, Cortez.

Dennis Dunaway:
The very first gig that the band did, before we became Alice Cooper, we played in 1964, a Halloween dance at Cortez High School, and at that gig we had giant spider webs on the stage that we made out of clothes line and we had a coffin that we made out of cardboard that we painted, because Alice and I were in art class together. We had a ghoul with makeup who came out of the coffin between songs, and then he would do

some shtick while we were deciding what song we were going to do next.

Because I guess we knew about theatrics but we didn't know about a song list then (laughs). We had a working—a small—but still working guillotine. A friend of ours from high school, his father was a carpenter and we got him to build that for us. So we had all of those elements already in '64. By the time we got to Zappa and stuff, we had a million of those kinds of ideas. We just didn't have any money to do any of our ideas at that point. But shockingly the audience came along before the name Alice Cooper. Alice Cooper was just the crème de la crème of our ideas of getting attention.

Our influences had a lot more to do with art. Alice and I were big enthusiasts of the Dada art movement and the surrealists, and a lot of it came from how those artists did their happenings. Salvador Dali was known for having these events where he would get all these people together and then he would do something crazy, and that had more to do with it than any bands, I think, except maybe The Who, because they smashed their guitars and we thought that was exciting. So that was of course when we saw the vision of bringing theatrics to rock 'n' roll.

People talk about Screamin' Jay Hawkins or Screaming Lord Sutch. It does seem like an obvious influence, and I really don't like it when bands deny their obvious influences. So I'm not doing that, but we really didn't. We weren't aware of Lord Sutch at all, and Screamin' Jay Hawkins was just a very vague thing. We had heard his name, but it wasn't like we said, 'Oh yeah, this guy is creepy; let's do that' (laughs). Ours just came from the Halloween dance in '64 and we thought this is great and it just stuck. To this day Alice still uses those exact same elements in his show. So it was just because it was Halloween and then every day was Halloween. We enjoyed doing that so much that it kept coming back.

1965 - 1969

During this period, rock grows from adolescence to bed-headed teenager-dom. Acid hits the scene and we get the likes of Cream, The Doors, The Grateful Dead and Pink Floyd, and then on a heavier tip, Blue Cheer and Led Zeppelin. The Spiders do their largest period of grind and woodshedding, '65, '66, and become The Nazz in '67. By March of 1968, the band is renamed Alice Cooper, with Neal Smith rounding out the original lineup when he moves in with the guys at one of a few different band houses in this period, December of 1967.

Things quickly heat up, with notorious gigs about town resulting in an almost adversarial relationship with the rock establishment, led by Bill Graham and the psych bands from LA and San Francisco who find the band's use of props offensive. But the hippie generation is about to get dark, the perfect environment in which a band like Alice Cooper might translate, connect, flourish. The Manson murders happen in August of 1969 and the Altamont concert results in violence and one death, into September of '69, with the Rolling Stones framed as evil, Mick an out-of-touch shaman, the Hells Angels suddenly less glamourous.

Over in Detroit, Dick Wagner puts out a record with his band The Frost, The Stooges debut with a self-titled, MC5 proposes a slashing and burning live album in *Kick Out the Jams*, and *Creem* magazine is born, all of this happening in 1969.

In Alice Cooper world, the band audition for Frank Zappa in July of 1968, quickly pick up a couple of on-the-make managers in Shep Gordon and Joe Greenberg and by November are recording their debut album. Into 1969, Frank has his new label going, Straight Records, along with his first act for it, a band he essentially humours, just like The GTOs, Wild Man Fischer and on some level, his own Mothers of Invention.

Alice Cooper begin touring across North America and into Canada as their debut album, *Pretties for You*, emerges. The album is pretty much a late-fer-dinner slice of psychedelic rock, but there's something different about the look of the band—arguably, they are the first rock stars, if of an easily dismissed ilk, because the music doesn't quite back the bravado, the long hair, the flashy clothes, the visual assault of five of these in front of your eyes. Again, with the hippie generation growing cranky, strung-out and violent, it all makes sense, even if L.A.'s furry freaks would gather enough indignation to—as the story frames it—kick Alice Cooper to the curb, where they would gather up their meagre possessions for a move to Detroit.

February 9, 1965. The Earwigs play at the Washington Grad School Talent show.

April 30, 1965. The Earwigs place first at the Sears Combo Contest at ChrisTown Mall, in hometown, Phoenix, Arizona.

May 1, 1965. The *Phoenix Gazette* runs a piece on Neal Smith and the Laser Beats. Into the fall, the combo win a battle of the bands. Neal is about to graduate from Camelback High School, which he discusses in the *School's Out* song, "Alma Matter," credited solely to Neal.

Neal Smith:
Ever since the British Invasion I wanted to be in a band. And I started playing drums when I was 12 years old. It was well after that that the British Invasion happened, and I was just totally knocked out by what was going on. At that time there was shock value with the Rolling Stones compared to like the Beach Boys. The Beach Boys were one of these clean-cut bands, American boys, and all of a sudden these rowdies from the UK come over and just make total chaos everywhere. I wanted to be part of something like that. I went to a Rolling Stones concert in Phoenix, Arizona, in the mid '60s, and I just couldn't believe the girls around me were screaming and going so crazy. I'm going, well the music's good, I like this band, but I don't get why these girls are doing that, but I like it. I'd like to be part of something like that some day. That was my motivation.

June 13, 1965. Yardbirds first studio album, a US compilation called *For Your Love*.

Alice Cooper:
We were always Yardbirds-oriented; we were always Who-oriented and to me that was hard, hard rock. We just didn't like medium rock. We liked the Yardbirds because they had out-of-control guitars and they had feedback as part of their leads, and I went, that's good stuff right there and you had Keith Moon drums, and everything was driving. So that was the beginnings of it.

Neal Smith:
We were a product of the British invasion of the mid-'60s. Arizona was a test center for a lot of the British invasion music that came over, before it was released in other parts of the country. So we heard tons of that music and were really aware and bombarded by a lot of bands, including all the bands that didn't make it. There were bands that played in Arizona like The Undertakers, which were a great English band, which never really made it, and The Yardbirds and The Zombies or some of the other great bands from that era that had commercial success. They were like the Stones or The Who, but they still had commercial success with their music and we were lucky to be baptized in fire by that environment musically.

Mid 1965. The Earwigs play their first shows at clubs around hometown Phoenix.

Alice Cooper:
We went to high school together. We were on the track team together. We were in journalism class together. We went to college together. We went through the Vietnam draft together. We did all that. I accidentally shot Neal when we were out shooting rabbits while we were drunk. There's so much history between us. We starved together, then all of a sudden we went from being the most hated band in LA to the number one band in England. So, how does that happen? We were at the right place with the right stuff.

September 1965. The Spiders issue, on Mascott, their first single, "Hitch Hike" (Marvin Gaye)/"Why Don't You Love Me" (The Blackwells). The band is an ambitious bunch of grounded, regular guys looking for a way to wake people up. The competent garage rock sides are produced by Jack Curtis, working at Audio Recorders of Arizona. Early on, The Spiders carve an identity by being the local band that specialised in The Rolling Stones, ceding Beatle territory to others, such as The Pendletons and The Vibratos. As well, cropping up were Sunnyslope and The Excels, who became The Tubes.

Dennis Dunaway:

Big influences came from the fact that Alice and I were in art class together in high school. Alice was like 16 when we met. We were in art class together, we ran long distance, cross country on the same team. We were in English and eventually journalism together. But art had a lot to do with our concepts. Salvador Dali, Dada, and television had a lot to do with it.

There was a local television show in Phoenix, Arizona called *Wallace and Ladmo,* which was on for years and years. When we were little it was called *It's Wallace?* and it was directed toward kids. But as he got older and as his audience grew up, he started getting more and more clever with double entendre. College students would tune into the show, and little kids would still laugh at the same joke for a completely different reason.

But the great influence we got from that, everybody in the Alice Cooper group, like everybody in Phoenix, grew up with *Wallace and Ladmo.* But the great thing is whenever their skits would bomb, it was almost better than when it worked because that was the humour of it. That was an element of our shows—we weren't afraid to bomb. So we would bring out maybe ten props and try them, and if something bombed it didn't matter because there were nine other props that night. So we actually got a lot of confidence from that show. Of course there was the horror films and gangster films, Cagney and Bogart—Glen Buxton was heavily into those—*Three Stooges,* things that sort of fuelled our immaturity throughout our career.

September 4, 1965. Having transitioned from The Earwigs to The Spiders, the band play a landmark early gig, at Jaycees, the VIP Club, supporting The Yardbirds. By this point, the band had moved on from their Rolling Stones phase and were playing, Alice claims, a dozen Yardbirds songs, which indeed makes up a bunch of the band's set on this night.

Dennis Dunaway:

We opened for the Yardbirds and we all of a sudden decided that the theme of that particular set would be silverware and forks from the VIP restaurant. So we came out, we had plastic forks stuck in our hair. Glen brought out a tray of forks and spoons and he played slide with a spoon, which he always did from that night forward. Even on songs like "Black Juju," Glen is playing slide with a spoon. Jeff Beck loved that idea so much that when the Yardbirds went on, Jeff Beck had come over and taken the tray of silverware and he used it when he played. He held his Telecaster up and did triplets, and let gravity bring it down. Then he was throwing spoons and letting them ricochet off the strings.

But that was one set. Then another set, there was a big cast iron old bathtub with the feet on the bottom. This thing weighed a ton. We decided that Alice would be in front of it pointing like George Washington crossing the Delaware. So we heave-ho'd this thing up to the stage and Alice climbed onstage and we did our set, he got back in, we heave-ho'd it back to the back room.

It was just always stuff like that. Then eventually we started building props. We built very early on a strobe effect. You used to be able to go to army and navy stores and get these ammunitions canisters that were metal. So we got one of those that had a light in it and cut a hole in the end and put a motor in it so we had this spinning disc with slits cut out of it, and that would do a rolling effect. It was very soothing compared to the erratic effect of the electronic strobes.

One of the things that was bad but we thought was good—bad in the club owner's mind—Jack Curtis at the VIP Club—it would catch on fire every night because it got so hot inside the thing. All this smoke would come out and we thought that was cool, but we drove him crazy, the first guy who really believed in the band. But he couldn't fire us over anything because we were packing the place. They were coming to see what we were going to do next.

December 4, 1965. The Spiders and Neal Smith's band, The Laser Beats, play together on the same bill, on Teen-Age Day at the Phoenix Art Museum.

February 1966. The Spiders play three hometown shows in Phoenix, at three different venues, supporting The Byrds.

Dennis Dunaway:

We played at this local club in Phoenix, Arizona which was the hottest club going, and we managed to become the house band there. But the ongoing thing that we could see was that they would have a house band for a couple of weeks and they would spit out that week's flavour of gum and get somebody else.

I had the idea of keeping the band changing so much that it doesn't get old. Within two weeks we'd be like a new band. So we started doing theatrics every weekend. We did eight sets a weekend, and we would do something new each weekend, and then that escalated to something each night. Then that got escalated to something each set. So we would go out in the parking lot between sets and find an old tyre and bring it up and roll it across the stage or we would come out with toilet paper all over and throw toilet paper into the audience. Just stuff like that so we had to keep outdoing ourselves.

Summer 1966. Michael Bruce joins The Spiders, replacing John Tatum.

Michael Bruce:
It's funny, when I went down and auditioned for The Spiders, they were the house band at the VIP Lounge, for Jack Curtis down on Seventh Street. The Jaycees ran it; it was a place for teens to go on the weekend, Friday, Saturday night, try to keep them out of trouble, steer them away from drugs and all that. And The Spiders, we jokingly called them The Rolling Clones, because that's all they did. But I really liked the Rolling Stones too— when Brian Jones was in the band still. *Between the Buttons,* I used to listen to that every day.

Late August 1966. The Spiders venture to Copper State Recording Studios in Tucson to record their second single. While in town, the band play a gig supporting The Yardbirds.

Dennis Dunaway:
I think back in the early days before we did *Pretties for You.* We were quite a good southwest regional garage band. I think we could have knocked out a hit or two like The Music Machine or those bands, and we could have had big success that way, and we could have done it at a time when we really could have used the money. But we chose the artistic direction. We had this driven vision, and that was more important than putting food on the table at the time.

September 1966. The Spiders issue, on Santa Cruz Records out of Tucson, their second single, the fuzz-rockin' "Don't Blow Your Mind"/"No Price Tag." Both songs are originals, the A-side, at 2:35, credited to Dennis and Alice, the B-side, at 2:06, to Glen and Alice. Meanwhile, Alice signs up for art courses at Glendale Community College.

Dennis Dunaway:
My biggest influences were painters like Dali, Magritte, Ernst and Miro. I've always been an artist and the band was another way of expressing art. It didn't matter what instrument I played. I ended up with bass because everyone else chose their instrument before I did. So in order to learn how to use that tool for expression, I sat down with Glen Buxton and a phonograph and he helped me learn blues patterns from Bill Wyman via Rolling Stones recordings. I learned a lot from McCartney too, but more through listening to his parts rather than playing them. But hearing Paul Samwell-Smith of the Yardbirds made me realise the bass can go anywhere you take it and that concept set me free to pursue my own direction.

Alice Cooper:
I became a creative writer; I was a journalist. That was one of my… I was a journalism major and an art major also. You put those two things together and you start realizing that the press is your buddy, it's not your enemy. I used to tell the press, look, the more things I do the more it's going to sell your papers, right? I'm your best friend.

January 4, 1967. The Doors issue their self-titled debut album. Jim Morrison and the band would be an influence on the Alice Cooper group, as well as friends of the band in the late '60s, when they both plied their trade in and around southern California. The Doors never took Alice Cooper on tour, but they did indeed play a few shows together. Robby Krieger remembers one show at a hockey rink (with plywood over the ice surface) in Las Vegas where the band's chickens escaped and they had to jump into the crowd to corral them. The bills with Alice came to be because Doors manager Bill Siddons liked the band. Robbie became one of Alice's early golfing buddies, playing with him in the early '70s at Valencia. Krieger says he was a pretty bad golfer at that time, still drinking a lot, but of course got much better later on. They still play a couple times a year.

Dennis Dunaway:
You're talking about Hollywood in the '60s, so, like everyone in that exciting scene, we ran into tons of bands

and actors. Jim Morrison was the only person that ever got away with blocking the view of the television in our house. Anyone else would have gotten yelled at by Glen, Alice and Neal. People that knew us would step quickly around the television. Jim sat on top of it.

March 17, 1967. The Jimi Hendrix Experience's "Purple Haze" is issued as a UK single; recorded January 11 and February 3, at De Lane Lea and Olympic Studios in London, UK.

Late March 1967. The Spiders play their first out-of-state shows, venturing to Los Angeles and Concord, CA.

Spring 1967. Alice quits college as the band starts to take off.

Michael Bruce:
We used to take peyote and drive to this mountain. There was a park there with picnic tables, and there was only one that had electricity. So we'd plug in our amps and we'd take some peyote and just jam all night. Just crazy experimental stuff. I remember one morning, we saw this thing glowing from behind the mountain, and as it came up, we thought it was the mothership. As it got higher and higher, the heat from the desert was making it shimmer and it actually turned out to be, I think, Venus, one of the closest times it was near the Earth. But we were so stoned we thought it was a UFO.

May 12, 1967. Jimi Hendrix Experience's debut *Are You Experienced* is released in the UK. The bar is raised in terms of both guitar pyrotechnics and pyrotechnics.

Mid-1967. The Nazz, or just Nazz, issue a single pairing "Wonder Who's Loving Her Now?" with "Lay Down and Die, Goodbye," both originals. The band is now setting up shop in LA, but the single is recorded at Viv Recording Studios in Phoenix.

August 5, 1967. Pink Floyd's debut album, *The Piper at the Gates of Dawn* is issued.

Neal Smith:
Not a lot of people talk about Charlie Carnell, our light guy. The light show was very flashy. We were influenced by the first time we saw Pink Floyd with Syd Barrett, in Santa Monica at the Cheetah Club, and there were some very cool things they did with lights. So we did a spin of our interpretation of that. The shiny clothes became a format, a background, for the lights to land on. That's what we were thinking. On *Pretties for You*, 1969, Dennis has a full silver suit on. The clothes were an intricate part of it.

Michael Bruce:
I loved *Piper At the Gates of Dawn*. We met those guys. I was fascinated by their whole trip, the stage show and the lights and whatnot, and we started getting into a little of that ourselves with our band. When Pink Floyd came here, their roadie Les Braden, he stayed in America. He worked with Pink Floyd and he stayed as an illegal immigrant and lived with us and became our roadie/mentor and it worked out just great. We got to meet Eric Clapton and Jack Bruce—we went up to Jack's room and he played us the song "Wheels of Fire." We got to hang out with Hendrix, and this was all because of this roadie.

August 22 – 27, 1967. The band, now called The Nazz (named for Yardbirds song "The Nazz Are Blue") perform over six nights at the Cheetah Club, in Venice, California. Regular shows continue at that venue through the end of the year.

Late Summer 1967. Neal Smith moves to LA, staying at The Nazz's band house in Santa Monica.

November 5, 1967. Pink Floyd perform two shows at The Cheetah Club, between gigs in San Francisco. They stay at The Nazz band house.

December 1967. Neal Smith replaces John Speer as drummer for The Nazz.

Neal Smith:

I went to Camelback and everyone else went to Cortez. The other drummer they had was a good friend of mine, and he was a different style of drummer. I was always very much a showman. I always wanted to be the biggest, baddest and the best. Even more than that, I wanted us to be the coolest musicians on the planet. I think ultimately the group Alice Cooper was the hippest band of the era. Nobody was cooler than us.

I probably fit in with Glen, Dennis and Michael musically better than the other drummer. He was very good, but he had a different philosophy. I have a philosophy about making it, but it was to be a little more experimental with the music and a little more album-oriented music, but still to have the hits. The first time we started going out into the desert we would have a couple of beers and a couple of joints and just have fun. Alice—he was Vince at the time—was not even there. The other drummer was still in the band and I was just going out to play with some friends. It was nothing more, nor nothing less than that.

Dennis and I were oil and vinegar. We were totally different. When we play together we just know where each of us is going and it is amazing. He makes a change and I make a change and it just flows together. We are on the same wavelength when we are just jamming freestyle on music. I think we are one of the most underrated rhythm sections in rock 'n' roll. The chemistry just gelled better once I was there. I really understood what they were doing.

Early 1968. The Nazz get kicked out of their LA band house and retreat to Phoenix. All five members escape the military draft, Neal most dramatically, after accidentally getting shot in the ankle by Alice. Also in '68, the VIP club ends its seven-year run.

Dennis Dunaway:

Alice and I both went to the draft board and we just dressed the way we always dressed. We dressed crazily all the time, on the street and onstage. I had a white satin shirt on that had white tassels all over it. Of course people didn't know what to think of that. It didn't even look like something a woman would be properly attired in. The combination of everybody together added up to something where hardly anybody wore anything that anybody had seen someone wear before.

Like Glen Buxton with all of his safety pins holding his pants together was quite a statement, even though it was really a necessity in those days because we didn't have money for food. We spent it all on beer. I had powder blue boots, I had satin green pants, I had a copper sequin shirt and then my hair was down to my waist. Nobody's hair was as long as ours either. So the ongoing joke with us and Jimi Hendrix—we used to run into him at the Landmark Hotel in Hollywood—was we would make fun of how he dressed, and of course we were dressed at least as crazily as he was.

Back, sure, back then it was shocking, especially where we started out in Phoenix, Arizona. It was tough. A lot of cowboys around, a lot of people that liked to get in fights, and we were the perfect target for everyone. Normally, before we came along, they fought amongst themselves, but when we came along everybody agreed that we were the target.

It was a threat to a lot of people who didn't know what to think of our sexuality. Even though we were heterosexual we didn't look like it at all. So therefore a lot of violent threats came our way and humiliating comments. You couldn't go anywhere. That actually drew the band into a tighter bonding because we hardly went anywhere unless it was a pack, where all five of us went everywhere together. But the consolation was girls were attracted to it. We didn't anticipate that but we certainly were happy about it.

Elvis got in a lot of fights. He was in the south and he liked to wear pink shirts. Elvis always had that corny element of fighting in all his movies, but that was real. He was down in the south and he was the target that the Alice Cooper group was. When you're in the south, even if you don't dress crazily, even if you tried to conform by cowboy standards, they would find something wrong. "I don't like the way your hat is tilted—what are you going to do about it?"

Confrontation thrived down there. The weekend wasn't successful unless you could go back to work on Monday and talk about a fight you were in. And that's what Elvis came up through. I loved Elvis, I love doo-wop. I'm the age where I was around when all that was happening. Elvis platters were coming out and my babysitters were bopping around the house, and it was quite exciting.

January 1968. Blue Cheer's debut, *Vincebus Eruptum* is released. A shockingly heavy album for its day, it is considered by many to be the first heavy metal album of all time. Here, we will assign it much weight, but deny it that title due to lack of skilfulness, lack of modern metallic flourishes, and assumed lack of visceral heavy metal intention.

February 1968. Dick Wagner's early, heavy band, The Frost, play their first show at the Grande Ballroom.

March 11, 1968. The Nazz relocate to Los Angeles after a couple months back in Phoenix.

Neal Smith:
When we moved to Los Angeles, there were twenty or thirty thousand bands in those days. It was like geez, what do we have to do? First of all, there was already a band called The Nazz, so we had to change the name. So we changed to Alice Cooper and that was a little bit different, and we were always thinking about being memorable more than anything else. We didn't care if people hated us or liked us. We just wanted them to remember the name Alice Cooper. The more we sunk into debt and the more we hit a ceiling as far as the amount of money we made, we just got frustrated and we started doing crazier things.

March 16, 1968. The freshly renamed Alice Cooper play the Earl Warren Showgrounds, in Santa Barbara, California. Also on the bill (somewhat as co-headliners) are Blue Cheer and The Nitty Gritty Dirt Band. The band literally change their name after the typically psychedelic poster advertising the show is printed. They are introduced from the stage as Alice Cooper. A story is floated that Neal dropped acid consulted a Ouija board on who Alice Cooper was and the answer came back, "thirteenth century witch." Never happened, says Alice, who, in his scotching of the myth, says the Ouija session story was attributed to show booker Dick Phillips and his sister. However, the idea was soon played up on press releases, resulting in a gig where a pile of witches showed up to a gig to basically worship with—or worship—Alice, which spooked the band.

Dennis Dunaway:
We were in a blizzard of new band name ideas. But when Vince suggested Alice Cooper, everyone paused. But our image was already triggering lots of threats so we weren't sure if we could survive with that name so the blizzard of names continued. But with suggestion after suggestion, the Alice Cooper name kept gaining strength in comparison. When I got home that night, I told my parents that our new name was Alice Cooper, and when I saw the look on their faces, I was sold. So the next night when the band got together, Vince had my added enthusiasm. Everyone agreed on one condition, that Alice Cooper would be the name of our group to be shared equally. Years later, at the band's farm in Pontiac, Michigan, we even signed contracts to legalise that agreement.

Alice Cooper:
It was the perfect name for us. We could have been The Husky Baby Sandwich or The Scabs but I said why give it away? Why should we have a scary name? I said we should have a name of the old lady that lives down the street that's the sweetest old lady that knits every day. But you're pretty sure there's bodies buried in the basement. I could have said Betty Smith or anything but I happened to say Alice Cooper. I said a little old lady named Alice Cooper that maybe makes children into pies when nobody knows it. I thought that's a great name. Then I thought Lizzie Borden, Baby Jane, Alice Cooper. It had a rhythm to it. It had a scary little sound to it. And people weren't expecting us. When they heard Alice Cooper they thought it was going to be a blonde folk singer, and they got us, you know? I said that's the perfect name. The idea was, let's not be obvious. I said let's make Alice Cooper—which is a perfectly sweet, little old lady—let's make that the scariest name in America.

Neal Smith:
Alice Cooper. What does that mean? It was wide open. It was untamed territory. We could create whatever Alice Cooper was. We could make it a monster, we could make it a lamb, whatever. I liked it myself because it was like The Who. It was a name that was never used before—just a woman's name for a band. And the shock value that we talked about at the time was these five crazy long-haired guys with makeup, shiny clothes and playing loud, weird music (and Zappa loved us), was that we'd get onstage and that's Alice Cooper. When they thought a character like Mary Travis from Peter, Paul and Mary would be on a little stool with acoustic guitar and long, blonde hair singing about puffing some dragons or something like that. So when people came to see us, that wasn't what they were expecting.

April 1968. Alice Cooper move into their new band house in Topanga Canyon. Matching the extremity of the band's music and vision, the guys went beyond regular bunk beds to triple-decker.

April 12, 1968. The band is in a car accident en route from Phoenix to LA. As the story goes, Alice signs the police report, "Alice Cooper." In Alice's (likely fanciful) recollection of the event, a lady cuts them off as they are driving at five in the morning, on a Good Friday (Cooper is correct about that—April 12, 1968 was a Friday), the van flips over three times, skids on its roof, and everybody is thrown out of the vehicle. Alice's dad had set them up with the vehicle, got it insured, a brand-new yellow van that cost $3000.

Nobody is hurt, but because they are all scraped up they have to get tetanus shots. Alice cites the fact that they emerged without so much as a broken bone, despite their vehicle being totalled, as the second miracle in his life, the first being his recovering from peritonitis, which he frames as God "putting his mark on him."

April 20, 1968. The band—Dennis Dunaway, Fabian Buxton, Neal S. Myth, Alice Cooper and Mike Bruce—are featured in a Phoenix alternative paper called *A Closer Look*.

Dennis Dunaway:
Musically? The Yardbirds, the Doors and the Stooges. Neal liked Sandy Nelson, Gene Krupa and Keith Moon. Michael liked the Beatles. Glen liked Chet Atkins, Les Paul and Jeff Beck. Alice liked Burt Bacharach and Leonard Bernstein. We all liked Bernstein and Gene Barry's James Bond soundtracks. I liked avant garde electronic music. Frank Zappa was thrilled to hear that I loved doo-wop and electronic music and he spent a whole afternoon digging stuff out of his record closet and playing it just for me.

May 23, 1968. An important homecoming show finds Alice Cooper supporting Iron Butterfly at the Phoenix Memorial Hall.

June 27, 1968. Alice Cooper support the label boss, Frank Zappa, at Wrigley Stadium in LA.. The two parties would turn out to be a good match for each other, because although Alice Cooper and Frank Zappa were, from the art, freaks, Frank and at least Alice, the person, were not doing drugs, while all around them almost everybody was. Plus with the rest of the Alice Cooper band, it stopped at pot and acid and in general, the guys were very dependable and hard working.

July 12, 1968. Alice Cooper audition for Frank Zappa at his 1914-built log cabin on Lookout Mountain and Laurel, in Laurel Canyon, across the street from Harry Houdini's castle. Zappa signs the band. The band meet the GTOs, with Pamela Des Barres taking a shine to Neal and Alice getting together with Miss Christine, who does some of the band's early makeup and helps with feminine clothing choices. As a speed freak, Miss Christine was always working and working fast, sewing clothes, coming up with combinations of wraps and feather boas, sometimes sewing outfits directly onto Alice. Much of the wardrobe work she did with Alice would take place at the Landmark Hotel.

Alice Cooper:
We thought at first everybody's going to love this. Then we started realizing that a lot of bands—I won't mention any names—but a lot of jam bands that were really big from San Francisco really hated us, because what they saw in us was the fact that people loved it. And now they were going to have to not wear their Levis and their sandals. Now they were going to have to do a show. Now they were going to have to actually work at it.

Because we were bringing a show in. It was like Broadway, only demented Broadway, and it was pure rock and it was louder than them. So it scared everybody to death. The press hated us for that. They said if you guys have to do all that, that means you're not good players. We went through that—until Frank Zappa picked us up. And everybody respects Frank Zappa as being the best guy, the smartest, most intelligent guy in the business. Well Frank Zappa was the only guy that would sign us.

Michael Bruce:
Alice was hitchhiking around, and he got to know the GTOs and Miss Christine invited him to the log cabin. She eventually got us the rehearsal and said, have the band come over at six. So we were so excited, that we couldn't possibly imagine he meant six PM. We got over there in the wee hours, set up our stuff, and were playing the music that you hear on *Pretties for You*.

So all of a sudden I see—there's the staircase, because this was down in his basement, this guy walking down—he's got his hair tied back, drinking a cup of coffee, and he goes, "What the fuck is going on here?!" We said, "We're the Alice Cooper band. You wanted us to be over at six." He goes, "I meant six in the evening!" That's what I remember. But he listened to it; we were performing all that material you hear on *Pretties for You* and we could do it live. He was impressed with the fact that we could do those arrangements over and over and he said, yeah, I want you on the label.

Mid-July 1968. Shep Gordon and Joe Greenberg walk into a fashion shop called Inside Outside, wind up talking to Cindy Dunaway. Shep and Joe had been spinning their wheels at the Landmark Hotel and knew they had to do something. Cindy said she had a brother with a band, Frank Zappa wants to sign them and they need a manager. Joe blurts out, "I'm a manager!" Soon after they talk to Neal on the phone and the band bring a tape down to the Landmark for them to hear. It was irrelevant what was on the tape, because the most interesting thing about them, besides how long their hair was, was that Frank Zappa was going to sign them in three days. On the band's part, they saw these guys were living at the Landmark, plus they bought the Shep's and Joe's complete like about being the west coast managers of The Lefte Bank.

In Shep's telling of the story, there's a convergence of events. Yes, they went into the store and met Cindy. But also, when they had checked into the Landmark, Shep says they were doing a little drug-dealing, and they were partying in the hotel, and Jimi Hendrix suggested if the cops asked how they were paying to live at the Landmark, tell them you're a manager. Then Lester Chambers of The Chamber Brothers, who were also at the party, said that they had this band living in their basement, Alice Cooper, that they should talk to.

Indeed, at first, Joe and Shep intended to use band management as a front to continue selling pot. Shep says there was a period there when he and Joey were paying the band $10 a week just to say they managed them, saying Alice would walk down from Topanga Canyon to the hotel to collect the money and then they'd spend it on Boone's Farms wine (this befuddles the timeline somewhat, as lore has it this all happened in a matter of a couple days). In any event very quickly, prompted by a scare where they almost got arrested, Gordon and Greenberg shifted gears from their nascent pot operation and took on this new project, Alice Cooper, even if the dealing continued low-key, along with a side job Shep had, selling copies of the *Los Angeles Free Press* underground newspaper.

To sign the contracts with the band, Shep and Joe meet with parents of the band members because they are too young to sign. Alice figures the parents were satisfied because they were Jewish and from New York, plus they looked the part. Joe figures that they saw that he and Shep were as young as the band, so they probably didn't know how to rip their sons off.

Immediately, Shep and Joe begin new jobs in the city as co-managers of Alice Cooper. A period of awkwardness ensues with Frank Zappa having first told the band their new manager is Herbie Cohen, who is running Straight/Bizarre with Frank. But the band says no, indicating that their new managers are these guys they met a few days earlier. Shep and Joe hash it out with Herbie Cohen, now newly belligerent because he's just been told he's not managing Alice Cooper. Shep in fact says that Herbie went after him with a chair, and that the GTOs had to intervene.

According to Alice, Shep and Joe are offered $30,000 but Herbie wants the publishing. They settle on $3000 with the band hanging onto their publishing (it was recommend by a lawyer named Sam Norton that when he goes in to negotiate, keep the publishing). Shep tells an incredulous band that if he was offering $30,000, they were worth ten times that. Alice Cooper didn't know what publishing was, but they were soon glad that they kept it (in telling the story, sometimes Shep specifies that they kept two-thirds of the publishing, not all of it). In a simpler telling, Joe talks about simply taking an offer of $6000 and that the band was happy. Alice says Joe and Shep celebrated the deal by buying new wheels for the band, a '54 Cadillac limousine for about $800.

Dennis Dunaway:
Our music was just way over the top, bizarre. That didn't help, but I think the biggest factor was that people came, they would hear the name, and they would come expecting to see Joan Baez or something. And then they'd come in and see what we looked like. Nobody wore chrome clothing or sequins and stuff like that in those days. Except maybe Liberace (laughs). But then when they would see what the band looked like, people would start screaming insults and line up for the doorway.

As a matter of fact, the first time Frank Zappa was in the audience, our potential managers, Joe Greenberg and Shep Gordon had come because Zappa was going to consider having us on his record label. The place was packed when we started, but within three songs it was emptying out so fast I looked behind us actually wondering if there was a fire or something. So because of that, I got this idea of breaking down the barrier between us and the audience. So I wrote a song called "Return of the Spiders," which the lyrics were, "Stop, look and listen." So I thought okay, that will get people to stop (laughs). It didn't really work.

But then we decided okay, we're going to start breaking down the barrier by throwing things into the audience, so we'll make them part of the show. So they'll feel like they're part of the show and then they'll want to stay because they're in the show. That led to me putting mirrors on my bass so the reflection would go into the room. Then that led to the giant weather balloons that we would throw into the audience that were full of smoke and money and confetti and all kinds of stuff. So that's how that developed. That was really to keep people from leaving the room, initially.

August 3-4, 1968. Alice Cooper play the Newport Pop Festival, at the Orange County Fairgrounds in Costa Mesa, California. The festival is cited as the first to draw over 100,000 people. Their set is four or five numbers. Joe and Shep had begged the promoters to put them on the bill. The promoter said that he had enough bands and would you please leave. Day of show, the band show up at security with all their gear and Joe tells the guy he's got "The Joseph Cotten Blues Band" with him—James Cotton Blues Band were on the bill, but Joe blanked and mentioned actor James Cotton instead. They are let through. They go up on stage, set up and start playing. They are screamed off the stage by the promoter.

September 1968. Track Records issues *The Crazy World of Arthur Brown.* Arthur's histrionic vocal style—from his falsetto to his scream to his growl—becomes an influence on and inspiration to both Bruce Dickinson and Ian Gillan. The single, "Fire" (the album's heaviest and most demonic track) issued the previous month, hits No.1 in the UK. An additional point about "Fire" is that its heaviness is partly derived from an ominous keyboard riff (courtesy of Vincent Crane), rather than electric guitar. The video for the track has Arthur pioneering the use of pyro, which shoots from a helmet on his head.

Arthur Brown:
Alice likes to explore images and he's very good at choosing—or having chosen for him some-times—images that visually are very potent. His best images are very simple. I remember doing one concert and he had the wind machine blowing and his hair was out here and things were just flying around and it was a very moving spectacle. Some of his things are more like illusionist conjuring stuff. He went through that phase.

I suppose that if you're looking for kinship with me, it's a delight in theatre. Delight in not just standing with pleasant imagery, but exploring the unpleasant and having a sense of humour about it. Not being sort of terribly invested in the damage one can do, but more just looking at the world and taking images from it. I think he went through a period the same as I did where there was too much visual imagery and it became like a pantomime. His musical background was obviously what he explores—different from my own—but similarly very energetic music.

Alice has been quite straight forward in that regard, in citing influence from what I was doing, in terms of things like makeup, which we were sporting before Alice used it. When he came over (to the UK) and we did some concerts in '71, he said wow, that was real psycho, you know. So I can see some of that in his performance, but I can also see the fact that he took it in his own direction. It's his own thing. I'm very flattered that he sees a connection.

Dennis Dunaway:
We had heard about Arthur Brown, and we of course had to send away for his album. We used to send away for the British albums all the time. I love his first album, which has one side that is incredible; the other side is not as good, but we had heard of him and liked him of course, for his theatrical stuff. We were also friends of The Doors by the mid-'60s, so they had their theatrical inclinations as well, and we also knew of Pink Floyd. As a matter of fact, they stayed at our house, on their very first tour. Syd Barrett was still in the band, and they were doing something very different from us, their lighting was theatrical. We prided ourselves on being the very first band to take our own light show on the road with us. We had our own light show since the VIP Club in Phoenix, Arizona. We had a guy, Charlie Carnell, who was very advanced. As a matter of fact Chip Monk used to come to our rehearsals in later days, and we would see Charlie's new lighting effect that he invented in the Stones show (laughs). And Chip Monk was admitting he would do that. He would tip his hat to Charlie. It wasn't like he pretended that he made up those ideas.

Alice Cooper:
I'd never seen Arthur Brown. I had never heard of Arthur Brown. It was one of the strange things. Arthur Brown and I happened at about the same time. He was going on in England but didn't have any hits over here. We were going on over here but didn't have any hits in England, and we were wearing almost the same makeup and doing very theatrical things.

So when I saw Arthur Brown I did a double take. I have a doppelganger. I think when he saw me it was sort of like, wow, there's somebody over there doing this thing too. He set his hat on fire, I had the boa constrictor. I really liked Arthur Brown. I think Arthur had the best voice in the business. His range was amazing, but he really only did that one thing. He did the fire trick and that was about it, whereas I thought every song should have a piece to it.

Gavin Baddeley:
One hit wonder is certainly unfair and unkind for such a talented figure, but Arthur Brown is remembered for "Fire." As the God of Hellfire. If that had a political message, it was to a certain extent the same political message you were getting from the Rolling Stones, touching upon the crackling energy of revolution that people felt on the streets. If you talk about the God of Hellfire the same way as Mick Jagger singing about sympathy for the Devil, you're giving everything an extra sort of charge of blasphemous or even Satanic energy, which means you're not just attacking the status quo and the government, but you're also implicitly provoking religious sentiments. It's a two-barrelled attack. But Arthur Brown is an example of an artist who is taking proto-psychedelic sounds and giving them an aggression and energy which perhaps they lacked. The summer of love was most people's abiding memory of the late '60s, however accurate they may or may not have been, but this was the suggestion that summer of love might turn into something else. But if you wanted to get a bit carried away here, "Fire" is evocative of the burning barricades and so forth, which again you find in the Rolling Stones' "Street Fighting Man." It's the idea that somehow there's a dangerous energy out here which we can unleash, at least partially, through music.

October 1968. Alice Cooper move band house again, setting up shop with Shep Gordon along as well, at John Philip Law's house on Observation Road in the Hollywood Hills. There's an interesting story as to how Vincent Furnier became the Alice Cooper in the band called Alice Cooper. Shep says that they had met with a publicist, Pat Kingsley, who sent everyone out of the room saying, I can't deal with five guys called Alice Cooper. The idea was for Shep to pick the best talker of the bunch, and that person will be Alice Cooper. The band themselves suggested Vince.

Dennis Dunaway:
In the early days, there was a period when we were very confident as a band, and quite solid when we worked at the VIP. Because when we started, we would do cover songs, and Alice was very confident that if we did a Rolling Stones song that he was Mick Jagger. If we did a Paul Butterfield song, he was Paul Butterfield and played the harmonica and everything. So he had a lot of stage confidence through acting, because he was pretending he was someone else.

But when we got to LA and decided we were going to shed all of that and move onto our original image everything seemed fine at rehearsals, but when we got to a live show, Alice would spend most of the set with his back to the crowd. Then we would go back to rehearsals and things seemed normal again. Our gigs were few and far between in those days, because LA had thousands of bands just looking for an audition (laughs).

I came up with this idea of having a different character for each song. We had a song called "Nobody Likes Me," the one where Alice is singing through the window in the door, we had a song called "Levity Ball," which was inspired by the movie *Carnival of Souls*, and so Alice would envision that he was a person who could see all of these ghosts dancing in his room. Alice still uses the gestures he had for that song.

We had a song called "Fields of Regret," our most popular song, for the people who did remain in the room in those days (laughs). We would sing out, "Fields! Fields!" People loved "Fields," because it was a dark song and Alice did this dark character. So he would change characters, and then when we would drop the song, the character would be dropped and a new character would be invented for whatever song replaced that. But I noticed... I didn't develop the character. The band really had a lot to do with developing the character that became Alice. It was definitely a collaboration, but I was the first to recognize that that's what the audience wanted. So I said, we should do more songs that are that character. As a matter of fact, we should do that character all the time. Alice is the one that of course had the talent to pull it off. Alice Cooper became the character that we decided to do all the time.

Neal Smith:

It was in a pile of junk behind our house. It was sitting down one day with a couple beers and thinking, "Nobody Likes Me"—because it's well documented we played lots of shows and people walked the other way when we were playing—and so we thought, well, we wrote a song called "Nobody likes Me," and it was a forlorn song. So we thought of this character just sitting at the door, the window, looking out of the home, nobody coming to my house to play with me, I'm just bored. So we fixed it up and painted it and put feet on it so you could stand it up. I remember some of the airports we went to, down would come the luggage and all of a sudden there was a door coming. You'd see these golf clubs and then some baggage and a door.

November 1968. Alice Cooper record what will be their debut album, *Pretties for You*. Completely run over, recalls Shep Gordon, Frank foisted upon the band his brother to "produce." Completely green, the guys played what they had on the first day and then it was declared, that's your album. Shep says perhaps there was a second day, but as he recalls, Frank looked at his watch and said that it was 9:15 and that he'd be back at 5:15 and that whatever is done will be the album.
Alice remembers Frank's involvement as a bit more substantial, saying the album took three days and Frank was there but moving them through the songs swiftly, as well as convincing them to just play them live, picking the best of two or three takes.

Neal Smith:

Pretties for You was a very complicated record that we rehearsed morning, noon and night and that's all we did. I would always want to be as well-rehearsed as possible going into the studio and we took that passion and work ethic into all of our albums. It also started our affiliation with Frank Zappa. Frank wanted to change the name of the band to Alice Cookies and he wanted put every song on a single disc and in a tuna fish can. We we're like, "What the fuck are you talking about man?" We flipped. He wanted a tin with 13 discs in it. So that was our first fight with a record company. He wanted to change our name and that was never going to happen. Alice Cookies was not going to happen. Anyway, it was recorded quick and released and we had our first album.

Michael Bruce:

We were at a meeting over at Zappa's house. We walk in, and you know that Edward Beardsley painting on *Pretties for You*? There's that huge painting hanging on the wall. We didn't know at the time that was going to become our album cover (laughs).

So anyway, we're downstairs, and he goes, "About the title of the band, guys; I've got this thing." So he pulls out this, like, cookie tin. Like that crackers or sweetbreads come in. It was about the size of a CD. He says, "So here's what I want to do. I want to call the band Alice Cookies."

At the time they had this thing called a hip pocket record player. You slide these tiny records in and you could take them to school and carry it in your back pocket. Basically a record fit into this thing and you pushed it down and there was a phonograph needle and it played the record. So it was going to be a tin of those, and each song would be on one of these little mini vinyls, smaller that a 45. The players were in the back of some magazine. It wasn't like you could go down to Sears and buy one or something. Well, we had a bad feeling. So we dragged our feet and moved past that hurdle.

But we did like the painting. His daughter Moon Unit had taken a crayon and scribbled on it. But that ended up being our album cover. The funny thing is, after Frank died, they went through all his estate and everything and that painting is missing. They never found it and they don't know where it went or who took it.

January 12, 1969. Led Zeppelin's self-titled debut is released. Arena rock is born.

February 7, 1969. Amidst all manner of shows, small to large, in their adopted hometown of Los Angeles, Alice Cooper travel to Denver to play the Denver Auditorium with Iron Butterfly and the Steve Miller Band.

Gavin Baddeley:
There was a certain level of opportunism about Alice Cooper, at least in the early years. They were originally a bunch of guys from Phoenix who decided they wanted to start a band. The most obvious model for this was the Beatles. So the idea was they'd be a Beatles-type band, but they sort of missed the point and called themselves the Earwigs and then the Spiders.

Then it became clear the next big thing was that all these crazy limey bands seemed to be dressing like chicks. Well, we'll give this a go as well. So there's this sort of half-hearted drag they put on. Again, it's all attention-seeking. But the shift from a band who were playing all these whacked-out Beatles-influenced songs to Alice Cooper, the artist who was being guillotined onstage every night while busty nurses walked about with huge syringes, it's a series of evolutions.

Early 1969. The Frost, featuring Dick Wagner, issue their debut album, *Frost Music.*

Dick Wagner:
The first album is poorly recorded or at least poorly mixed. It doesn't really have a great sound but I think the songs were pretty inventive and really showed a change in my writing, a motion forward that eventually led to all my writing with Alice Cooper, and my range of stuff with Lou Reed. I call that an experimental record. I came out of The Bossmen doing real pop, commercial, English-sounding Beatles-type stuff. I put The Frost together because I wanted a band that could really play this new music of mine and The Bossmen weren't really capable of that.

May 1969. The band move to Cincinnati, Ohio, after being "thrown out of LA." But the rental turns out to be a scam, and they are tossed out by the university students rightfully returning to take over for the school year.

April 12, 1969. *Billboard* magazine reports that Frank Zappa and manager Herb Cohen have formed Straight Records, and that their first act is Alice Cooper.

Michael Bruce:
What happened was the *Freak Out!* album by Frank Zappa and the Mothers became a huge hit. The hippies liked Frank for putting down the establishment. But after getting to know Frank, I realise that he was putting down hippies. You know, because he didn't drink or smoke or do drugs.

But he made a ton of money and now he's gonna get taxed really heavily. So he decides he's going to start Straight Records and sign every weird band, like Captain Beefheart, Wild Man Fischer, GTOs, Alice Cooper band. Tim Buckley was the only really legitimate guy on the label; he was really musical.

So they would come through one door and, "Okay, sign a contract, Herbie is your manager, see you." Boom, boom, boom. Then a couple days before we were supposed to sign with Frank, we met Shep Gordon and Joe Greenberg and we talked with them and they agreed to go represent us. Because they were saying, hey, you know, you guys, they're going to bury you and they were right.

So we had this meeting at the Landmark Hotel, met Joe and Shep, and then Shep walked into Frank's place and he says, "I'm managing the band." Frank was very upset. Because they didn't want anybody meddling with their label and their business. After being on the label for a while, I find out Herbie and his bother, Mutt Cohen, they'd get royalties and they would just sit on them, invest them, and when the bands started whining and crying about it, finally, they would give them their money. But it was like trying to pry yourself loose from *Jaws* or an alligator to get money from them. I guess we were really a pain in their sides, Herbie and Frank.

Also being on his label, we were his discovery. You'd read a review or anything about the band, it was

Frank Zappa discovered us; he was a notable person at the time. So our next ambition was to get as far from the label as possible so we could do our own thing. Thanks, Frank, for discovering us—now we're going to get the hell out of here.

March 1, 1969. *Creem* magazine begins publication, in Detroit. The magazine is started by Barry Kramer (dead at age 37 in 1981), and Tony Reay, with financing provided by The Grande Ballroom's Russ Gibb. The magazine's ample coverage of heavy metal would last through at least 1981, with much good-natured fun made of the genre's hairy personnel. Arch-rival *Circus* would also cover much metal, but with less of a hipster sense of irony.

April 18, 1969. Alice Cooper play the Aggro dome in Vancouver, British Columbia, supporting Frank Zappa and Canadian heroes, The Guess Who. The following night the trio play Seattle.

May 1969. Screaming Lord Sutch and his famous buddies record some pretty rocking tunes, however they wouldn't be issued until early 1970.

Gavin Baddeley:
Screaming Lord Sutch was always— this sounds cruel—an interesting failure. He's an example of how you can perhaps use shock to make up for your limitations in other departments if pressed. Screaming Lord Sutch—who incidentally wasn't a Lord by any stretch of the imagination—was a compulsive attention-seeker and by his own estimation far from a brilliant singer. But he worked out that if you threw some more elements into the mix, then you could try and carve a career out of it.

But he was always lurking on the periphery. The closest he came to success was with a song called "Jack the Ripper," which in its own camp way is quite sinister. He used to come onstage in a coffin dressed in Jack the Ripper garb. We don't actually know what Jack the Ripper wore because we don't know who it was, but everyone thinks he wore a top hat and a cape and obviously had a big knife, and used to chase girls dressed as Victorian prostitutes around the stage and so forth.

Another significant aspect of Screaming Lord Sutch's act is his backing band included a who's who of significant sort of proto-heavy metal performers of the late '60s. But the tragedy with "Jack the Ripper" is it was actually banned by the BBC. There's a misconception that being banned is the automatic road to success, that you're a controversy, a success from scandal. That only works if you can still get your work out there and people buy it. With "Jack the Ripper," being banned by the BBC it kind of canned any money he might have made out of it.

Mid-May 1968. Alice Cooper play Philadelphia, with the MC5.

John Sinclair (MC5 manager):
I first heard of Alice Cooper when he was on Frank Zappa's bizarre label, with *Pretties for You*. That was pretty far out to begin with. Then when the MC5 played a show in Philadelphia with Alice Cooper, there were about 100 people there—total flop (laughs). But we liked them and they liked us and we said, "Man, you guys gotta come to Detroit. They would love you guys in Detroit." It turned out to be true. Because they were bizarre and they rocked. They were a great, great band. "I'm Eighteen," "School's Out"—those are great records. But Vince is

from Detroit (laughs). I think that was bred into him before he moved to Arizona with his parents. Those other guys fit right in. They were all hard rocking guys, Rockin' Reggie and those guys.

June 6 – 16, 1969. The band play venues around New York City.

June 21, 1969. Alice Cooper play the Toronto Pop Festival at Varsity Stadium in Toronto, Ontario.

June 25, 1969. Alice Cooper issue their debut album, *Pretties for You,* on Frank Zappa's label, Straight Records. The band is pictured heavily glammed-up, more so—and somewhat pre-dating—the more famous glam bands from the UK. Besides working with the GTOs and Neal's sister Cindy on their clothes, an early event that helped push the wardrobe was the purchase of, as Alice recalls, 50 pounds of old *Ice Capades* outfits bought at 25 cents a pound.

Dennis Dunaway:
Those albums were exclusively limited to a small group of people with impeccable taste (laughs). We spent most of our time rehearsing and batting ideas around. We wanted to show the world something unique. So creating those crazy abstract songs was a fun process. Our day could end with a new song or it could just be a long day of improvising. But improvising is how we gained our intuitive feel for each other's playing. Ideas started with "What if…" And each and every idea was a challenge to be topped, or made crazier and we became razor sharp at it.

I really liked "Fields of Regret" because it was dark and eerie. The middle part is a good example of how we used instruments like orchestration—bass, guitar, cymbal repeating in that order. "Today Meuller," Toodie Mueller was/is a friend from our earliest days. She was innocent and bubbly and she got us to gigs in her Baby Blue Mustang, so we wrote a happy song about her.

"Nobody Likes Me" belonged on *Pretties for You* as much as "Strawberry Fields Forever" belonged on *Sgt. Pepper*. But it somehow fell by the wayside. I wrote it to symbolize how audiences were treating the band then. Alice sang through a window in a door, "Nobody likes me, it's all my fault" and we answer, "Oh yes, we all like you, we like you a lot." But by the final verse, it's revealed that we hated him. We wore masks to sing our responses to Alice because we represented the audience. The masks were shaped like birds symbolizing how people would fly out the exits when we played.

You see that it says produced by Alice Cooper. The band name belongs to all of us equally. That's just one example that confirms that. Each of us have always received 20% of the royalties on every song on *Pretties for You* because the credits say "Music, lyrics and arrangements by Alice Cooper" as well as that production credit like that right on the label.

We wanted to use Salvador Dali's "Geopolitical Child" for the front cover of *Pretties*, but they claimed that it would cost too much, so we used a painting that Zappa had just purchased—he probably took a tax deduction on it. For the back cover, the band did a photo session at an art gallery. We loved one particular photo but Bizarre lost it. None of us were happy with the alternative one they used.

Alice Cooper:
Frank Zappa loved *Pretties for You* because it was just so bizarre. He said, "I couldn't even teach the Mothers of Invention to play this stuff, it's so weird. *Easy Action* as well; you know, you listen to those albums, and you say this is a good psychedelic band here but no direction at all.

Neal Smith:
We were all thrusting an image and Alice was obviously the focal point on stage. But coming out of Hollywood, we had, Dennis and I… our hair was longer than anybody in rock 'n' roll. Glen and even Mike had long hair. So there was that feminine side, but also music was very powerful. But we weren't trying to do anything except look different than any other band.

My idol growing up was Brian Jones of the Rolling Stones, and I thought he was so cool. He had longer hair than the Beatles and it was blond. I thought man, I want my hair even three times or four times as long as his and my clothes even more outrageous than his. To this day, when it came to rock 'n' roll, I always was a flashy dresser.

The band got into that glitter thing. It was because we love Hollywood. My sister would go to the back lot sales at Fox and MGM and Warner Bros., when they were selling their costumes, and get us a lot of stuff back there. That was all glitter stuff from the '30s '40s and '50s. Nobody really talks about it, but look at *Pretties for You*—Dennis is all dressed in silver on that album. I can't think of too many albums in 1969 or prior to that that anybody was actually dressed like that.

Michael Bruce:
Zappa was sick. He was there about three days. He was just wanting to get it done and he said he was sick and he left. Herbie Cohen, comes down—he was gonna produce the album. He ended up falling asleep on the couch. Thank God for Ian Underwood. He was the keyboard player in the Mothers, and he went on to do synthesizer in a pile of hit movies. He finished the album for us and did a great job.

August 1969. The Stooges' self-titled debut is released.

Alice Cooper:
Nobody did punk better than Iggy and The Stooges. We grew up with those guys in Detroit, and the first time I saw Iggy and the Stooges, I just went, this is… I don't even… there was no such word as punk at that time. So I just called it Detroit street rock. Because it was very simple; there was nothing complicated about it and it was in-your-face, and it had some anger to it and our rock did the same thing. We were a little more sophisticated than The Stooges, but there was always an angry clever twang going on in our music.

Dennis Dunaway:
The Stooges were the originals. That was the first band that had that punk attitude, and they had it in spades. When we came to Detroit, our band had a Hollywood glitz image. We were all wearing chrome and sequins. This was before David Bowie. I don't know why everybody always gives him credit for it, starting that look, but we landed in Detroit, and we see these hard rock, high-energy audiences, and all of the bands are doing that. The MC5, SRC, Ted Nugent, and even Suzi Quatro with the Pleasure Seekers, Frost, Bob Seger. It was a very, very alive, high energy, with everybody on their feet with their fists in the air. If you came out and did a ballad, it wasn't a good idea (laughs). But we showed up and we had this whole completely different thing going on. Luckily they liked us, and we were admitted to the VIP Club there that was going on in Detroit.
    The first thing that happened was Iggy started wearing silver lamé gloves, and MC5 was totally glittered

out. But it was an even exchange in my opinion, because we took the high-energy edginess of the music scene and incorporated it into what we were doing, and we got darker because of it as well, because the bikers liked us a lot.

Back in those days, in the Eastown Theater, where we played a lot and they played a lot, there was a stage that was about two-and-a-half, maybe three-feet off the floor, and Iggy would dive into the audience. But there was no such thing as a moshpit yet (laughs). The crowd would part and Iggy would hit the floor. You could even hear it over the volume of music. Then Iggy would walk around and pick a fight with somebody.

One night Alice and I were walking into the club, because we were going to play after they did. Iggy was looking around to start a fight with somebody. Alice and I stopped to watch that going on, and he came around and looked at Alice, and you could see, he was ready to start a fight with Alice. Then they stood there looking at each other for a few seconds, and he just smiled and moved on.

But MC5 were doing this extreme high-energy show with a lot of political overtones. It was interesting too, because the politics of that day was the same in Canada as it was in the Detroit area. But in Canada it was more like "Imagine" and John Lennon had a big influence, and, "Let's stop the war; let's make love instead of war." In Detroit it was, "Stop the fucking war!" (laughs). So it was the same message; it was just a completely different attitude behind the delivery.

So yeah, the Stooges were the originators of the punk thing, and even though Alice and Iggy had a very similar thing, we followed the Stooges at the Fillmore West once and that was where you could really see the contrast of the differing characters. They were both edgy, they were both threatening, but when the Stooges did their show, it was like they nailed you to the wall on the first song and then every song after that. When we followed them, we came out, the first thing we did was shift gears and pull everything back onto our terms, rather than trying to overpower the Stooges, which nobody could do. So we shifted gears and pulled things back, and then Alice's character sucked them into this deep, dark thing.

August 2, 1969. *Pretties for You* appears at No.194 on the Billboard charts.

Mike Pinera (Iron Butterfly guitarist):
I met Alice Cooper in '69 and he came over and opened for Blues Image at a club, the Experience here in LA on Sunset Blvd., and everybody was so scared of these guys. They had these long fingernails with polish and then the black makeup under the eyes, but to me, man, I just saw some cool guys. The band would see them coming and say, "Don't let them in the dressing room. Don't let those guys in here." I'd wait until my band was gone, then I'd bring them in and share our sandwiches and our coffee with Alice and the boys because they didn't have any food… they didn't have any money for food and they were stuck there all day until it was time to play.

August 8, 9, 1969. The Charles Manson/"Helter Skelter" murders in L.A., which represent the death of the innocent '60s, although the event is one of a handful of cultural touchstones to do so. America finds out that hippies are not all peace and love, a revelation that would also come to Black Sabbath, who will represent a new pessimism, cynicism and fatalism amongst the ranks of the very hairy.

Dennis Dunaway:
Just before '68 when the Alice Cooper group first started traveling to California, to Hollywood, we got there right at the tail end of this amazing era of the Sunset Strip. It was just, you walk down the street and it's unbelievable. Buffalo Springfield over here, the Doors over here, and the amount of people all dressed up, hippies and all kinds of people—I had never even heard the word silicone before. It was amazing. California girls.

Then it all changed with the Charles Manson thing. All of a sudden all this love and peace and everything got darker. There was also this big crackdown in Los Angeles in particular—and I'm sure other parts of the country—where they wanted to suppress what they thought was a threat. Therefore you started seeing things like paddy wagons pull up and put everybody who was in line to go into the Whiskey A Go Go in the paddy wagons and haul them all away.

You couldn't walk down the street without being checked, and if you didn't have your ID with you… to this day my wife and I always carry our IDs because of the LAPD back in those days, because you'd be shipped out of town. Buffalo Springfield had "For What It's Worth," "There's something happening here, there's a man with a gun over there." Well that was about Pandora's Box, a popular club on the Sunset Strip where there was a big crackdown.

Therefore you had the Doors. It became the establishment was against us, a lot of bands thought, and therefore our music is going to be our way of fighting back. So lyrics started getting more political. Not ours. We weren't really politically motivated, we were more culture motivated. We just saw that the peace and love generation was burning itself out. Bill Graham is convinced that we ruined everything, our band in particular. He hated us. We weren't really angry at anything. We were just totally into perpetuating this vision that we had. All we cared about was music.

September 6, 1969. An article appears in *Billboard* reporting that Alice Cooper are beginning legal proceedings to break ties with Straight Records.

September 13, 1969. Alice Cooper mount a historic stand at the Rock 'n' Roll Revival festival, Toronto, Ontario. This is the site of the famous Alice Cooper chicken incident, in which a chicken thrown off the stage by Alice gets torn apart by the crowd. The false story that Alice could never live down, however, was that Alice tore apart live chickens on stage—and worse.

Dennis Dunaway:
The Toronto Rock 'n' Roll Revival footage is an insight to how we applied our artistic influences to the show. That night we used a metal folding chair with the concept that a common item can take on significance when it's featured in the spotlight with the whole band looking toward it while playing a big fanfare. Making a chair seem that important sparked curiosity and assumptions. It had to mean something, didn't it? We also incorporated a football that night, which Alice kicked into the crowd. That kick was the cue for an explosion of musical and visual chaos. It was a rock 'n' roll revival and not many Canadians knew about us so it was completely unexpected. We were fearless about trying things in our show. It was like an evolving string of assaults to the senses. Very few people outside of the Alice Cooper group realised how fast and furiously the show evolved. People would comment about how different one night's show was from our previous night's show. If they had returned the following night, it would be different again.

But what happened that night… see I grew up with chickens. My grandparents raised chickens when I was a little kid, and when I moved to Arizona we had chickens, and then later on in the Detroit area, Glen was doing this thing where he would tap the top of his neck with his right hand, fingers on his right hand, and it would make a sound that reminded me of chickens clucking. So I thought, just another one of these things where we would during that era, still from the VIP days, or the club in Phoenix, we would just grab things backstage and incorporate them into the show.

Well I got this idea that it would be funny to have chickens sitting on Glen's amp when he did this finger-plucking part, which was the solo he did in one of the tunes. So I got this guy to go out and get chickens and set them on Glen's amp. The great thing is, these chickens looked totally oblivious to what was going on onstage, which was total chaos. They would look at Glen when he did that sound and tilt their heads like they were trying to understand what his guitar sound was saying to them.

So we loved that, and that led to Neal and I having a pillow fight sharing a cheap motel room in Cincinnati. We were just bored so Neal hit me with a pillow. So I hit him back and a feather came out of the pillow and floated in the air. Then we were hitting each other as hard as we could. Actually I think we were even getting pissed-off at each other, or upset at each other, and more and more feathers came out.

So we go, wait a minute, that's it. Feathers came out of the pillow, and so I got the idea of chickens, feathers, let's rip the pillow open. Then Michael Bruce got the idea of using a fire extinguisher to blow the feathers to kingdom come. Of course once Alice and I established the idea of doing theatrics onstage, everybody joined in. Neal had an art background. Michael was the least likely to join in, but he came up with some great ideas as well. So that was one of the pretty amazing things, I think, that you could have five personalities that were so different from each other, but all were on the same page when it came to doing the craziest theatrics we can think up.

I had an acoustic bass amp, which was the bass amp to have in its day, and it started sounding muffled. So I took the grill cloth off and the amp was full of feathers. The CO_2 tank had blown the feathers right through the grill cloth. So every month or two I had to empty it out.

So the chicken sound led to us using chickens. Unlike the stories that everybody has chosen to believe over the years, we said we didn't back in those days, because we had so much pressure from the Humane Society and everything, but the chickens were our pets. Glen kept them in his hotel room, he put them in his bathroom, and they even had names. We used them every night.

But that particular night, Alice got this idea to toss one into the audience, which was a bad idea. But I do believe his part of the story that he really thought the chicken would fly. Because that's just how he was. He didn't grow up on a farm like I did (laughs). So he thought he would toss the chicken and it would fly away, whereas the chicken landed in the audience. What we didn't anticipate, or intend, was the audience ripped it apart like it was a valuable souvenir.

On that particular night, there's footage of it called *The Chicken Incident* by D.A. Pennebaker, and if you slow down the frames, you can see Glen playing a lead guitar break, and you can see how it's come out of the pillow case, and you can see that that pillowcase has something in it besides feathers. You can see Alice take the chicken out and toss it into the audience. He was supposed to take the chicken out and just set it down or let it loose on stage, so it would be walking around when we were doing this feather storm.

So the chickens were just another element in our ever-evolving props. The *Rock and Roll Revival* wasn't the first time we had used them, but it was the last because we really didn't like what the crowd did to our pet chicken, Pecker. Following the chicken incident at that show, we continued our heavy schedule of playing every gig we could get. But we noticed that lots of people were showing up at our shows with rubber chickens. It took a few nights before we figured out what was going on.

But we intended to do something different for every show, and we had gotten comfortable with winging it. We would use anything as a prop. We would even grab things on our way to the stage—a watermelon, a bicycle, a garbage can, anything. If we used something and it bombed, fine, we had so many other things that it didn't matter. Many people were convinced that our odd choice of props had some significant underlying meaning. They would come backstage and say things like, "I know why you opened the umbrella over Glen's head while he did his solo." In reality, we were just having fun. That was the art of it. Then stories and rumours inevitably started to fly. Some make me smile and some make me see red.

Neal Smith:

My recollection of the story is that we were playing these large clubs and we would release doves, like an anti-hippie statement, when we released the feathers. It made sense. It'd be feathers and some birds flying out. I remember that our roadies couldn't find any doves for that show, but they found some live chickens. I think we were doing a version of "Animal Pajamas" or "Lay Down and Die, Goodbye." But I think it was "Animal Pajamas," which they call "Freak Out Song" on Science Fiction and all the bootleg albums that you find from that era. It was actually a remake of the Spiders' first hit, "Don't Blow Your Mind." That was a local hit in Arizona, but we rewrote it as "Animal Pajamas" and did a big freak-out thing on it. I did a drum solo, and we had guitar solos and Dennis does this amazing bass solo, and it was just a free-form thing.

It ends up with the CO_2 and the feathers flying, and also Alice had a flare gun too and it came down into the crowd, and it didn't quite burn out before it landed. Nobody ever talks about that but I actually still have the flare gun (laughs). But the chicken came out, Alice throws it out into the crowd—I don't know what happened to it.

The thing about that, there was a group of people there that were physically challenged folks in wheelchairs at the front. John Lennon had been there, we were on stage with big celebrities during that show. So they had a section, which was great, so everybody was invited to the concert. Alice says that it went in there and they stomped on the chicken and killed it.

All Alice did was throw it out into the crowd, and where it landed and what happened, I don't know. But I remember that the roadies couldn't find any doves to release, because it was the Rock 'n' Roll Revival/ peace festival. I love Michael Bruce, who had this representation of it: Alice always said he was from Detroit, a city boy, he threw a chicken out and thought it would fly. Michael says, "How many times have you ever seen a chicken fly by the window?" So I don't didn't buy that story that Alice didn't know chickens didn't fly. So he threw it out and I don't know what happened, and the worldwide press across United States and Canada was crazy.

But I don't remember that story Dennis says about them being on Glen's amp. But I remember the chickens that one night. We may have had them as just a bizarre thing, but I know they were on stage. I know that the roadies put them on there; they didn't just suddenly appear. So whether we used them several nights… they maybe were on Glen's amps, because at that time Glen was still on the left-hand side of the stage before Michael was pushed over there. At any rate, we never killed a chicken—that was the thing.

Alice Cooper:
First of all our manager, Shep, was one of the guys that put the show together, and they were going to pay him. He says, "Don't pay me. The only thing I want you to do is I want Alice to go on between John Lennon and the Doors." On a Saturday night and we were really not that well-known. We were notorious, but we weren't well-known then. So the Doors go on, and everybody, oh, it's the Doors. They were friends of ours.

They got done and then we go on. We do our set and we do the feathered pillows and the CO2's coming out, and the next thing I realise, I look down and there's a chicken. Now I didn't bring the chicken. Nobody in my band brought a chicken. Somebody in the audience went, let me see, I got my keys, I got my wallet, I got my drugs, I got my chicken. Who brings a chicken to a show? I swear, we have no idea where the chicken came from.

There's a chicken onstage, I'm from Detroit, never been on a farm in my life. It had feathers, it was a bird, it should fly. You know? So I picked it up and I went, okay, and I tossed it lightly into the audience thinking it'll fly away or somebody will get a great souvenir. I got Alice's chicken. It went into the audience and the audience tore it to pieces. Blood everywhere and threw what was left onstage.

Of course now the next day in the paper it was Alice Cooper kills chicken. In the melee, everybody will swear that I ripped the chicken's throat out and ate the head and did all this stuff. It never happened. Frank Zappa called me the next day and he says, "Did you kill a chicken onstage last night?" And I went no. He said, "Well don't tell anybody; they love it." I got my first lesson in, okay, they love it. You know, now I became much more notorious than I was before.

I realised that it was maybe the best thing that ever happened to us, the sacrifice of this poor chicken. Now the kicker to the story is this. I would never hurt an animal. I'm an animal lover. But the first five rows at the concert were all people in wheelchairs. They're the ones that killed the chicken, which makes it even more bizarre. Because now the crippled people crippled the chicken in anger somehow.

I thought that is so weird because Canada seems peaceful and loving and wonderful. Did we bring that out in them that they would kill a chicken? That was even more bizarre to me. That story then, to this day, when we play, are you going to kill chickens tonight? I say how come nobody's hassling Colonel Sanders? He's killing billions of chickens. He's like the Hitler of chickens. One poor chicken got thrown in the audience and I'm the chicken-killer forever.

But in the end I totally get the folklore behind it. I've done much worse things than that since then, but the chicken thing seemed to be the one. That was the launch button for Alice Cooper. Now I looked on the side, there's Jim Morrison on this side and John and Yoko on this side going, yeah! They loved the performance art of this whole thing.

September 14, 1969. Alice Cooper play the Toledo Pop Festival, which includes on the bill, the MC5, the Amboy Dukes, The Frost, The Rationals and Früt.

Dick Wagner:
The first time I saw Alice Cooper was at the Toledo Pop Festival, I think, when they had the fans blowing and they threw out the chicken feathers. I'd say they were already pretty shocking by that point. Alice got hung or I think it was electrocuted. So I thought that was just great, very clever. Because like, my old band, The Bossmen used to do little skits and stuff, so we were attuned to the idea of theatrical rock.

Dennis Dunaway:
Shep Gordon and Joe Greenberg—we talked Zappa into signing us and he said we needed a manager and we had three days to find one. My wife, Cindy, who was—and is—Neal's sister found Joe and Shep. They and Zappa came to see us perform at the Lenny Bruce memorial show at the Cheetah Ballroom in Venice,

California. All of these bands were playing that day, Iron Butterfly and quite a few great LA bands. The place was packed when we started playing. Within three or four songs the place had evacuated. We're thinking, well, we just blew a record deal.

But Shep Gordon—probably more than Joe Greenberg—thought this was amazing. The most amazing thing he had seen. All we had to do was harness that power. That we could drive those people out of the room that fast all screaming insults at us. So he started advertising the band that drives people out of the room. So people started coming to see us to see why people left.

Then our album *Pretties for You* did not get very good press. I think one writer said, "Songs Disney had sense enough to leave in the can," which, that was a stake right into my heart because I thought this was the greatest album in the world at the time. So we're all depressed, and Joe and Shep are like, "No, are you kidding? This is good! If he wrote something good about you guys, we wouldn't be able to use it." We're like, oh, really? Sure enough as time went on, bad reviews… not like we had any choice. We would work extremely hard on our music and then somebody would talk about that we used the snake. So it was always negative press. Even when we'd get positive press there would be something negative in it usually, or there would be another story that was completely negative, because people still didn't like us because of our image.

October 31, 1969. The Black Magic & Rock 'n' Roll Festival, otherwise know as The Black Arts Festival, Olympia Stadium, Detroit, which includes America's most prominent occult rock act Coven. A poster for the event reads: "Witches, Devils, 6 PM – 3 AM. Tickets 5:00." Acts listed are: Arthur Brown, Dr. Tim Leary, Frost, MC5 (whited out), Ralph Adams, Mystic Peter Murkos, Amboy Dukes, Bonzo Dog Band, Stooges, Coven, Pink Floyd, Savage Grace, Kim Fowley, Alice Cooper, Sky, Teegarden & Van Winkle, Satan (Ainsley), SRC, Frut, Bob Seger, All the Lonely People and Pleasure Seekers. A second poster reads: "Mike Quatro, Russ Gibb and Mike Keener present A Black Arts Festival" with the highlighted bands being MC5, Stooges, Frost, Bonzo Dog Band, Bob Seger System, Arthur Brown, SRC, Pink Floyd. One fan has documented that the show turned out to be a rip-off, with no performance by the likes of Pink Floyd, Bonzo Dog band, Alice Cooper, The Frost, MC5, Arthur Brown or The Amboy Dukes.

December 1969. The Frost issue their second album, *Rock and Roll Music*, which, like MC5's *Kick Out the Jams*, is recorded live at the Grande Ballroom.

Dick Wagner:
The Frost was always heavier live that we were on the record so we captured a bit of the live heaviness on that album. We were like the most popular band, but we were also the outliers. We were the ones doing the rock 'n' roll with melody and harmonies, very sort of sophisticated for the time. I was fortunate enough to be one of the two guitar players in town who was really getting recognition, the other being Ted Nugent.

We did some touring but not that much. The band could've been much bigger, had we had the opportunity to really tour. But we didn't have the proper management at the time and we really didn't have an agent. I was basically doing everything. Doing all the calls for gigs. Then the band broke up because Bobby and Donnie wanted to go home and go fishing. They didn't want to go out on the road, and have to suffer going through the winning of new audiences. Because it's a task, every time you play brand-new place, especially if they don't know who you are. But The Frost had a certain magic about the band, and we pretty much scored every time we played. We made fans; people loved us. Even San Francisco, where we open for B.B. King; even that audience loved us.

December 6, 1969. The Altamont Speedway Free Festival in Northern California, headlined by the Rolling Stones, results in lots of violence, one murder, and three accidental deaths. The event-gone-wrong is considered the death of the '60s, or at least the death of '60s psychedelic rock, an idea foisted up the Manson murders as well. It is a rare large festival of the day with no heavy rock, just heavy security.

1970

Alice Cooper begin 1970 by watching Black Sabbath's debut record come out. I'm joking, but it's sort of important in the wider scope of things, because with both acts being on Warner, it will become framed for the first half of the '70s that these are the two spooky and dark competing rock acts operating amongst everything else. Despite the presence of Bowie, not really doing much until 1973 as the original Alice Cooper group wanes, plus no Kiss or Blue Öyster Cult for a while, this is basically it, along with a slight blip for Arthur Brown.

In March of 1970, Alice Cooper issue their second album *Easy Action* to zero effect. But being in the right place at the right time, with the sordid Straight Records run by Frank, (not exactly a straight shooter) and the nasty Herbie Cohen, Alice gets sold off at a discount to Warner Bros. and all of a sudden they are on a major.

This happens concurrent with the move to Detroit and a trial by fire than finds the band increasing their intensity levels to match that of the harder Detroit rockers. The "chicken incident" of late 1969 still causing an uproar, the band play a fest in Cincinnati that gets them on TV.

But the most important gig turns out to be a low-key club show in September at Max's Kansas City in Manhattan, attended by Bob Ezrin, who is sent down to get Shep off of Jack Richardson's back and tell these pests once and for all, no, you are not going to be the next Guess Who. Turning the tables, Bob loves the band and takes on the project as his first rung up the ladder (eventually putting him over *The Wall*).

As they mourn the death of Jimi Hendrix, Bob and his new charges knuckle down at the band house and at a nearby studio in Chicago on what will become the hit *Love It to Death* album, debuting before the year is out with anthem for the ages, "I'm Eighteen." Alice is now a midwest band—it's not exactly rust belt at this point—soon to become an east coast band, but emphatically not an LA band. For the next three years it will be about pragmatism, hard work and not a ray of sunshine.

January 30, 31, 1970. A raucous gig at the Eastown Theatre in Detroit finds Alice Cooper and The Stooges on the same bill.

Dennis Dunaway:
    The obvious competition was killer back then. You had Hendrix, The Beatles, The Stones, The Kinks, The Who and everybody else, and in retrospect they all had their own unique styles. Even though there were

clone bands back *then, as well as there are today, it seemed like the aim was to become more individual. So our goal was* just to stand out from everybody else. And some of our influences were those obvious ones, but we also became very geared towards incorporating art into the show.

One of the many things we did was build a big giant wheel. We called it the Electro-lucent Mind Machine. It was made out of plywood, and it had to be eight feet tall or whatever size the largest sheet of plywood comes in. We cut it into a circle, then we painted it with all kinds of abstract hieroglyphics. It also had hidden things so that under a black light these words would show up that were invisible in regular light. We had a motor on it, and we would get the thing spinning, and we had a very early strobe light, before other people did, that we had made out of an ammunitions case from the old army and navy store.

So this really came from our interest in the Dada art movement and incorporating art into what we were doing. Because I was an artist when I was in grade school, there were years where nobody even knew my name. They just called me The Artist. So to give up art to pursue music, I wasn't ready to do that. Alice and I decided we were going to bring our art with us, and incorporate it.

February 1970. Screaming Lord Sutch, one of England's favourite underground wild men of rock 'n' roll through the '60s, finally issues his debut album, entitled *Lord Sutch and Friends*. Characters like Sutch and more so Arthur Brown represent the UK's answer to Alice.

Dennis Dunaway:

Skirmishes with society was an everday occurance with us (laughs). All we had to do was walk down the street, even in Hollywood. The way we dressed and the length of our hair... it was longer than anyother band at the time. When we walked down the street, people would either get upset or they would like it. But there was hardly ever that we would pass anybody who didn't have a strong reaction. Then of course after the chicken incident happened in Toronto, every time we showed up to play—animal rights people and the Humane Society and the fire marshalls and everybody—it seemed like there would be so many people there to stop us from doing the show. The promoters always had to convince them that it was just a show.

Neal Smith:

We were very anti-hippie all the time, and as things progressed, we were always decadent. But we were decadent even when we were poor. It was Dennis' idea, when you open up the album cover on *Love It to Death*, the most unusual thing was Alice's eyes and when you look inside the pupils, you see a picture of the band. We were doing that all the time.

We just wanted to come up with things that were different. People called us Dada rock in the middle and in the beginning, and they also called it third-generation rock, and they were trying to come up with a name because they just couldn't figure out what the hell we were doing.

I guess we were considered freaks because of that early sound plus given that we were associated with Frank Zappa. But I never associated myself with anything other than rock 'n' roll, I just wanted to be a rock 'n' roller. As far as my image, I consider two people, there

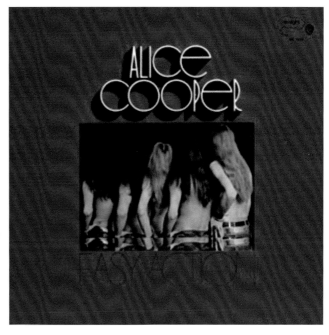

are cool people and there are not cool people, and I always thought our image was just trying to be ultra-hip all the time. The more money we had, the cooler we looked. Sitting there with a $5000 jacket on and sitting in a Rolls-Royce, I'm no fucking hippie, I'll guarantee you that. I'm wearing a diamond ring that has 18 diamonds in it. So like I said, we were always decadent, we were always rock 'n' roll, and it was just trying to be different. It was a rock 'n' roll interpretation. Hippies were the fans. Actually I never considered too many bands hippies. So I look at it a little bit differently. But of course back then, Zappa signed us because he thought it was freaky. It's a band called Alice Cooper and the singer's called Alice Cooper. It's a very androgynous band and we're there with the GTOs and Wild Man Fischer, Captain Beefheart, all these freaky bands, and our first couple of albums were pretty crazy. But again, I never considered us hippies or freaks.

Friday February 13, 1970. UK release date for Black Sabbath's debut, *Black Sabbath*. Sabbath, also a Warner Bros. artist, would long be linked with Alice Cooper as premiere scary hard rock bands through the first half of the '70s.

March 1970. Leicester's Black Widow issue their debut album, *Sacrifice*. Black Widow were known for being the most overtly Satanic and theatrical UK band of the time although not that heavy. Still, the band's act, where they performed a Satanic mass, would generate the scared hysteria Alice would experience in his heyday.

March 27, 1970. Alice Cooper's second album *Easy Action* is released.

Dennis Dunaway:
I don't know who hired David Briggs. He had just finished producing an album for Neil Young and Crazy Horse and that's what he should have been doing. We all got the impression that he didn't like anything about us. Despite that, he got an album out of an unprepared band. As for those songs, Alice wrote "Shoe Salesman" with an evident double entendre lyric about a dealer. Glen was pretty faithful to Alice's original acoustic guitar part on that, as well as on "Laughing at Me." But Glen raised the bar with his Chet Atkins influence.

"Beautiful Flyaway" was Michael's piano tune, which I've always loved. He reminded me of a little Mozart brat when he was recording it. Michael is singing and playing piano on "Beautiful Flyaway." David Briggs played piano on "Shoe Salesman," which was one of the welcome few times he seemed to care about the sessions.

I liked "Lay Down and Die, Goodbye" because it contained a free-form sound collage that was disturbing. I would have been happy if the whole album was like that. "Lay Down and Die, Goodbye" includes the line, "You are the only censors; if you don't like what I am saying, you have a choice, you can turn me off." That is an excerpt of Tommy Smothers' farewell speech in response to the network pulling the plug on the controversially ground-breaking *Smothers Brothers Comedy Hour*. I think it was David Briggs' idea to use it.

We tried with "Lay Down And Die, Goodbye," to write a proper song, but we still weren't good enough at our craft of songwriting to be able to pre-determine how the song was going to come out. Writing a song for us would be like shooting a shotgun at a canvas and just seeing what it looked like. Briggs called the song psychedelic garbage, and he looked like he wished he could turn it off. I think his negative comments seeped into the feel of the recording.

For the cover of *Easy Action*, the photo of the band facing away was Neal's idea. It proved to be very effective for emphasizing our androgynous look. Especially since nobody had ever seen anything like that before. But really, Easy Action is my least favourite of all of them. For one thing, we were forced into the studio when we only had about a third of the material to do an album, because of contractual obligations. We had a lot of ideas for songs, but I don't think there are more than one or two songs on that album that we had actually written before we went into the studio, so we made that album up on the spot and we didn't have anywhere to rehearse. So that's how that was slapped together. So we already had good intentions, but we just didn't have the means to pull it off, by then. Even though I do really love some of the songs, and I love the way Glen played on "Laughing at Me" and "Shoe Salesman," stuff that is a completely different style for the band. It was very Chet Atkins-influenced on Glen's behalf.

Neal Smith:
We wanted to improve our production so we got David Briggs. When we did "Lay Down and Die, Goodbye" he called it "psychedelic shit." So that gives you an idea about how much he was into what we were doing or understanding what we were doing.

Michael Bruce:
When we did *Easy Action*, David Briggs idea of producing a record was, he'd come in and he'd kick back in the chair, put his feet up on the console, in his cowboy boots, and he'd start rolling some big doobie and smoking it, and he'd go, "Okay, that's a take, next song!" So, we were about ready to get out of the music business. I played "Beautiful Flyaway" through once, and he goes, "Okay, okay, that's good!" I had to talk him into letting me do it again.

Spring 1970. The Alice Cooper band move to Detroit. Suddenly they are part of a harder rock stew that includes The MC5, The Stooges, the Amboy Dukes, SRC and Bob Seger.

Dennis Dunaway:
We left LA, because *Pretties for You* didn't take off for us and we were travelling on the road, basically just doing any gig that we could come up with. We were touring with what I called the Zorro method, because we would play in Oregon, and then we would go to Boston, then LA and Florida. Sometimes it was an M, which was just a sideways Z. But we had to just take whatever gig and then get there. So we jumped in the car.

But Detroit had a lot of fans who liked what we were doing more than other parts of the country at the time. So we came to Detroit and here we are this glammed-up Hollywood act, and then here's MC5 and the Stooges and this artistic sort of inspiring of each other. We all of a sudden saw this high-energy thing happening in Detroit that was even maybe more loyal, dare I say, than the San Francisco groups were to their bands. Well, San Francisco and Detroit had the audiences that were the most loyal to their bands; let's put it that way. But if you played in Detroit, it was fists in the air for every single person in the audience—but you'd better not play a ballad, or like Glen Buxton used to say, a girl's song.

So we drew that energy and that made our music improve. But Iggy started wearing silver lame gloves and MC5 started wearing shiny fabrics in their outfits, so there was a meeting of the arts there and it was good for us. We started playing all these festivals that Mickey Quatro mostly put on. It would be Cradle and Catfish and Savage Grace and Mitch Ryder and the Stooges and MC5 and on and on. But mostly the same Detroit bands.

But every time it would be sold-out, packed and fists in the air. So that became our bread and butter. So we started staying at this dive hotel, the Grass Ship—I hope it's not still there. Anyway, that was our home for a year. Living out of suitcases, really. Then we got the farm in Pontiac outside of Detroit.

Alice Cooper:
We realised we were just a fish out of water in LA. We were this band that was not groovy, we were not into peace and love, we were not into love-ins, we were not into, "Isn't everything groovy?" We were more interested in switchblades, blondes and Ferraris and we just didn't fit in. We were notorious because we didn't mind a little violence onstage, and that was the last thing LA was about. LA was about Buffalo Springfield. The Doors was about as close as they came to anything violent, and Jim was just volatile. But we were out-and-out *Clockwork Orange*, pre-*Clockwork Orange*.

So we didn't fit in at all. We finally said the first place that gives us a standing ovation, we're going to move to. We got this gig at the Saugatuck Pop Festival in Michigan and that's what happened. I'm from Detroit; that's my hometown. We did our show and the audience loved it. Just total opposite of LA. This audience was a black T-shirt, black leather jacket, greasy black hair audience who saw us and went yeah! Attitude! This band had attitude and they loved that. Then when they found out it was from Detroit, I was the missing son. I was the missing finger in that glove.

Maybe that's where that string of violence comes from in me, is it's built-in, it's in the DNA. And the sensationalism of it. You don't just sing the song, you act it out. If you're going to say "Welcome to my nightmare," give the audience a nightmare. Don't just say it. If you're going to do "Gutter Cats vs. the Jets" and it's *West Side Story*, do the knife fight from *West Side Story*.

Neal Smith:

Detroit's always in our hearts. It was Detroit and the Midwest that broke the band. Before we even brought Bob Ezrin in we were surviving by selling a few albums on Frank Zappa's label and having a part of the country that really "got" what we were doing and enjoyed it. At the time The Stooges and the MC5 were big bands in Detroit and we moved in, we came in from out west and we set up camp there and we started playing all of the top places and playing all of the big festivals.

I asked a couple of people in the area, "Why do you guys like us so much?"—just out of curiosity, because most people don't care—"You have some great bands here with the MC5 and The Stooges." And they said, "Well, you're doing what they're doing, but you're doing so much more!" I understood what they were saying. So the Alice Cooper fan base was established right between Detroit, Cleveland and Toronto—that was our launching grounds.

Michael Bruce:

When we moved to Michigan, it was a whole different style back there—the music was different. A lot of people were going over the UK and bringing music back. In the Ann Arbour area, we got roadie Martin Priest, and he built a really kick-ass PA for us. Now, when we played a show, one night to the next night we could sound just as bad-ass. Consistency is what really made it happen. But the props and whatnot that we used, the music always had to be the backdrop for that and it had to be spot-on. So he did a great job and that was a real factor in our early days.

Plus we were stuck out on a farm. We lived in Pontiac, it had a dirt road and a well for water, but it did have a big horse paddock in the back, indoor, where they trained horses. It was the size of a football field. There was a workshop at the end of it, and we could play our little hearts out. That's where we burned a lot of midnight oil.

The house was two bedrooms and then the bathroom, and I think Glen was sleeping in the dining room. I don't know where everybody else slept. If I think back, it was six or seven of us at the time, and certainly there wasn't that many bedrooms, so we didn't play in the house. We were poor. We used to go to the Farmer Jack's grocery store and steal the meat from the department because we couldn't afford to buy any at the time.

Jaan Uhelski (Creem magazine journalist):

They were really minimal players when they first came to town. They had a house out near where I worked. They were just unbelievably strange flowers that had taken a route in some sort of suburban oasis, had a band house and practiced all the time and pranced around and wore amazing clothes. I would see them come in masks in the mall where I worked. This is right around the time they had Ezrin produce them. But they were a joke. They were just not really good before this, not until probably the third album that they actually got good. They were almost unlistenable, but again their show was so great; it was like a phenomenon. I'm not sure if they were never not dark also. They were always funny but the songwriting got so much better, and they started to make anthemic things. You could really see the development in them but when they first moved there, they were the proto band.

As for Alice and Iggy, they were rarely in the same place. Every time I interview Iggy, he says that Alice just wanted to be next to him. I think it was almost a strange hero-worship. They rarely talked; again it wasn't the same circle. They were on bills together but that's it. Alice was born in Detroit. I have a feeling that they just fell on their faces in LA and that they were a joke because of their association with Zappa. And Zappa thought they were a joke after a while, after embracing them, and just dropping them.

They didn't have many moves left. Detroit had a reputation. He's always loved The Stooges. I think he really wanted to get back to that hardness. They were really a hard band at that point. I think they hadn't got their theatrical direction down yet. God bless your countrymen, Bob Ezrin, if he hadn't come in and whipped them into shape, they wouldn't be the band they are.

But they rented a farm out in the outskirts of Detroit, which was incredibly cheap rent. All of them could live there, and they brought Bob Ezrin down, and Bob moved in with them, and he really did drill them. He taught them how to write songs, he put them through their paces and made them practice all the time. It was like the military. I remember them being really poor. I used to manage a boutique when I worked at Creem, and I remember Alice and Neal Smith coming in, and me giving them free clothes, because they were just down on their luck financially. But they were a presence. They weren't of us, they weren't Detroiters, but they played there a lot.

Dennis Thompson (MC5 drummer):
The powers that be in New York, when they came to Detroit and found us, well then they hired The Stooges and The Frost, and more bands got signed as they came to Detroit and recognized the talent. Alice Cooper got signed. They were an LA band who came to Detroit to get muscled-up. Because when they first came out here and played, they were god-awful. They were a sideshow, clown carnival band. They came to Detroit and the attitude in Detroit was kick out the jams or get off the stage; you know, play and play well, play really well. And they really, really improved, really tightened-up and got some strength to their music.

Wayne Kramer (MC5 guitarist):
I think Alice Cooper moved to Detroit because Detroit was the portal at the time. It was the gateway, and there was a lot going on. There was a lot of work. You could perform regularly all over the area. It was a good hub. You could shoot down to Cleveland, you could go to New York, over to Chicago. Living was inexpensive. You'd have a band house. The MC5 lived in a converted dentist's office. I think our rent was $125 a month, with a rehearsal room downstairs for another $75 a month. That's pretty reasonable, even by 1968 standards. I think Alice and the guys were intrigued with the music. They saw what was happening with the MC5. The first time I ever played with them, we were both appearing at a club in Philadelphia. We were in our dressing room, they had their own dressing room, and they sent their roadie over. He said, "Yeah, I'm with Alice Cooper. Is MC5 wearing all your spangly clothes tonight?" "Yeah man, we're wearing our shit. Are you guys wearing…" "Oh, we're going to wear ours, too." "Okay, cool." Checking out the competition.

K.J. Knight (Amboy Dukes drummer):
Alice Cooper, I'll tell you what, they went through a tough transition. When we played with them, a lot of times, man, they would be booed off the stage, and I don't think people understood or had a grasp of what they were trying to do. But after they had a couple of hit singles, and after they started playing out so often, they picked up so much popularity that it was just unbelievable. They become very successful, a huge group.

Johnny "Bee" Badanjek:
They were up the road, I-75, out near where Pine Knob is or DTE, the outside venue; they rented an old white farmhouse off of Brown Road, Pontiac, and he had a big barn. They converted the barn into a rehearsal space and they used to have these parties all the time. There'd be like 500, 700 people, everybody from Detroit go out to the farmhouse on the weekends. There'd be drinking, jamming, girls, the feeding of Alice's snake in the aquarium. That was the highlight; they'd throw a rat in there or something and girls would go screaming and stuff, great time. But they also started getting their sound together, and then they did *Love It to Death* and got popular really fast. Alice's father was a preacher and earlier they were between Detroit and Arizona so he was aware of the scene. They stayed here for a while, but then they started getting really big and they were travelling.

One time, when I was playing with Detroit featuring Mitch Ryder, and we doing opening shows for Alice, and we were in Washington, DC, the old hockey arena. There was two shows, an afternoon show and a night-time show and it was packed. Ten thousand kids. Alice is on the part where they're going to hang him.

We already played our set. I'm sitting on the anvil cases with some of the biker guys who were security and we're watching this. Alice is up there, they put this clip behind him to catch the rope, and so he's hanging. He's actually got his hands tied because they've got handcuffs on his hands, right? So the clip slips and he's actually hanging. His face is turning red, and everybody on his crew is going, oh, the boss is getting into it today, this is incredible.

I'm looking at him, me and Dirty M, and I'm going something's not right. It looks like he's going get me down, get me down, I'm really hanging. Everybody's going he's really into it! The audience is mesmerized. I'm going get him down, he's dying! They finally realise it, and these guys run up and take him down, and Alice is done. His face is red as a tomato, his hands are still tied. He's going, "What took you guys so long?"

May 20, 1970. Four students killed by the Ohio National Guard at Kent State University in Ohio, where protests over the American invasion of Cambodia were taking place.

Neal Smith:

I think that sooner or later something like Alice Cooper would have happened. The revolutions, the Vietnamese war, the turmoil of the '60s, Kent State, this was normal TV now. You could see students killed in a university. You see all this tragedy all around you every night on the news. That didn't happen in the '50s; it was happening in the '60s and the '70s. People were bombarded by all this stuff and that's why Alice says we were almost a reflection of what was happening in society. We were in the right place at the right time and we did the right things at the right time. If it wouldn't have been us, maybe the next extension after the Doors would have been another band.

June 1, 1970. The US release date for Black Sabbath's *Black Sabbath*, prompting long and loud visits for the only band to rival Alice in the spooky rock sweepstakes.

June 13, 1970. Portions of Alice Cooper's performance at the Cincinnati Pop Festival, at Crosley Fields in Cincinnati, are broadcast on local TV.

Dennis Dunaway:

We were mostly banned by television stations who didn't want to touch us with a ten-foot pole, because of our image. That's why there's not very much footage of the original Alice Cooper group, as visual as we were, and that's perfect for an interesting show. They had this show called the *Midsummer Rock Festival*, which was in Cincinnati, Ohio, and what happened was, there was supposed to be a baseball game and I believe the baseball players went on strike. So a major network's sports hour, where these hours are worked out, the promoters brought in this rock festival and the television station decided they were going to broadcast it and they used sportscasters.

There were a lot of bands on the bill, the Stooges, Traffic, Grand Funk Railroad, Mott The Hoople, on and on and it was televised nationally. We decided that we were going to play a song that we had never played before, "Black Juju." We never even rehearsed it before. I discussed the arrangement in the car on the way to the show. Then we had gotten this idea, probably because we were used to stealing pillows out of hotel rooms. We decided to steal the sheets and Alice would put a sheet over each guy while we were performing this song, and somebody in the audience got a hold of a sheet, and they pulled it out of Alice's hands.

So he threw a sheet under Neal's drums and climbed under there, and the cameraman climbed under there so he could broadcast Alice. He showed Neal who started blowing kisses to the camera. He had this blue eyeshadow on, and we didn't know this until after the fact, but evidently a lot of the affiliated stations across this country pulled the plug on us right then and there and they said it was rare that people would pull the plug between commercials—they would usually wait till the next commercial.

And Alice getting pelted with a cake was a surprise to everyone. But when the cake hit Alice, he didn't retaliate like anyone would expect. Instead, he grabbed a gob of it and smashed it in his own face. It was the most unexpected thing that he could have done. That was our fear of failure. It made us invincible on stage. Like Alice said in his acceptance speech at the Rock and Roll Hall of Fame induction, "We won't promise that we'll never embarrass you. We're Alice Cooper—that's what we do." We used embarrassing situations on stage for dramatic effect anyway, so the cake fit right in.

So we always had things like that. Even in the early LA days. We played this show, probably because they thought, again, Alice Cooper was a folk singer or something, and we showed up. It was a really popular daytime talk show and they had us lip-synch our song. We really didn't want to do that but they forced us to do that, and so all we could hear was the drums. We couldn't hear the track, because they had such a little thing. Anyway, Neal was very upset about that and he was cursing. The curtain closed but what we didn't know was that Neal's mic was live out into the audience. So we got banned for that (laughs).

Mid-1970. Zappa's Straight Records is sold to Warner Bros.; Alice Cooper inherits a major label deal.

Neal Smith:
Warners Bros. bought out Straight Records, which was Frank Zappa's label and there was ten bands, which I still think was one of the most amazing business deals ever done at the time. Warner Brothers bought out ten bands from Straight Records for about $50,000. This was already after we'd recorded *Easy Action*. Linda Ronstadt was with a band called Stone Ponies and also James Taylor was in one of the groups that Frank Zappa had at the time. So they kinda got Alice Cooper as a bonus because they'd really wanted Linda Ronstadt and James Taylor.

Dennis Dunaway:
Bizarre was supposed to be in charge of it, but it seemed like our first two records were pretty much promoted from our managers' telephone and out of the trunk of their beat-up old Cadillac. *Pretties for You* got some publicity when Woolworths refused to carry it with the girl's panties showing. So it was censored with a sticker, which caused a slight boost in sales.

Later on the Alice Cooper group went to a Woolworths to see if they were stocking *Easy Action* and they had a big poster of us in the front window. A kid was standing on the sidewalk staring at it so I got the other guys to sidestep between the kid and the poster. We waved at him and pointed to our poster. He freaked out and begged us to wait there while he ran to get his friend. We took off.

Michael Bruce:
We were on our own on the first two albums. So, it was five minds turned loose in the studio and you got a helter skelter stampede. There's a whole lot of ideas, but not one particular one that is followed through.

August 7 – 10, 1970. At the Strawberry Fields Festival in Bowmanville, Ontario, at which Alice Cooper was on the packed bill, Shep Gordon talks to producer Jack Richardson about working with his new charges. Richardson, from the advertising field and as straight-laced a rock producer as one could imagine, declines but suggests his assistant, Bob Ezrin.

August 10, 1970. The Alice Cooper band appear as themselves in the movie *Diary of a Mad Housewife*.

Neal Smith:
There was so much to write about—about the band and about Alice, really—that the sky was the limit. We were getting mainstream press even before we'd even recorded *Love It to Death,* and at that point we hadn't even sold 20,000 albums with two albums, and the press was bigger than our success was. Also being in the movie *Diary of a Mad Housewife,* which was released in 1970 helped bring a buzz on the band in the underground. College stations were playing Easy Action, but we weren't ranking at mainstream at all when it came to the actual music.

Bob Gruen:
Alice Cooper, that was somebody people were scared of. Because he was a boy with a girl's name. Because he brought a sexual connotation into it that Kiss didn't have, in the sense that you were more afraid of the New York Dolls because there was a sexual connotation. With Kiss it was more about rock 'n' roll, it was about fantasy, it was about scary monsters, but it wasn't about your son turning gay, going for a gay guy. Alice Cooper, one of his early publicity pictures, he was half

man, half woman, where on one side he was a scary looking guy and on the other side he had lipstick and his hair was fixed up a little more and he looked more like a girl. That was an image that frightened a lot of people, that a man could take on a female role and be open about it.

August 14, 1970. Space rockers Hawkwind issue their debut album, a self-titled that captures them not quite fully formed yet. The band would rapidly build a following as a theatrical although more so, loud and psychedelic band. Hawkwind and Alice Cooper as represented on the first two albums bear similarities in that they both proposed a post-psychedelic era psychedelia.

September 8, 1970. Alice Cooper play at Max's Kansas City in Manhattan; in the crowd is a young Bob Ezrin, who sees the band perform for the first time. Before the show, Bob attends hit Broadway show *Hair,* so he brings along the *Hair's* Canadian lead Allan Nicholls. Emerging from the subway and following the laser beams in the street, they turn the corner and there's Max's. The brief from Jack Douglas and his partners back at Nimbus 9 is to "get rid of Alice Cooper."

Dennis Dunaway:
We were still hitting rock bottom. We were starting to lose our faith at one point, especially a particular night when we came to New York City. New York City was a tough nut to crack for us. We played several gigs there and the sound systems were bad and the acoustics were bad and the audiences were just really cold to us. They just weren't on our side at all. We were booked into Max's Kansas City. The dressing room was full of beer cartons, of empty beer bottles, so we had to tune up on the stairs. There were about five people in the club. Neal in particular was very upset. Who advertised this? So the band decided that it wasn't worth playing that night.

I was always giving my Newt Rockne, "One for the gipper," and I would always say the smaller the crowd the bigger the rumours. I remember going to Buxton and saying, "Well, why don't we not play and start a rumour that we did?" Anyway, that night we played but we were all upset. It was an angry set. One of the people in the audience was Bob Ezrin, who was just a kid at the time.

He came up afterwards and he said, "Oh I loved that song, 'I'm Edgy.' It's such an edgy show and it was perfect with this song, 'I'm Edgy.'" As it turned out, he meant "I'm Eighteen." But he says, "I'm going to get you guys a record deal," and we're like yeah right, kid. We'd buy you a drink but you're not old enough butwe ended up getting a record deal.

Alice Cooper:
He heard us at Max's Kansas City. He heard "Eighteen" and he went, "Oh, what's that song, 'I'm Edgy?'" I said, "You mean 'Eighteen?'" He said, "Yeah, that song is so dumb, it's a hit." But we would play it and he would go, "No, dumb it down." We were trying to be the Yardbirds.

Neal Smith:
Jack Richardson thought we were just a bunch of transvestite, drug-taking, beer-drinking weirdoes from California. And we wanted Nimbus 9, Jack Richardson's company, to produce us. We had done two albums that artistically we were happy with, but financially and commercially, we didn't have a gold album, that's for sure. So, we wanted somebody that was doing hit records, and who was doing hit records in the late '60s but The Guess Who? They just kept having hit record after hit record, and we were like, "Who is producing these records?" So we found out it was Jack ¹ Richardson of Nimbus 9, up in Toronto.

So we did a big press to get him to come and see us live, and we were playing at Max's Kansas City in New York, and it was just a showcase for somebody from the record company to come on down and check us out. We wrote so many times, "Jack, will you come and see us?" "No." "Jack, will you come and see us?" "No!" We asked him tons of times and he didn't want to. Our managers Shep Gordon and Joe Greenberg were in his office every day up in Canada. They went up there specifically to pressure him, well "convince" him, let's put it that way, to see the band.

So he said, "Fine. I have this new guy Bob Ezrin; I'll send him down." He's thinking to himself that Bob Ezrin is classically trained, he's a technician, there's nothing about this weirdo group that he's going to like, and he's going to see them and go running back to Toronto with his tail between his legs. That's the story Jack Richardson told us! So Bob comes down to see us at Max's Kansas City—and he loves the band! He gets it. He goes back to Jack, and he says to Jack, "There's a new huge wave of music coming and this band is the tip of it, and either we get on board with it or it's going to pass us by."

September 18, 1970. The death of Jimi Hendrix, arguably the person who invented flashy heavy metal. Also on this day, Black Sabbath issue their hit second album, *Paranoid*. The '60s is in the rear-view mirror and soon, so is Alice Cooper's '60s music of the first two records.

September 19, 1970. Alice Cooper play at The Warehouse in New Orleans, Louisiana, as part of a rip-roarin' bill with The Stooges and the MC5.

Late 1970. Dick Wagner's band The Frost issue their third, last and heaviest album, *Through the Eyes of Love*.

Dick Wagner:
The third album was the one that I produced, did a lot of the arranging and stuff in the studio, you know, not much preproduction with it. The album was pretty heavy actually, but it had a terrible album cover, just terrible. That was Vanguard; whoever they had working in the art department at that time came up with that beauty with the gas masks—it was just stupid. We had a good laugh over that one.

Early November 1970. Alice Cooper work with new producer Bob Ezrin, at RCA Mid-American Recording Center in Chicago on tracks that will comprise their third album. The brief however is to get a four song demo done, so Warner can green-light the band proceeding toward the full-length.

At this point, Bob is relieved that Jack Richardson hasn't fired him after coming home from New York and raving about this band he was instructed to turn down. However Jack said he wasn't about to produce them and that it was up to Bob to handle the job if he liked these guys so much.

Bob's first trip to the infamous band house was memorable to say the least. He's taken aside by one of the roadies, out to the barn where's he's handed a knife blade of dirty white powder that he has to snort as a sort of dark initiation. The drug turns out to be horse tranquilizer and Bob swears he drove back to the city and doesn't remember a minute of the trip.

Michael Bruce:
Shep had been going up to Canada and he met Jack Richardson and some of the people at Nimbus 9. Supposedly the story was, whoever fucks up has to produce the Alice Cooper group (laughs). They heard our first two albums and they weren't too impressed. But I guess Bob screwed up, so he went down and caught our show, and that's where he thought the song we were doing was "I'm Edgy."

He came out to the farm. I was so excited, I rode out to the airport to meet him and talked his ear off all the way back. We started working out there with him and it was great. We went through all the material and analysed it and added and took out parts. He was a classically trained pianist. His father wanted him to be a doctor but he was a rebellious kid so he became a rock 'n' roll producer. But before Bob came out, we were struggling. We had done two albums that didn't exactly set the music industry on fire.
Unless they were piling them up and burning them.

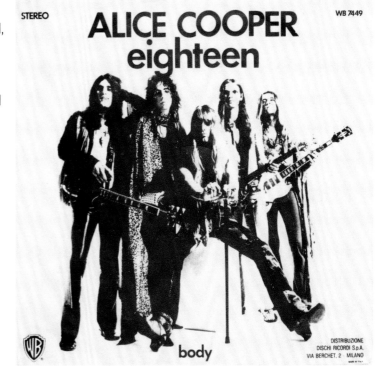

Bob Ezrin:
I was in that world every day and that was my reality. But all of us just felt Alice Cooper and this Detroit music was the true American sound and radio was catching up. When I was working with those guys and living with them in Detroit, hanging out with them and Nugent and the MC5 and Jimmy Osterberg, Iggy… and I had produced Mitch Ryder right after the first Alice Cooper album. So I spent a lot of time there and from that point of view, being my first real experience in an American city, being into an American city's culture as opposed to just being a visitor,

everything was rocking and hard. Everything was larger than life. The people were loud and brash and the bands were heavy, and to me that felt like the seed of the next revolution.

I just thought this was where everything was, this was a true expression of where American youth was. I didn't see it as a dangerous thing to do. I thought it was absolutely natural. Maybe that was good. Maybe in our ignorance, we just stormed ahead and were doing what we did instead of worrying about what was expected of us.

Alice Cooper:
It didn't surprise me at all to walk downstairs and find Dennis in a frog outfit. When that sort of thing happened you would just walk by him and go, "Oh, hi Dennis." It never occurred to any of the rest of us that such a thing would ever be odd to anyone else. If you knew Dennis then you were used to that sort of thing. It must have been a bit of a shock to Bob. Imagine just walking in and finding a frog. Then he would discover that everyone else in the band had very distinct personalities. Luckily, we all worked well as a unit. I consider the *Love It to Death* album the first Alice Cooper album, because when we hired Ezrin to be our producer, he changed the sound, the look, the feel—the whole thing. He was the one that defined what we actually sounded like.

November 11, 1970. Alice Cooper issue as a single "I'm Eighteen," (at this point, just "Eighteen") backed with "Is It My Body." The single performed well, spending eight weeks on the chart and reaching No.21 on *Billboard*. In Canada, the single vaulted to No.7. Its success moved Warner to tentatively allow the band to record a full-length.

Alice Cooper:
"Eighteen" was just a riff we used to jam to, to warm up. I remember when we first started to do "Eighteen," it was in Detroit; we used to rehearse in this dump. Everybody had a bottle of Boone's Farm Apple Wine. It was just the worst; I don't think it's ever seen anything except chemicals. We'd all have a bottle of that and that was just the chord progression (sings it), and it was a good riff for everybody to warm up and jam a little bit on. Bob Ezrin kept hearing that and he kept saying that's really a good riff. He would listen to us rehearse and he'd say let's make something out of that.

Again, it's one of those things that I would like to say, it was during the war, the end of the war, and there was always that controversy of, "I'm a boy, I'm a man." I can go get killed for my country but I can't buy a beer. So "Eighteen" was that juxtaposition of being both. Then, when it sounded like a complaint, then it turns the corner. It says I'm 18, I've got angst, I don't know what I am, I don't know if I'm a boy or a man, and I like it! That was the selling point of that. It was the fact that instead of I hate it, it was I'm 18 and I like it. Everybody related to that and said, "Yeah, I dig being screwed-up."

Dennis Dunaway:
Following the lack of acceptance for *Pretties for You*, we decided to write songs in a more relatable style. We would have come much closer to achieving that on Easy Action if we had had a rehearsal space and another month or so. But by the time Bob saw us at Max's Kansas City, Michael had spearheaded the development of songs like "Caught in a Dream" and "I'm Eighteen." Neal had written "Hallowed Be My Name" and I had written "Black Juju" as a vehicle for the Alice character.

1971

At this point one can safely say that Alice is in that apocryphal spot that a clutch of '70s bands experienced (and complained about with a chuckle), where they put out two albums in one year and to boot, did it while barely falling off the road. Alice is all the rage in 1971, playing bigger and bigger shows off the back of their boy-to-man hit anthem "I'm Eighteen." The rest of *Love It to Death* doesn't have near the same impact, but it paints a picture as dark as the album cover, of a band uneasily sophisticated for heavy metal, so they aren't.

First half of the year, "I'm Eighteen" reaches No.21 on the charts, the band gets big royalty cheques and Jim Morrison pops a clog in Paris. Into the second half, the band find time to record what will become *Killer* while also touring Europe for the first time.

In an exaggerated version of what happened last record out, *Killer,* issued in November of this year, would be dominated by a single not quite characteristic of the rest of the album. "Under My Wheels" would be a happy glam boogie rocker, after which a deep dive into the rest of the album (save for "Be My Lover") reveals a record more nightmarish and shocking than its predecessor, which had a few things on it that were still psych in spirit. And Lord save us, what an album cover, as Neal introduces us to his snake Kachina, a trademark beyond cane and greasepaint and glam-gone-wrong that is added to the band's bulging bag of tricks.

March 8, 1971. Alice Cooper's third album, *Love It to Death* is issued. *Billboard* calls the band "the first stars of future-rock." Biggest hit on the record is "I'm Eighteen," which, although essentially a morose ballad, paints the picture of the young rocker who might be a fan of Alice, Sabbath, Deep Purple or The Doors. The initial issue is on Straight Records but the album was quickly reissued by Warner Bros., new owners of Straight.

Alice Cooper:
Love It to Death changed a lot of thinking about what was going on in music. It was a really hard-edged, Detroit, eerie... you know, it had classical things in it, but you could tell that this band was not classically-oriented. But all of a sudden you would hear this classical piano that would come in, over top of all this horror. That's why it's really unique. At that time, I've got to be honest with you, *Love It to Death* was a really hard record to make.

When Bob Ezrin got hold of us he said, "Look, everybody wants to love you guys, but there's nothing to hang the handle on. You guys have no musical handle." So he took us for eight months. We sat in Detroit in a barn, ten hours a day, and we learned how to play. I developed a sound, Alice's vocal sound, Dennis developed a bass sound, Glen had a guitar sound, Neal had a drum sound. So when *Love It to Death* came out, it was the first time people heard it and said, "That's Alice Cooper." It had its own sound. When you heard

Jim Morrison, you always knew it was Jim Morrison. When you heard Mick Jagger, that's Mick Jagger. This time they heard it and said, "That's Alice." So we had an identification there; people could identify with us now.

But I wouldn't say we were heavy metal. I think the first time I ever saw the moniker heavy metal was *Rolling Stone* talking about us. It was in a big *Rolling Stone* article, and they called us heavy metal and it had parentheses around it, so that was pretty much the first time I ever saw that term. I think really, the first heavy metal band was probably Iron Butterfly. "In-a-Gadda-Da-Vida" was heavy metal (laughs). But we always liked The Who and The Yardbirds and then I think Led Zeppelin took it to another level and then you started getting your Black Sabbaths. But we were always right in that soup. Hard rock was never far from heavy metal.

Michael Bruce:

It was our third album and we felt it was a make-or-break situation. It was also our first adventure with Bob Ezrin and I knew that the way this man worked, I could tell he was putting everything he had into it. It was a lot of hard work and it paid off.

Neal Smith:

During and after *Love It to Death*, we were starting to find our niche. We were all art students in college and high school, and we were also fans of the old horror movies, all the way from *Frankenstein* to *Wolfman* and not only that, but the westerns. I was a big fan of John Wayne and all the early guys, Roy Rogers and the Cisco Kid, and all those movies had hangings in them.

But the vibe of that album had a lot to do with the culture of Detroit and us being in Detroit. Of course Motown is there, but this is like the anti-Motown. I think drugs played a part in it too. Because when we were in California, the drugs around California were more mellow, more natural, marijuana, pot, LSD. But when we went back to Detroit, there was a lot of THC, harder chemicals, and people even had the heavier stuff than that. So the harder drug culture played a part in the harder sound.

Detroit is a big industrial city, as opposed to California with the beach and the sun, where it's beautiful all the time and it's mellow and laid-back. If you're starving in California, at least you're warm. If you're starving in Detroit, Michigan in the middle of winter, you're starving but you're freezing. So it's a totally different vibe there. It's one that inspired us to greater things. We basically wrote *Love It to Death* in the Midwest. So it was a very different vibe. We were in the right place at the right time for our writing. And also for the crowds—the fans that took us into their heart before anybody else did were those crowds.

Bob Ezrin:

I don't think that Detroit music was what was inspiring the band, particularly. The band didn't know that they needed to change. It was a combination of their strangeness and my more classical and structured musical upbringing. We put all that together and it came out sounding like the new Alice. I just felt the songs were all over the place and there was no focal point to them. Plus I didn't feel like Alice Cooper really had a sound. Or if there was a sound, it was back in the *Pretties for You* days and it was so outrageous that they weren't going to succeed with it.

We did want to succeed. We weren't just making music for our own indulgence. We were making stuff that everybody would hopefully love. That was the goal, to make stuff that people were going to love all over the country, and they would buy records and come to the shows and enjoy the ride with us.

So none of those other guys influenced this band musically. If anything it was the other way around. At the beginning, we were doing stuff that people were going, wow, wait a minute, that's unusual. Only because it was just basic goofy, very simply-structured stuff. It was all I could do at the time. But it had any integrity to it and a flow to it. The material really hung together and so it served the music well. Plus it was theatrical.

Dennis Dunaway:

I preferred crediting everyone. Dividing up who did what never mattered much to me. I let others decide the breakdowns because I was obsessed with thinking of the next thing we were going to do. There are a lot of songs that my name probably deserved to be on as a songwriter, but then there are others that I feel like I'm generously included. Michael once said, "It's pretty much a wash concerning my credits."

The ones credited as band songs truly all came together as band songs. We pounced on every song thinking of every possibility to make it better and we stuck to a hard rule that every idea had to be played by the band. Only then could a majority vote eliminate it. Then everyone would move forward with a posi-tive attitude—no grudges. That wasn't easy, but it was an extremely important key to our success. Few songs came through our mill with little changed—"Caught in a Dream" and "No More Mr. Nice Guy" did)—and many changed radically several times over, like "Elected" and "Lay Down and Die, Goodbye." But most were group efforts from scratch.

"Black Juju" was mine. I remember, I plugged my bass into a small guitar amp and cranked it to a sinister distortion. Like Dave Davies "You Really Got Me" guitar sound, but with a bass. I was alone in an old motel that had a little room with a water heater. I removed the metal plate from the heater and used the glowing pilot flame as the only light in the room. I imagined the flame as an inferno, and that inspired the riffs.

A week later, I discovered a hot old attic in an off-campus dormitory in Cincinnati. I went in there with pencil and paper and my Frog bass. It was dimly lit in a spooky way and I got into an Edgar Allan Poe frame of mind. That's where I wrote the lyrics, which included the concept of Alice hypnotizing the audience with a swinging pocket watch. The band liked it as it was. Ever since we had dropped "Fields of Regret" I had been talking about giving the dark side of the Alice character another dramatic vehicle, and finally there it was.

April – August, 1971. Alice Cooper tour intensively the US Midwest and the eastern seaboard, including the band's usual high propensity of festival dates along with a handful of Canadian dates.

Dennis Dunaway:

The idea as it struck us was black and white. That's why the front of the album is dark and the back is light. We had songs like... the white part of it would be songs like "Caught in a Dream," it's an uplifting song—it's not a dark character song. But we also had "Black Juju," so the set was like that. It started out bright and then it got very dark, shifted gears, after about four rockers, then it shifted gears and got very moody and very dark and then it became uplifting at the end, after Alice got killed (laughs).

We had an electric chair. I came up with the idea. We wanted to put on a morality play-type thing and that was developing in the music. With "Dwight Fry," Alice is going crazy, and then "Black Juju" was just very dark with nothing necessarily going on as far as being a victim or whatever. But still, it was conducive to this all of a sudden very dark thing that was going on.

So we were thinking, well, why don't we have Alice do something bad? Then he'll be punished for it. Like a million operas or whatever (laughs). So we're trying to think of how he should get killed, and I thought of the electric chair. We're like, yeah, we can't even afford food; where are we going to get an electric chair? I said, I'll build it and I did. It is in Canada now, in Ottawa. I saw it just recently. But I have the second one. The first one was a little bit rickety because we didn't know what we were doing yet, but then the second one we built to be sturdier for the road. Then we built two collapsible ones after that. So there were four electric chairs altogether.

But by *Love It to Death*, we already had these songs for the dark character that was Alice. I wrote "Black Juju" and Neal wrote "Hallowed Be Thy Name." We had several songs that were aimed at this dark character, and that's really how it developed. It started way back on *Pretties for You*, but it took us a couple albums to get there.

Yet even in *Love It to Death* on "Ballad of Dwight Fry," you can hear this vulnerability in Alice's performances. That's what he could do extremely well, and that's why people still love him, still love his shows today. There is a vulnerability and that would vary, into the era when Alice was drinking too much. Glen would be criticised for drinking too much and maybe playing a little bit loose on occasion, but Alice could be falling down drunk forgetting the lyrics and unable to even stand up on stage and people loved him, because of that vulnerability.

Neal Smith:

It was either The Grande or the Eastown—I think it was probably the Eastown. There was a big movie screen that came down from the ceiling. It was a movie theatre at one point. The opening band would sit in front of it. The headlining band had their equipment back behind. The headline band that night was the Who. From behind the stage you could see right through the screen. In front of the screen, because it was pure white there was a light show on it and you could not see behind it.

We finished the show—this was the *Love It to Death* tour—with "Black Juju." Goose, my drum tech goes, "Did you hear Keith playing along with you?" He said, "He was playing with you, note for note, on 'Black Juju.' I was backstage and you were in front of the screen and he was behind the screen and it was like a mirror image with him playing right with you." With all of the music from Glen and Dennis and Michael, I could not hear the drums behind me as Keith was not mic'ed up. That is the story. Goose said it was amazing. It always reminds me of a scene from a movie. If that had been filmed, it would have been awesome.

April 24, 1971. After a steady two-month rise, "I'm Eighteen" reaches its chart peak of No.21. By this point the band was making $15,000 a show. *Love It to Death* was rapidly going through reissues due to both the label change from Straight to Warner, and due to the cover art, where some thought that Alice's thumb peaking through his clothing, looked too much like a penis.

Alice Cooper:
What a silly thing that was. First of all, what an insult! They looked at my thumb and figured that's my unit! If I woulda known that, I would have had a much longer thumb.

Neal Smith:
Everybody said his thumb looked like a penis. I said, well, if that was my penis, I'd be totally embarrassed (laughs). But I just couldn't believe that; it was one of those fluky things. We had a few things that accidentally happened in our career and that was one of them. All of a sudden they had banned the album, they had to change it and airbrush it out. Give me a fucking break—that's the most ridiculous thing in the world. With Alice Cooper, people were trying to find things that were outrageous. From that standpoint, if they really thought Alice is sitting there holding his dick in the picture, I wouldn't be in the picture with Alice if he was holding his dick. But at any rate, it was one of those great things in the end.

      Also if you look on the back cover, I'm holding a cane. See, in 1968, we had a hunting accident when Alice shot me in the foot. I still have the bullet in my foot. I used to use a cane for quite a while to help me walk and I just wanted a prop to use. So if you look on the back cover, I'm sitting on that seat, holding my hands out with the cane going straight down. Then on the front cover, there on the left I had the same cane, but I had it over my shoulders, and I'm draping my arms over it. So that was the first time the cane was used on stage and to this day Alice still uses a cane. So that was the evolution of where that came from. Also on *Billion Dollar Babies,* Alice had a cane that turned into an American flag which was cool. Even on *Love It to Death,* Alice was toting a sword.

April 27, 1971. "Caught in a Dream"/"Hallowed Be My Name" is issued as the second and last single from *Love It to Death.* The song stalled at No.94 on the charts.

Alice Cooper:
There were all rock heroes and no rock villains. My heroes were the Beatles and the Stones and all these great bands, and I said well that's great but there's something else I'm missing here. I'll make Alice the ultimate villain. He'll be Dracula, Jack the Ripper, all these guys rolled into one, but he'll be a rock singer, and he'll write these songs that are sort of irritating the parents a lot. And what music fits horror more than rock? It's perfect together. And I was surprised that nobody did it before me.

Michael Bruce:
After *Love It to Death,* Bob was determined to prove himself, and he wasn't going to let this be a flop. We really worked hard on *Love it to Death.* And it was, hey, we're just five guys from Phoenix, Arizona. We used to refer to ourselves as like "the band who couldn't shoot straight" as in that movie, *The Gang that Couldn't Shoot Straight.* You know, the bumbling idiot that makes it big. And we were five of those idiots.

June 1971. *Love It to Death* is issued in the UK, where it would rise to No.28 in the charts, again, in part, driven by the success of the album's all-important hit single.

July 1971. Each of the members of the band receives royalty cheques of $8000.

July 3, 1971. Acquaintance of Alice and the band, as well as monumental rock icon, Jim Morrison dies at age 27, in Paris.

July 11, 1971. Alice Cooper play the Long Beach Auditorium, supported by Savage Grace and Black Oak Arkansas. In attendance is a 14-year-old Randy Rhoads who decides then and there that he wants to rock 'n' roll for a living. A decade later, Rhoads would be in a band with Black Oak Arkansas drummer Tommy Aldridge.

July 19, 1971. A particularly robust bill in Canada's capital, Ottawa, Ontario, finds Yes and Black Sabbath supporting Alice Cooper. This was followed up in August by additional shows with Sabbath, along with Humble Pie and Edgar Winter Group. This is roughly when Alice started using a boa constrictor in his set, with his first snake Kachina. Apparently the snake had been thrown on stage back in January, and Neal had decided to keep it.

Dennis Dunaway:
I do remember a gig where the bill was Black Sabbath, and Alice Cooper headlined, and there was this opening band that nobody had ever heard of. I remember walking into the arena and seeing the audience basically people socialising and finding their seats. This band was on stage that I thought, "Oh man, we've got to follow these guys?!' And it was Yes and I was thinking, geez, these guys are playing so good and nobody is paying any attention to them.

September 7, 1971. Brief recording session at RCA Studios in Chicago where the band work on "Desperado," "Halo of Flies" and "Under My Wheels."

Michael Bruce:
I ended up with a lot of song fragments and I used to string them together in sort of a loose format. I'd use them to warm up with and that's where "Halo of Flies" began. Then of course we added other parts to it for the finished song, but I don't remember trying to measure up to Emerson, Lake and Palmer (laughs). We basically made an instrumental with a little vocal part in the middle and it took on a life of its own. That went back to the band's early beginnings because we used to do jams and Bob used to say it's cool to speed up and slow down as long as you do it together. As far as I'm concerned we were masters at that and "Halo of Flies" was certainly one of them.

September 13, 14th, 1971. Alice Cooper support Led Zeppelin at the Berkeley Theatre, in Berkeley, California.

October 22 – November 7, 1971. The band tour Europe for the first time, beginning on the continent and ending at The Rainbow in London, England, one night with The Who, another night with Arthur Brown.

November 1971. "Under My Wheels," backed with "Desperado," is issued as the first single off of *Killer*. The song is credited to Michael, Dennis and producer Bob Ezrin. Guest guitar on the track is provided by Rick Derringer.

Dennis Dunaway:
We had a lot of positive things going on with outside musicians. Bob wasn't the only one that advocated that. The only time it was ever upsetting was later on when the majority vote of the band was dismissed. Rick Derringer plays the lead guitar break with the heavy effect on my song, "Under My Wheels." We became friends during a six-night stand with the McCoys at Steve Paul's Scene in NYC in '69. Rick was Glen's friend too, and when he stopped by the studio in Chicago to wish us luck, "Under My Wheels" was in progress, so we told him to get in there and plug in.

     Neal always tells the story about Michael and I flipping a hotel couch forward to make a fort for privacy. We spent most of a day under there working up "Under My Wheels." Michael did a lot of woodshedding back in LA and became a much better guitar player. Then he did the same with the piano and then he applied those instruments to his songwriting. He was extremely persistent with each song. He was loud and didn't care who was around to hear him pounding out parts. He could drive you nuts with it. You wanted to choke him sometimes. But by the time we met Ezrin, Michael was on top of his game. He was also the most aggressive at getting the band to do his songs. If he didn't have an idea, then he was willing to work on mine. But if he had an idea, he was like a steamroller. Sometimes I thought he would sabotage my ideas, which would have been unacceptable if his ideas weren't so strong.

Alice Cooper:
When you're writing for a character, for somebody other than yourself, then it's different. I might write the greatest song that I've ever written and then I will realise that Alice would never sing this. It could be a great song for Guns N' Roses or the Foo Fighters, but it's not a song that Alice would ever sing. Being a songwriter, you just

write the song and it comes out the way that it is. If it's usable, then a lot of times we can twist the lyrics around enough to make it sound like Alice, but a lot of times you can't.

Bob and I would sit there and be very objective about Alice. We'd talk about him in the third person without getting personal about it. I would say, "Bob, that whole second section there is not Alice." Bob would listen to it and say, "You know, you're right. Let's change that." If I were writing for Captain Hook then I would be able to do it because I know how he thinks about things, but you couldn't just write anything and have Captain Hook sing it.

Michael Bruce:

Well, I jokingly referred to myself as… you've got the drummer, bass, lead singer, lead guitar player and I was the lead rhythm player. Of course, I was the only other guitar in the band, so… (laughs). But if you think about it, Neal very much so played more from the top part of his kit rather than… he would still have the bass drum, but he wasn't John Bonham. Plus no syncopated type of bass drum parts. He could do it but he didn't have that… a lot of the times it was the writing that didn't bring it out. Then Dennis was all over the place doing runs in the songs. And so my parts were simple—I was the guy that was holding down the fort.

November 5, 1971. The band record a performance for UK music show *The Old Grey Whistle Test*; the footage airs four days later.

November 8, 1971. Alice Cooper's fourth album *Killer* is issued. Also in early November, the band move into the band house to end all band houses, the 42-room Galesi Estate in Greenwich, CT.

Alice Cooper:

Now *Killer*, by some standards, by real rock reviewer standards, some of them say that that is the best record we ever did. That was the fifth or sixth biggest selling record that year, and that really was just pure Alice. We weren't doing anything on that album that we just wouldn't have done naturally, except for the fact that we had Bob Ezrin putting it in a really good package. You know, we would write the song and it would sound really cool, but then Bob Ezrin would take it, and he was our George Martin. He would take the rough song that was a good song, that had three good parts in it, then he would arrange it and get it on tape so it really was good. That was our Canadian connection there. Without Bob Ezrin we would not have been done. So I always give Bob Ezrin all the credit in the world for any musical ability that we had.

Dennis Dunaway:

My favourite is *Killer*, in the respect that that was the first album we did where we knew people would be listening. On *Love It to Death*, we went into the studio coming off of two fairly unsuccessful albums. Even though they made the charts, they weren't putting food on the table. When we went into the studio for *Killer*, we knew people would be buying the album. So our playing abilities were improving just at a time when we met Bob Ezrin, but then by the time we got to *Killer*, we had learned a great deal about proper studio techniques. Plus we quickly learned how to dissect a song and properly reconstruct it. We were like sponges for that knowledge and Bob Ezrin was a revelation.

The song "Killer" came from a vivid dream that I had. I woke up and wrote it down as lyrics. Not long after that, the band was packing up after a long rehearsal day at our farm in Pontiac when I asked Michael to stay after. I played "Killer" for him and we worked it up pretty fast. I wanted it to be longer but Michael applied what he had learned from Ezrin. The next day, we showed it to the others and the band took it to the next level. I love how Glen's and Michael's guitar parts compliment each other on that song.

Many critics went to great lengths to insult our playing abilities. Many of them seemed convinced that our theatrics were just a crutch to smokescreen our deficiencies. If our name had been something like Hurricane Cooper, and we just stood on stage in T-shirts and jeans looking down at our instruments, they might have heard what we were playing. We overshadowed ourselves by giving people a real show. Just wanna hear music? Stay home and put on the record.

As for the approach on "Halo to Flies," early in our career, we prided our ability to assemble medleys of our favourite British bands. We did a Kinks medley, a Who medley, a Beatles medley, and we thought our transitions were pretty clever. So years later, having a bunch of extraneous riffs and melodies kicking around, we decided to apply our knack for segues and we came up with "Halo of Flies." It was the first time many critics finally admitted that we could play. And it proved that the band were self-sufficient in writing our own complex arrangements.

Then "Dead Babies," in this day and age, it's impossible to realise how tough the censors were back then. We were trying to be shocking under the critical magnifying glass of radio stations, advertisers, church groups, parents and even many of the kids that were our age. Plus we actually did have our own sense of decency. It was a balancing act. As tame as some of our things appear in retrospect—like five androgynous-looking guys with a girl's name—it really was shocking then. It demanded more thinking than the public cared to do, so many just tried to write us off as a joke. Others threatened to kill us. Girls loved us. But nobody could ignore us. As for threats, our entire career was riddled with threats of all kinds. We had so many threats that we became immune to worrying about them.

Johnny "Bee" Badanjek:

After Detroit, they moved to this strange house in Connecticut. I guess it was owned by some old gangster or something. There was hidden tunnels behind the fireplace; it was the weirdest house, with tunnels all over the place. It was a huge mansion they rented for the band, and so just before they split up, they were there for a year or so. I think Shep was in New York, and they probably just want to be close to the management. They were on the road more than they were in Detroit anyway, constantly touring. So they probably just thought it was time to get out of Detroit.

December 1, 1971. The *Killer* tour ensues, beginning at NY Academy of Music, support by Dr. John and Wet Willie. This marks the first use of the gallows as well as the debut of Alice's "clown" makeup, i.e. solid black with two strong vertical lines rather than the spotty star look.

Dennis Dunaway:

I still have the poster. When the band first stayed in New York City, one of our early visits, maybe within the first three, Alice and I shared a room that particular day, and when we got to the room, first thing I would do is look out the window. I'm not sure why, but we were about three or four floors up and across the street was the Civic Center in New York City. It's still there.

But there was a poster advertising a ballet, and there was white-faced clown. I thought wow, that's pretty striking that I can see the eyes on this clown from this far away. Because it wasn't a real big poster. So I got Alice to come and look, and he was more interested in television. But later, I kept watching the theatre, and when they finally opened, I went down and asked them for one of those posters, and I brought it back to the room, and I talked to Alice. We went out and found some mascara and came back and Alice did his own version of that makeup. Like I say, I still have that poster to this day (laughs).

But that's how that started. The whole thing was the idea of... because when we were in LA, we would drive people out of the room. Which is hard to believe in Hollyweird, that we would be too outrageous for it or that anybody would be too outraged. But they were, just because we were five guys who looked the way we did with our girl's name.

But Neal's right, we were anti-hippie. In LA in particular, there were freaks and there were hippies, and you didn't want to call a hippie a freak and vice versa. Even though there were a lot of similarities back in those days—you know, change the establishment and the way things are done and make it a better world—but hippies by that point had become very, very typical, and were also showing signs of burning out, because of their drug use. So we found that to be hypocritical. You know, you go to the supermarket and you have to read the ingredients in the food, but it's okay to do heroin—we found that to be totally absurd. So freaks were of a different order. Even though we drank a lot of beer, we still weren't in the hippie movement. So yeah, there was a distinct difference between a freak and a hippie. A freak was like the Mothers of Invention. In LA, in particular. You could get away a bit more with calling a hippie a freak. You didn't want to make the mistake of calling a freak a hippie. Even though they had a lot of the same ideals, they had different attitudes about it, and we were more of the freak part of it.

We made fun of ourselves too. We made fun of everybody. We in particular made fun of ourselves. If anybody walked out of the room that was in the band, they knew when they came back that the whole time they were gone we were just whittling them to shreds. Then when they walked back in the room, usually it was Glen Buxton who would say, "Shhh, he's back."

Alice Cooper:

Well, to me, it was always, I looked around and said, "Look at all the Peter Pans. Where's Captain Hook?" You know? Look at all the rock heroes; where is the definitive villain? There was no phantom of the opera and I said, I was born to be that. I am not going to be the pretty boy lead singer. I'm not going to be Paul McCartney, this guy or that guy. I looked at myself and said, Alice needs to be the prime villain of rock, the Moriarty of rock. You know, why not develop this character?

I think that two things that developed the character's look more than anything else was that we had a real fascination with *What Ever Happened to Baby Jane*?, the movie. You look at Bette Davis in that movie and she's like an old woman trying to look like a little girl. She had the white caked makeup all cracking and the black smeared eyes and the red lips, and I went, that is so frightening (laughs).

So that look was involved, and then we saw *Barbarella*, and I saw The Black Queen, Anita Pallenberg, and I said, "That's what Alice should look like." You know, a combination of those two. That's how we started shaping the look of Alice, and pretty soon, I realised that nobody had worn eye makeup. No one had become the dark court jester of rock 'n' roll. I said man, that's just the perfect image for me.

Nobody had done theatrics. The Who were the closest thing to theatrics, because of the fact of their smashing the amps up. That was the most chaotic theatrical thing that had happened. I kept thinking, why can't this show be more visual? Why can't this show be more surrealistic? If Alice looks like this, why wouldn't he have a snake? Why wouldn't he have a sword? Why wouldn't he have a this and a that? And pretty soon we said, since nobody is doing this, and since there's nobody to compare us to, let's just do whatever we want. Let's let the lyrics be the script for the show. So, if I said "Welcome to my nightmare," well, don't just say it, give the audience the nightmare. You know, visually show it to them.

Then of course, we ran up against the whole world of, "Oh, they're not really good musicians; they hide behind theatrics." We fought that battle for years and years and years until people like John Lennon and Paul McCartney and Bob Dylan started to say, "You know what? Alice Cooper makes great records." Then we had a couple of No.1s, and very rarely would you find a band that was as theatrical and upsetting to the public as us, like the Sex Pistols were, with hit records. That was the one thing we had that other bands didn't have, was the fact that we had 14 Top 40 records.

December 4, 1971. With *Love It to Death* on its 38th week in the charts, at No.145 at this point, *Killer* joins it, entering at No.83.

December 19, 1971. Stanley Kubrick's *A Clockwork Orange* makes its debut, suitably in Gotham, in New York City.

Alice Cooper:
We looked more like Clockwork Orange characters than we did a band. In fact Clockwork Orange used an awful lot of Alice Cooper in the movie. The guy's name was Alex, he had a snake, he carried a cane, he had the glove. There was so much Alice in that movie it was incredible.

December 27, 1971. With *Killer* now at No.26 on the *Billboard* charts, "Under My Wheels" enters the singles chart at No.88.

Dennis Dunaway:
We had this concept: we were going to make every song about a different killer, and "Desperado" was the gunslinger and "Halo of Flies" had the James Bond/License to Kill guy and whatnot. Even though Michael came up with this incredible song, "Be My Lover," which we were thinking, well, I don't see a killer in there, and you're really stretching to say it's a lady-killer. But that song is so good we couldn't say it can't go on the album (laughs).

So the snake, we thought, okay, the ultimate killers are a shark or a snake. Well, Neal had a snake. Okay, the snake is going to be on the album cover and the handwriting on the album cover is me writing with my left hand because I wanted it to look like a demented ransom note thing. So when we did the photo session with Pete Turner in New York City, who took the band photo on that album as well, we had them do the picture of the hanging at the same time, and then we had them do the picture of the snake for the cover.

Now, Neal was holding the snake and that was not a little snake. So holding his arm out and trying to hold still for as long as it took, Neal started losing his patience with them. Because they would wait until the snake's tongue came out and then they would snap the picture and it would be too late. And Neal kept telling them, "No, you fuckin' missed it!" He'd say, "Well, you're making the mistake of waiting until you see the tongue and it's too late. Just snap when you don't see the tongue." Anyway, they took a ton of pictures of the snake and when we looked through all of them, all of the contact sheets, there was one picture where the snake had his tongue out and that's the one that's on the cover.

1972

In 1972, Alice Cooper continue their rise due to a constant injection of themselves into the news, through stunt and through achievement. To kick off the year, *Killer* goes gold, and a second deceptively light and campy song from the record makes the rounds as a single, "Be My Lover" harming no one.

As the band shift headquarters to the Galesi Estate in Connecticut (a better band house), they come up with a conceptual follow-up to "I'm Eighteen" in "School's Out," issued and celebrated before the album of the same name would drop. When it did drop, once more the band would see strong but not stellar sales, the record driven by the fortunes of one hit and really no more (actually less than *Killer,* which had arguably two, two-and-a-half). In summary and in broad terms so to speak, Alice Cooper now had three albums that sold respectably more or less because of one hit single, with, indeed, almost all the rest of the material doomed to be deep, deep album tracks. But of course the band and Shep Gordon, hard workers and enthusiastic participants in life, social animals, make the best of it, pranking Piccadilly Square in London and pouring panties over the Hollywood Bowl.

Into the second half of the year, *School's Out* vaults to No.2 and the band, like good bands in the '70s did, went back to work, assembling a follow-up album and, just to keep on the tips of tongues, issuing another single in "Elected," this one, again, fortunately working, setting up hopes for continued success once the next record was completed and released. Further success comes when in November, *Love It to Death* joins *Killer* at gold as the band hit Europe for the second time. Alas, however, the heavy workload begins to take a toll as both Glen and Alice find themselves chucking down way too much booze. It affects them in different ways however. Alice copes, remaining the life of the party, while Glen goes hazy and ineffectual.

1972. Dick Wagner commandeers a short-lived and heavy band called Ursa Major, who issue a self-titled debut produced by Bob Ezrin. Gone from the formative stages of the band before the album was famed piano man Billy Joel. Ursa Major toured nationally in support of Jeff Beck and later, Alice Cooper.

Dick Wagner:
Ursa Major was great, but it never got distributed. We signed to RCA and we were making this record and the guy who signed us and brought us into the label left the label just as our album was finished. The guy who replaced him was the former jazz critic of the *New York Times* and he hated us! He couldn't stand this music. He was a jazz critic (laughs). So we had a bad transition of promotion there. It killed *Ursa Major.* Bang, that record was no-go and it went cold.

A lot of people said that it had been a tremendous influence on a lot of bands. I can see that maybe it was, given that it was 1972. But Bob produced that. He's got great ears. He's brilliant and I learned a lot from him. He was younger than me when we ended up doing that stuff and together we really created a lot of good stuff. I have the utmost respect for his abilities. I remember Bob going around with a fire extinguisher blasting people. He had a habit of doing that stuff, to create as much commotion as possible.

1972. At a presentation at the Hyatt House in LA, Alice Cooper is awarded with the key to the city.

January 21, 1972. *Killer* reaches its peak position of No.21 on *Billboard* while "Under My Wheels" has moved up to No.59.

January 27, 1972. *Killer* is certified gold.

Neal Smith:
By *Killer*, now we had the big weather balloons that we filled with confetti and fake money. But even before that, the evolution of the sword came from people who would just sit there and weren't really storming the stage. We wanted people to storm the stage. So early on we actually took real money, put it on the sword, dollar bills, and Alice was flinging real money at the crowd. We did that throughout the history of the band—we always threw real money out there. Alice now has fake money on there, but we always had real money. So that's where the sword came from because it was the obvious thing, like a shish kebab skewer; Alice would peel it off and throw it to the crowd.

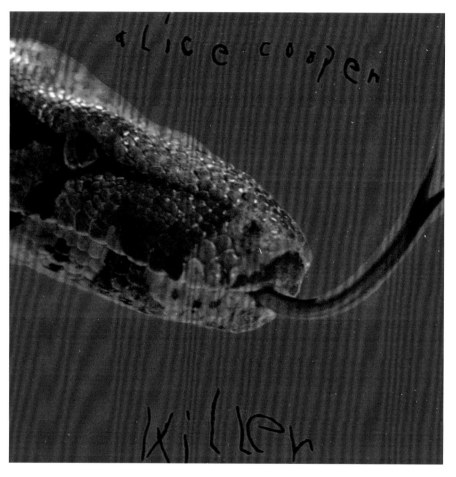

We used the balloons, and then of course *Killer* we added the gallows, which the Warner Bros. props department built for us. We did that death dirge for "Killer," as Alice was taken to the gallows. We'd come out as characters because now we had recorded music. We had the song "Killer" coming through the speakers, but we're not playing the song. I came out, had the snare drum on, I'm playing the death dirge on a black-draped snare drum, Dennis is the priest—he put a priest costume on—and Michael has a lit torch and Glen is actually the hangman.

He escorts Alice to the gallows, walks him up the stairs and then puts the rope around his neck and then pulls the lever to hang Alice. That's all brand-new stuff that had never been done before. A band actually playing their music, and then going through a theatrical piece for the execution of Alice for the song "Killer." So that was pretty dramatic, and then of course when Alice falls through there and the lightning crashes, and the lights, it actually looked like a lightning storm, and then after he's hanging there, he's got blood dripping from his mouth and all over his clothes. So I would say that was a big turning point in the violence of Alice Cooper. The electric chair was one thing but actually having him hanging there and the blood coming from his mouth… rock 'n' roll had never seen anything like that before.

February 7, 1972. *Killer* is released in the UK.

February 21, 1972. "Be My Lover" is issued as the second and last single from *Killer*.

Late February 1972. The band gather in Joe Smith's Warner Bros. offices in Burbank, CA for a gold disc presentation in honour of *Killer*. But the physical awards aren't back from the plant yet, so they mug with golds of Jimi Hendrix's *Rainbow Bridge* instead.

March 1972. Richard Avedon takes the famous shot of Alice Cooper naked, with snake, the new one being Yvonne.

Alice Cooper:
Here's a guy named Alice, he's got hair down to here, he has absolutely no respect for any authority at all, he's calling his own rules. That's not bad enough, but they have hit records on top of it and every time that he does something that his parents says, well you're not going to see him, the kids go yes I am. All of a sudden you become the forbidden fruit.

That's what people are afraid of. They're afraid that their kids are going to start wearing eye makeup and start wearing black top hats and all black goth clothes. They were right—they did. But all those kids turned out to be doctors and lawyers and politicians; they all ended up being okay. It's just art, but art sometimes really scares people.

March 3, 1972. As part of a north-eastern swing, the band play Harrington Auditorium in Worcester, Massachusetts. Support comes from Blue Öyster Cult, who begin to regularly share bills with the band.

Neal Smith:
We just wanted to be memorable onstage; I think that was the first thing. We were certainly aware of Screamin' Jay Hawkins and Arthur Brown, and in those days, in the late '60s, nobody even had a word for Screamin' Jay Hawkins or Arthur Brown, who would come on stage with this big flaming helmet he had on top of his head (laughs) and a big sceptre or whatever he was holding. Lyrically The Doors were doing the same thing. We may have been more influenced by the dark side of The Doors and taking it into a further dimension.

Dennis wrote "Black Juju" and we would all brainstorm. We had the idea of putting the sheets over us; this was even after the door for "Nobody Likes Me;" and we still used the feathers. We had "Dead Babies," even though it's not about killing babies; it's about parental neglect, child neglect. So we thought okay, we'll just do a theatrical thing for "Dead Babies" and for "Ballad of Dwight Fry," and we'll execute Alice on stage. We'll put the singer in an electric chair. Without a doubt, we were big fans of the horror movies and that sort of thing. Our influence went beyond musical to theatrical with movies and Broadway.

March 11, 1972. "Be My Lover" creeps onto the *Billboard* charts at No.81.

April 1972. Most of what will become the *School's Out* album is recorded this month, working at The Record Plant in New York, just down the highway from the band's new home base.

Dennis Dunaway:
We had a lot of fun making "School's Out" mainly because we all related on the exact same level. Glen, Alice and I started the band in high school and Michael and Neal went to nearby schools. I'm not sure the historical success of the single detracted from the other cuts though. Royalty cheques reflect that many of the other cuts are still getting various kinds of exposure. I thought the album flowed together pretty well. And it has a lot of musical texture.

Alice Cooper:
We had done everything we could do in Detroit. We had our first hit record, "Eighteen," out of CKLW in Windsor, through Rosalie Trombley, who still to this day, is as important to us as Frank Zappa was because she took a chance on that song, "Eighteen," which became a number one record there. She was playing Simon & Garfunkel and The Supremes and all those bands, but she heard this record and her son liked it. Her teenage son said that's the coolest record, so she added it. The next thing you know it got requests and it was a major hit. Now if you were a hit on CKLW, that was the biggest station in the Midwest. That was Chicago, Detroit, St. Louis; that's how big that radio station was. If you got a hit on CKLW, you had a national hit. Everybody looked there to see what was going to be a hit. So we had become a national product because we had a national hit.

Anyway, when that happened we decided New York was more to our liking. LA was still not going to accept us. New York, though, had that underground, the Velvet Underground scene, the Warhol scene. There was actually something going on there, with the Ramones and all this who came a bit later. But when we plugged into New York, then, we were at Max's Kansas City, we were at all these New York things. We had the money now. But we didn't really want to live in New York because it would be very hard to rehearse. So we leased a house up in Greenwich, Connecticut that was a 32-room mansion called the Galesi Estate.

April 2, 1972. Alice Cooper play the calamitous Mar Y Sol Pop Festival in Puerto Rico.

April 8, 1972. Old manager from the Zappa days, Herb Cohen sues Warner Bros. and the band for royalties from *Killer,* based on his interpretation of wording from the original Alice Cooper contract.

May 16, 1972. Alice Cooper issue the title track from their forthcoming *School's Out* album as a single, backed with "Gutter Cat." The song would become arguably the most beloved anthem of the band's catalogue, reaching No.7 on Billboard, No.3 in Canada and No.1 in the UK. The song essentially singlehandedly make the album a success, given that no other singles were floated and indeed, every other song on the album would become deep
obscurities in the catalogue.

June 3, 1972. As *Killer* holds ground at No.42, "School's Out" enters the charts at No.88, rising to No.63 the following week. An integral part to the song is the children's chorus. To do this, Alice and Bob had five
professional stage kids over to a studio in New York, with their protective and wary mom's looking on. In addition to Rosalie Trombley (immortalised in Bob Seger song "Rosalie," also covered by Thin Lizzy) helping the band out of Windsor, Ontario, Joe Greenberg cites Chuck Dunaway out of WIXY in Cleveland as being instrumental to the band breaking first in the Midwest. As well, hooking up with Michael Quatro as a booking agent out of Detroit aided and abetted the cause.

Alice Cooper:
"I would say that "School's Out" was… you know, when you're writing a song, and there's a momentum in the song where you know that it's a hit? At times, very apparent, other times not, where you write the song and you say, "Oh, this is a really good song," then all of a sudden it falls off the album and it's a hit and you go, "Oh, great." "School's Out" was designed to be a hit. It was designed to be an anthem. It was designed to
appeal to every single person in the world because everybody has sat through school on that last three minutes before school is out. The longest three minutes of the year is that last three minutes on May 30th or whatever it is. So I said, if we can capture the joy of the kids screaming, knowing they have three months off of school, well, that will be a big hit.

Michael Bruce:
Bob's a perfectionist and he's thorough. There was no detail left undone. Everything from the tempo of the song to how he thought about the song to what's going on in the song was all covered. "School's Out" wasn't just, "Hey, it's the end of school—play it like that." We had a chorus of kids and everything was premeditated and thought-out. Bob was also a child prodigy keyboard player. He was quite the pianist and we laid everything out on the piano like it was a Mozart movement.

We could have done those albums without Bob, but would they have turned out like they did? Not at all, no way! He was our fifth Beatle. He was our George Martin. When he was done, I was like, "This is what I wanted my song to be like." Take "No More Mr. Nice Guy;" it's basically a rock song, but the way it's done and the way it's produced, it's just done so well that there's not a bad part in it and I take enormous pride in that. It's textbook; it's Rock 101.

We were the culmination of dark and light and that's what we did in our shows. We'd start off with what we called our white set and kill Alice some way and he'd come back, be reborn, and then we'd be in our dark set. Bob is the one who musically really made that happen. He filled in all the blanks. If there was a part that was going to be, "Okay, make this scary," he'd have the moans or give some sort of idea of how to do the baby thing. He'd do those little vignettes on the piano like, "Mommy, where's daddy?" He made that stuff happen.

Bob takes all of those ideas and puts them in a nice neat package with a title. I used to hate outlines in school because it forced you to focus on writing a paper and come up with a theme, subtitles. I'd want to put the whole thing down on paper and be done with it. Bob was our teacher in that aspect. He taught us how to go through it thoroughly and make a complete piece of music out of it. I think that's why it's so good.

June 6, 1972. David Bowie issues *The Rise and Fall of Ziggy Stardust and the Spiders from Mars*, probably the definitive, most well-known "glam" album, glam being a mostly UK music and fashion craze that existed from about 1972 to 1975. Stateside, Alice Cooper and the New York Dolls were considered the closest thing to what the likes of Bowie, Mott the Hoople, Slade and Sweet were doing.

Alice Cooper:
Actually, I invented Bowie. Bowie used to come to our concerts when he was David Jones and he was a little folk singer. And all of a sudden after he saw Vince turn into Alice, he suddenly became David Bowie. So I just want to get the history straight there. I was the first one who really invented the Jekyll and Hyde character and then Bowie did the chameleon.

June 19, 1972. The band find out that the 750,000 panties they'd manufactured to be part of the *School's Out* packaging have failed government inspection because they were too flammable. The manufacture figures out how to save the job, with a flame-retardant spray.

Late June 1972. The band work at their new mansion headquarters and at Record Plant on "Elected" just as the *School's Out* album is issued.

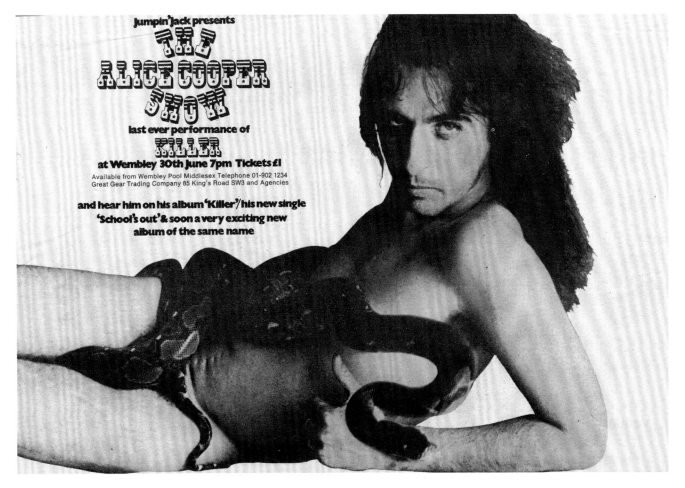

Alice Cooper:

One thing about the *School's Out* album that is interesting, was the fact that there was a real Yardbirds presence there, especially with the song itself. If you really listen to the bottom of that song, it's all Yardbirds, which was our biggest influence. It was the only song I ever did that I was sure was going to be a hit. A lot of other songs you sit there and you go, "I think, maybe that could be... I'm not sure." "School's Out" was, "Oh yeah, this is a slam dunk right here." If this isn't a hit, then I don't belong in the business. So we were right about that one. That's one in a row there.

Jackie
Alice Cooper

But the other thing with that album, was when we did the reference to *West Side Story,* and we did the Jets song and the whole fight thing, we never realised that our audience had no idea what *West Side Story* was. I thought everybody knew *West Side Story.* It was just like part of America to know *West Side Story.* People would say, "Oh, I love that Jets song." And I go, "Yeah, it's *West Side Story.*" "What does that mean?" And I go, come on, you're kidding me. I realised that 90% of my audience had no theatrical knowledge. They wouldn't know *West Side Story* from *Bye Bye, Birdie* or any of those.

I may be the only straight guy in the world who knows show tunes. But I go to a lot of plays and I love musicals, because to me, I do the closest thing to a musical. When I go to see a real musical on stage—and it might be the worst thing in the world; it could be *Mama Mia*—I would go, okay, how does this music connect in this theatre, with the way they set this up? I watch the worst stuff and go, oh, I know how to connect that up. I think of something on stage. With me it's going to be something like a dead body on stage that's going to be flung around. I would pick up something from a show that you would never connect up with Alice Cooper (laughs).

I'm telling you what. We've already had offers on taking *Welcome to My Nightmare* to Broadway and redoing it as a new version of it, and that may happen. So that might not be that far away from being a reality. I would love to take it to the West End of London and just do it over there in London for a month and then on Broadway for a month. Then take it to a town and do it for two weeks at a time, a week at a time, in each town.

But back to the album, "School's Out" was really the biggest hit. There are a lot of what I would call stage hits on there. There are a lot of songs that the audience wants me to do. There's about five or six songs I get requested for all the time on that and there are 28 albums. If I just did one song off of each album, that's a full show. So I've really got to pick and choose what songs I'm going to do.

Michael Bruce:

That was great. That was one of the more fun albums to make and Glen was really on the mark. We rehearsed and did some recording out in LA and some in New York. Songs like "Blue Turk," "Gutter Cat vs. the Jets," Bob brought in that *West Side Story* element and we loved it, and I liked "Luney Tune." It was just the real spirit of the band, some of our blues with our New York sort of feels.

That and *Killer,* the band was still pretty much intact and I think that after *School's Out* we started working really hard and we were doing like two albums a year and we started leaving Glen behind. I don't think he could keep up and I just don't think he was prepared to work that hard. He either couldn't or didn't want to.

Dennis Dunaway:

"Elected" was recorded, pretty much, everything except the vocal, at the estate. I remember the actual take that we got on the recording. Because I remember when we got to the end, and I started doing this high bass line, and later in overdubs we added horns, with everybody in the band following the bass line. The song was on its way out, and when I started doing this bass line, I knew that we had finally gotten the take, and I had chills going up my spine, thinking, "Wow, we finally nailed it."

Neal Smith:
The nucleus of that song was "Reflected" from *Pretties for You*. In fact, "Reflected" was originally called "Elected!" The agreement that we had as a band is that anything we wrote on *Easy Action* or *Pretties for You*, we all share the songwriter's credit equally on it. Whether someone wrote a song, I think Dennis wrote "B.B. on Mars," but

we all took credit, because it was the early stages of the band and we all worked on all the songs a lot, equally as much. A song like "Apple Bush," that was a song I had written, but it was the whole band that made it come to what it was on the album. Then anything that would be spun off from that era, whether it was recorded or not—as I say, "Elected" was like a rewrite of "Reflected." Because that was a rewrite of "Reflected," it still fell into that category, so that's why everybody's name was on it.

   But yeah, we brought it back out, dusted it off, rearranged it, and changed the feel a little bit, but it still had a lot of the characteristics of the original song, and then changed the name to "Elected." After "School's Out," which was a timely song with the ending of the school year, the election was coming and we wanted something timely, because we'd found a formula with that, first with "I'm Eighteen" to "School's Out," now "Elected." So that is why we chose to use that subject; it was working for us, and nobody else was really doing it to that intensity that we were.

Late June 1972. The band try a new prop, a 20-foot cannon which was supposed to shoot a dummy of Alice across the auditorium. It malfunctioned at one of the band's rust belt shows and was quickly sold to The Rolling Stones, so Mick could sit atop it.

June 28, 1972. The band arrive in the UK and record a performance of "School's Out" for *Top of the Pops*.

June 29, 1972. A famous stunt in Alice Cooper lore finds a truck festooned with a photo of Alice on a billboard "stalling" in Piccadilly Square. Shep says that this was staged in a panic because ticket sales were poor and something had to be done to generate some press. A driver was found who was willing to get arrested, and in fact the faux breakdown of the vehicle was staged three times.

Alice Cooper:
We pulled every trick in the book in England. We stalled a photo of Alice half-naked with a snake around him in Piccadilly Square on a Friday afternoon. Stalled a truck and stopped London. It was the cover of the London Times the next day. It was a pure Hollywood publicity stunt. But the British loved that. The British love to be put on like that. When they saw the show, we gave them the show they wanted. It had everything they were expecting in it. Everybody thought we were from England because we were such a big hit over there.

July 23, 1972. Alice Cooper play one of the most memorable gigs of their career. The venue is the Hollywood Bowl. Supporting were Captain Beyond, Jo Jo Gunne and Wolfman Jack, who rode in on a camel and introduced the band. A helicopter broke the law by flying too low (and was fined for the dangerous manoeuvre) as he dropped thousands of pairs of paper panties over the crowd, in celebration of *School's Out,* each copy of which came wrapped in a thin cloth pair of panties. Bernie Taupin recalls being there with Elton John and the two of them leaping up to grab the panties as they fell from the sky just like the rest of the crowd.

Dennis Dunaway:
I couldn't say we had made it until we played the Hollywood Bowl. When we went back to LA as a successful band and played the Hollywood Bowl, that was the night I said, well, I have to admit that we've made it (laughs). Elton John was there that night, and he was backstage raving about our costumes. And all of a sudden, he was flamboyant from that night on (laughs).

Neal Smith:
He came over to Alice and I and said, "Thank you for showing me what rock 'n' roll is all about," and from that second on he was glitter.

July 28, 1972. *School's Out* reaches its highest point on the charts, No.2, locked out by *Honky Chateau* from Elton John, who had been in attendance at Alice's Hollywood Bowl show the previous week.

August 1972 – January 1973. Alice Cooper and Bob Ezrin work at their Connecticut band house, The Galesi Estate in Greenwich, as well as The Record Plant in New York and Morgan Studios in London on tracks to be used on their forthcoming sixth album.

August 5, 1972. Alice Cooper play the Akron Rubber Bowl in Akron, Ohio, supported by J. Geils Band and Dr. John, memorable due to a reprise of the helicopter panty-drop stunt.

September 2, 1972. Alice Cooper play a triumphant show at Varsity Stadium in Toronto, Ontario. The show, so loud, with 24,000 in attendance, making it the highest grossing show at that venue up to that point. Two nights later, the band play the Montréal forum in Montréal, 18,000 in attendance.

September 19, 1972. "Elected," backed with "Luney Tune," is issued as an advance single from *Billion Dollar Babies*. Issued just in time for the November US presidential election, the song hit No.26 on the charts the week of the vote. As promo, the band created a story-themed music video similar to those that would become big business in the '80s. The song is a loose rewrite of "Reflected" from Pretties for You.

Dennis Dunaway:

"Elected" was a natural follow-up for "School's Out" because of its similar potential for repeating airplay. Every time school ends, they play it. So what about every time there's an election? It was pretty simple so I might say we all thought of it together. They both continue to get periodical bumps in airplay. I didn't like that video because like Glen said, "Even the chimp's in it more than the band."

Because our controversial image was repellent to parents, and therefore advertisers, we had a rough time getting anything filmed, or on television. So the money wasn't invested there. But I know we could have introduced some bold ideas if we, as a band, would have been left to our own invention, and so we did videos. But unfortunately, every time a camera was around, outsiders would be there to impose their interpretation of what they thought Alice Cooper were all about. With all due respect to their talents, they missed it completely. Why would we record "Black Juju" and project a sexually threatening image with a sinister stage show, and then ride an elephant like the Monkees? It was embarrassing and damagingly counter-productive to our cause. How can you shock people after that?

As for "Luney Tune," John Lydon of the Sex Pistols is always citing that as the scariest song he's ever heard. I wrote that song and Alice wrote the bridge. I still have the very original lyrics, which also may have come from a dream. I have lots of notebooks filled with what I call my dream poems. Alice used lines from those poems in many songs. I wrote the song on bass and Alice delivered the lyrics as I had imagined them, with convincing sincerity. We had one of our rare disagreements over the line, "Couple shots and I don't feel no pain." I'm not sure why I didn't like that—it's a strong line anyway.

November 2, 1972. A show at the Hofstra University Auditorium in Hempstead, NY is filmed for the first *ABC in Concert*. When the show aired on November 24th, some affiliates yanked coverage, shocked at the opening act of the program. For those who ran the footage, complaints were numerous.

November 4, 1972. The band arrive in London, England and proceed to Morgan Studios where they work on some of the material that would appear on *Billion Dollar Babies*. The famed photo shoot used in the gatefold of that record also takes place, conducted by David Bailey at his studio. Shep says that the money used in the gatefold of the album had to be flown over from the States and delivered under heavy guard with guns.

Dennis Dunaway:
I don't see anything shocking about it myself. It was just a snakeskin wallet, and I guess people got shocked because it had the crying baby. Alice is holding the crying baby, which was baby Lola, whose mother, Carolyn Pfeiffer still works for Alive Enterprises after all these years. She worked in publicity with the Beatles, with Derek Taylor. That's where we got her from, and that was her daughter. It was so blatantly, "Hey, we're rich (laughs), and we're rock 'n' roll." We had a picture with a big gigantic pile of money, and a crying baby with Alice Cooper makeup on. But overall, it seemed pretty mild to me.

　　The white clothes and the rabbits, that actually came from an idea I had when the band lived together all the way back before *Love It to Death*, going back to that concept of the white and the black on that album. Cindy, my wife, who was Neal's sister, at the time had rabbits on this farm that the band was at in Pontiac, Michigan. I got this idea for the white part of the album which I thought would be the back cover, all sitting in a white bed wearing white, and we would have these bunny rabbits in bed with us.

　　So it would be the opposite of the dark. See, I wanted to contrast happy and innocent and dark and evil. So we brought in a photographer and we did this shoot. I have seen some of these pictures crop up all these years later. But at the time the guy wanted to be paid a few hundred dollars, and we're like, "You've got to be kidding, man. Look in our refrigerator. We don't have any food! Take pity on us and do a spec deal." And the guy wouldn't do it.

　　I was so pissed-off, after we went through all this trouble. I told him, "Well, we're going to redo this picture someday, and then we're going to use it and you're going to be sorry" and so eventually we got around to it. We even got rabbits in London. That was David Bailey, who photographed the Beatles and all kinds of people. That shot was taken in London. But the night before, I was up all night, because Cindy was in my room sewing, making those outfits, because she made all the clothes for the band and I'm trying to do a photo thing at nine o'clock in the morning with no sleep. None of us had any sleep, really; we were partying in London. But the hard part about that photograph was trying to get that much American money in England.

November 6, 1972. *Love It to Death* is certified gold in the US, having peaked at No.35 in the charts.

Neal Smith:
I was the first guy in the band to buy a car and it was a Silver Cloud Rolls Royce. That was a goal of mine. That was in late '72 after *School's Out*. When I left school in 1967, I had a picture of a white Rolls Royce next to my bed and eventually it happened.

November 10 - 26, 1972. The band conduct their second European tour, supported by Flo and Eddie. Opening night in Glasgow (the only UK show) includes a riot by 300 fans, an overturned limo and the first three rows at the venue vandalised. Shep recalls Alice refusing to fly over to the UK because they didn't have any Budweiser beer there. Shep confirmed that he was right and got a connection to look into it, an American who was opening up the first Hard Rock Café there. Eventually some was acquired from an American base in Germany and the tour was back on.

November 13, 1972. After the band's show at the Olympia Theatre in Paris, Omar Sharif throws an after-party to which the guests were asked to arrive dressed as Raquel Welch. Later, in 1975, Welch (who Alice called Rocky) would fall for Alice hard, who was now in love with Sheryl and had to spurn her advances, despite Shep urging Alice to try keep her entertained and show up to her events, given that Shep was now managing Welch and wanted to keep her happy. Alice recalls one incident where he and Dick Wagner were golfing at the Doral Park Country Club in Florida with some bankers, and out of the blue, Raquel runs up to the cart and says, "I'm your caddy today!" Also, according to Alice, at this Olympia Theatre show, somebody jumped up on stage and rushed Glen, throwing a burning guitar at him.

December 1972. Alice is admonished by manager Shep Gordon about his alcohol intake and he flies off to Jamaica for a rest and rethink. Meanwhile, Glen in hospitalised in London and once back home in Phoenix he is rehospitalised with a pancreas gravely damaged due to alcohol abuse. Buxton never quite recovers and his participation in band matters is reduced.

Gavin Baddeley:
Alice Cooper is more heavily influenced—at least he's said he's more heavily influenced—by things like TV, films, soundtracks and so forth. He's very much an American decadent. Unlike the European decadents of previous generations who smoked opium and read poetry, he drunk Budweiser and watched TV all day. But the results are a dissolving personality, a descent into depravity and confusion.

But of course his motivation has changed over the years. I think even he'd be the first to admit that. During the '70s, with the band's first major success, he was drinking more and more, losing contact, perhaps, with a lot of what we call real life. The show itself certainly was shocking; it was very much that they wanted to get people's attention.

One of the things he describes is that in the early years they'd do these various shows and they'd be the one band that would empty the room in minutes and it sort of worked out. That was something to be proud of in a perverse way, and it was also the thing that attracted the attention of Frank Zappa. Later on, I think it was largely a commercial decision on their parts; it was putting on a show. It was the Grand Guignol. He used the term about his stage show on a number of occasions.

One could say that part of Alice's mental degradation is represented by or seeded in the prosaic version of how the name came about. Alice Cooper just sounded so all American, and Alice Cooper, the character, was sort of about the side of being all-American that people didn't like to talk about. Alice Cooper is a persona being separate from Vincent Furnier, the preacher's son, who he was off stage.

My suspicion is this became increasingly important for him as his problems with alcohol became more and more pronounced, and he was having problems differentiating between different sections of his life. If you look at some of the albums from this period they talk about the trouble of, you know, coming back down to earth. A lot of popular musicians will tell you there is an issue whereby they don't like to talk to anybody after a performance. Because it's such a powerful, powerful thing, and that you can't maintain that level of intensity 24 hours a day, seven days a week. This is pronounced if you're playing a character like Alice Cooper. What he does on stage is not something you can do in your private life and hope to remain sane.

Michael Bruce:

Glen Buxton—Funny guy; you know, he played the spoons or whatever other hardware was laying around. Funny story, we were downstairs rehearsing, and his high E string, the real thin one, kept popping out of the bridge, the saddle on the bridge. He would play it and it would flip out. So I said, "Glen, you gotta get that taken care. You don't want to have that happen when we're playing." So a couple days later, we're playing along and I go to him, "Did you get that fixed?" He goes, "Yeah, yeah." I went over and looked at his guitar, and he drove a nail in his guitar right next to the string. If that gives you any indication… (laughs).

Then he cut a hole in his Gretch and put a Fender pickup in there. There's nothing he wouldn't do; he could do anything. It was all right as long as you got what you were looking for. He was an interesting player. As we started doing less cover stuff as we were changing from the Nazz days and Spiders… we used to do four sets and then we would do one original and then two original and then three original. He was really fine on the covers but it was a little harder for him when we started writing.

December 12, 1972. The band return home to the east coast after their European tour, whereby Alice gives Bob Ezrin the *Billion Dollar Babies* from overseas. Ezrin takes them to The Record Plant in New York City and continues to build the record.

Dennis Dunaway:

I'm not sure I would describe it as being more difficult or easier, but we had a mobile truck parked in the driveway of an estate in Greenwich, Connecticut, and it was one of the first studio albums recorded with a mobile truck. I don't think it was the very first one though. So the whole house had… there was a microphone in the hallway because it had a certain amount of echo. There was a microphone in the solarium because it had a certain amount of echo, and we basically talked to a video camera, which was early on technology. We recorded most of the bed tracks right there.

We did the vocals at the Record Plant East in New York City, and we also recorded a lot of the vocals at Morgan Studios outside of London. But when the band was doing a European tour over there, we realised we needed one more song for the album. So after the tour, when everybody had the flu, we rented rooms in a hotel, but as it turned out we were the very first people who stayed there, and we had the entire hotel to ourselves, and we wrote "Generation Landslide." Then we went back to London and recorded that. I was very happy with the way that album came out. I loved "Generation Landslide;" I thought that could've been a hit for us.

But being in various places is what a band does, so that wasn't a problem, especially since we recorded most of the tracks in our own house. As for other players, Rockin' Reggie was a friend and a good influence on Glen. We knew Mick Mashbir ever since our Arizona days. Bob Dolin added what we were looking for in keyboards. Steve Hunter is a very unimposing guy. He fit in better than Dick Wagner, who is a nice guy but he just didn't get our humour. His severe sort of seriousness was foreign in our world, and it created an awkwardness all around. Ezrin insisted on his involvement, and he certainly could play, so we went along with it. We all liked Donovan and we were honoured that he sang. We just tried to keep doing what we had always done—keep moving forward and try to stay focused on each task at hand.

As for outside material, "Hello Hooray," Alice and I chose "Sun Arise" for *Love It to Death* so weren't against outside material. For *Billion Dollar Babies*, we were trying to come up with a good opening song so Bob's suggestion to do "Hello Hooray" was a welcome solution. Of course, we did it much different than the demo that we had heard. But it turned out to be stage show opener too. The fog would roll out and then this song would start and it would be the introduction to the set. Then we used pyro where Alice would point his cane at the audience and this flame would shoot out above their heads. That would kick the show off. But you know, we were safety-conscious. This wasn't really pyro like a charge; this was more like flash paper, and actually it was flash paper, like magicians use. We could have been the first band to use laser beams, which Blue Öyster Cult ended up doing. But we were concerned about the safety factor that was in question in those days, so we passed on that, as well as other things. Our show had this dangerous look to it, this aspect, but we didn't really throw anything into the audience that would hurt anyone. A lot of people threw things back that would hurt us. Glen went to the hospital one time because someone threw a hammer and hit him in the knee. Neal got a dart in his back, Michael Bruce had an M80 thrown and it blew up right next to his head, in Toledo.

Back to the album, "Generation Landslide," we had just finished a European tour and we were all sick and exhausted so we went to the Canary Islands to rest. "Rest" was management's code for finish writing the album. We had our equipment set up on the hotel top floor where, unfortunately, men were still working. So, with the sounds of hammers and saws all around, the Alice Cooper group wrote "Generation Landslide" together from scratch. It proved that Alice Cooper was still at our best when we were left alone.

Neal Smith:
Unlike "Billion Dollar Babies," "Generation Landslide" is a perfect example of a song that did start with a beat. We had finished the *Billion Dollar Babies* album, and we had recorded most of the tracks in New York. We recorded some of them at The Record Plant in New York. We had recorded some of them at the estate in Greenwich Connecticut, and then in Morgan Studio in London, where we stayed at the Brinks Hotel. We needed one more track for the record and we were on tour in Europe, and we took some time off. We went from London to Canary Islands, just specifically to write one song.

We said, well, where the hell are we going to be able to actually rehearse in a hotel? It's impossible. So we found a hotel that was just almost completed in construction, and all the penthouses on the top floor weren't really finished yet. They were okay, had electricity, and they were finished to the point where we could go in and use one as a rehearsal area. But it wasn't really ready for somebody to stay in the room. So we stayed in a hotel, and took the equipment up there to use as a personal area. And we spent the day and didn't come up with anything really great.

Then somebody suggested, or I suggested, well let's just try a little bit different beat. So we really didn't have any ideas. There was nothing going on. So I just started going (sings the drumbeat), and Michael started strumming chords, and then in 15 minutes the basic idea for "Generation Landslide" was written. Now, that one specifically, the drums inspired the song. "Billion Dollar Babies," like I say, that didn't happen. That was pretty much straighter, and then I came up with the idea for the intro to the song, and that really solidified the song. So "Generation Landslide" was written around the drums.

I love Alice's harmonica playing. He's a great harmonica player; he should play it more, but he doesn't. He played on "Eighteen" and he'd done it on a couple of tracks, but I don't think he did any on *Killer* or *School's Out*. So on the guitar solo, we were hugely influenced and knew a lot of Yardbirds songs. So the break in the song was inspired by The Yardbirds and the solos that they would have, where they'd go "Bum bum," then they'd stop and the harmonica would play—it was like an old blues thing. We'd never tried anything like that as Alice Cooper, even though we knew those songs for years. Lyrically, I think my two favourite songs are "My Stars" and "Generation Landslide." It was such a great song to play drums on too; just let the kit run right through there.

1973

Parallel to the theme of Alice as "the world's most interesting man," the Alice Cooper band packed more living into 1973 than any band in any of their given super nova years. Okay, maybe not (Kiss had quite the 1976), but let's just go with 1973 as an incredibly energised super nova year for Alice Cooper.

First off, the band is methodically imploding. Alice and Cindy move out of the band house down to Manhattan. Cooper also gets involved with Salvador Dali for a loopy hologram project, inconsequential save for the fact that it's just more thrown on the pile of the cult of Alice, band optional.

The big news is that in February, Alice Cooper issue what will be their biggest album. And why is it big? I'd say it's a combination of it being their time, the fantastic and decadent packaging featuring provocative images of snakeskin, babies in makeup, piles of money and the band in virginal white, plus the fact that the album contained, to some degree, four hit singles versus the usual one to two.

An extravagant tour ensues, the band's biggest and best, aided by magician The Amazing Randi, but further cracks appear with the addition of a keyboard player and more shockingly, Glen Buxton being ghosted by guitarist Mick Mashbir. Nonetheless, surprisingly little is discussed in the press about any of this. The band are plastered all over the newspapers and magazines and the album goes gold.

And then, as testimony to how much sensual and information overload five bodies can stand, before the year is out, *Muscle of Love* will emerge. Turns out there is indeed a limit, and the album is not great, it is to be the last for the original band, and the record is never toured. "Teenage Lament '74" is issued as a single, but it's never a runaway success, soon to be joined by the impressive and impressively heavy title track as the only songs to live on in classic rock rotation.

January 1973. Alice and his girlfriend move out of the band house and into a penthouse suite in Manhattan. The seeds of a rift between Alice Cooper, the man and media maven, and Alice Cooper, the band of school chums from Phoenix, are sown.

January 16, 1973. Alice Cooper issue as a single "Hello Hooray" backed with "Generation Landslide." The dramatic and glammy concert anthem would reach No.35 on the *Billboard* charts, after entering at No.72. Alice Cooper's version of this song is nearly unrecognisable as the Rolf Kempf original or the purely folky Judy Collins rendition. The lyrics are the same but Alice Cooper completely overhaul the melody, the tempo, the rhythm and the arrangement.

Neal Smith:
Rolf Kempf. Of all the albums we recorded, there were only a couple of other songs written by somebody else. And that song was presented to us. I still have the reel-to-reel tape with the original song

on it; I guess Judy Collins did a version of it just before we did. We didn't normally do someone else's material because we were such avid writers, ourselves, but for the beginning of the album and for the beginning of the *Billion Dollar Babies* show, it seemed to be perfect.

It was a great track; Bob liked it, so we played it and learned it, and it sounded great. It was a perfect intro to our show. It really said what the band was all about, and what we had done and what we had accomplished and the lyrics were all written by him. Alice stood aside as a lyricist—and Alice is a great lyricist—and went with the lyrics that were written, and it worked perfectly. So, it opened the show and on the album, as the song fades out, there's cannons that are firing, very, very subtly in the background.

February 1973. The band rehearse for upcoming tour dates. Bob Dolin is brought in to play keyboards and guitarist Mick Mashbir is brought in to compensate for the fading skills of Glen Buxton.

Mick Mashbir:

In May 1972, I drove across America on my way to London and ended up staying at the Cooper mansion for a couple of weeks. I knew Michael Bruce and Neal Smith from playing together at parties, etc. in high school. Later when I lived in the desert, Mike or Neal would come by and we'd jam on Kinks or Yardbirds songs. Are you getting a picture of the influence of the British Invasion on musicians in Phoenix? (laughs). After a couple of weeks I went off to London. The Coopers followed a few weeks later to promote *School's Out*. We hung out some more, and then they left. I had been living in a tiny studio for about three months when I got the telegram to "Come back to work on the new album." I was stoked. London was starting to happen for me musically but I personally didn't understand the warm beer concept (laughs) so, it was time to go. I felt no hesitation at all. In fact, I felt it was destiny being fulfilled.

About two years earlier I went to see the band in Tucson, Arizona for the Killer tour. I bought some really good street acid—don't try this at home, kids!—and had a great time. Rock security wasn't what it is now. I looked like one of the band so I headed backstage after the show. The guard opened the door for me, no questions asked! Anyway, while talking in the backstage scene I had this very strong feeling that at some point I would have a real reason to be there. I could have been a guitar roadie, but fortunately for the roadies, it didn't turn out that way.

On my flight back to America, I thought about Glen, since he was a lead guitar player and so was I, and wondered how he felt about me coming in to play. The first thing I did when I arrived back at the Cooper mansion was go directly to Glen's room. I knocked on his door. He opened it and said, "Mick! What are you doing here?" I said, "I came back to play on the new album." He said, "Cool!" and that was it.

After a couple of weeks of rehearsal at the Cooper mansion, the Record Plant mobile truck showed up and we began recording Billion Dollar Babies. We had a pretty difficult time getting any decent takes. Part of it was probably the new chemistry. This was the first record that Glen hadn't shown up for. I'm sure that weighed heavy on their minds. By the end of the second week things were going so poorly that Bob Erzin wanted to pull the plug, but it was decided to press on once the band got to London.

We arrived in London and started recording at Morgan Studios the next day. Name any famous English artist and they all recorded at Morgan. The change of studios made a big difference and things started to come together. We started listening to rough mixes in London and you could hear the magic in the tracks. Morgan was the site of the infamous superstar jam with myself, Alice Cooper, Neal Smith, Keith Moon, Marc Bolan, Harry Nilsson and Rick Grech. Even though I started that jam, as usual I am in none of the pics or articles. It began during a break while I was talking with Marc. I started playing a riff similar to his hit "Bang a Gong" and he asked if he could play Michael Bruce's guitar. I said yes and off we went. Rick Grech ate a couple of my peyote buttons, picked up Dennis Dunaway's bass and Neal sat down at his drums.

We had been playing for about an hour when a highly inebriated Keith, Harry and Alice showed up. Bob Ezrin was very excited! This was the era of super group jam records and he figured he had one of his own beginning to form. Well, he set up a mic for the three singers, started rolling the tape—here comes genius! Well, the first thing out of Keith Moon's mouth as a singer was "I blew a dog." I was bummed he wanted to sing instead of playing drums. I think Neal would have given up the drum chair for Keith, no problem. Anyway, it all went downhill from there. Ezrin got pissed-off, stopped the tape and threw everyone out of the studio! So much for that super-duper session.

After a couple more weeks we went back to New York and finished the album at The Record Plant. As far as what makes the album so great? It must have been my involvement (laughs). I think a fan could give you a better answer than I can. I do know though, that the record was a victory lap for the band and our playing skills were well honed and our overall confidence was up, which contributes greatly to the vibe of any record.

But yeah, it was actually Mike Bruce that made that happen. GB was basically on strike. He didn't want to be in the same room as Michael or Bob Ezrin and they were rehearsing for the next record. Mike was also looking to the future because he didn't know what GB was gonna do. He knew I would fit in with the other guys from Phoenix. I ended up playing on every track except "Elected," "Sick Things" and "Generation Landslide". My favourite song was "No Mister Nice Guy". I was happy with all my parts. GB was around as little as possible. We were recording in the bands mansion and he didn't bother to come downstairs.

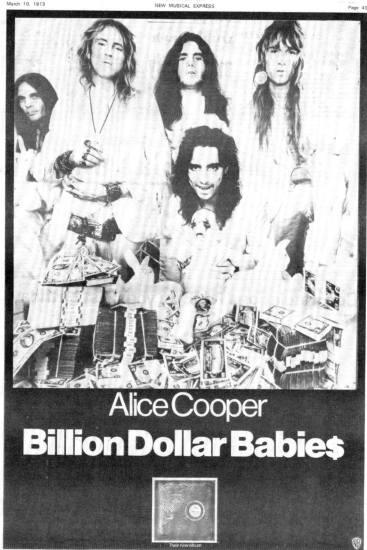

Alice Cooper
Billion Dollar Babie$

Their new album

Neal Smith:

When we did the *Billion Dollar Babies* tour, Bob Dolin was the person who played keyboards. You know, Michael Bruce had always gone back and forth, as far back to "I'm Eighteen," between guitar and keyboards. He's the one who played it on the record, and he played it live on stage and he would go back and forth from his guitar to keyboards. So, by the time we got to *Billion Dollar Babies*, we could afford to have a keyboard player on stage. So Bob Dolin was a friend of Mike's from Phoenix, and I don't know who else might have known him, but he's a great keyboard player, so he ended up on the Alice Cooper Billion Dollar Babies tour in 1973.

Glen really did not contribute anything, unfortunately, on the *Billion Dollar Babies* album, except smashing his guitar on "Sick Things." He was having some health problems and alcohol abuse problems, and the demons of rock 'n' roll were really starting to take its toll on him. He could still play "I'm Eighteen" and he could still play "School's Out" pretty damn well, but the new stuff he wasn't keeping up to speed with.

So we had two guys come in to play songs on the record. I think Dick Wagner was there, Steve Hunter was there, and they came in because that was the Nimbus 9 camp. When Alice went out to do *Nightmare*, he used all those same studio guys on it. So, we still had the feeling of the band, but the frosting on the cake was those guys. Which was fine. Because I like the stuff Dick Wagner did on "School's Out" and "My Stars," that's his solo on that one. But Mike Bruce is also playing on a lot of it as well.

The point I'm making is that Glen was not able to play a lot of those songs when we went on the road. So we added Mick Mashbir, a friend of mine from high school in Phoenix and he was in a couple of great local bands out in Arizona. We were lucky to get him to come on the road with us. He had a great look, and he's a really easy guy to work with, and a great guitar player. So he came on the road with us and he filled in the gaps where Glen wasn't able to play. So that's how they ended up in the band, as backup musicians with the original Alice Cooper.

James Randi:

I was in a magic shop in New York City on 34th Street, and one afternoon I'm talking with some colleagues there. The phone rang, the proprietor took the phone call and he turned to us and he said, "Anybody here want to work with a rock artist?" He didn't mention any names or anything. Frankly if he said Alice Cooper I wouldn't have known the difference. But I said, "Yeah, tell him I want $100 to talk to him." The other guys laughed and then he put his hand over the phone, and he says, "Okay, he'll pay." I said, "Hey, damn, that's okay. Just wants to talk to me, I'll do that." I said, "Where is he?" He said, "He's so and so by the Enterprise" and whatnot. So it was just frankly down the street. I was near 8th Avenue, I should say, at the time.

I hustled myself down there and I found the place appropriately decorated with dead plants. Purposely done, I found out later on. That was the sort of atmosphere to the place. I walked in and introduced myself to Shep Gordon and we hit it off right away, and he said, "What do you think you could do for us?" I gave him a whole thing, and I said how I could get in touch and get a hold of an original Will Rock guillotine. That wouldn't mean anything to you—technical term in the trade.

He said, "Okay, what do you want for it?" I said, "What are you offering?" He made me an offer which was very, very satisfactory. I said, "Fine, you're on; we're in business." He told me when the tour started, he invited me to go… where was it? It was some place north of the city, in Connecticut, where they were holding fort. They had rented an old mansion there and pretty well wrecked the joint from what I saw. Somebody had put a hole through one of the walls so he could see the TV in the next room. But that was sort of the way of groups in those days.

Dennis Dunaway:
The band was in a hotel room in NYC and we were all sitting on a bed watching television which was typical of the band, especially Alice—he's still glued to the screen whenever he has any downtime. The TV was the god, it was always on, we all liked it and we all got a lot of ideas for the band from television. All of a sudden there was a guy who started talking in the back of the room and one by one we looked around to see who the heck it was and it was Randi. We had all decided that we wanted to do something different and he just happened to be a powerful personality that stuck, I guess. He came in and started doing magic tricks and stuff. Randi is a great self-promoter.

Alice Cooper:
We were the *National Enquirer,* where other bands were the *LA Times* and the *Chicago Tribune.* Alice Cooper was the *Weekly World News.* We were the "Boy Born with Dog's Head." We were more exciting, much more sensational. I understood the power of the press. I was a journalism major in school, and I totally understood what sold papers and that was sensationalism. So Alice Cooper gave them sensationalism.

I wasn't stupid. I was saying, if I have an image like this, I'm not going to sit back and be subtle about it. We've got to be outrageous. But, we have to be able to pay it off with great songs. It's like that in sports. If you get 20 rebounds a game, yeah, then you can have leopard-skin hair. If you can knock out anybody in the ring, then you can call yourself The Greatest and be as outrageous as Muhammad Ali. Same thing with music. If you can deliver hit records and hit albums, you can pretty much do anything as outrageous as you want to.

February 14, 1973. *ABC* re-airs *ABC in Concert* and the complaints pour in yet again.

Dennis Dunaway:
The Alice Cooper group had a lot of detractors. We had a lot of people who hated us and weren't afraid to let us know it any chance that they got. So it was hard to all of a sudden think that we had made it. Also, because we were putting so much of our profits… all of our profit basically went back into our massive staging. No band before had their own stage, or even lighting on the road. If you think about it, Hendrix, The Who, none of those bands; they would show up and use whatever lighting was available and whatever staging was there. So, a lot of our money went back in.

February 17, 1973. The *New Musical Express* gives away an exclusive flex-disc version of "Slick Black Cadillac," as the Alice Cooper team continues to work the UK market, regularly buying ads in the UK music weeklies and doing a high volume of press.

February 18, 1973. Alice continues to make good use of his ties to New York City, getting an invite to a performance by George Burns, who he give an "Alice Cooper Living Legend Award." Cooper also had one made for Jack Benny, who he also met that night, but that award had yet to arrive. Also around this time, Alice and Shep meet Salvador Dali and his wife Gala over dinner at the St. Regis hotel to discuss Alice's likeness being used in a hologram project Dali was overseeing. Gaia instructs the duo not to discuss money with Salvador, in fact, only to respond to things he brings up. Gaia pours Dali hot water, after which he pulls a jar of honey out of his pocket, pours some in and snips it off with a pair of scissors. Gaia eventually takes Shep aside—Salvador would only call Shep Mr. Blenly—and they leave the room to talk money. In subsequent meetings, always at Trader Vic's at the Plaza Hotel, Dali pays for dinner only with his autograph, by signing a napkin.

February 26, 1973. Alice makes himself available to Salvador Dali for the technical work necessary to create the Alice Cooper hologram. Cooper is wearing over $1M of jewellery borrowed from Harry Winston. Subsequently there's a presentation at a museum, with national press in attendance. Rather than pay for the making of the hologram, the Cooper grant cede rights to it to Dali and take three holograms. The work, called "The First Cylindric Chromo-Hologram of Alice Cooper's Brain," can be seen at the Dali museum in Spain; as well, one is in the collection of the Dali museum in St. Petersburg, Florida.

Dennis Dunaway:

I fully understood Alice having his own celebrity status and I had no problem with it. That's what we had strived for. The problem came with the decision to cut us out. In the real world, I was excruciatingly quiet, but the band knew me as a relentless crusader for a crazy cause. How else would you talk a preacher's son, a football line-backer and two punks from Ohio into wearing sequins?

February 27, 1973. Alice Cooper issue their sixth album (in four years), *Billion Dollar Babies*. The album would reach No.1 on the *Billboard* charts and hit No.1 in the UK as well. Canada would respond with a No.2 ranking and Germany, No.9.

Alice Cooper:

It was probably the most timely record we ever did; *School's Out* and *Billion Dollar Babies* just hit at exactly the right time. We were at the very top of our popularity. All of a sudden *School's Out* had broken everything wide-open. That was a No.1, and then *Billion Dollar Babies* followed it up. When those two things happened right there, suddenly there was a new respect for Alice Cooper. All the rock critics that said, "Well, maybe, just by accident this group could have a hit. Maybe, just because their show is so good, and because Alice is so bizarre, okay, we'll give him that."

But when we followed up with *Billion Dollar Babies*, all the critics were saying, "You know what? This is the best album I've heard all year." All of a sudden, even the musicians, who were always, "So what, Alice Cooper?!," they were now going, "Hey, these guys are good." To me that was important. Because I knew that the show was going to overshadow the music. When they started actually loving the music, that's what I really cared about. It's a no-brainer that they're going to love me getting my head cut off. If you hate Alice Cooper, you're going to love that. But when they actually played the record and said this is my favourite record, and when you get guys like John Lennon saying "Elected" was his favourite record, that's great. That's the recognition you've always wanted.

Dennis Dunaway:

We all wanted the same thing—to make great records. It didn't matter who came up with the best idea for a bridge or a lyric. We tried every idea and voted on what was best. That's what got us to the top. The problems came when that democracy fell to dictatorship.

For instance, four of us did not want "Mary Ann" on *Billion Dollar Babies*. We had some killer rock songs and the best one of them should have been where "Mary Ann" was. Betraying our long proven rule was a

major problem, and damaging. As that type of thing escalated, so did our resistance to it. But Alice wasn't resisting. The more he was separated from the rest of us, the more we saw our band, and all of the benefits of what we had all strived for, being taken away from us. The louder we rebelled, the more they called us out-of-control rock star egomaniacs that they had no choice but to replace. We just wanted our band back.

But "Mary Ann" was actually played by a keyboard player from Nimbus 9 recording studios, Jack Richardson and Bob Ezrin's studio, in Toronto Canada. He was one of the guys who worked with the studio and did a lot of keyboard tracks whenever they needed something like that for The Guess Who and so on and so forth, a really nice guy.

Personally I was fighting tooth and nail to have another song put on the album instead, because I thought we had some great songs that we were bumping to put that on. Like "Woman Machine," that ended up on *Muscle of Love*, although I also don't know if they were really as good as I thought they were at the time.

But I really thought we had more band songs, that would likely become something people would remember the band for. Even though in retrospect, I like "Mary Ann." Actually, I wrote a bass part for that. I had worked diligently to come up with something different, which actually reminded me of an early song that Michael Bruce did on the *Easy Action* album. I think it's "Below Your Means," which has a part where Michael reminds you of a little Mozart guy, playing piano, a spoiled brat kid, and then the bass does this little comical run. Okay, well, for "Mary Ann" I had a similar thing, a very Broadway bass part gone crazy. But as it turned out, we decided that for texture, we wouldn't record the bass part. I'm sorry that we decided that actually. I would have liked to have recorded that. But time was of the essence as well.

Then we also had "Sick Things," which Bob Ezrin and Alice wrote together. Ezrin was on piano, and Alice came up with the concept and the lyrics and everything. We went to Morgan Studios outside of London, we decided that we wanted to get more bottom on the bass. So we actually set the track up and I played the bass part really fast, and then we slowed it back down, so the bass could have more bottom.

At that point I also re-did the bass tracks to the movie, *Good to See You Again, Alice Cooper,* which didn't have all the shtick in it at that point, but it was basically the live concert that we did in Texas, where they had a technical problem with the bass tracks, and I had to redo all of the bass for that soundtrack. This was an actual movie release, but it was only released briefly. Rock movies are generally not successful.

The last song on the album, "I Love the Dead," has one of my favourite bass parts I ever wrote. That one had a lot to do with Dick Wagner, actually. He played a lot of the great guitar lines in it. So we had that new influence. The band was very tight amongst ourselves. Usually everything that we did was the band in a room, and anybody else was an outsider. But then when Ezrin came along, he was accepted as a part of the band, and when Dick Wagner came along, he was accepted as a member of the band and so was Rockin' Reggie. So we were like that. It was a tight clique, but we didn't keep people away if they were into it and they had creative ideas that we liked.

Neal Smith:

On *Easy Action*, there was a song Michael wrote called "Beautiful Flyaway" that was very Broadway, very theatrical, and so we thought that with everything we had on *Billion Dollar Babies*—"Sick Things," "I Love the

Dead," "Raped and Freezin'"—we needed something a little lighter. But it had to have that Alice Cooper twist on it. So if you listen to the lyrics you certainly know what the twist is on that. But again, that goes in to the theatrics of what Alice Cooper was and what we could do musically as well as theatrically.

"Sick Things," there was a huge ballroom where we would actually rehearse our live shows. And the fireplace was so big you could put a small car in there, and 40-foot ceilings. We'd bring all the equipment up and do our full rehearsals right there, before we would go on tour. But we'd also use that room to record. We'd made a drum riser about ten feet high and then put microphones all around this big monstrous room and that was the drum sound we got for "Sick Things." I'm just banging away doing these big rolls across tom-toms that are echoing in that room and it was just monstrous. There was just no way could you get a bigger sound than that—maybe in the Grand Canyon or something!

Michael Bruce:
Our *Sgt. Pepper* (laughs). The quintessential Alice Cooper album. "No More Mr. Nice Guy" was a tune I had written and had been around since *Killer* but it was just not a song that would fit on any of those albums. But when *Billion Dollar Babies* came around, it was its time, and that song—and "Billion Dollar Babies" really—set the mood for the album and then we built it from there. I think it was more of a public album—we were celebrating our success. It's worldly and in-your-face at the same time.

It's got great pieces like "Mary Ann" and Alice wanted to put his macabre twist on it and yet the album had songs like "No More Mr. Nice Guy" and "I Love The Dead." It ran the gamut. But each of the albums were so distinct that even *Muscle of Love*, and not doing it with Bob Ezrin, was distinctive in its own way because it wasn't Bob Ezrin. It was Jack Douglas and Jack Richardson who were people we worked with all the time with Bob. It was the same sort of thing, but without the big theatrical piece. Each album seemed to have its own character to it. I think it's what The Beatles had going. Each album had a real character and a flavour to it that stood out. When you listen back to *Rubber Soul*... we weren't doing it to that extent, but we were on that track.

But yeah, we also had on there "I Love the Dead." From what I remember, that was a song that was worked up by Bob, Alice and Wagner together. But they didn't have an ending to it and I came up with the major chord change (sings it). The cheery part I wrote and I noticed I didn't get any credit on it, but that's okay. Those guys were working so much on the feeling of the first part of the song that they never got to where the song was going as a whole.

I had written a lot of stuff with the band and "I Love the Dead" is a good example where I didn't get any credit on that because people thought that I wrote so much of the stuff that it's not going to matter "to Michael." I wrote some stuff for a couple of Neal songs and Dennis' song "Black Juju." I worked with them but didn't get any credit because that was my job in the band. I was one of the writers and I was on salary to do that. If I didn't like the song they'd come up with, then it was my job to work on it whether or not I got any credit.

Dick Wagner:
They were looking for more accessible music than what they had been doing all their career which was a little bit left field. Then Ezrin stepped in and they did "I'm Eighteen" which was very accessible. They wanted more of that and they hadn't been able to come up with anything until I came in and did the stuff that I did and it turns out they were ballads. I wrote some of the rock stuff too obviously 'cause I'm a rock 'n' roll player.

I knew Alice from before because we had met in Detroit when I was in The Frost. He came backstage and later that year I was flown out to Greenwich, Connecticut to the mansion where they were living and wrote "I Love The Dead" with him out there. From then the relationship just developed. So, was I afraid? It's always scary to sit down with a new person and write because you don't know what to expect. It was the perfect collaboration between Cooper and I. It was immediate because we would just start laughing at shit. We would laugh and laugh until we'd settle down and then we'd write a great song. We'd always come up with these weird titles, have a good laugh and then make great music.

Alice had the idea. I just started playing the music, and wrote the music. He came up with the title, and when you're singing "I love the dead," what music are you going to write? (laughs). There's only so many ways you can go.

Jackie Alice Cooper

Mick Mashbir:

I know that Mike Bruce presented a lot of the songs in finished form, lyrics and all, like "Be My Lover," and if Alice felt they fit what he and the band were trying to present, then he would leave the songs as is. If the lyrics didn't fit, Alice would rewrite them. I can't give you any specific examples of the rewrites but I know that it frustrated Michael and that led to his desire to express himself with a solo album. The easiest way to understand this is, Mike embraced the Beatles' music, and the rest of the guys were a Stones band before he joined. I remember that during the tracking rehearsals Alice didn't sing. He sat and listened and worked on his lyrics. What competition there was led to a more creative working situation, as it often does in bands.

February 27, 1973. The band perform a dress rehearsal gig at the Capitol Theatre in Port Chester, New York, no audience, to work the bugs out of the difficult *Billion Dollar Babies* show.

James Randi:

You've got a character that's called Alice Cooper, and it's not Vincent Furnier. It's Alice Cooper, and you've got to develop the character and the character always takes on the character in tune with the music that's being played and the themes and such, so that's all part of developing the character. You're in show business, not just going out there and doing music.

I'd never even been to see a hard rock show before in my life, frankly. I knew nothing about it. The kids were eating it up and they caught on. About one-third of the way into the show they were catching on. It's all a put-on. It's an act. The dolls, the chickens, the whole thing and they loved it. Once they caught on to the fact that this is all a big extravaganza show, literally a show, then they felt more at ease with it. There were some kids that were die-hard idiots, of course. They were all doped-up and they were exposing themselves and tearing their clothes and doing all kinds of crazy things, but they were gotten rid of by security pretty fast.

But most of the fans laughed at it. At first they didn't quite know whether to laugh or to be scared or whatever, but then Neal would be winking at them… Neal was quite a good character in the show, too, and Dennis Dunaway, still a very good friend of mine. He would always carry on. He would get close to the crowd and say personal stuff. He'd call down to the front row and say something like, "Are you terrified?" Things like this, *so he* lightened it up and they left very happy. That was a very happy audience. They wouldn't have left early. You couldn't have gotten them out of there with a can opener.

Alice kept it going, on stage and off. He was always very conversational and he was busy, busy, busy. Press all over the place and all kinds of problems with the show to get it onstage sometimes. We'd travel during the middle of the dead winter and we had all kinds of problems. We all pitched in. I even shovelled snow along with the rest of them when we had to. It was a cooperative deal. We all worked. We never asked about why we were doing it. We did it because the show had to go on.

Mick Mashbir:

I'd only seen Bob Dolin play in one band and Mike Bruce wanted a keyboard player for the live show, so we auditioned him. Bob was a gifted player with a fabulous ear. On tour we got along quite well since we were the hired guns. Whenever there was a press conference at the hotel, the local promo man would show Bob around town so we would not be interviewed by the press. On the tour everyone from both bands got on tremendously. The openers Flo and Eddie hired Bob and me about five years later.

March 1973. *Billion Dollar Babies* is certified gold, however platinum wouldn't be achieved for another 13 years.

Mick Mashbir:

The tour was a great experience. For me, it was like taking the express elevator to the penthouse and paying for your own room. That's a whole other story! (laughs). I had only been playing in bars and clubs and in the middle of the Phoenix desert before that. Having said that, I was more than ready to take that ride. At first the band wanted me to wear a gorilla costume! I was having none of that, but looking back on it, I probably would have gotten more publicity out of it. But no one would have known what I looked like.

The first night was a humbling experience. The crotch of my pants split as I climbed up to the stage. But as far as Glen was concerned, he was secure in his place in the band. I was just a supplemental player to him. We got along just fine. I remember once we got to the gig and everyone piled out of the limo and went in the back door. Glen and I went to the trunk of the limo to get our guitars out. We both had the same workingman approach. We carried our own guitars.

Anyway, the limo driver starts to drive off! We're screaming and chasing him. Finally he backs up, opens the trunk and we get our guitars. He drives off again. Glen and I get to the back door, it's locked and no one is there. It's one of those glass doors. We look at each other and start banging the glass with our guitar cases, hoping someone would hear us. Oops! The glass shatters, we open the door and just as we step in, someone comes around the corner, "What happened to the door?!" "It must have been some fans," we said as we shuffled off to the dressing room, laughing the whole way.

Neal Smith:

On the last two albums, *Billion Dollar Babies* and *Muscle of Love*, Glen's only contribution was smashing a guitar on "Sick Things" which is a lot like what Pink Floyd went through with Syd Barrett. They got another guitar player and went on, but we couldn't figure out how to do that with Glen. Dennis and I started working with another guitar player, Michael started working with another guitar player and Alice started working with other guitar players—everybody did it, but we couldn't do it as a band.

Mick Mashbir played on *Muscle of Love*. He had been on the *Billion Dollar Babies* tour, he had been on the *Muscle of Love* tour. He went down to South America with us, so he was already in the organisation, but he was being paid to come onstage with us and play the guitar parts Glen didn't know. Glen still played "School's Out" and "I'm Eighteen" and stuff, but there was a lot of pressure with everybody to try and figure out what the fuck we were going to do. Other bands had done it and moved on easy, but Glen was such a huge part of this band. After the fact, there's ways we could have done it. Was that 100% the reason for the break-up after *Muscle of Love*? I wouldn't say that, but I think it had an awful lot to do with it.

Michael Bruce:

Another occurrence that I always thought really put the nail in his coffin was that first trip to New York. You know how the movie *Blade Runner*, I think it is, takes place in this hotel that has the old-style elevators with the wrought-iron cage; it's a hotel in New York. We stayed there and they had these huge rooms that had three doors on them, eight beds inside.

We went in to crash. I remember we got in really late and all of our luggage and guitars were sitting there, and in the morning, Glen's guitar was gone. So we were pissed-off and we decided to check out. We went down to sit in the lobby and right across the street was the Howard Johnson's. So we get something to eat, and when we came back, somebody had stolen his suitcase out of the lobby. Just his. What are the chances? You have all that luggage sitting there, that they would get Glen's. Somebody was a serious fan or they didn't like him; I'm not sure which (laughs).

But think about it. He lost his sound, he lost his image, all his clothes, and it was really hell for him during that time. I remember him experimenting with different guitars and he just couldn't seem to lock in. We would play shows and he would end late or start early and have feedback and he was really struggling with it. But I think that was another factor that wasn't a big help to his psyche at the time. Plus his other extracurricular activities. It was not a good time. We persevered through hoping he was going to get better and it didn't really happen.

March 1 - June 7, 1973. Alice Cooper mount an intensive Canadian and US tour in support of *Billion Dollar Babies*, main support coming from old pals Flo and Eddie. Stage props would include dolls, mannequins, Alice's famed guillotine, as well as a surgical table, dentist rill, axes, whips, a bubble machine and a new snake named Eva Marie Snake.

James Randi:

The show was an 'I love the dead' sort of thing. Alice was perpetuating his character. I was quite taken with it because it was a very, very professional group. I didn't see any dope being used at any time. The roadies were always into pot and whatnot, and that's okay, but I didn't… Alice was boozing pretty heavily at that time, but beer only. Never anything stronger than that. But I never saw any dope being used; I never saw anything really nasty taking place. There's stuff I wouldn't approve of and wouldn't have liked to see, but I was in approval of everything I saw and I got along very, very well with everybody there. They liked me and I liked them and we were a good working team and we had to do some very strange things, but it's a long story.

But I was concerned about his consumption of beer. They would pop open a can for him, give it to him and he would chug-a-lug, put it down, and they'd take it away and give him a fresh can right away because he

was always afraid of somebody putting something into the can. Which could have happened, theoretically, so he was very cautious about that. He was a little concerned about the fact that he was consuming a lot of booze, and the next morning he would pretty well almost always be hungover, and he was feeling bad about that. I felt he was very uncomfortable with that.

Anyway, I hit it off well with the guys and everything. Glen Buxton gave me a lot of problems because he was always high and the guys knew it. They came to me first and said, "Glen will always be little dopey and a little crazy. Just try to understand that." Shep had determined to keep him for the Billion Dollar Babies tour, because he was advertised and he was in all the photographs and such. But they hired Mick Mashbir to play the guitar from a back room doing Glen's part, and Glen never knew that he wasn't being heard on the system. It's a strange story. They actually had him surrounded with monitors and little speakers on the stage pointed up at him and he was hearing himself. But he wasn't hearing what Mike was doing from the back room, and that was going out to the audience. Very sad.

Dennis Dunaway:

I'm not sure it was so shocking other than this totally outrageous band had made it to the top. We were doing the guillotine at that point, but it was the same formula that we used before with the light and dark. We would kick it off really positively with "Hello Hooray." If you were in the audience, this big giant bank of fog would roll off the stage and then we would all be standing there wearing white playing this ballad, and then do some rockers.

Then all of a sudden everything would shift gears and we would change into dark clothing, and I would switch from a white bass to a black bass and everything would do that same shift of gears into the dark side of things. Alice would be an evil type of person, and then he would get caught and punished for his crimes.

In the end he would come out in white tails and a white top hat and confetti would drop and all of a sudden everything would be positive again. So we would have this happy ending comeback. People came to see this thing everybody was talking about, and they were seeing something they had never seen before. Even people who had seen us before would see something they had never seen before.

That was still a heavy duty time with the animal rights people, where it was impossible to convince them that we didn't kill animals onstage, that we never intended to do that. It was just an accident that happened—that plagued us forever. So there was a lot of that still with officials. Plus because of the Jim Morrison profanity thing, it was common in those days for promoters to withhold a fairly large amount of your pay, and if any foul language went out over the microphone, if Alice had said a four-letter word, which he never did—Alice has never cursed. Then the promoters would keep that money.

So Alice got around that where he would go to the front of the stage and say, "What's the dirtiest word you know?" He would hand the microphone into the audience and they would say the dirty words (laughs). On those nights, it would end up with the promoters and everybody arguing whether or not that was a loophole (laughs). But Alice did that more just to bug the promoters for trying to withhold that money than anything.

But we never got any heavy banning by the religious right or anything, because Alice's father was a minister. It was almost impossible to be shocking in those days, with the amount of censorship and everything, although we basically found a lot of loopholes. It seems tame by today's standards, but back then it was quite shocking that we would have a song called "Dead Babies." But we would get around it by making the lyrics about parental abuse. The message was moral. But all people tend to hear is the chorus, "dead babies," and then Alice has a baby doll on stage. We had to be shocking without being banned, and that was the hard part. It was very hard. So it was safe enough that we were able to get away with it.

Neal Smith:

Alice sweeps that under the rug a little bit, but we were getting death threats. We were getting banned from a lot of cities. The founding fathers, the mayor or the first selectmen from some cities would come see our show. It got more negative publicity than it was really threatened. Once the Toronto incident with the chicken came out, they said Alice Cooper bit the head off a chicken and drank the blood from the neck. That's the stuff, once it's out there in the press, people believe a lot of this bullshit.

It was great for us. It was phenomenal. You can't buy that publicity. But the fact is, the show was basically theatrical and we weren't harming anything. There was one article I read saying there were baby ducks and chicks on the stage, and with our big platform shoes we were just smashing them to pieces. In actuality, we had stuffed blown-up animals of little bunnies and teddy bears and we smashed those onstage, but they weren't real animals. So it's always interesting how the press sometimes interpreted what we were doing on stage.

We definitely had death threats. Plus the fact that people couldn't figure out whether we were gay. I was shocked when I found out that a lot of people in Canada thought that I was a girl and I can attest, that's not true (laughs). But there was a lot of fear about the band. They didn't understand it. They couldn't put a label on us and they couldn't figure what the hell we were doing. When we were with Frank Zappa that was one thing, but all of a sudden we have a hit with *Love It to Death* and "I'm Eighteen" and *Killer* and "Under My Wheels," all of a sudden this band that everybody thought was going to go away is selling millions and millions of records and the songs are going up the chart, into the Top 50, the Top 30, the Top 20, and then "School's Out" was in the Top Ten. We became a real threat.

There were some cities in the Bible Belt that banned us. But also the mayor would come to see one of our shows, and they would say, "Oh, it's not that bad," and we would go ahead and play the city. I think Utica, New York was one of those cities. So it was always an issue. But we were not going to change what we were doing. By the time we did *School's Out*, I was carrying three handguns with me because the threats were so severe. But in those days, you could just throw them in your bag and walk on the plane with that and nobody would check anything. I would sleep with them under my pillow.

I had Kachina, my pet boa constrictor with me. That was another thing that we added to the show. So she was always with us, and then we wrote the song "Is It My Body," and right around Killer, we decided to bring the snake on. And she travelled with us anyway. If you are on the road with us and we were paying for your food you had to work somehow (laughs). So Kachina came out and she made the cover of the *Killer* album.

March 15, 1973. Because of a cancelled show in Knoxville, TN, the band return home to Connecticut for a short break to work on songs for the next album. Alice, however, returns to New York City.

Dennis Dunaway:

It would depend on the songs. I always maintained that Alice Cooper was the name of the band, and all of the songs were written by Alice Cooper, which meant all five members. Everybody had a lot to do with the song-writing. There are hardly any... there are a few songs that pretty much Michael came in with the song and we added our parts, but most of the songs were gone over, taken apart and dissected and reassembled hundreds of times over until we got the song just the way we liked it.

Alice's contribution, a lot of times, if we went into the studio and didn't have any clue what we were going to do, we would start by jamming and Alice would sit in his chair with his beer can sitting on the floor and a pad and pencil, and he would be thinking about what the song should be about or whatever. We would be playing, and then all of a sudden Alice would jump up and say, "Okay, how about if the song goes (sings some chord structures)," and then he'd direct us like Burt Bacharach. Burt Bacharach is one of Alice's heroes. So even if Alice seemed quiet in some respects, in other respects, whenever he had an idea, it always seemed to work. It always seemed to be a valid direction for the song to go. Usually his talent lies in coming up with the concepts for the songs.

You know, back in those days, I was trying to come up with a book of poetry, which was based on dreams. All these nights of playing and not getting back to the hotel room until three, having to get up at eight and stuff, what would happen is, we would rarely have a sound night of sleep. So when I would start to fall asleep, I would start to have a dream or something, and I got in the habit of forcing myself to get up and try to write a poem related to that dream.

I had a whole book of those, and Alice always kept that book by his chair. He would sometimes just be paging through it and he would see some lyrics that would inspire him. He would take the concept of the poem, and a lot of times just pull a lot of lines out of it and turn it into a song. Some of them were pretty abstract ideas, but he would make them more relatable to people. "Killer" was a song like that; that one, the lyrics are pretty much a dream poem, as I called them."

Alice Cooper:

Well, Dennis is so clever. Dennis has always been *the* artist in the band. By the way, he's a great artist, graphic artist. He always came up with the weirdest stuff. All the stuff on any of the early albums that was really out there was Dennis. All the stuff that was really commercial was Mike Bruce and myself. When it came to songs like "No More Mr. Nice Guy," that was a single; that was Mike Bruce and me. Mike Bruce wrote a lot of those riffs. We were very open about… you know, we blueprinted "Substitute" by The Who there. When it came to things like "Blue Turk," that's Dennis and me.

All the trippy stuff was always Dennis. He was a big Pink Floyd fan. He was the first one that came to me and said, "Listen to this." It was *Piper at the Gates of Dawn* and I listened to it and went, "Wow, that's really cool. That's the best psychedelic band I've ever heard." Dennis was the guy that could have joined Pink Floyd and fit right in. Dennis was every bit a Roger Waters, or even maybe bordering on Syd Barrett, just very creative, very smart, and a great showman onstage. He used to bring in Stockhausen and all this electronica and we would sit and listen to it. I wasn't always interested, but I would sit and listen to it with him.

March 21, 1973. "No More Mr. Nice Guy," credited to Michael and Alice, is issued as a single off of *Billion Dollar Babies*, backed with "Raped and Freezin'." The song reached No.25 on the US charts and No.10 on the UK charts. A full court press is put on the hit record, with announcements of TV ads for both the UK and the US.

Michael Bruce:

Well, it's funny, "No More Mr. Nice Guy," that's my song. I wrote it, and that song was written back when *Killer* was happening, and of course, it didn't fit that album. It didn't fit *School's Out*—maybe it could've fit *School's Out.* But then *Billion Dollar Babies* came along. Well, "No More Mr. Nice Guy," the music on it, that part stayed the same because I wrote the whole thing and it was perfect, I must say. The whole song was like, "I used to be such a sweet, sweet thing—that was just a burn. Break my back just to kiss her ass and got nothing in return. All my friends told me, man, you're crazy for being such a big fool. But I guess I was, because being in love made such a fool. Now I'm no more…" See, really, that's life. But then Alice re-writes it and changes it into a song about the press. Great, if you're the lead singer…"

Dennis Dunaway:

"No More Mr. Nice Guy" is pure Michael Bruce. Other than ideas for bass parts, like me playing some unusual notes in it that made the chords sometimes sound like they changed when they didn't, or changed to a chord that had different textures than it normally would have, had I just played the root note. You know, Michael came in with that song, played it, and that was one of those things that was a done deal. When you finished it and heard it, you knew it was right. Michael always had—and still does—that crystal-clear guitar sound that just cuts through.

And Mike Bruce had a very offbeat sense of humour. He was funny. So, when we were driving around in station wagons, hotel rooms, year after year, all together all the time, long hours on the road, I think what held it together was a highly entertaining sense of humour within the group. I was the guy who, if I said something, the conversation stopped because I was so quiet. But my sense of humour is so off-the-wall, it's like, people just think about it rather than laugh. However, I was the one who was the observer. I contend that I remember a lot of things that nobody else in the band remembers. I remember it much more clearly, because I was observing instead of doing (laughs).

Now the flipside of "No More Mr. Nice Guy," "Raped and Freezin'," that song came together at the end. It's also definitely a Michael Bruce chord structure, which I always really liked, because Michael's chords, a lot of times, had a swing feel to them. He would land on chords and stay on them long enough to allow the bass the room to do things, as opposed to chord changes that are coming so fast, the bass doesn't have much choice but to comp the chord changes. "Raped And Freezin'" was one of those good feel songs where Alice, of course, enhanced Michael's lyrics. Then I think it was Bob Ezrin's idea, at the very end, to have the 'ole' from the bullfight come in.

Neal Smith:
The character in the song "Raped and Freezin'", Alice I guess, gets picked up by somebody while he's hitchhiking. Of course it has a south-western Mexican flair in the music. I always loved to bring a different feel in as far as the percussion went. Of course we were from Phoenix, Arizona, so from "Desperado" on *Killer* to "Raped and Freezin'" on *Billion Dollar Babies*, once in a while some of the things from the areas where we lived in different parts of the country would filter into our music.

April 3, 1973. A press conference and party take place in NYC for the opening of the Dali Hologram Exhibition.

April 21, 1973. *Billion Dollar Babies* hits No.1 on the charts.

Dennis Dunaway:
When *Billion Dollar Babies* hit the top, we were already deep into *Muscle of Love*. But by then, the band were buckling from pressures far more severe than that.

April 28, 29, 1973. The band film performances in Dallas and Houston for the *Good to See You Again, Alice Cooper* concept film. Meanwhile, "No More Mr. Nice Guy" is at No.55 on the singles chart while "Billion Dollar Babies" is at No.3.

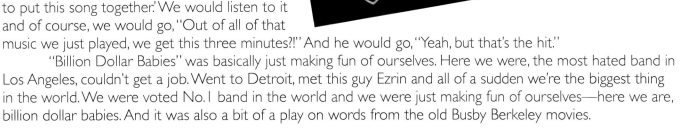

Alice Cooper:
"Billion Dollar Babies" was actually a song that was written off the drums. Neal comes in and goes (sings it), we wrote the song directly off that riff. We used to do that a lot. Dennis Dunaway would write a bass riff, let's say on a song like "Blue Turk," and we would write the song around a bass line, and this time it just happened to be off the drum riff.

Everybody was very good about contributing original things. Then we let Bob Ezrin take a 15-minute bit that we did and tear it down to three minutes. He would take the best stuff out of it and say, 'Okay, now we're going to put this song together.' We would listen to it and of course, we would go, "Out of all of that music we just played, we get this three minutes?!" And he would go, "Yeah, but that's the hit."

"Billion Dollar Babies" was basically just making fun of ourselves. Here we were, the most hated band in Los Angeles, couldn't get a job. Went to Detroit, met this guy Ezrin and all of a sudden we're the biggest thing in the world. We were voted No.1 band in the world and we were just making fun of ourselves—here we are, billion dollar babies. And it was also a bit of a play on words from the old Busby Berkeley movies.

Michael Bruce:
I told Neal that I go to music stores and hear those drums. But it has a lot of little riffs to start as opposed to one monster riff like in "Smoke on the Water." It's a solid song and when I hear it today it really holds up. It's so powerful and it couldn't be denied. We were hot at the time and it could be about 'billion dollar baby' meaning you got it so you flaunt it, or about a girl. It had a lot of different faces that could be put on the song. Those lyrics, it's hard to remember them, "Slimy little monster greasy as a weasel in the alley been infected by the rabies"—it's a mouthful, but Alice is a word creator. He does great lyrics. More than anything what I really miss is having somebody who can get up there and sing and create great lyrics for a piece of music. That's one thing I really miss about working with him.

Neal Smith:

I didn't write anything except the drum intro to the song. That was the hook, but the original song, as we were working it out, the song pretty much had a straighter beat to it. A friend of ours, who you'll see on some of the credits, Rockin' Reggie Vinson… he was a good friend of Glen's. His name is on a couple songs on *School's Out*, and he did some background vocals with us, and he's a good song-writer and a good guy on his own.

The original idea for the song… I can't remember its name, but it was called "Rag Doll" or "Rag Doll Girl" or something. But it was a straighter song, and then we gave Alice the idea to go in that direction and then he came up with some great lyrics on it and then I did that beat. I had always heard this different movement on it. So as we were working it out, the song didn't start out with that beat. I think if "Billion Dollar Babies" would have gotten written by everybody in the band, and our friend Rockin' Reggie wasn't there, it would've been a different story. But it was his song, and it was part of my job to add to it. It's a great question, as a matter of fact. Sometimes people think the song is written around the intro, but it's not. Still, the song came to life when I finally put that part on the intro.

But I had always loved the Rolling Stones intro from Charlie Watts to the song "Get Off of My Cloud." I thought that was very cool, and as a drummer I always used to like to write songs for drummers, because people listen to songs and think, "That's cool." But if I was a drummer listening to an Alice Cooper song, what would be cool about it? I always tried to have something special in there that would get someone's interest. So this one gave me the opportunity. I'm a rudimental drummer; I learned all the rudiments when I was first trained, early in my music education. I always loved flams; "Mississippi Queen" and some other great songs had a big flam all the way through. "You Drive Me Nervous" from *Killer* was flams all the way through the song. For people that don't know what they are, it's like a double stroke; you use both sticks with one syncopated just right after the other on a single stroke, and it sounds like two hits at almost the same time. It's one of the basic rudiments of percussion.

So I wanted to have a drum intro, and we were fooling around with the idea of songs that would feature different guys in the band in the beginning, in the intros to a particular song. I pretty much had liberty to do whatever I wanted to a song. Bob Ezrin heard the song being a little bit straighter played all the way through the song, but I liked the idea of this flam intro and then sort of keep it going through the song. Bob said, "Well, ya know, if you're going to play it, you have to play it perfect." I did play it perfect and it ended up being the intro to the song as well, and gave it a certain flashy character and feature that I think helped it stand alone. "Billion Dollar Babies" is such an interesting song and interesting album.

Dennis Dunaway:

Rockin' Reggie, whose name is Reggie Vinson, was a friend of the band, who we met in LA. But he lived in Detroit, not far from the Pontiac Farms where the band lived, when we wrote the Love It to Death and the Killer albums, and he became a very close friend of Glen Buxton, and he used to hang out at the house all the time. Then when the band moved to Greenwich, we called him Rockin' Reggie; Alice tagged him with that name. Actually Rockin' Reggie is the one that tagged Glen with GB, who… everyone called him GB, pretty much from then on.

But we were writing the *Billion Dollar Babies* album, and we knew that we wanted that to be the title of the album—Alice had come up with that name but we didn't have the song. Rockin' Reggie, and Glen wrote this country and western-flavoured ballad. First of all, it would be good to know that Rockin' Reggie wrote incredible songs, where you would swear that it was Roy Orbison. His voice has that range and that style. So we're at the estate, trying to work out this song one morning. Back in those days, we would rehearse about ten hours a day, and we would start reasonably, around noon. But anyway, everybody is sitting down and we're running over this song over and over, and it was a good song, with a nice…and then I said, "I don't know if this has got the fire that we need for the title track of the album." So I jumped up and said, "Okay, we've got to light some dynamite under this song." I had Bob Ezrin and everyone in the band looking at me, "Okay, what's the idea?"

Here I am standing up and making this little speech about it, and I didn't really have a clue (laughs), so I just turned the bass amp up and played this riff, just started making up this riff. Then the next thing we knew, we had Glen doubling the riff, and that song changed radically, because of that bass line. But Neal hadn't gotten his drum part together. We were in the studio actually recording the song, going for takes, and the drum part still wasn't together.

Bob Ezrin decided, well, we can't keep just running through this, trying to get this drum part together, so he told Neal that he wanted him to straighten the beat out, so we could get the take. Neal refused; he stuck to his guns. "No, no, I know I'll get this; just stick with me." He did, within a couple more takes, and he nailed that, and I think it's one of his most creative drum parts.

As for recording, Donovan was in the studio, Morgan Studios outside of London, and there were a lot of people there. Rick Grech from Blind Faith, Keith Moon was there, Harry Nilsson, Mark Bolan, Flo and Eddie, you know, Mark and Howard, and anyway, it was sort of a celebrity bash going on there. But we had brought Donovan in, specifically, to sing some of the verses and doubled on some of the choruses of *Billion Dollar Babies*. Great guy too. He was into it and very professional, as you expect I guess.

Keith Moon had on those Groucho glasses with the nose, okay? He had those on but the nose was a

penis and he had had a few drinks that evening. As a matter of fact, so many that he could hardly sit on the drum stool, let alone play (laughs). Harry Nilsson was also drunk and kept falling on the control board, and we kept kicking him out because he messed all the dials up; he could hardly walk. But when Harry Nilsson sat down at the piano and started playing and singing, here's this beautiful voice and all and these incredible songs coming out of him.

That song was verging on heavy metal but we were never comfortable with that term. Alice in particular always put down heavy metal, which is ironic, because of some of the styles of music he's gone to since then. Which I don't criticise. I'm just saying, he always seemed to be the one that always puts it down.

Heavy metal by the time we were coming up was getting a cliché connotation, as were things like drum solos. So we didn't do a drum solo. Neal did on "Halo of Flies," but normally when you would have had someone's drum solo, we did it with the bass and with a different feel than what some other drummers were doing at a time. Also, when we did do a drum solo, when it really did come down to drums, I had this idea for everybody in the band to play the drum solo. So everybody would grab sticks and we would stand around his kit and we would all be pounding out this pagan beat while Neal did the soloing in between. Actually, Alice's whole band used that idea on later tours.

James Randi:
When Alice went out there and he had to make these big fountains of flame come from his fingertips I had to equip him with the two devices strapped to his fingers that did those things. So I was the last one that would speak to him before he walked onstage, and then he would march up the stairs looking like the Frankenstein monster and out onstage and "School's out forever" and all that sort of thing, and boom with the flashes.

So I had a number of duties to do, but the two parts I played were the mad dentist and the executioner, and in both of them I was completely disguised and I did not get listed in the program. I didn't want to be listed in the program. I didn't want to be somebody's second banana because I'm used to running my own show and I didn't want to take a second seat, so to speak. But during the interviews and the press and the media meetings and whatnot I was there and I was doing silly tricks for them. Fluffing the thing up, you know.

May 5, 1973. Alice Cooper takes the tour to his home state of Arizona, playing Tucson, and according to James Randi, Phoenix, possibly on the 6th or 7th (although in the quote below, he may be describing the Tucson show).

James Randi:
I'll give you a little episode to chew on. When we came to Phoenix, Arizona, Alice came to me with a very worried look on his face. I said, "What's up?" He said, "This is my hometown." I said, "Yeah, I understand that." He said, "My mom's going to be here." I said yeah. "My mom doesn't know what I do. She knows I'm a musician but she's never heard any of the records; she's never seen the show." I said uh-oh and he said, "Yeah uh-oh. Would you sit with her during the opening of the show and as much as you can, any time you're off stage would you go and sit with her? We'll put her in the third row or so and you'll have a reserved seat there,

and just soothe her." I said sure.

I had to babysit his mom, a lovely lady. After all his father, as you probably know, was a Mormon minister and the mother was very much a member of the family and that sort of thing, and I knew she was going to be in for quite a shock. So I went and sat with her and introduced myself to her. I sat down unnoticed from the audience.

Then the show started, and Alice came out onstage with the torn costume and the smeared makeup and everything, and she sat there and said, "Oh, Vincent, oh why is his shirt torn like that?" I said that's part of the costume. "Oh, well he could get it fixed." She was extremely, extremely naïve at that point. Then when he started to attack the dolls and stomp on them and whatnot, she said, "Oh, why is Vincent doing that?" I said, "It's all part of the act. He's just having fun with the kids, but remember it's all an act. It's just an act" and she said oh, my. She was quite shocked by it and quite subdued by it, and rather disturbed.

Then I went and did my dentist stuff, and I came back to sit with her again after changing to regular clothes again, and that was before the executioner thing. I looked at her, and she was laughing and chortling and carrying on. She loved it. She sort of settled into it and said oh, okay, it's an act. I guess he's an actor and that's my kid up there. She was quite happy with it.

When I went to the audience to rescue her right after the guillotine when Alice came marching out with the tails and top hat and everything, resurrected, I went and grabbed her and took her backstage so she didn't have to deal with the crowd, and she was quite pleased. At his 60th birthday party, I was invited out to Phoenix to celebrate that and I met his mother again. She remembered me, and she said, "Oh, my, you don't know how happy I was to see you." She said, "I didn't know what was going on. I thought this was some sort of a monster I'd raised, and you talked me out of it." So it was a very good arrangement. I had a hell of a time.

Dennis Dunaway:
Yes, the famous one was when the snake pulled up missing, because it was in Alice's bathroom. They couldn't find the snake and we had to move on to the next gig. The next thing you knew, we read in the paper that it had come up in a different room in the hotel, in Charley Pride's room. He freaked out because the snake came up out of his toilet, and evidently it had gone down the toilet in Alice's room.

But as far as any other problems, I'm not going to be able to remember the name of this stadium, but I think it was in Pasadena, wherever the Queen Mary used to be parked, in California. Anyway, our snake had just eaten or something, so right after it ate, or right when it was ready to be fed, we wouldn't use it on stage. But we had this big thing there, so Warner Bros. said they would supply a snake.

So there was this big basket on the floor of the limousine, and the band was in the back riding to the gig. Everybody is bored and stuff, and it was like, "Well, you wanna look at the snake?" "Nah, later." "Ah, you wanna look at the *snake?*" "Yeah, let's look at the snake." And we look in this basket and it's solid snake. This was the biggest snake I'd ever seen in my life. It's like, "Whoa, wait a minute, what's going on here?!"

During the show, when the roadies got this snake out of the basket, there were like five guys trying to manhandle this snake out to the stage. So they walked it out to Alice, Alice sang to the snake, and then they went backstage and spent the rest of the night trying to get this snake back in the basket. That one wasn't a boa constrictor; it was an anaconda. That thing must've been… I bet it was 20 feet long (laughs).

June 1973. British MP for Pontypool Leo Abse attempts to get Alice Cooper banned from the UK, offering the band valuable free press. The notorious Mary Whitehouse, name-checked by both Deep Purple and Pink Floyd for her censorship antics, gets involved as well. Meanwhile, Michael Bruce crafts plans for a solo album and Alice swans about town hanging out with celebrities, often at Max's Kansas City. He also travels with his girlfriend Cindy to Acapulco.

Alice Cooper:
We just said we're going to go to England. All right, "Eighteen" was a hit over here and it got to be a hit over there. Already the urban legend had started in England about, oh, I heard that he kills cats and eats them and things like that. Incredible. We didn't have the internet then so it was all urban legend. By the time that we were scheduled to go over, they had tried to ban us. Mary Whitehouse and Leo Abse said, "No, Alice Cooper's not coming to play in England." Thank you! They couldn't have been better. We sold out every ticket at Wembley, the record went right to No.1 and the public said how dare you tell us what we can see and what we can't see, right?

James Randi:
I think it was Baltimore where Shep Gordon called a special meeting. He said, "Oh, we're in deep shit now." I said, "What's the matter, Shep?" He said the mayor of Baltimore, who was a young fellow in his early 30s had given Alice a key to the city. That's the last thing that Shep wanted. He said, "No, the parents have got to hate him! They've got to want their kids not to go and they've got to forbid their kids to go. That makes sure the kids will go. They'll find a way of getting there if the parents absolutely forbid them to do it!"

That was Shep's psychology. He wanted them to be against Alice—that is the adults—to despise him and hate him and the whole thing, and so he fostered that image. But when he found out the mayor wanted to give him the key to the city, he didn't know what the hell to do.

Shep was in heavy control. Shep was just wonderful. I had to admire him. He cooperated with the media and such, he knew the media were our friends. What they would say would influence attendance and he tried to direct that. Of course, he was doing the PR thing. Shep was a wonderful, wonderful manager. Just top-notch. Alice couldn't have asked for a better guy.

But Alice Cooper made his own news. As soon as he arrived in town… well look at the plane. The plane had on its tail a huge dollar sign, on both sides. I used to sit up front with the pilot, who was a fellow named Kirk, and on the door was Alive Enterprises. Captain Kirk, the Enterprise. Get it? But that just happened to be a coincidence.

But I'd sit up front with Captain Kirk, the captain of the ship, the pilot, and we would have a lot of laughs, and I'd listen in on radio interceptions. He'd gesture my attention out the window to another plane that was flying… I say alongside, but that's half a mile away. You could see the plane there and the pilot would come in and say, "Hello, unknown aircraft to the starboard. This is TWA flight 466 to St. Louis. May we ask what is your airline, the dollar sign on the tail? We don't know that airline. We don't have it in our books here." So he'd get on and say, "Oh, this is Alice Cooper." They'd say, "Alice Cooper?! Oh wow!" Get all excited (laughs). That's just part of the joy I had in working with this group. They were wonderful people, wonderful people.

June 8, 1973. The band move back to Los Angeles (in piecemeal fashion), with Alice moving into a house next to conservative firebrand Barry Goldwater. Co-manager Joey Greenberg and road warrior Charlie Carnel, now legends in the business and part of the organisation since the beginning, leave the fold. Rumours start flying that Alice has legally changed his name to Alice Cooper, further staking claim on the brand for himself.

July 1973. Lou Reed issues his *Berlin* album. Producing is Bob Ezrin and the guitarists on the project are future Alice Cooper guitarists Steve Hunter and Dick Wagner.

August 1973. New York Dolls issue their self-titled debut. Like Alice Cooper, the band represent a hard rock sound married to a glam look, although by this point Alice Cooper had been methodically dismantling their glam visuals since 1969. Indeed with the "hot mess" that is the New York Dolls, androgyny and decadence collide and explode, and what's more, the band is American. Again, similarities with Alice Cooper.

Entertainer Liza Minnelli, left, sings with rock star Alice Cooper in a New York recording studio. Liza, the daughter of Judy Garland and star of movie "Cabaret", dropped by to sing backup for a song on Cooper's new album. (AP Wirephoto)

Neal Smith:
I actually knew David Johansen on a social level hanging out in the city. I liked their image. It was like Twisted Sisters and The Plasmatics. You had your Dolls and the Ramones and all that vibe coming out of New York, which was great. But I really didn't think they could play; they were a flash in the pan. They were an offshoot that our inspiration, our influence started to create. People that may have been reluctant to do something, to go in a transvestite or gender-bending direction, have long hair and be effeminate but still tough, still hard rock 'n' roll, I thought that was all healthy stuff. Because rock 'n' roll has no limits.

Late August 1973. Neal marries his girlfriend Babette.

Alice Cooper:
Neal Smith was the epitome... if there was ever any drummer that challenged Keith Moon as far as ego, it was Neal Smith. Neal Smith was not only six-foot-six, but he would wear the six-inch heels and with blond hair down to his waist. You know, he would call up Keith Moon and say, "How many drums do you have?" Keith would say "32;" Neal would say, "I have 33." Then he would stand up on his drum set. Now you have to picture him. He's already seven feet tall, in all chrome, and that hair. Then he would lift up his arm as high as he could and twirl his stick. He was the ultimate show drummer. He wasn't as good a drummer as Keith Moon, of course, but he was the epitome of what I call the glam drummer of all time.

Neal Smith:
I'm 6'3", pretty big on the drums, and I had like a six-foot arm span. I have huge arms and people say, "Your playing looks like an octopus." But I think, one of the biggest things that I had influence on were the huge drum

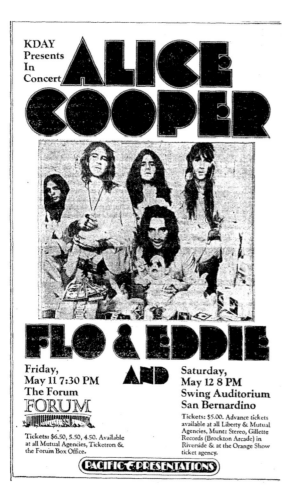

sets. Let's face it, Keith Moon's first drum set was seven drums and my biggest set was 21 drums. I was watching an Elvis special from 1973, and the drummer had a set of Premiers or Slingerlands. The guy had three mounted toms on the bass drum, so even Elvis' drummer was inspired by it. Nobody had three toms mounted on the bass drums. Because Slingerland flipped out when I told them I wanted three drums on one bass drum.

I think that's the stuff that Alice misses today. The other dimension. I also used to do the real spinning of the drumsticks. Not a lot of drummers do that. What they do, I call it a wuss-ass little thing between the fingers. It's like a little windmill or something. But I judged myself from what I played more than how I looked on stage. But I think I had a lot of energy on stage. I still do. I think I bring some charisma to the stage.

Early September 1973. While in Toronto to rehearse at Nimbus 9 material that will emerge on *Muscle of Love*, the band are presented with platinum awards for Canadian sales of over 100,000 copies of each of their last four albums.

Neal Smith:
We brainstormed and we talked an awful lot about what we did musically and theatrically—we did it every single day—and as far as the ideas and where they came from, it wasn't Alice by himself, it wasn't me, it wasn't Glen, it wasn't Dennis or Michael—we were all throwing out ideas all the time. So we were in the great Northwest and playing either Oregon or Washington state, and we're in the airport driving back. This is when we're getting ready to record *Muscle of Love*. Glen was passed out; he was lying on the limo floor and I think I had my legs over him. He was too out of it to even get in the seat, which often occurred. No matter what, Glen was always engaged in the conversation, and we're talking about somebody, and Glen said, "Oh, they can suck my muscle of love." And that's where the title *Muscle of Love* came from.

If we threw it out and we liked it and it worked, nobody thought any more of it. So that's what we created. As far as the press went, man, we gave them so much to work with. A band like ours, they could just spin it and take it off on their own. So yeah, we had a lot of publicity. But basically it was all true stuff. We weren't making it up—except when Alice said he was Eddie Haskell. He was just so bored talking about the same bullshit every time, about the snake and about beer.

Mid-September 1973 – October 12, 1973. Back in LA, the band work at The Record Plant and Sunset Sound on tracks that will comprise their seventh album, *Muscle of Love*.

October 4, 1973. Alice work with Ronnie Spector and Liza Minelli in New York City on backing vocals for "Teenage Lament '74."

October 12, 1973. Police raid the band house in Greenwich and arrest Michael Bruce, Bob Dolin and Mick Mashbir for possession of cannabis with intent to sell; four pounds of the stuff is confiscated.

Dennis Dunaway:

We were able to function (laughs). In the real early days, the *Pretties for You* days, we were probably like most people in Hollywood, California in the '60s; we were pretty spacey, even on stage. But soon after that, the band really got more professional, going in the studio and stuff. We went in straight and we worked on music straight, in the studio or on stage. However in the later days of excess, that changed for some of the members and not others. To this day, Neal and I pretty much believe that the inspiration comes from the music. Even though people fool themselves and think that the inspiration comes from drugs, you don't need drugs—drugs in the long run hinder you.

October 19 - 22, 1973. Alice travels to Japan, to do some TV and to promote the forthcoming *Muscle of Love* album. Reported to be the largest press conference ever for an entertainer, Alice's pow-wow with the press was attended by an estimated 200 reporters.

November 19, 1973. The original Alice Cooper group issue what would be their last album together, *Muscle of Love*. Quite impressively, it is the band's seventh album in just a little over four years. Jack Douglas and Jack Richardson share the production credit after the band split with Bob Ezrin, the breaking point being Michael's refusal to accede to Ezrin's request for changes to his song, "Woman Machine."

Dennis Dunaway:

I like the album except it really needed Glen. That's why it didn't flow like a complete album. But he had dropped out entirely by then. For the first time ever, I found myself going against the majority vote, which was to replace him. But the band began as friends and I wouldn't have given up on any of them. I wouldn't want them to give up on me, and I refused to give up on Glen. We all loved Glen, but the Don Quixote in me refused to allow the big business machine to rule over friendship. I knew he would be lost, and as it turned out, he was. My insistence on keeping him only added to the fractures in the band.

As for the songs, "Hard Hearted Alice," I really like the lyrics on that song. The chorus may have held a more biting significance to us in the band. It had a two-fold insinuation. I've always felt the recording was too soft and whispery. The live version had a lot more dynamics when the guitar solos really kicked in. Although this looks like an album of shorter songs, because of their complex arrangements, "Muscle of Love" and "Man With The Golden Gun" seemed longer than their actual running times. "Crazy Little Child," I thought the style of that song was too typical for us but I liked the challenge of going for that classic bass playing, which I got Jack Richardson's guidance on.

Jack Richardson of course is credited as the producer of *Muscle of Love*, but Jack never gets credit for co-producing *Love It to Death* and *Killer*. The band didn't vote for Bob's departure. This is what happened. We were rehearsing at Nimbus 9 studios in Toronto. We were happy to see Bob

walk in because we had just worked out a song. But as soon as we started playing "Woman Machine," he stopped us to make changes. We hadn't even gotten past the intro!

Michael confronted him over it, emotions escalated, and Bob got insulted and walked out. There was no vote and no reason to think it was anything more than a temporary flare-up. But somehow, it turned out to be beyond our resolve. In the end, *Muscle of Love* shipped fine but a lot of record stores returned them to Warner Brothers claiming the box had a defective stain on it, and of course the stain was intentional. Some stores didn't like the depth of the box because it took up too much space per unit in their record bins. Those returns were a major blow to the album's momentum.

But yeah, *Muscle of Love* was different because Jack Richardson produced it without Bob Ezrin. Jack Richardson produced The Guess Who, who are renowned in Canada, but like I say, Jack Richardson also produced *Love It to Death* and *Killer*. Bob Ezrin was the little boy wonder apprentice. In fact, Richardson was the man who made sure the album came out a viable product.

We had a feeling that we were getting back to the way we had worked before we got so on the road-oriented. We were putting out two albums a year, plus coming up with a new concept and new staging and new costuming and everything for each tour, to promote each album. So that had to happen twice a year too. Plus I don't know if there were any bands doing more gigs than we were. We were doing like 65 shows out of 90 days-type thing, and our days off we were either travelling to the next city or writing an album, to go back into the studio.

Jack Douglas:

It was the death album. It was the last group album and everyone knew it, so it was a bit of a downer. The fun part was that we were doing it at Sunset Sound, which is a great studio; I loved it. The other thing about it was that I had a chance to be hanging out with John Lennon during his adventures in Los Angeles.

Mick Mashbir:

I wrote the verse in "Never Been Sold Before" and co-wrote "Hard Hearted Alice" with Mike. I knew nothing about the music biz so I didn't really know what to ask for. The album credits were on the book cover insert and I was credited as "additional guitar." Shep didn't want the public to know that GB wasn't involved. My favourite moment was when we have been trying to get a basic track for "Muscle" and Neal kept fuckin' up the take. Then after about a dozen or so tracks, I fucked up and Neal threw an empty vodka bottle at me. There was a lot of tension because this was the follow up to *Billion Dollar Babies*. As for the production change there, Jack's style and vibe was much more rock 'n' roll than Ezrin's. Don't get me wrong, Ezrin was a trained musician with a lot of talent, but he just wasn't fun to work with. If you can't have fun while workin' or playin', what's the point?

But in the beginning I was just happy to be a part of it all. After the *Billion Dollar Babies* album and tour, GB won an award for his slide work on the "Slick Black Limousine" flexi-disc. That was my work that got me thinking that I might be getting the short end of the stick. During the recording of the *Muscle of Love* album there was talk of making me a permanent member but Alice left the band before that could happen.

As for why Glen is credited on the album, there were a bunch of writing sessions with only the band. I was not asked to be there. GB was there but I don't know what he contributed if anything. They were trying to get him back into participating and probably thought giving him songwriters credits was a way to keep him interested. But, since he didn't know how to play any of the songs when we were rehearsing for the *Muscle of Love tour*—I had to teach him the songs—I don't think he actually "wrote" anything.

Michael Bruce:

It was a good album, but it's just unfortunately about the box, although it did go to No.20. The box probably should have been lost after the first shipment of records because it was hard to merchandise. You learn these things after, but that's show biz. As for that photo shoot, we were like sailors on a holiday letting it all hang out. That's where the idea for the cover came from.

The music was the material we had at hand. When the Stones do an album, it's basically a collection of what they've been doing for the last year or six months or whatever. Maybe it's because there was such concentration of stage energy, but I certainly didn't think Queen did a stage show for any of their stuff. But their stuff was certainly very theatrically-oriented. Because I always looked at the sales of the records. You don't hear too much theatrics over the radio do you?

So it's the musicality of the album that to me said it all. We got to No.1, and when you look at all the people behind us when *Billion Dollar Babies* went No.1, it was pretty impressive. So that's the bottom line. We were selling theatrics when people came to see it, we were selling records when people came to buy our

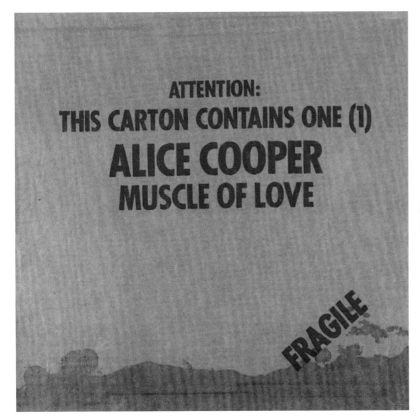

records so I think it was like love and marriage—can't have one without the other (laughs). It was a partnership of music and theatrics.

But the neat thing was that you were always wondering what the band was going to do when they came to town. When you think about this, could this have happened ten years later when MTV was out? We would have had to make videos of what we were doing and then you would have lost the whole element of surprise. I think we made it in the time that was our time and it was over when it was over.

Neal Smith:

Bob Ezrin, unfortunately, did not get to work with us on that album. I love a lot of songs on that album. It shipped a million copies, and I think 800,000 sold but they had to ship some of them back. Which was in part because of the packaging—they weren't expecting this funny box. There were a lot of people that sent them back because they thought there was a stain on the box. Well, that was intentional, but some people were too freakin' stupid to understand that. So, there were some logistical problems with it that had never occurred before.

But I thought the album was great. I would've loved to work with Bob on it, but we worked with Jack Richardson and Jack Douglas, two really good friends and two great producers. I never thought there was anything wrong with the album; I still love it to this day. "Muscle of Love" is one of my favourites. I'm crankin' out double bass drums on that song all the way through and it's got nice changes.

The only thing I didn't really like on that album was "Crazy Little Child." I thought that, for us, was a little bit out of the norm. Even though for my solo stuff I've recorded songs like that, I think for the Alice Cooper group, I just never really saw where that fit. With "Mary Ann," I understood how that worked, but something that was that different?! It was a cool song in its own way, but I think if it had been replaced with another song it could've changed the colour and the character of that whole album.

Now I don't think anyone in the band wanted us to be a disco band, but a song like "Big Apple Dreamin'," there was a place called The Hippo in New York, a discothèque, in the early to mid '70s. It was actually called The Hippopotamus. We would go there and hang out when we were in New York, because we lived in Connecticut, and where we lived at the time was only about a half-hour drive in to the city. So we would hang out there a lot, be in there a lot on the odd days.

We thought it'd be a goof to have a song where, it's not with a disco beat, but it's like the Stones when they did "Miss You," just sort of a nod to the music scene that was going on at the time. It was an experiment for us, and I think it's a cool song. Again, an experimental song for us—we weren't that band. But we were always willing to listen to stuff. Lyrically, it was interesting, that's for sure. Then "Woman Machine" is great because of all the percussion. That was a fun song to do, experimenting with different percussion.

Bob Gruen:

I took a lot of pictures for him. Not so much the album covers but publicity pictures for a number of years. But that sailor shoot, yeah, that's mine. That was their idea, to set up as sailors. They did a short tour in December with a sailor theme; the way sailors drunkenly come ashore and take over the town. We come into your town, want to party it down, that feeling. I just showed up there, they were in sailor suits, so I took pictures.

That's the thing about Alice; he has all kinds of props. It's like a theatrical production. He acts out every single song. In the early days it was a bit more low budget but they were very effective tricks. There's one part of a song where he would take a feather pillow and he had a high-pressure air can, like it looked like a fire extinguisher or something, and he would cut a big hole in the pillow and then hit it with the air from the gas can and literally blow feathers all around the room. Within a second he filled the entire Fillmore with tiny feathers.

Then he would swing a spotlight around his head—again, a simple trick that cost a dollar for a spotlight that you gaffer tape an extension cord at the back—and he would swing it around his head so the light was alternately hitting the feathers and hitting the back wall and swinging around so it would just flash on these feathers. So you had all these thousands of little dots flashing in front of your eyes. Very effective, and the whole thing cost less than five dollars. All you need is a new pillow and some more air every night.

He had all kinds of things. At the end he would hang himself. I think in the early days he had an electric chair. He ended up finally graduating to a guillotine, because Alice plays a lot of roles of nasty, evil people, and he gets punished for it. There's a moral to the story—he doesn't just get away with being an evil person. He advocates evil things and then he's literally executed onstage.

November 25, 1973. Alice meets Lemmy for the first time, at a Hawkwind after-party in New York City. Alice and Lemmy would become notorious denizens of the Rainbow Room on Sunset Strip, but Alice in the late '70s and early '80s, Lemmy in the late '80s until his death in 2015.

December 1, 1973. Black Sabbath issues their fifth album *Sabbath Bloody Sabbath*. Two points of interest: 1) the record's album cover would successful out-frighten anything Alice Cooper would ever do and 2) Geezer Butler, quipping about the vinyl shortage at the time, said that the record was delayed because all the vinyl was getting used up making Alice Cooper records.

Dennis Dunaway:

I don't remember the vinyl shortage but the price of oil definitely went up. We were on the road and there was the truckers strike, because of the high cost of fuel. We had two semis on that tour, and whenever they would pull into the gas station, there would be all of these truckers picketing. Then they'd have to tell them, "Oh man, this is for a band, rock 'n' roll" and everything, and then they supposedly—this is what I heard—they would be allowed to fuel up. But we had a few gigs where we had makeshift staging. Because we actually had two sets of stages. One would go to one city and set up and do the gig, while the other one was driving to the next city for the next show. That was a really tough tour because of that.

December 7, 1973. *Muscle of Love* is certified gold, while entering the *Billboard* charts this week at No. 76, while *Billion Dollar Babies* was still charting, down at No. 158. Concerning sales, in addition to people reacting negatively to the faux water damage stain on the *Muscle of Love* album cover, there was a problem with getting enough records into the stores. Instead of rack-jobbers pushing a dozen copies into a store, there would only be, say, five, because that's what fit in a rack. Then there would be a lag until the album would be restocked. As well, fewer copies fit in the standard cube boxes used to ship records, adding to the cost and the confusion. Ultimately, there was an element of the packaging causing a supply problem rather than a demand problem.

Neal Smith:

Warner Brothers was always a struggle. If you talk to Dennis or Alice or Shep—especially Shep—every album, they wanted to release us. "Well yeah, 'I'm Eighteen,' *Love It to Death*, that was a fluke." *Love It to Death* sells 500,000 copies and goes gold. "That's a fluke. That's the end of you guys." And we'd say one more, so we do *Killer*, and it goes gold and platinum, with "Under My Wheels." "Oh, that's a fluke. It didn't really have a hit as big as 'I'm Eighteen,' so I don't know why it sold so many, so we don't give a shit." "Okay, one more." "School's Out" goes double platinum, one of the biggest singles they ever had. They still think it's a fluke, so we have to renegotiate again to do *Billion Dollar Babies*. It was always like that.

December 8 – 31, 1973. Alice Cooper perform what is known as the *Billion Dollar Babies* Holiday Tour, which essentially becomes the tour for the *Muscle of Love* album. The set list to split evenly between the two recent albums, with a few earlier hits at it on. Support comes from ZZ Top.

James Randi:
Alice was quite interested about the history of the guillotine we were using there. That beautiful guillotine; it's the only one of its kind. It was invented by a man named Will Rock, R-O-C-K, a magician of olden times. And I'm talking about the '20s now. And he was famous for this one particular illusion. For many other things too, but he had invented the idea because when—I'm calling him Alice. I do that with the public, but we called him Coop of course—when Coop would have his head fastened in there, he would sing the final lines of the song, "I Love the Dead," and he would be looking out at the audience and they would see that was his head in there, and I'd be holding him by the hair, holding his head up so they could see him. Then I'd simply drop the hair and I'd stand back and look at the audience, and grab the rope and the guillotine blade would come down. The head that went into the basket was Alice Cooper's head, the real head. Of course Alice was attached to the other end of is as you might imagine, but it's a startling illusion.

And the audience in the front row would gasp—"Oh Jesus!" They thought it had gone wrong. I'd reach into the basket and pull out the dummy head that we had moulded with the hair and the blood coming from the neck and whatnot, and I would slap it in the face and drop it back into the basket, but it was very, very realistic. It was so realistic that that really shocked the audience. They'd really go wow! A huge shout would come from them when the head went in the basket.

But I knew what I was doing, I got there, I set up the guillotine, I tested it. Made sure that we had four safety gimmicks on it so that it couldn't possibly approach his neck at all, and Coop trusted me. He got into it the very first night and he said, "It's all in your hands." I said, "Yeah, or it's all in your neck." But no, he was very confident with what was happening, and we didn't add anything else to the show. We had to improvise a few times because some things went wrong. Other things didn't arrive, props didn't arrive and things like that, but we always made it.

The stage they use these days is much less than the big stage show we had. We had a plexi-glass stage, solid plexi-glass, two inches thick all over the place with mics coming up from underneath it. Spotlights and whatnot rotating like crazy. All kinds of wonderful effects. They can't get that into the theatre by just unpacking the show you know? Because when we went to these places we were always in big coliseums and places and we would move into just a bare area there and we would construct—they would, I had nothing to do with that—they would construct a huge plexi-glass stage that occupied a couple trailer trucks. It was huge. It was a big, big, big production.

They were doing very well. They were doing so well that in one of the cities in Europe—I've forgotten which city now—they actually weighed the money because they didn't have time to count it before they left. Shep was in a hotel room there and he had a scale. We were all laughing. We thought it was so damn funny to weigh your money, you know? They'd have 100 of whatever, kroner notes, and they'd say, "That's 15 pounds, 100 kroner notes; I wonder how much that is? And they only weighed it to get an approximate figure.

Dennis Dunaway:
We took our entire stage. The whole stage was ours. The stage was made out of plexi-glass with steps that lit up, that bands have copied since then. The Stones I think even copied that idea. But we had an entire stage that had multi-levels. We had two semi trucks to fit it all in.

We also had our own lighting, which we had taken on the road since the really early days, because we used to take the old iron theatre lights, from theatres that didn't use them anymore. These things weigh a ton. And then Charlie would shimmy up of the posts and clamp the things on, put all of the lighting up like that.

These days you have hydraulics and the lights weigh nothing; you can just pick it up with your little finger. And then they have vari-lights where the computer changes each light to whatever colour you want, which isn't what we did.

We had tons and tons of stuff that had to go up on the scaffolding, which our roadies also shipped and set up night after night. We took our own PA, which actually we rented from ShowCo... we weren't the first band to take our own PA with us, but we were one of the very early ones. And this staging also has scaffolding that went way up high.

We had giant mirror balls—this was before disco. These things must've been four feet in diameter, and then we had chrome and gold mannequins hanging up in the rafters, which I still have in my basement at home. We had these boxes with stars on them. It was like a gold box with giant gold glitter on it, and then a white plexi-glass star, and then the lights would flash inside these boxes.

But the more important props, were the mannequins, which I thought were extremely effective. They got chopped up nightly with a hatchet by Alice, which had certain connotations that I'm not sure that the show has now. A rag doll isn't the same as a mannequin. It doesn't have the same powerful imagery and so forth. But I still have the little baby doll mannequins and most of them have hatchet chops in them.

Then we had the guy impersonating Nixon. Oh he was great. I don't know how much he got paid but hanging out with him was a blast; he milked it. One time we were walking with him down the street and there was a traffic jam in New York City and he walked out into the street and started directing traffic and you could see people looking at him going, "Whoa," and they would all do what he wanted them to. When he would go to a restaurant, he would just walk in and point to a table and all these people would see him, freeze for a minute and then the whole place would be abuzz with everybody hustling (laughs). He had a blast with it. If he was sitting still and you would really study him then you could see the differences, but because of his boldness and he would always keep moving, he would really look like Nixon.

Mick Mashbir:
First let me say that touring in the winter in the Midwest and Northwest is not pleasant. Some days the weather was so severe that I didn't expect anyone to show up at the arena, but the fans did. We were using a modified version of the *Billion Dollar Babies* stage and because of the storms the stage didn't make it to the gig, but the equipment did so we performed as a flat stage rock band. I think those were some of the best shows for me and the band. It was the first time I could go to the edge of the stage and engage the fans. It was hard for Alice because he relied on the props to do his thing and they weren't there. When we went to Rio, we were a flat stage band and we kicked ass. I wish there were some bootlegs of that show. Actually the state of the band was cool because the *Billion Dollar Babies* book hadn't come out yet. I was sharing a house with Mike and Bob Dolin and we continued working on songs in our home studio. That is where I began teaching myself to produce and engineer.

December 11, 1973. "Teenage Lament '74" is issued as the only single from *Muscle of Love*, achieving a middling No.48 on *Billboard*. The other songs from the record would essentially fade into obscurity, save for the heavy rocking title track, which would become a modest but perennial success at classic rock radio.

December 13, 1973. A show in Toledo, Ohio is halted after only ten minutes when a riot breaks out. The trouble begins when fireworks were lofted onto the stage at ZZ Top's set, and then once Alice Cooper started, a flurry of projectiles prompted the band to walk off and not return.

December 23, 1973. Shep Gordon, who recently had picked up Helen Reddy as a client, throws a part for her at The Troubadour in LA. In attendance are Micky Dolenz, Harry Nilsson and John Lennon. The core of the "the Hollywood vampires" takes shape, referring to Alice and his circle of friends who became drinking buddies about town.

December 26, 1973. Very frightening hit horror movie *The Exorcist* opens for business. Alice attends the premier with the movies female star, Linda Blair. The two are essentially the top horror stars of 1973, working with different media.

1974

Bizarrely, the Alice Cooper band finish up at work by playing a clutch of dates in Brazil, April 8th in Rio to be their last. Alice meanwhile finds out how famous he really is, by doing mainstream TV along with a sort of promo/press solo tour of Europe, on behalf of the band still at this point, early in the year.

Kiss issue a debut album and Aerosmith issues their fine second, *Get Your Wings*. New York Dolls and Montrose both issue their second albums too. Alice Cooper, with their boxy and somewhat tepid melange of radio-friendly rock propositions, recorded only sensibly; all of a sudden don't sound as bold as they still look.

A goofy movie called *Good to See You Again, Alice Cooper* doesn't help the cause although a greatest hits album keeps the façade up and at 'em. Still, behind the scenes, the band is breaking up—slowly. Everybody seems to want to spread their wings and make solo records. No one knows at this point how horribly ineffectual Dennis, Glen, Neal and Michael will be at this, how almost nothing comes of it for decades, and how any record that did manage to fall into record stores would suck.

Nay, it is only Alice who would make this work, something Shep instantly realised as quite likely, with his manager hat on, knowing full well that Alice the complete man, with the name Alice Cooper, is thereabouts 80 to 90% of the band or the brand or the talent at hand, in the eyes of the public.

So, not like he absolutely was thrilled with the situation, but good-natured Alice rolls with the punches and goes back to work, now faced with building a solo career, even if a small part of him might have thought it was temporary. Put together with Dick Wagner, connected by Ezrin, Alice gets to writing what will become, arguably, the record tied with *Billion Dollar Babies* as the best (or at least historically most well regarded) to bear his now legal name.

February 1974. Lou Reed issues his *Rock n Roll Animal* live album. Lou's band includes four future Alice Cooper collaborators, guitarists Dick Wagner and Steve Hunter plus bassist Prakash John and Finnish/Canadian drummer Pentti "Whitey" Glan.

Dick Wagner:
In some ways, Steve Hunter and I come from the same school. Having played together so much, it's hard on some of those records to tell who's playing what. I think he's more of a technically proficient guitar player and I might play a little more… I don't know if you would call it soulful. I'm more of a rock 'n' roller than he is but he can certainly play rock 'n' roll, obviously. He's got a little more country roots, a little more blues roots. I have blues roots too but I really came up as a rock 'n' roll guitar player.

Steve Hunter:
Well it's a little difficult for me to compare against Dick because whatever it was that was different about our playing is what helped us played well together. I think his tone, generally, tends to be a little brighter than mine. Mine's a bit darker and warmer and his is more a searing, singing sort of tone. And the two of us, because of

that difference, played well together. You didn't have to think about it too much, because we just worked naturally together and it just seemed to work from the get-go.

As a player, I like to be melodic. For me, the guitar is a very, very expressive instrument. Because of the nuances it's like a singer. There are so many nuances and so many ways of singing a phrase, and the same with guitar. I love playing melodies on guitar. That was my main love and that love came out of blues, because blues solos, normally, are pretty melodic. You could almost always sing them. That has been my mainstay, that's what I'm about, that's what my playing is about, and it's a feeling and emotion thing. I think that's some of the reason why I got hired, especially in the '70s.

Again, tone, I had a friend of mine say, "You know what your tone sounds like? Your tone sounds like a great big black woman singing." To me, that was the highest compliment that anybody has ever given me on my tone. I thought oh, okay, that's a woman tone. So it's a woman's voice, and that's what it's always been to me. When somebody said that, I thought, how cool is that? So maybe that's how I would describe my tone.

Early February 1974. Alice takes Cindy on a vacation to Mexico where they both get food poisoning. Alice golfs, having been introduced to the sport on a recent trip to Hawaii.

Mid-February – Early March 1974. Alice is busy being a celebrity. He films a segment for game show *Hollywood Squares*, he films an episode of Snoop Sisters, he and Helen Reddy present Stevie Wonder with a Grammy, he meets Elvis, he attends a Kiss record release party, and he generates salacious rumours due to his nights out with Liza Minnelli. Shep and Alice both regret doing the *Hollywood Squares* gig, Shep saying that it showed too much of the real Vince.

Alice might have continued down this path if Bob's and Alice's first plan for Alice's next phase had seen the light of day. The plan was to do a movie about a rock star, named Steven, who is also a pilot, and who crashes his private plane in the snowy mountains. After a couple of months, he has to cannibalize the girl who was with him, with whom he was having an affair. He emerges from his rescue a cannibal serial killer who wakes up and finds that what he thought was a nightmare actually happened. Alice and Bob flew

up to meet with director Daniel Mann in Vancouver, where he was filming scenes for *Journey into Fear* on a boat in the harbour. Nothing comes of the Alice vehicle, but Bob and Vincent Price bond over Ezrin's Montecristo No. 2 cigars, with Bob also telling Price that he'd like to put him in a hot rock 'n' roll song one day.

Dennis Dunaway:
I think the day that it lost a lot of its impact was when Alice went on the *Hollywood Squares* and *The Muppet Show*. All of a sudden the curiosity factor of, "Who is this?" and "Is this guy for real?" was answered. The answer was no, it's a character; it's not a real guy. But that didn't matter to us because it was entertainment. We were evolving and would have continued to evolve, especially if the band had stayed together long enough to sign that next record deal, which would have brought us the money we needed to do some of our phenomenal concepts that we, up until then, just never could quite afford to do.

February 18, 1974. Kiss issue their self-titled debut album. All of a sudden, Alice Cooper have some competition. The significance of Kiss' entrance onto the Alice Cooper timeline is that the original Alice Cooper Group is over and done with before Kiss even gets going. Still, over the next essentially two-and-a-half years, the battle for the shock rock throne will be waged between Kiss and the Alice of *Welcome to My Nightmare* fame, with the head-to-head not really gathering in intensity until after Kiss' *Alive!* hits in May of 1975. Shep recalls that much of the Alice Cooper band's tour apparatus and supplier base simply shifted over to Kiss, as people associated with the now defunct group looked for employment. He recalls that this was a deliberate procedure, through consultation between himself and Kiss manager Bill Aucoin.

Neal Smith:
Ace Frehley was a good friend of mine, and he still is, and he told me one time plus I heard him say in interviews, "Alice Cooper band, they had one Alice Cooper with the makeup and we wanted four Alice Coopers on stage." So maybe we didn't take our individual images far enough to really stand out as far as the press went. Still, the bigger the band was getting, everybody individually was getting more attention as well, because I gotta tell ya, Dennis and Glen are two of the most interesting characters on the planet.

Peter Criss (Kiss):
Number one, Jerry Nolan from the New York Dolls was my closest friend. I don't know if people know that but we grew up together in Brooklyn. We went to school together. He gave me my first drum lesson. I was jealous, actually, when he got the Dolls because they were so cool. They were such a force in New York to reckon with. Everyone loved the Dolls in New York. It's funny, New York was the only place in the world they were famous. I think their album *Too Much Too Soon* was a good title for them because that's what they were.

But Jerry was the type of guy for who image was extremely important. As important as the music, I think more so with those guys. Looking great, they looked adorable. They looked like chicks with the eyeliner and the chick boots. We tried it, but we looked like we were in drag. Looked like four guys in drag. Gene's a big guy. He looked like an old whore from some whorehouse.

So we realised that makeup, the glam, didn't look great on us. It wasn't going to fly for us. But we knew we wanted to do something that no one else ever did in the world, and we had a chemistry to it, and we wanted to be the Beatles. We wanted to be four guys that each one of us was like John, Paul, Ringo and George, and everyone loved each one of us separately, but all together they loved us like immensely. We thought, wow, what a great idea. It was like when we saw Alice Cooper. He was the only one who had makeup on. No one else did. So we thought what would it be like if four guys had the makeup on and the four guys all shared the limelight?

Larry Harris (Casablanca Records):
To show you how they upped the ante, we were with Warner Bros. in the beginning with Kiss's first album, and so was Alice. Well Warner Bros. before the first Kiss album came out actually approached us and asked us to ask Kiss to take the makeup off. We were incredulous because it was, wait a minute, you've got Alice Cooper, he wears makeup, what's the problem with Kiss? Well Warners felt this was over the top and it was too much makeup. Of course we said no, we're not going to do that.

But actually Neil Bogart, so he could cover himself, did say to Bill Aucoin, by the way, Warners asked if you'd take the makeup off, and Bill said absolutely not. So Neil could go back and tell Mo Austin, oh no, the band said they wouldn't do it, even though Neil knew they'd say no anyway. But they wore just that much more. Alice had some makeup on. You could still tell his features, and what did he use, a boa constrictor or something? Big deal. You can walk in the streets of certain cities in America, whether it be San Francisco or LA, in those days, especially San Francisco, and see people with a boa constrictor walking around in the street. Alice's thing lasted only a short period; him being that outrageous.

March 1, 1974. Aerosmith issue their second album, *Get Your Wings*. Dick Wagner and Steve Hunter play on "Train Kept a Rollin." The album is produced by Jack Richardson and Ray Colcord, with Bob Ezrin credited as executive producer.

Alice Cooper:
It's funny, if there's one band, musically, that's the closest band to Alice Cooper, it would be Aerosmith. When I talk to Joe and Steven Tyler and all these guys, and we talk about our high school days and our 20s, what our roots were, it's exactly the same. We learned every Yardbirds song there was and so did they. If we went into a room and somebody said, you know, "I Ain't Got You" by the Yardbirds or "Shapes of Things" or "Happening Ten Years Time Ago," we learned those songs and they said, "So did we" (laughs). So I could tell by Aerosmith, how their records were, their influence. You know, they listened to Them with Van Morrison, they listened to The Kinks, they listened to The Who. And everybody was influenced by The Beatles.

Dick Wagner:
I think I played on four tracks on that album, actually, including "Same Old Song and Dance." Steve Hunter played on it and so did I. They used us because we were more advanced, we could come up with the stuff more quickly, whatever, and Joe was still learning. He's a great player now. But it takes a while to get to the stage that Steve and I were playing at, because we both had been doing it a long, long time. We're both on "Train Kept a Rollin'." We're doing the solos and I think we also play on the rhythm tracks too, but Joe also had rhythm tracks on that song.

March 10 – March 21, 1974. Alice takes his celebrity tour overseas, after a band tour was cancelled. He hangs out with Dutch soccer pros (one of which presents him with a gold record for Dutch sales of *Billion Dollar Babies*. In Finland, he winds up meeting Colonel Sanders of KFC fame, and then in Paris, he is spotted nightclubbing with Aristotle Onassis. In London, he drinks with Bernie Taupin, practicing for when both would do that and more back in Los Angeles as part of the Hollywood Vampires.

March 30 – April 8, 1974. The band perform five dates in Brazil. The April 8th show in Rio De Janeiro would represent the last show ever of the original Alice Cooper band.

James Randi:
That was a close one in Brazil. The kids almost started to die like flies. They were all being pushed by a massive crowd. I never saw such a big crowd of people. They were being pushed up against the supports at the front, the three-quarter inch plywood. We had to literally reach down and grab some of the kids and pull them up onto the stage because they were getting crushed. It was a very bad scene.

Dennis Dunaway:
We just got driven into the ground. We were working so hard, we just couldn't do everything. Also the other thing that is a distraction from art is when you become that popular, how do you sleep when there's people knocking on your door all night? How do you write a song, how do you discuss, even, a song at a breakfast table like we did before we got so popular, when there's a whole bunch of people standing there asking you for your autograph?

It's a bittersweet thing, but it's a wonderful thing; it was our goal. But it makes it very difficult to be able to keep focused on the project at hand, which is the art of it. We did as well as we could but there's a tendency for things to get very complicated as far as logistically being able to sit down. Part of the chemistry of that band, and I think any good artistic collaboration, is friction. Because we were all passionate about getting the best thing. It was all for the right thing, but we had loud discussions and we could drive people out of the rehearsal room. It wasn't anything where we were really upset at each other. We were just voicing our concern for my idea. I think my idea's the best, you think your idea's the best, and then we'd discuss it and try both ideas, and then everybody would vote.

Then the good thing about it was if my idea wasn't the one that we used, that was the end of it. Same with everybody. That was the end of it. But try to do that at a table when there's a bunch of strangers standing around you. There was a lot of that, and the difficulty of being able to sleep. You were in different time zones all the time. You were travelling and moving this giant stage. We didn't have the crews then that people have that set up a show like that at Madison Square Gardens these days.

Michael Bruce:
I really liked *Muscle of Love*, but by that time Glen was out of the picture. I think we were going in a direction

that Alice didn't feel as comfortable with. I remember Shep came in and said, "Oh, this is the end, man." "What's the problem, Shep?" "Oh, the album just went to No.10; we just had a No.1" and it was ruining his day. *Billion Dollar Babies* was No.1, that plus the fact that he lost a publishing lawsuit with Herbie Cohen regarding the early material.

So he was like moving on, moved out to LA. Even though he was still managing us, Alice is out there. Then we get the phone call, he doesn't want to work with us anymore. I think it was just the writing on the wall. By that time we'd built Alice Cooper up into a namesake, a household word, and he wanted to move on and Shep was ready to do that for him. Even Deborah Harry, in her book, she says the same thing. Shep was constantly trying to get her away from the band. That's, I guess, what managers sometimes do. They develop that person into a star rather than all the guys in the band.

We had agreed that we weren't going to stop until we were all millionaires. I think Alice and Shep forgot that we wanted to be millionaires too (laughs). I think back now—our future wasn't carved in rock. It was more like etched in sand. I think that we weren't going to go past *Billion Dollar Babies* even though *Muscle of Love* was the band reaching out, trying to prove itself.

Alice had become like a Frank Zappa—It was all about him. Any interviews and stuff, he would talk about everybody on the planet before he ever mentioned anybody in the band. It was disheartening, because we came up through the ranks of the first couple of albums, I sang, and jokingly we used to refer to Alice as the lead maraca player in our band. He wasn't playing an instrument. He didn't always sing either.

But I have to say, he became a great lyricist and a very, very good singer. But the thing is, we just felt like we wanted to express ourselves a little bit broader, musically, than, you know, Alice stabbing at the heart of the love generation and stuff like that. Which was provocative and it made for great print, but you know, it was just another kid rebelling against either his parents and/or the country, with like when we did "Elected."

But I would write a song like "Desperado," which, I did a lot of lyrics on that, but even the more melodic stuff and softer stuff that we did still had his view of the world. We wanted to say something, the guys in the band. I know Dennis did. He was very frustrated. Neal did. We basically wanted to take a year off to see what we could do. We were very naïve of the fact that Alice doing a solo album… I think we all thought he was—and this is crazy that I even entertained this thought—but we thought he was going to do his solo album as Vince Furnier (laughs). That wasn't going to happen.

May 1974. *Good to See You Again, Alice Cooper* premieres, after which further editing happens. Essentially this turns out to be a soft launch. Also this month, Alice and Groucho Marx strike up a friendship and an episode of *Hollywood Squares* Alice shot in March airs, with more staggered throughout the coming months.

Neal Smith:
We had done so much to create an image for the band intentionally and unintentionally that when the movie came out… the lights, the sunlight and we're outside, I was like, "What the fuck?" We've done all this for years to create an image and an attitude and this was like a home movie. It's not very Alice Cooper-ish as far as I'm concerned. When did we ever say we were into comedy, and very, very bad comedy too, by the way? It is what it is and I'm glad it's finally released.

Dennis Dunaway:
We could afford to carry off more of our ideas as the gigs picked up. But obviously it was, okay, well, we executed Alice in an electric chair, what are we going to do next? So that led to the gallows and that led to the guillotine and it would have kept escalating had the original band stayed together, or been allowed to stay together, rather, and moved into the era after we would've signed our first lucrative contract. We could've taken it to the sky but that didn't happen, so unfortunately a lot of ideas prematurely bit the dust. But every tour that we did, every album that we did, and every album cover and the way we dressed, was designed to fit a particular album. It kept evolving just like it did in the days of the VIP, when the band kept changing. We were the only band that did that, although the Beatles did that. They influenced us as well, because it seemed like every time the Beatles put out a new album they looked like a different band.

June 1974. Reports surface that Alice is planning a solo album, while both Neal and Michael are well along on solo projects. Various sides to the story as to why the band would break-up are offered below, but Shep is adamant that a clutch of problems contributed. He says that the band needed convincing night after night at the end to do the show with full theatrics rather than just go out in jeans. All the years of being disrespected as musicians had built to the point where they wanted to make it all about the music, Mike and Neal in particular. Dennis, famously framed as the artist or the Dali in the group, could have gone either way but ultimately sided with the band. Glen by this point was so hobbled by booze and, posits Alice, downers, Seconals, that he barely ventured an opinion on anything.

Shep also figured that Alice was doing all the work, that the band wouldn't do interviews, the guitars were being played by outside players, the guys would only continue if they were allowed to make solo albums, and that they didn't think Alice was a good singer or lyricist. Furthermore, Shep figures it was the band that broke their gentleman deal that they would continue until they were all millionaires.

Financially, at this point, Shep figures that each equal partner had about a quarter million dollars to his name, so they were far from their goal but not exactly broke, which is sometimes how he characterised the situation (and certainly a truism of sorts most of the time pre-*Billion Dollar Babies*).

There are various reasons that the band was not as well off as the hyperbole would have it. First, they were selling gold and barely platinum but not astronomical numbers of records. Second, the show was very expensive to put on—which the band was all too aware, another point of contention in the break-up being the reticence of the guys to invest in something as elaborate as *Welcome to My Nightmare*. Finally, huge paydays for concert performances were not the norm yet. With ticket prices of only a few dollars, Shep figures at the high end, for a marquee show of the day, a band might get $50,000, and indeed even a tenth of that for a marquee act performing only a few years earlier, at the turn of the '70s.

Dick Wagner:
I really don't know the story in that. He became Alice Cooper. Because originally the whole band was called Alice Cooper and he became the persona. The way it was approached to me was that he wanted to go solo and just be Alice Cooper and that he wanted a better band to be able to play better places. That he wanted something better, something more sophisticated. I don't know if that's all true or not.

Dennis Dunaway:
I didn't want to, but being completely driven into the ground physically and emotionally, we had no choice but to take a break. We all agreed to take one year off and then we would get back together and do our next Alice Cooper album. That wasn't unreasonable, and it was a solid investment for the band's future. Never in a billion years would I have thought that Alice would take the ball and run with it.

"School's Out" was the biggest selling single in the history of Warner Bros. Records. Our *Billion Dollar Babies* album was No.1 in the US and the UK. We were on the cover of *Forbes* magazine for topping the Rolling Stones' and Led Zeppelin's tour records. We had worked incredibly hard for a decade. I've never squandered any money away. So we were questioning where the money was, which is very different than wanting to cash out. Their eventual story, that "they wanted to cash out" rationalisation, came way after the "they refused to do theatrics" campaign, which was the first excuse. But yeah, first it was the idea that after our break, we thought we would all return refreshed, sign a significant new record deal, and finally have the funds to do what we had always strived toward.

Michael Bruce:
You can't say the situation with Glen wasn't a factor. On the other hand you can't say that was the only reason. He just wasn't doing his job anymore and we tried to get him some help, but he just didn't want it. I think everybody decided to go on their own. I know I did and when we wanted to get back together, I don't think Alice wanted to do it without Glen. So, he just went on and did his own thing, which in the long run turned out pretty good for me being one of the main writers. Every time Alice plays, he's promoting the catalogue, so I've done well. He's kept it alive.

But Glen wasn't really doing his part and when we went in to do any recording he wasn't writing. He was just doing whatever Glen would do and then we'd go into the studio and have these songs written and there would be no Glen part. So Wagner or Steve Hunter or Mick Mashbir or Bob Dolin or whoever—we had a bunch of different people come in, not just Wagner—and they would provide something that Glen would do. Glen carried on and he was on the *Billion Dollar Babies* tour 'til the end, but his participation was somewhat limited. But for *Muscle of Love*, Glen was ill and in the hospital and when he came out we didn't know if he'd know his stuff or not and we basically had to be prepared either way, so that was why Mick Mashbir came in.

July 1974. Alice and guitarist Dick Wagner go to the Bahamas to write songs for his proposed solo album. Dick has reconnected with Alice through Shep. Dick had finished a stint with Lou Reed and had written about thirty songs for a proposed solo album. He is living in Connecticut at this time, so he goes into the city to meet with Shep at the original Alice office and ask his advice. It's a no-brainer that Dick and Alice should get together.

Dick Wagner:

I had known Alice from the Detroit days and they asked me to come in and do some writing with him and I wrote "I Love the Dead" with him and Bob Ezrin, although I'm not credited on the album because I sold my part of the song to them because I needed some money. So I'm not on the credits but I'm definitely a writer on that. So that was the beginning of that, and Alice remembered writing with me and how much he liked it, and when they were going to replace the old band and put a new band together, they asked me to be his writer, and put together an album and to help put together a band. I had just finished Lou Reed's stuff and I thought, we'll bring the band over from Lou Reed to Alice Cooper, which is basically what we did, which worked out great, because it turned out to be the *Nightmare* band.

Alice and I went to LA, did a little bit of writing out there, wrote "Only Women Bleed" and "Department Of Youth" and a couple of things from that album, at his house. But we weren't getting enough accomplished, so we went down to the Bahamas. So we're down in the Bahamas thinking, what should the concept of this album be?

Alice came up with the idea of *Welcome to My Nightmare.* It happened on a day when he and I went out in lawn chairs, sitting out on the lawn. We had these cottages out on the beach in the Bahamas, and this huge storm came up. It was 80-mile-an-hour winds for 24 hours straight; a hurricane passing by. We're sitting out there in the wind with acoustic guitars (laughs) and Alice said, "Welcome to my nightmare." (laughs). I played this little riff and we just fell into it. He's like, "Eureka, that's it," and he went in and called Bob and called Shep and said he had an idea for the concept of the album. So he came up with the idea there in the Bahamas.

August 1974. Warner Bros. issue *Alice Cooper's Greatest Hits.* The album features a Jack Richardson remix of the tracks, and a subsequent refloating of the remixed "I'm Eighteen" as a single.

Ernie Cefalu:

Drew Struzan did the outside and Bill Garland did the inside. Two different illustrators, which makes that piece even more desirable, because Drew's only worked on the same piece with another illustrator three times. The first one was the first *Star Wars* poster, when he worked with Charlie White, who could draw figures. So Charlie did the background and Drew did the figures. So that piece and two other pieces, Black Oak Arkansas' *Early Times* that we did. Bill was very much a very versatile illustrator, and Drew was a mentor to him. We all worked at Pacific Eye & Ear together, and they did it like an animation cell. Drew did the background, and then Bill did the cartoon characters on an overlay.

But what happened was, we did that album cover, we submitted it to the record label, and the record label said, "Well, you know, you're going to have to change... any-body that is still alive, you have to take out." So we had to change 23 faces. It wasn't just as easy as going in and changing the face. You had to find somebody who was the right physical height and weight. For example, on the front, I think we have Judy Garland dancing with Alan Ladd. Well, originally it was Mickey Rooney. Judy Garland and Mickey Rooney were teenagers together in movies—all the Andy Hardy movies and stuff—and they were sort of a known couple so it was a no-brainer to have Judy Garland dancing with Mickey Rooney.

Well, when they said Mickey Rooney is still alive, you can't have him in there, you have to change it, we had to find somebody who is his same height and weight and physical makeup. So it wasn't just as easy as changing heads. Those two drawings are graphite pencil. It's not that easy to work with graphite, once you start erasing. So it was really tedious. You can't just go in an take the face out and just redraw it over. You had to lift the graphite that was on the board off, and then redraw on top of it. So it's an interesting cover. It was really neat watching Drew do the work.

THE HIT MEN OF ROCK
HAVE PUT ALL THEIR BULLETS
INTO A BRAND-NEW PIECE

Alice Cooper's Greatest Hits

W 2803

12 KILLERS AT LARGE ON WARNER BROS. RECORDS & TAPES
LET THEM TAKE YOU FOR A NICE LONG RIDE...

Late August 1974. Dennis weds long-time girlfriend Cindy. They are still together 45 years later. Meanwhile, Alice is in Toronto working with Bob Ezrin and session musicians on his first solo album. Work winds up mid-September.

September 18, 1974. *Good to See You Again, Alice Cooper* receives a full-blown official launch with extensive merchandising and ad campaigns.

October 1 – December 31, 1974. Sessions take place for the complicated *Flash Fearless* concept album, for which Alice takes part, to be released in early 1975.

November 12, 1974. After a steady climb, *Greatest Hits* reaches a lofty No.3 on the *Billboard* charts.

November 30, 1974. Alice's new right-hand man Dick Wagner marries Elizabeth Marsh.

December 19, 1974. Released to theatres is the ninth James Bond movie, *The Man with the Golden Gun.* Having already written a song just in time for school letting out, and another just in time for the presidential election, Alice Cooper turn their attention to film, issuing a song with this title fully a year previous.

Neal Smith:
That was the new movie that was coming out and every time a new movie would come out they would have somebody that was a very popular singer who would do the theme song. Of course, nobody would ever have Alice Cooper do a theme song to a James Bond movie! So we just said, "What the hell!" The next movie coming out was going to be called *The Man with the Golden Gun*, and we knew that was coming and we wrote a song about it and we just put it on the album.

It would be a long shot that they would actually use it in the movie. Although we didn't think that would ever happen, the biggest slap in the face was that Lulu of all people ended up singing the theme song. We lost out to Lulu (laughs). That was a low blow to us. Our song was just there. Believe me, if anyone was looking for anything there, they knew it was out. So everybody knew it. Whether it was officially submitted, I can't tell you that. But it was out well before the movie, so they had plenty of time to have it. But I don't know if there was a real full-court press to get it done. Because we just knew the ramifications of a band like us... it'd be like the Rolling Stones or the Doors doing a theme song for a James Bond movie—not impossible, but not very likely.

Paul McCartney got one, but you know what? First of all, it's a great song and it's perfect for *Live and Let Die*, and secondly, I think he worked very closely with John Barry on the song, which makes a big difference. If we had John Barry in the studio with us, it may have been a politically brilliant move on our part, or business move on our part. But it didn't happen.

1975

One can never predict what will happen, but as it turns out, Alice will experience his greatest solo success of his 35-odd years after the dissolution of the original band, immediately, with an action-packed album called *Welcome to My Nightmare*. Studded with confident, well-recorded songs in a number of styles, sprinkled with ear candy, *Welcome to My Nightmare* would cough up a huge hit for Alice, in the ballad "Only Women Bleed."

"Department of Youth" and the title track would also be mooted as singles, but neither would exactly catch on. But acting as that second hit single would be the elaborate stage show, which would be taken all over North America and come August, into Europe, marking Alice's first jaunt there as a solo artist.

In the spring, Alice would meet with the band to explore any sort of future they might have together, but it was plain for all to see that Alice and Shep had their hands full with a hit, even if the beast was hoovering up money at a white-knuckle rate, steeling the army Alice was commandeering to deliver night after night.

Also helping put bums in the seats was the launch on April 25th of *Alice Cooper: The Nightmare*, a narrative made-for-TV version of the album. The record proved to be a natural for this type of treatment, and kids were captivated, even if by autumn, Kiss were going to come around and steal Alice's thunder with their *Alive!* album and touring bombast of their own.

Still, nose to the grindstone, Alice and Shep triumphed over the tour's massive expense, and by the end of the year, with everybody absolutely spent, the band performed a residency at Lake Tahoe. As for the man himself, despite a now grave problem with booze, Alice had found, in the presence of a classically trained dancer brought into the *Welcome to My Nightmare* maelstrom, a new and lasting love in his life.

January 2, 1975. Alice conquers another medium, appearing on big-league talk show, *The Mike Douglas Show*, following that up two days later with a performance of "Unfinished Sweet" on *The Smothers Brothers Show*, significant in that he did it without the band.

Dennis Dunaway:
For that one, I used a Vox Fuzz, a fuzz tone wah-wah pedal on the bass. The beginning, I used to think it was humorous, and I think Alice was the only one who shared my humour, to make a bass sound like something that no one would ever think to use a bass for. Like I used to do bird calls on stage with the bass. It didn't sound like a bird, but, I thought it was funny, and so did Alice, that I would be attempting to do bird calls on the bass. On that song, I decided that the bass should sound like a juice harp, a mouth harp. So I used that effect on the beginning, and then we actually overdubbed a real mouth harp on it, which, actually, I chipped my tooth doing, and still to this day I have that chip in my tooth. But that's because of improper positioning of the instrument (laughs). So when the band comes in, I switched the effect off so that it goes to regular bass bottom.

Now the song, "Unfinished Sweet," is of course about somebody going to the dentist and the nightmarish aspect of that, as a kid. Neal's sister, who eventually became my wife, when we played it live, was the dancing tooth. I had that idea because there used to be these Chesterfield cigarette commercials on television, where they would have these dancing girls, that you can see their legs, but the top part was covered with a cigarette box, for Chesterfield.

I thought, well, let's use that and we'll have the dancing tooth come out. So that took place in the middle part. Then we also had The Amazing Randi, who worked with the group, and a guillotine that was designed for us, he was in charge of operating it. Well, he came out as a mad scientist with this giant drill and drilled Alice's mouth. Then the dancing tooth would come out, and Alice would have a giant tube of toothpaste and a giant toothbrush, and he would chase my wife around the stage and end up brushing her while erotic sounds went over the PA (laughs). James Randi is the one who debunked Uri Geller. He's the guy who used to have the million-dollar cheque ready for anybody who could prove a paranormal event (laughs). Maybe he still does.

Neal Smith:

First of all, "Unfinished Sweet" is actually my song. I was writing a couple of songs, and the nucleus, the original idea for the song was mine. Then Michael came on board and helped me with the music and then Alice came on for the lyrics. It took a really cool direction which we all really liked a lot. Plus we were all James Bond fanatics, so it went into that middle part that was like a little James Bond idea, when the character is under gas at the dentist office and has his dream (laughs)—that was cool, that was great, that was Alice's concept. But the original idea for the song and music were mine.

We were all big fans of the monster movies and James Bond and *West Side Story,* so all of those things came in to inspire our music throughout the years. When I'd written the song originally, Mike Bruce and I started working it out and he came up with some elaborations on the music and some arrangements. My original lyrics on the song were totally re-written by Alice, and he went in another direction. We did the same thing on the song "Alma Mater" from *School's Out;* I had written the song and I got total credit on that song, but Alice did have something to do with the lyrics that were in the song.

On this song, the idea of going to the dentist scares people and it was about going under and while you're having your teeth worked on, you're having this dream and it becomes a James Bond story. Bob Ezrin's the perfect person to work on with that.

I love John Barry who wrote all the great James Bond songs and music in the movies. So that certainly inspired us on that song. Of course, on stage the Amazing Randi came out with the giant drill like you see in the movie *Good to See You Again, Alice Cooper,* and he takes this monstrous drill and puts it on Alice's mouth and you hear the sound of the drill noises on the record, and that was on stage as well. To this day when I listen to that drill sound, it makes me cringe a little bit. But it turned out to be a great song, and a great one for the stage too.

January 20, 1975. Alice signs on with Atlantic Records as a solo artist. Presenting the record to Atlantic as a soundtrack album allowed manager Shep Gordon to escape the ire of Warner Bros.—for now.

Dennis Dunaway:

Welcome to My Nightmare was contractually negotiated when we signed our deal with Warner Bros. Records. It was negotiated as the band would be allowed to do a soundtrack, with any other record company, without breaking the record contract with Warners. The band decided... we had been pushed so hard, like really burnt-out on the road. Even though I was gung-ho to keep going, I was the only one. Everyone else wanted to take a year off. Michael wanted to do a solo album, because he wrote a lot of great songs that the band wouldn't use because it didn't match up with the image that we wanted. When Michael decided that he was going to do a solo album, then Neal also decided that he wanted to do one. So we decided that we were going to take a year off, we'll get back together, everybody will be fresh because we were also on the verge of renegotiating our contract with Warner Bros. So we wanted to go in with a fresh, whole new tour idea, whole new concept and everything.

As we took that time off, when the band got together and did what was the subsequent record, the *Battle Axe* album, it was impossible for us to get a hold of Alice all of a sudden. We didn't know at that time that Alice was exercising the contract negotiation that was negotiated on behalf of the band, to use this soundtrack. That's why *Welcome to My Nightmare* was a television show, so that it would fall into that soundtrack loophole that we had negotiated into our Warner Bros. contract. We just were never able to get back together after that.

But one of the aspects is that unless you have this incredibly mega smash hit during your first major label contract, you don't really make money until the point where you've fulfilled your contract and it's time to go shopping, or renegotiate with that record company. Well, everything coincided with that, so Charlie Parnell, the guy that did the lights for the Alice Cooper group since day one, was paid as an equal member—he was considered one of the band. Shep Gordon had a partner, Joe Greenberg, who was a sharing partner in the management commissions and everything. Joe also had a great deal to do with the success of the band over the years.

So, here we have eight guys, eight people who were going to cash in finally after all of this work and all of this putting money back into the show, and hoping that we would renegotiate the contract that would give us enough money to do the big shows we had in mind. We were still, even on the *Billion Dollar Babies* tour, as extravagant as that was, we had bigger things in mind. So as that contract was finally renegotiated, all of that, all the gravy was split between two people instead of eight—Alice and Shep Gordon.

Mike Marconi:
I wasn't privy to all the goings-on on the legal front, and believe me there was a lot going on behind the scenes. They were disappearing into rooms and talking for hours, going into the city and talking to attorneys. What it seemed to me at that point, you've got a manager, a good one, and let's face it, Alice was the star of the show. It's like Stevie Tyler and Aerosmith—Stevie Tyler is the star of the show! There's nothing wrong with that; there's going to be a focal point in every successful band.

I think it was a question of, "Look, Alice, you're the star, and you can get anyone to play with you and put them on salary!" Alice had been doing well, because he's Alice, riding on the success, in my opinion, of the hit songs that were written by Michael Bruce, "Schools Out," "I'm Eighteen," "No More Mr. Nice Guy."

At the same time Alice "sold" those songs—he put it over. So it's a team that needs to work together to make this big rock 'n' roll wheel move. It just didn't work out that way. I think the Billion Dollar Babies band thing started out as "something for them to do until they got back together again," and then turned into, "Well, maybe there isn't a getting back together again and this might be another way for us to perform, stay on the road and write music." But I know there were a lot of animosities and things with Alice.

Neal Smith:
When there were rumblings of any lawsuit, I said, "There is no way in the world I will ever sue one of my best friends." It was not going to happen. If somebody else wanted to do it without me, then whatever. But I think it's one of the best decisions I ever made in my life.

Spring 1975. Chrysalis Records issues *Flash Fearless Vs. The Zorg Women Pts. 5 & 6*, a casual comic book concept collaboration of a bunch of rock stars including Alice, who contributes on two tracks, "I'm Flash and "Space Pirates."

March 4, 1975. Alice Cooper issues his first solo album, *Welcome to My Nightmare*, which enters the charts at No.63. Three weeks of intensive routining and rehearsal ensues, in LA.

Alice Cooper:
"Well, that was my first album away from the band. It was really me rolling the dice and going, boy oh boy, it sounds like a great idea but I've been with the band all my life, and people don't necessarily like it when the lead singer of the band goes off on his own. But I didn't go off on my own. The band went off on their own, and I was basically sitting there with Alice Cooper. They didn't want to be Alice Cooper anymore; they didn't want to do the theatrics, they didn't want to spend the money on the show.

I'm sitting there going, "Well, guys..." They're saying, "Let's tone it down," and I'm going, "What?! I'm thinking of going twice as heavy this time!" Instead of going backwards, I wanted *Welcome to My Nightmare* to make *Billion Dollar Babies* look like child's play. They were going, "No way, we don't want to do that. It's too hard, it's too much work, it's too much money, it costs too much." I just went, "Hey, I'm sorry guys. You guys want to go and do your own albums, go do them." I said, I've got this idea for this album that's really going to be like an Edgar Allan Poe story line and the stage show is going to cost every penny I have, but if it works, it's going to be phenomenal (laughs) and it did.

We toured that album for two years and it nearly killed me. It was amazing, because people had never heard numbers like what they were hearing, as far as grosses and how many people saw the show. We were working six nights a week, selling out every show, for two years. We worked so hard for two years, that it literally almost killed me, just because of the fact that I drank so much just to try keep up with it.

Dick Wagner:

It's about a kid into his psyche and dreams. I don't really see how it fits. It's a concept but to me it was never really a totally completed concept. Because the songs weren't all totally done for this concept. Like "Some Folks" really wasn't. "Cold Ethyl," "Only Women Bleed"… those were all part of *Nightmare* and the meaning was really simple; there wasn't really anything deep about it at all. It's about this character that Alice portrays going to sleep and having a nightmare and waking up from it and hopefully escaping all these monsters. "Steven," "The Awakening," that's just the finale for the concept. He's got to come out of that nightmare. That's really what it's all about and the character is Steven. He's the guy through the whole thing.

But "Some Folks," that was written with Alice and Alan Gordon, and I think Bob was involved. Alan was a songwriter in New York City and he wrote a lot of the Turtles stuff way back; very bright guy, very nice guy. How that came about, it was just part of that concept, Alice and his bizarre tendencies towards blood and stuff. "Some folks love to see red," it just came off the top of Alice's head. Elsewhere, "Department of Youth," that was the second song that Alice and I wrote in LA. In fact, we might have written it first before we wrote "Only Women Bleed." But it was part of that initial writing session for the *Nightmare* album in Hollywood. And then "Years Ago" I wrote in the Bahamas as part of those sessions down there. I just came up with this guitar figure, this A minor weirdness. I just started playing that and Alice said, hey, that's pretty cool. By that time we were basically into the idea of the concept now; the *Nightmare* thing had been conceived in that storm.

Bob Ezrin:

When we got to *Welcome to My Nightmare*, we decided to experiment with more overtly theatrical stuff, and we had this band put together that was a strange amalgam. We made the switch because we didn't have a band anymore, and we had this concept for a film. It actually started off as an idea for a film, and we began writing the soundtrack which then morphed into *Welcome to My Nightmare*.[1] So it began theatrically, it began with a whole different approach of more like a show, Broadway show, musical film, then hard rock album.

When we assembled the musicians and all that, it was so much fun doing that, it was just fun, fun, fun. Great musicians, stuff flying off the floor. It was fabulous, plus it was successful. It was like his biggest record, I think, in album sales up to that point, except for maybe *Billion Dollar Babies*. The audience liked it too, and we took it on the road and it made for a great live show.

There was so much more he could do with it, and now he carried the show himself. If you think about it, it's a whole 'nother animal. So he needed stuff like dancers, props, all that. Then once we were in that frame of mind, in that theatrical and musical place, it was a natural progression to go to *Goes to Hell* and *Lace and Whiskey* and so on.

But it's not heavy metal by any stretch of the imagination—it's rock. The two heaviest songs on *Welcome to My Nightmare* are "Devil's Food" and "The Black Widow." "Black Widow," except for the chorus, where it goes (sings it), that's where it turns into Broadway. But the other part, if I had done that with a real band and not studio guys, which was what we were doing, I think it would have been even heavier still and that would've qualified as heavy metal.

Kim Fowley:

I co-wrote "Escape," which is the song that ends *Welcome to My Nightmare*. Alice Cooper showed up in 1969 on the 4th of July in drag at a hippie event at the beach in Santa Monica, and 3,000 people ran out screaming into the sand like, "What is this?!" The hippies. Then Shep Gordon walked up and he said, "You're going to be No.1 in the world within three years because if you can get this type of response, wait until I market this and record it right." I was there in the room when that happened. No one really knows this but Alice Cooper were almost roommates of Janis Joplin and Big Brother and the Holding Company, because they slept in the next door room at this very same hotel that Janis Joplin died in. This was up on Franklin, next to the Magic Castle.

Moving along, so Hollywood Stars, Kiss got a song from them and "Escape" came out of the Hollywood Stars catalogue too, both songs co-written by me. So after the fact, guess what happens? Bob Ezrin, who's friends with Aerosmith's guy Jack Douglas, calls me up and says, "Quick, Jack is about to have a baby. Give me a band that you're too busy to produce that you've already A&R'd so these guys can benefit, Jack and his family." I said, "Why should I help you?" He said, "Because I did your Hollywood Stars song on my fucking Alice Cooper album and another one on a Kiss album and you made a million dollars, you prick." "You're right! Okay, no problem." So I turned over Cheap Trick to Jack Douglas, who had been an opening act for my band, The Runaways.

Dick Wagner:

I have no idea why that's there. I never saw him around there. I helped on that song too but I'm not credited on there. I don't know how Kim Fowley got into that song. I don't know how any of these people were involved in it. Because I remember Ezrin and I working on it in the studio one day. We were trying to come up with the melody for it. The chords had already been written. Maybe Kim Fowley wrote the chords for it.

Bob Livingstone:
It was a small horn section. It was Arnie Chycoski on trumpet, Erica Goodman on harp—Erica Goodman was there with us; yes, she was part of the horns (laughs)—myself on bass trombone, Eugene Amaro, I believe, was a tenor saxophone and Marty Morrell on percussion. And it was done at Nimbus 9, on Hazelton in Toronto and Dave Green was the engineer. We played to a basic rhythm track in our headsets. Any strings would have been added as sweetener after. Then actually, we were told that the Brecker brothers, Randy and Michael, who were in New York of course, were going to be adding solos on top of what we did. I remember they told us that during the session. When we had a little break, they were talking about how they were going to send down our parts and Randy and Michael Brecker were going to do their solos.

Steve Hunter:
We'd always just try to make it equal. But we didn't really have to do that on *Welcome to My Nightmare*, because Bob Ezrin was producing and he pretty much did that. He kept us balanced. It just worked out that way. There was some songs that Dick's approach to soloing worked better than mine and then vice versa. After we worked for a while it just became instinctive.

  That record was an unbelievable amount of fun. I don't remember ever having so much fun in a

session in my life. Part of that has to be Alice's incredible sense of humour. But we also had a sense of humour. Even though we're in there having fun and we're acting crazy, the second thing that I remember most is there was some incredible stuff coming out of that. The sense of humour kept it from getting too serious. There was always just a little tiny sense of humour in everything.

  I think that's important in all music, actually, even serious music. I think it needs to have a little tiny sense of humour in it so it keeps it sounding and feeling very human. I remember the sessions, playing those songs. Sometimes we would do 20, 30, 40 takes, just to get the right vibe and the right energy, and the funny thing is, I never got tired of playing them. They're just great songs, it was a great vibe, it was really my first major album. When we went in to work on it, we knew that this was going to be something special.

  But Alice knew instinctively where the line was with humour on the actual album. His character had developed to the point where he knew that character inside and out. There were times when there might be a line that he had written vocally, and he'd say, "Alice wouldn't sing that." So between him and Bob—and Shep too, for that matter—they all knew the character well, and if something was getting a little out of hand, those three knew it and they would bring it back in.

Ernie Cefalu:

There was a meeting and we talked about this nightmare being like a three-ring circus and Barnum & Bailey and stuff, and that's where I came up with this idea of him being like a ringmaster. Drew Struzan did this beautiful illustration with graphite pencil on canvas—Drew always stretched his own canvas—of Alice tipping his hat. The piece is probably 15" x 20". We'd taken some photography, and he did this tipping his hat, and Drew did this magnificent drawing. It took him a whole day.

At the end of the day, I remember everyone had left. Because Drew only worked nine to five. He had a family... but he did more work from nine to five than most people did in two days. He was very fast and very confident. I swear to God, I don't remember him ever making a mistake. Even when he did that Jack Davis thing. It's an impossible style. So you practice for a while, cut 23 pieces of board, 15" x 20", and he did 23 drawings without making a mistake.

He did this beautiful drawing of Alice on canvas. If it was flesh-coloured, you'd think it was real. I remember being with my partner smoking a doob and looking at it at the end of the day, and thinking, man, they're just going to love this. We thought he was going to go back on top of that and add a little colour. So he got in before we did the next day, and by the time I got in, he'd taken a sienna wash and put it over the entire canvas, where you could hardly see the drawing underneath. "Drew, what did you do?! What happened? You can't even see it!" He said, "Don't worry about it." I said, "You can't see the drawing." "Don't worry about it. That's my middle tone. That's my middle tone." What he did over the next couple of days is took all the colour and used that sienna as a middle tone, and worked the dark detail back in. It was fucking amazing. When he was finished… well, you see the painting. That's it.

If you look in the textured background, there's an actual pattern of insects and stuff he did as a separate illustration, and we put that together photo-mechanically. But the actual painting, if you look at the background, it has that chiselled style, and if you look in the background there are still pieces of sienna floating around.

Drew Struzan:

We wanted to make something classy, so we put him in a top hat and tuxedo, and made it very clean and welcoming, "Welcome to my nightmare." I do remember, because Alice was so very kind, he hung around when I penned it and we got to be pretty good friends, really nice, kind, quiet man. We got along really well, and he would come over and visit. But when we shot the picture of him, we actually went up in the Hollywood Hills where his house was. I just brought the camera, and I said take the pose, so we can get an idea. We needed a dark background, but we weren't prepared much at all, so I said, "Stand in the closet," so the background was dark and I took his picture. Then I just painted it, oils on canvas.

March 18, 1975. "Only Women Bleed"/"Cold Ethyl" is issued as the second single from *Welcome to My Nightmare*. The thoughtful domestic abuse ballad fares well, hitting No.12 on *Billboard* and No.1 in Canada. For the single release, the title was truncated to "Only Women" to lessen the wrongful association of the song with menstruation. The song becomes the first of a pattern of ballads for Alice making it into the charts.

Dick Wagner:

It started out with us needing an album. Alice and I were at his home in Los Angeles and we started writing some stuff. I had a song that I had written back in 1968. I had lyrics for it that I hated, but the music was really good. So I played it for him and he agreed: the music was great and the lyrics sucked. But he had an idea for a song title and he and I sat down and wrote the song in about twenty minutes and that was "Only Women Bleed."

Over the hill, behind his house, lived Mickey Dolenz so we went over to Mickey's house and recorded the first demo of that song, which we then gave to Ezrin, then he produced the record and the rest is history. I had the original demo tape of that, but it was in a storage locker in New York I had with tapes from twenty years of recording stuff. I hadn't had a chance to ship it and the place burned down and I lost everything. I lost all my scrapbooks from all my European tours; everything is gone.

As far as favourite solos I've ever done goes, I think that would be my Hawaiian Steel guitar solo in "Only Women Bleed." I enjoyed doing that; I think it sounds great. Interestingly, the vocal on "Only Women Bleed" is the rough vocal, from just the practice session for the song. So we got that track cut in one take. With that band, you pretty much didn't have to go through 25 takes. You're done in two takes.

Now "Cold Ethyl," I remember that Hunter came up with that beautiful lead thing at the very beginning, which was really cool. That really moved me. I thought the idea for the song was hilarious. I like my solo in "Cold

Ethyl." Steve's got great solos in it too but I like that one I did, because I accidentally hit the strings with my pick and got this very high frequency little thing going that sounds like it was on purpose, but it wasn't really (laughs).

Alice Cooper:
"Cold Ethyl" was, again, just part of the nightmare. It was a guy that was in love with Cold Ethyl even though Cold Ethyl was dead. It never really copped to necrophilia, but he wasn't just in love with her spiritually. He was definitely in love with her physically. I thought it was funny. I thought it was just gross enough and sophomoric enough to be one of those jokes you're not supposed to talk about.

That was the one where Ann Landers wrote the letter about, "How dare Alice do this with necrophilia?" I went, okay, wait a minute are you telling me... I actually wrote her a letter and said that if there's an enormous rash of necrophilia in the next month or so, then I'll take responsibility, okay? But I really doubt if there will be, because it's called satire. But when I was a kid... did you always try to find the joke that all your friends would laugh at, and then they would go eewww?! That was the joke. "Sick Things" was that joke. "I Love the Dead" was that joke. The unloading babies with a pitch fork, that whole thing when you're in school going, "Hey, what about sliding down on a razor blade into a..." You're always try to come up with the grossest thing. That's what "Cold Ethyl" was.

March 21, 1975. Alice Cooper, now solo artist, performs the first show of his back-breaking *Welcome to My Nightmare* tour, in Kalamazoo, Michigan. Support on the historic first US leg is Suzi Quatro. The elaborate show is expensive. Alice works with Disney people and *West Side Story* people. Shep re-mortgages his house to help pay for the show and, recalls Alice, Bob Ezrin kicked in a substantial amount of money as well, although Shep says no, that the financial leap was only he and Alice, spending every penny each of them had to make this a reality. *Welcome to My Nightmare* would run for a year before the guys would break even. On the negative, Shep knew that this new highly theatrical solo concept was a huge gamble, but on the positive, wearing his manager cap, he knew that taking just Alice and the name Alice Cooper was a huge business windfall, and that the band were quite voluntarily making a huge mistake in going their own way.

Dick Wagner:
That tour was put together as a show. It was strung together on the record loosely as a concept; it sort of worked as a concept but there are a couple songs that didn't really concept-out all that much. But for the show, we tried to put it together with the whole… Alice in the bed having his nightmare and on and on and on through all the characters and the dance routines. So yeah, it was put together as a concept and we played it that way. I wrote a bunch of incidental music, segue music between songs, stuff we did at the live show but was never on an album.

That would certainly be interesting to hear on a live album someday—a very good live album. I don't know if there are any good recordings of that at all, though. I don't remember them recording shows every night. When I was touring with Lou Reed, they recorded them every night. But with Alice, I don't think they did. If they did, I didn't get to hear any of them. But we played all those songs live.

Steve Hunter:
Dick Wagner and I did our little guitar duel. I believe it was my idea that, Dick, you know, if we're going to have a guitar duel, let's actually make it look like we're actually getting into a fight. You take a swing at me and I'll go down, and I'll have a blood capsule. We made a big deal out of it. We just made it funny, because during that time in the '70s, there were a lot of two-guitar and three-guitar bands, and they would trade off solos all the time. It would always look like it was a competition, like a duel although I don't think it ever was.

Other than that, basically, we just played the music, and there was so much wonderful stuff going on, on stage anyway. I really loved the theatre aspect of it. It was great watching every night. Yeah, that was the best of all the tours, because we were in black satin and black top hats, and then when Dick and I did the duel, we had full-length capes. I just thought that was the coolest look, especially for a rock 'n' roll band. We looked like gravediggers when we walked out.

Alice Cooper:
To be really honest with you, if we did a rehearsal, a nine-hour rehearsal, even in the old days, eight hours was on the music. The music always came first to us. The theatrics was easy. That was, okay, we're going to do this song, what are we going to do? Okay, that sounds good.

I tried to keep it guerrilla theatre, until we got into *Nightmare*, then it got produced, then it looked like a Broadway play. But when I discovered my voice again, then I said I'm surrounding myself with the best players in the world. That's when we got Hunter and Wagner on guitar and Whitey Glan on drums and Prakash John on bass, Joey Chirowski on keyboards. Bob Ezrin hand-picked those guys with me, and they were the top of the line players. So if you had those guys playing, then we had rehearsals just on singing to make it sound great. That's when I really discovered my voice again.

April 5, 1975. Alice plays the Olympia Stadium in Detroit to a sold-out crowd of 17,000. In the audience are Dennis, Neal and Michael. After the show they have what is essentially a band meeting. It's plain for all to see, however, that the Alice Cooper brand has shifted to the man, and that the band is no more.

Steve Hunter:

It was a gruelling time. We would do five shows in a week. We were just busting our butt in those days. But see, I got a nickname called The Deacon, because I don't drink. I did my little drug experimentation in the '60s and I got bored with it; it just didn't do anything for me. So by the time I got into all this, the Alice Cooper thing and Mitch Ryder and Lou Reed, I wasn't doing any drugs. So that's how The Deacon nickname came. So now it's a joke, a fun thing, the Deacon of rock 'n' roll, because he doesn't get high.

But with Alice, the bizarre thing was I never was worried about him. I never ever felt that he wasn't going to be able to carry off the show. Part of the reason is I never really saw that side of him. When I'm on tour with anybody, I tend to stay very much to myself. That's not because I'm aloof or arrogant or any those weird things. It's just in order for me to deal with the road, I have to spend a lot of time alone. All I really pay attention to when I'm on the road, is what did they do when they're on stage together? I didn't really know what was going on until later, until much later and people started telling me stories. I never realised it was so bad.

April 25, 1975. *Alice Cooper: The Nightmare* airs on ABC. The elaborate concept production goes a long way to reinforcing the content of the album and the show and the fanfare around it helps propel ticket sales even further.

Dick Wagner:

I was supposed to mix the soundtrack for the movie, but somehow that never came together and whoever mixed it's terrible. Bob Brown, or whoever that was. But Shep didn't really care about the sound of the movie. This was just a way to make some money, put a movie together, get it out there.

Just like with our live shows; it would've been better if we had better sound mixing. Of course, we played such horrible places, these huge arenas and stuff. It's hard to get a good sound, especially in those days. It was the hockey barns more so than arenas, actually. We played Olympia, we played Madison Square Gardens, Chicago, that big one, whatever the hell that's called. Suzi Quatro opened part of that tour. One day we had the Atlantic Rhythm Section and we had Roy Buchanan on one date. We had Roy Buchanan and Johnny Winter on another date; that was at Meadowlands in New Jersey.

We had ZZ Top open for us when we played Texas. That was before they hit it really big. It was the biggest grossing rock 'n' roll tour of its time. I don't think it lost money, but I know the show was very expensive to put together. We did about 110 dates over the period of a year, so we toured quite extensively. We rehearse hard too; we had two months of rehearsals, every day rehearsals at the Paramount Soundstage, I think it was, in Los Angeles, a movie stage. I'm sure that was very expensive.

One story, I remember when we were on the tour, Ringo came out to see us. He came walking into the dressing room at Wembley, singing "Only Women Bleed"; that was cool. When we were rehearsing on the soundstage in LA, we had lots of different people come by, Richard Chamberlain, Little Richard. I remember on the *Nightmare* tour when we played Chicago, whatever the big hockey rink is called, we didn't come out for a second encore and they piled up chairs and burned them. The crowd was going absolutely insane. They wanted us back out there and that was it. But we didn't go out there because we thought, you know, let's leave them wanting—and they started a fire.

May 5, 1975. Alice plays Madison Square Garden, after which for a second time the entire band—Dennis, Neal, Michael and even Glen this time—sift through the ashes and see if there's anything left. At this point, Michael is the only one besides Alice with clear solo plans.

Andy McConnell's Mum warned her pink peekaboo, fresh out of nappies son that the Crown Prince of Transylvania Towers was one of the most foul, dangerous perverts on earth. But Andy still went up amongst the vampire bats and into the tower where this being lay. As he entered he heard the eerie voice say...

HIS SATANIC MAJESTY REQUEST

"Don't the audience see it's become a joke to me. I don't even like being on stage anymore. I've had ... of this sordid stuff."

April 19, 1975

ALICE COOPER IN DETROIT BY BARBARA CHARONE

Detroit's favourite son comes home

SOUNDS Page 36

PICTURES: CHUCK PULIN

Neal Smith:

I had the mirror balls from the *Billon Dollar Babies* tour. The reason I got all of this is that they were ready to throw it in the dump. "They" being the Galesi Estate where we lived in Connecticut. We'd been out of there for a while, but our roadies were still there. They had an eight-car garage with a big storage area above it. We stored all of our *School's Out* stuff up there. We had the hanging gallows up there. We had the *Billion Dollar Babies* tour stuff up there as well.

     We were told one day that if it was not out of there in a couple of days it was all going to the dump. I had two roadies living with me, and we went and took as much stuff as we could and the guillotine was part of it. I already had my drums, naturally, but the stuff that was in storage was going to be thrown in the garbage, so I had to get it as I had protected all of it over the years. This was back in 1975.

     I've got the original *Billion Dollar Babies* guillotine. There have been others that have been supposedly the original ones over the years, but this is really it. It was a great illusion. That is how it all came to me. I salvaged it and hung onto it for over 40 years.

     I had a lot of storage in my basement area. I had tons of room for it, and most of the homes I have lived in were big enough to accommodate that. Over time I loaned some stuff out, like the light stairs from the *Billion Dollar Babies* tour. The band Dennis Dunaway and I had in the late '70s called Flying Tiger used the stairs. After we broke up, I had some friends who borrowed them and they ended up in Hartford, Connecticut. They are now in some Baptist church in Hartford. They are rocking and rolling on Sunday mornings with the *Billion Dollar Babies* light stairs.

June 14, 1975. *Welcome to My Nightmare* is riding high on the charts at this point at No.6 while "Only Women Bleed" is No.13.

Johnny "Bee" Badanjek:
I did a lot of sessions in Toronto. Bob would call me up and say, "Bring your drums up. I got this gig; I'm producing." What happened was the original band…from what I understand it'd be easier to talk to the original guys, but it was driving Bob crazy because it was taking so long to record, just to get things right. Somehow they started using session players. He was doing his album and he called me up and he goes, "I got some tracks I want you to play and you'd be perfect for it. I want you to come to Toronto and play on Alice's album."

Jack Richardson, great producer who did all the Guess Who stuff and Bob Ezrin, they've done so many big albums… when you walked into Nimbus 9 there was so much gold and platinum you had to have sunglasses on just to walk in there with the secretaries. Every wall was covered like this. Bob might have been looking to get more into that, get Alice some hits. I'm not saying he wanted to make Alice sound like the Guess Who or anything, but maybe the idea was to write some hit records which were cleaner sounding for what radio was looking for, AM radio, hit radio, as opposed to the rock 'n' roll of the original band.

Of course Steve Hunter, our old guitar player, was there; he was using Dick Wagner and Prakash John and of course the great bass player, Tony Levin. Great guys on this session. But Alice was drinking then a little bit. We'd get up in the morning and he'd start saying, "Hey Bee, want a Heineken?" I'm going, "Nah it's too early for me." "Come on, you gotta have a Heineken!" "It's too early! How could you start drinking? It's 11 in the morning!"

I remembered that there was this little kid right then. Alice was staying at his friend's house. A mother or a friend of his had a son and he would bring him to the studio. I was playing pinball with him—and I said to him, "Hey what's your name?" He said it was Keanu. I said, "Hey that's a pretty cool name." He said, "Yeah it's Hawaiian. Keanu Reeves." Playing pinball with Keanu Reeves. He always talks about that. He's in Rolling Stone or something, and said it was one of the greatest things in his life, him as a little kid hanging out with Alice and being at that session. They were great sessions because we were getting things done, you know? We were all professional players; we'd gone in there and did our job and knocked things out.

June 16, 1975. Alice throws a party for "1000 of my closest friends" at the Hollywood Palladium. Alice jumps out of a cake to begin his show, but also on tap are an Uncle Sam on stilts, an organ grinder, a mime troupe, a Dixieland band and an animal act.

June 23, 1975. Alice Cooper is the Pacific Coliseum in Vancouver, where he falls from the stage, breaking some ribs and sustaining a head injury. As Alice recalls it, he tripped over a wire, fell down about 12 feet, on a photographer, broke six ribs on his right side and gashed his head to the point where he needed 28 stitches. He tried to continue but very quickly concussion effects overtook him and Shep whisked him off the stage. He paints a picture of being in the hospital, covered in blood, still in his boots and red jumpsuit, bottle of whiskey in his hand, signing autographs for all the nurses. He says that the next day he woke up in the hotel and could barely move from the pain. Surrounded by flowers, Alice figured he was dead and lying in a funeral parlour. Two days later, an attempt was made to go to *The Return of the Pink Panther* with Sheryl, but as soon as he started laughing, the pain was so excruciating they had to leave.

Mid-1975. Michael Bruce issues his first solo album, *In My Own Way*, on Polydor, who will also, two years later, issue the album by the band Billion Dollar Babies. The album features Bob Dolin and Mick Mashbur, guest musicians on the *Billion Dollar Babies* tour.

Michael Bruce:
You just carry on with your life. I know I did. I was living in Lake Tahoe at the time and I spent a lot of time with my family which was great because my mother passed away not too long after. She was only 60 years old. It was a good time because we got to do a lot of family things together. I'm glad I had the opportunity to spend the time and to be there and I was coming down from Arizona and finally moved down there and married a girl from Phoenix. So it was good in that sense, but musically it was rough. I didn't want to run off and start another band, so at the time I just kept on working on my material and I went in and did an album of my own music, which ended up being *In My Own Way,* which is more the Beatles side, the acoustic side, ballads and whatnot.

Mick Mashbir:
I worked with Mike on *In My Own Way*, from conception to completion. I played lead on every track. We recorded in LA at the Record Plant. It wasn't the most pleasant experience because Mike chose the guitar player and drummer from The Young Rascals to produce it. They changed everything we had been working on for over a year, as far as songs and arrangements, and not for the better in my opinion. The album was conceived as more of a rock album but they turned it into a weak pop record. We could have had Bill Szymczyk—The Who, The Eagles, Bob Seger, Joe Walsh— produce, but Mike Bruce didn't want to wait for him to be available. After that, I was offered the Billion Dollar Babies band gig but I had just relocated to LA and I was not ready to go back east again. I was also a little burned-out on the guys in the band so I just turned it down. I thought the album was nice in its own way and after hearing how it ended I have no regrets.

As far as my performances on *In My Own Way*, I felt my work was just what those songs needed. The Beatles pop feel let me play my George Harrison-style slide work which I quite enjoyed. If you listen to the bonus tracks on the double album release, you will hear the tracks we recorded with Jack Douglas producing. Comparing the demo of "As Rock Rolls On" with the finished product, you will have a perfect example of how the work was watered down to a pop sound. The whole guitar solo section on the demo was left out of the final arrangement by Gene and Dino.

The Slade cover, "So Far So Good", came the closest in energy to what I thought the album should feel like. It was sad to me that other songwriters were brought in to the project. I was disappointed that Mike allowed that to happen, but it was his solo project, not mine, so I respected those choices and supported that with my playing. In the end none of the above really matters, because I don't think that many people have heard that record. I will add that the engineer David Palmer did a nice job.

July 29, 1975. "Department of Youth"/"Some Folks" is issued as the second single from *Welcome to My Nightmare.* The song didn't exactly catch on, reaching only No.67 on the charts. Alice says that the routine for "Some Folks" was the toughest part of the show because it—and he—had to be strictly choreographed. But the silver lining was that from the call for dancers, put out in the *Hollywood Reporter* and eliciting a couple thousand responses (according to Cooper), Alice was to meet one dancer (after three weeks of rehearsal) in particular that would change his life, Sheryl. David Winters, in charge of the dance segments, picked out Sheryl and Robin Blythe as the best, with Alice first starting to feel sparks for Sheryl through the acting they had to do together for "Only Women Bleed" and "Cold Ethyl." A presentation of an engagement ring at the Plaza Hotel in New York was soon to follow.

Alice Cooper:

"Department of Youth" was a big hit in Australia and it was a big sort of anthem. Not my favourite anthem. It had the best opening but it wasn't a great anthem. "Some Folks" was Fred Astaire (laughs). When Fred Astaire actually saw the *Nightmare* show he loved it. So my dancers who were dressed like skeletons in top hat and tails were sitting there whispering, "Fred Astaire's in the audience!" It was just the most incredible thing. Funny thing about people like Mae West, Jack Benny and George Burns, Groucho and Fred Astaire, was that they always saw Alice as vaudeville. They never saw him as being a threat. I think they hit it right on the button. The kids would be scared, and they would be sitting there going, "Cool."

August 14, 1975. There's a fire at Alice's Hollywood Hills home. Elton John, who lived next door, recalls being out and getting told the house next door was on fire also remembering that the house didn't actually burn down, although it was serious enough.

August 31 – September 17, 1975. Alice mounts his first solo tour of Europe, with main support coming from Heavy Metal Kids.

September 3, 1975. Alice takes his *Welcome to My Nightmare* travelling circus to Copenhagen, Denmark. In the audience is a young King Diamond of Mercyful Fate fame.

King Diamond:

That's one show I will never forget. I saw them in '75 before I played in any band. The first band I played with was friends from school, a band called Brainstorm. I didn't sing; I only played guitar. And that was in '76 that we started up there. I had seen Alice in '75, the *Welcome to My Nightmare* show in Copenhagen and that show blew my mind. That was the show where I decided myself that if I ever started a band I would use makeup. Not his style but makeup because the makeup he used never worked on me. It felt unreal; it felt like a person from another world. I was down front and reached up and touched his boot and it seems like he might have disappeared; it was magical to see. From right there I decided I'm going to use makeup. We started with the band called Brainstorm.

So Kiss was not my inspiration for the makeup. That's not where that came from. I definitely liked Kiss with the old, heavy albums. The show was incredible. I didn't see it as being about shock or horror. It was more like a show; he was spitting blood and breathing fire, but it wasn't shock like I was saying about Alice Cooper. With Alice, it was the magical things that went on, on stage. All the magician's tricks that went into it that make you go home and think, "How the hell did they do that?"

I remember from the *Welcome to My Nightmare* show there was this big screen that they were projecting a film on. I remember the song was called "Escape," and they were running after these four dancers they had on stage. But they were being projected up on screen running after him, chasing him. He had broken out of a coffin. Then he suddenly walked out through that screen onto the stage and disappeared on the film. Then they came out after him onto the stage, ran around chasing him, caught him, lifted him up, carried him back onto the screen. Right when they walked through that screen again they were on film.

Those things were so magical. Of course he had the guillotine and he's done the electric chair. There are so many things that are more horror. His wife back then was one of the actresses on stage and there was this song called "Only Women Bleed." It could also have been "I Love the Dead," but there was one where he smacked her around. But then you realised at some point that they had some tricks with the lights and that she had switched places with a life-sized doll and when he picked up the doll and smacked it around, it wasn't until the end that you realised it's a doll. There were some amazing things he did when I saw him. So Cooper is probably my favourite for the moodier, raw horror stuff because it's absolutely mind-blowing how he can put himself in the scene, how he can make it sound like he is there in the middle of what he is singing about. That's what I admire about him.

September 10, 1975. Kiss issue their fourth album, *Alive!*. The explosive double live album comes just in the nick of time with the band and their record label Casablanca rapidly running out of money. Basically, it was Kiss and Alice Cooper who were cheered and jeered as the two big shock rock bands of the '70s, although at this point, it was Kiss in their super nova phase, and Alice having instant huge success but as a solo artist.

Alice Cooper:
When came out, they did something that I considered to be very smart—they didn't try to say that they invented it. They started out by saying, "Look, if one Alice Cooper works, then four oughta work." It wasn't like, "Alice who? Gee, we never saw his show. Oh, he wears makeup, too?" But they did the whole pyro-Kabuki—comic-book characters whereas Alice was much more musical, for one thing. I always thought that Alice was more *Phantom of the Opera*, a little bit more cerebral, a bit scarier, because you never knew quite where Alice was coming from.

Sensationalism always works. I always used to say, if you have a Disneyland on the left side of the road and an airplane wreck on the right, more people would go to the airplane wreck, because there's some sort of morbid fascination in that. The Alice Cooper show was like that. If you had the choice between the Mamas and the Papas on this stage or Alice Cooper on that stage, you would be much more prone to watch this Alice Cooper thing, because you'd be like, "What is going on with these guys?"

September 11, 12, 1975. Alice performs two shows at the Empire, Wembley, London, which is filmed and issued as the *Welcome to My Nightmare* concert film. At the celebrity-filled after-party, Alice is presented with a UK gold disc for *Welcome to My Nightmare*.

October 1975. *Welcome to My Nightmare*'s title track, backed with "Cold Ethyl," is issued as the third and final single from the album. The song was pared down from 5:19 to 2:48 for consumption as a single.

Alice Cooper:
"Welcome to My Nightmare" was just the absolute theme for that whole album. It's a play on "Welcome to My Dreams." "Welcome to My Nightmare" was saying, here it is, we're going there, we're going to go to this nightmare. A nice little play on words. Actually it was pretty jazzy, and that was the Ezrin touch in that. My idea was that in the beginning of that, all the parts were very dark and Doors and Alice combined. But when it

came to the end of that song, it really just took off into a whole horns and jazz and rock kinda funky thing. But it still stays creepy. That's Bob Ezrin.

Johnny "Bee" Badanjek:
I just came in and Bob told me what the song was about. He told me he wanted Johnny Bee and he wanted me to kick ass. If you listen to "Welcome to My Nightmare," as we're going out I'm just wailing on the drums. As it's fading you can still even take your volume and turn it up more and more. Bob was outside standing on it, "Yeah more! More! Go! Go, go, go!" And then he said, "Well, what are your plans?" I said, "Well, I think I'm going to go home and start my own band." "Do you want to go on the road? They're going to do this tour and something after." I probably should have said, "Yes, that would be great."

Dick Wagner:
I did a version of that in my studio that I think is better than the one on that record. But of course that's after the fact. Maybe we got a little stronger in the interpretation after awhile. Did you think it was disco? Maybe a little bit. It was supposed to dance, you know? When they put the single out, they actually speeded the track up a key, to make it even more danceable. I'm pretty sure it came out in the key of F instead of E.

November 18 – 29, 1975. A planned Australian tour is cancelled. Meanwhile, Alice is going through a split with his long-time girlfriend Cindy Lang—both Alice and Cindy had been cheating on each other and they were generally incompatible, Cindy being into drugs and essentially a part of the decadent Andy Warhol set, with friends dying left and right from overdoses. Alice says that by the end of the *Welcome to My Nightmare* tour, he would look at his stage costume and break into tears because he knew he would have to keep drinking whiskey to get in his stage clothes and perform the show. Also by the end of the tour, he was starting to take cocaine as well as a couple of B12 shots before a show.

December 13 – 18, 1975. Alice takes a residency at the Sahara Tahoe, Lake Tahoe, Nevada, and on the first night, Vincent Price in a guest appearance. The huge Alice replica balloon sporadically used in Europe, is once again used for promotion in conjunction with these shows. On opening night, Vincent Price appears to do his monologue from "The Black Widow," one of three songs on the album that are some of Alice's heaviest of the '70s.

Alice Cooper:
"The Black Widow," especially, was just another one of those Bob Ezrin/Alice Cooper/Dick Wagner songs, where Wagner came in with the germ of it, and I came in with an idea. Of course, it's still being part of this guy's nightmare. You know, I always thought spiders were a good part of a nightmare. And then the idea of, wouldn't it be great if Vincent Price were on this? Nah, we could never get him. Sure we could. Let me give him a call. Soon as we called him, we read it to him, and he goes, "Oh, I'll be there tomorrow." It was just great to have that voice doing the narration. To me, it was one of the great high points in my career, Vincent Price and me doing a duet together and him just loving it. He had so much fun doing it. He kept saying, "Can I, can I change words?" I said, "You can do anything you want. You're Vincent Price!" So "The Black Widow" was just a part of this guy's nightmare. I felt that it was just disjointed enough to be a nightmare.

Dick Wagner:
It's funny, but half of "Devil's Food" officially, is Vincent Price's most excellent narration, a preamble to "The Black Widow." "Devil's Food" was just that perfect heavy metal rock song that just felt so good and had all these time signature changes, which was Ezrin. I met Vincent Price. In fact, when we did the show in Reno, Nevada, he came out to the show and did that speech in the middle of *Nightmare.* Just for one night, not every day. We were out there for two weeks. I met him during that time but not in the recording time.

1976

On the treadmill for so many years, Alice's body started talking to him for real in 1976. Married to Sheryl in March, Alice attempted to go back to work but a 30-date tour planned in support of his new album, *Goes to Hell*, is shelved when he is diagnosed with anaemia.

Cooper and his organisation will step aside as Kiss, now at their peak with a new Bob Ezrin-produced album called *Destroyer*, are all the rage, with Aerosmith and Ted Nugent reaping huge returns as well.

But Alice continued to keep skin in the game. *Goes to Hell*, the first of three similar "establishment" albums for Alice, records of regular radio rock, light humour and easy listening even on the rare occasion that the guitars came out, would go gold on the strength of ballad "I Never Cry." In essence, press on the radio, this song on the radio, attendance at events and TV appearances and the release of an autobiography replace touring for the year. The effect is that Alice continues to ingratiate himself into mainstream culture. He is rock star still, but more so, he is a famous person.

March 15, 1976. Kiss issue their well-regarded hit album, *Destroyer*. Much of the credit for the record goes to the production acumen of Bob Ezrin, who applies Alice Cooper-like theatrics to the sonic landscape of the album.

Bob Ezrin:
Alice Cooper was my first production client, and I learned my craft doing Alice Cooper albums in the early '70s. By the time I got to Kiss, I was an experienced producer. So what I brought forward from Alice Cooper was everything. The theatrics and that sort of stuff, that wasn't from Alice Cooper—that's me. Alice Cooper and I aligned on it perfectly, but we were both very theatrical. I shouldn't say both, that whole band were very theatrical people. But I came out of theatre. I was doing theatre and doing television and at the same time playing in clubs and stuff like that. I was doing that before I was doing Alice Cooper. So I'd always seen things in theatrical terms. I was particularly moved by movies and television and so were they. So those were our frames of reference.

March 20, 1976. Alice marries Sheryl Goddard in Acapulco, on a cliff overlooking the bay. As discussed, Sheryl came into his life as one of the dancers in the *Welcome to My Nightmare* show and quickly became inseparable. They are still together today. Acapulco was chosen in part to cede to Shep's request to keep it as quiet as possible. The couple were married by both fathers, given that both were pastors (although because they were out of the country, they were married by a justice of the peace back home as well).

Back in LA, Sheryl would be thrust into a life of celebrity as the two would frequent Le Dome, Alice rubbing shoulders with Frank Sinatra (who called Alice, Coop) as well as Jack Benny, Fred Astaire, George Burns, Steve Martin, Albert Brooks, Steve Allen and Groucho Marx. Alice says he'd come home and Sheryl would be sitting in Groucho's lap, and that Groucho used to chase here around the house, cigar in hand, in jest. These top comedy writers would hang around the house coming up with material and trying it on Alice and Sheryl. Keith Moon became the guest that wouldn't leave. Sheryl would have her own Hollywood connections, using her ballet training to get jobs such as being Goldie Hawn's dance double.

Steve Hunter:
I don't pay much attention to anything when I'm on the road. Because that's usually the safer way out (laughs). Part of me was a little naïve too. But after a while I could see that there was something developing. I've known her since '75. So I've known her as long as Alice has. In fact, I've known Alice longer than he's known Sheryl. We talk about it all the time. But you could see something was developing, and it was so wonderful because they're both really terrific people and Sheryl is such a sweetheart. You could see it sort of blooming. It was wonderful. I really enjoyed watching it happen.

June 1976. Alice publishes an autobiography called *Me, Alice.*

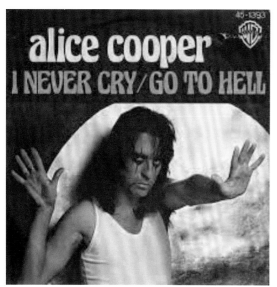

June 15, 1976. "I Never Cry"/"Go to Hell," pairing a rote ballad with one of Alice's heaviest solo-era rockers, is issued as the first single from *Goes to Hell.* Alice has said that "I Never Cry" was his confession of his alcoholism. The single peaks at a lofty No. 12 but only after Shep performs CPR on the dying single, by flying a bunch of radio program directors on an all-expenses paid holoday to the Bahamas.

Alice Cooper:
With radio in the '70s, you would put out a rock song and it was on the radio. When disco happened, the disco plague of the late '70s, they wanted to play Alice Cooper, they wanted to play Kiss, they wanted to play Aerosmith, but they went, "We'll play your ballads." So I had four ballad hits in a row that were top hits, and the rest of the albums were all rock 'n' roll. "I Never Cry" was a hit. The rest of that album was pure heavy rock. "How You Gonna See Me Now," *From the Inside,* and "You and Me" from Lace and Whiskey... I think I'm getting these right. Even "Only Women Bleed" off Nightmare. Four ballad hits in a row, and everybody goes, "Alice is going soft." I'm going, no I'm not; that's just the only songs they'll play from us. Same with Aerosmith, same with Kiss—their biggest hit was "Beth," which was a ballad. If you look at the time period, what was being played? The Bee Gees, Tavares, and all those bands.

Steve Hunter:
The first time I heard Alice singing it, I thought wow, man, this guy can really sing ballads. He caught me off guard. Because "Only Women Bleed," it's more of a big, tough thing. It had a harder edge to it. I just found it incredible that Alice could sing a ballad so well. Because I'd just never really heard him do it. I thought, wow, this is really nice. It was a really cool experience for me to hear him do that.

June 29, 1976. Alice Cooper issues his second solo album, *Goes to Hell.* The album brings back the character of Steven from *Welcome to My Nightmare.* As for the cover art, *Goes to Hell* keeps up Alice's fairly consistent trend of not appearing in makeup on album packaging. A 30-date tour for the album is scotched on doctor's orders when Alice comes down with anaemia. Years of heavy alcohol consumption and even heavier workload and social calendar had taken

their toll. It is said that the "Hell" that Alice was to go to with the planned stage set for the tour was a disco, apropos as disco was the new musical scourge threatening rock's dominance at the time. Interestingly, part of Alice winning Sheryl over involves an incident where the road crew, all good-looking Italian guys, says Alice, invited Sheryl over to Fire Island, where they summered. Alice, sensing a threat, flew straight over on a seaplane to keep tabs on Sheryl, where she taught him how to disco dance, Alice quipping that he was a regular John Travolta, doing The Hustle.

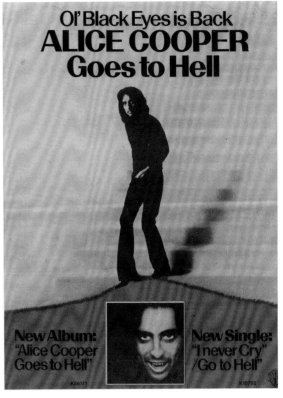

Steve Hunter:
The wonderful thing about working with Bob is that he got to know us so well, especially Dick and I, because we worked with him so much, and we got to know him so well, and then also with Alice, it got to the point where we understood the character of the songs. In other words, when somebody played a song to me, like let's say "Go to Hell" or "Lace and Whiskey," we could already feel where the song was going to go. Even if Bob was just playing it on the piano.

By that time we had done a tour with Alice, we had done an album with him already, and you really absorbed the whole thing. You just become a big part of it. Bob might want to try a different guitar part or something but we knew what direction each song was going to go into just from the first time we heard it. That's because we worked together so much—it became second nature.

August 6, 1976. Alice appears on celebrated late night concert show *The Midnight Special.*

August 17, 1976. Elton John plays Madison Square Garden in New York City, and performing during the encore are Divine, Kiki Dee, Billie Jean King and Alice Cooper.

September 18, 1976. Alice co-hosts the *Rock Music Awards* show with Diana Ross, also turning in performances of "I Never Cry," "Wish You Were Here" and "Go to Hell." Alice follows up three nights later with an appearance on The Tony Orlando & Dawn Rainbow Hour, where he performs "I Never Cry" and "Give the Kid a Break." At this point Alice's name is attached to a number of movie projects, many of which don't pan out.

November 23, 1976. *Goes to Hell* is certified gold, peaking at No.27 on the US charts, slightly better in the UK, at No.23.

Late 1976. Alice and Sheryl, plus Elton John lyricist Bernie Taupin and his girlfriend, vacation in Tahiti while Alice and Bernie write some songs. The collaboration will come to light on Alice's *From the Inside* album, which would take a whole different path from those early musings. Alice cites Bernie as his best friend during the drifting late '70s years in LA, saying he saw Bernie every day, as much as he saw his wife. Although Alice figures he never had an argument with Shep, during this period he didn't see him much, and that when they got together it was more to take care of business, where with Bernie he could get personal. As a member of the loose Hollywood Vampires drinking club, it fell upon Bernie to host everybody once the bars closed at two AM, given that his house was a two-minute walk from The Roxy, on Doheny Drive. By this point, Alice was dinking beer all day, switching to "seven and seven," Canadian whiskey in the evening.

1977

A year of reckoning, 1977 finds Alice pulling out the *Welcome to My Nightmare* costume for a fraught zombie run of the old show in Australia. On booze and psychiatrist-proscribed medication, Alice survives and then remains on the job, issuing another album celebrating his life in the mainstream. *Lace and Whiskey* finds Alice in the guise of gumshoe Maurice Escargot, apropos however of little on the album, which is pretty much *Goes to Hell* part 2.

"You and Me" is "I Never Cry" part 2, and the housewife-like ballad keeps Alice in the game for yet another year. Meanwhile, Alice's ex-band are now called Billion Dollar Babies, issuing a bomb of a record on Polydor called *Battle Axe*.

It's working for him and plus he's always been a social animal, so Alice stays on TV and stays in the public eye any way he can, culminating in a big show at Anaheim Stadium, before quietly heading off to rehab. Even though it doesn't stick, one would have to call Cooper's stint at Cornell a success, given that it lasts nearly a year. Alice's life is saved to fight another day. One might conjecture that without the mental and physical rigour of this weeks-long bout of rehab in the fall of 1977, along with the subsequent ten months of sobriety, his descent into the madness of crack cocaine in the low '80s would have surely killed him.

1977. Alice Cooper guitarist Steve Hunter issues a solo album called *Swept Away*.

Steve Hunter:
We used to make fun of disco on stage (laughs). I don't know if that had an influence on anything other than personal, when we were on stage and we could dig at it a little. But I think there was an undercurrent. I wasn't prepared for the fact that things were changing the way they were. I was caught with my pants down in the '80s. Suddenly the phone stopped ringing. I didn't quite get it, until I started thinking back, and I thought, well, I saw this coming, that rock 'n' roll was changing. Punk came around and did some cool things, and what we were doing was being morphed out of the picture and I didn't realise it.

It literally felt like 1979 I was working and everything was cool, 1980, I was out of work and it just seemed like overnight. I forgot to allow for the fact that music is always evolving. I was just too blind to see that. You've got to stay on top of it. Alice did go with some changes with *Flush the Fashion* and into *DaDa* and *Zipper*.

March 14 – April 4, 1977. Alice Cooper's *Welcome to My Nightmare* tour, the tour that almost killed him, closes out with a dozen very belated dates in Australia and New Zealand. A notable addition is new hit singled "I Never Cry" from *Goes to Hell*. Alice was under the care of Dr. Eugene Landy while in Australia. Landy, deceased in 2006, was notorious for his controversial and controlling methods, as famously applied to Brian Wilson. Dick quickly intervened and informed Shep, who flew out and fired Landy. Although things slightly improved, Alice still could barely function from the drink on this tour. Shep says one time that Fat Frankie from the road crew got relegated to the job—Shep says he rigged it, using an odd/even number game—to be the one to knock Alice out and throw him over his shoulder, put him in the car and get him to the show, where he was slapped back to life and pushed onstage.

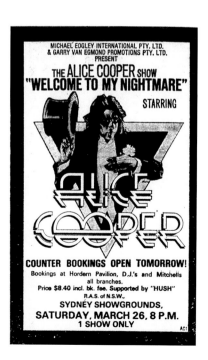

Dick Wagner:
Alice was exhausted. It was a long tour. By the end, when we went over to Australia, he couldn't even do it. I spent two hours every night before show time, convincing him to do the show that night. He was not going to go on stage because he just didn't feel well and thought he would throw up and there was good reason for it. The psychiatrist, Landy, the guy that treated Brian Wilson, was on tour with us, and he was giving Alice pills, and he was drinking and taking pills at the same time. So it was very interesting. Alice didn't feel like he could do it anymore. It was hard. He was tired of being the Alice Cooper personality. He wanted to be himself but didn't know how to. It was a struggle every day. I called Shep to tell him what Landry was doing to Alice and Shep... that was the only thing he ever thanked me for, was me taking care of Alice during that time and getting him up on stage.

Steve Hunter:
For some reason or another, I didn't do Australia, and I don't know why that was. I was really bummed because I'd never been there and I wanted to go. But I had gotten involved in something else and couldn't go. I think it was Bob Kulick who replaced me. I don't even remember what the hell it was I had to do, but I couldn't get out of it. I was under contract to do this, and it was only for a couple weeks. But yeah that tour was very long.

April 5, 1977. "I Never Cry" is certified as a gold single, while *Goes to Hell* reaches gold status as well, as an album.

April 12, 1977. "You and Me," backed with "It's Hot Tonight," is issued as an advance single from *Lace and Whiskey*. It is the third very successful, musically very conservative ballad for Alice, reaching No.9 on the *Billboard* charts, and No.3 in Canada.

Steve Hunter:
Bob Ezrin's creativity just goes beyond. He's got this innate ability to hear the album as a finished product, just from hearing a song on a piano—it's the most amazing thing. That's exactly what he did with *Berlin*. All he got was Lou playing an acoustic guitar and singing the songs and he heard that whole album, as it is, from just those songs. That amazes me, that he has that ability. To hear the finished product before he even gets started.

April 22, 1977. Alice keeps up his regular charming appearances on mainstream talk shows, visiting the *Dinah!* set. Four days later, he's on *The Gong Show* and in June, at the top of the heap with an appearance on *The Tonight Show with Johnny Carson*, where he performs "Lace and Whiskey" in character as Maurice Escargot.

Bob Ezrin:
I don't think he consciously felt that he was moving away from hard rock. I think circumstances for him made him go… we weren't a band anymore. It was a bunch of studio musicians that we pulled together, and we wrote it on the spot and played it. The essence of hard rock is there has to be a group. There weren't very many successful solo hard rock artists that piece together bands on a project by project basis. Those that try to do it make fairly mediocre records.

   The essence of hard rock is that there is a group consciousness, an us against the world mentality. For the most part, they either live together or they are constantly working together and they're flying together, bussing together, doing all that stuff that gave them a commonality, a common conscience. We didn't have that anymore. Heavy metal is a frame of mind and a way of life; it's not just a musical style. You don't just decide to be heavy metal. You have to be in that place.

April 29, 1977. Alice Cooper issues *Lace and Whiskey*, not a concept album, but at least a concept cover, on which he adopts the persona of film noire gumshoe Maurice Escargot. The album would peak at No.33 in the UK but only No.42 back home.

Steve Hunter:

If I had to pick one, I'd probably pick *Goes to Hell* more over Lace and Whiskey, although I think *Lace and Whiskey* had more of a sense humour. *Lace and Whiskey* was meant to be funny. Because *Goes to Hell* has quite a few really good rock songs on it, like the title track. There's just some really cool moments on *Goes to Hell*. I really like "I'm the Coolest." It's sort of about the devil and all that, but the solo I got to play was this really slinky bluesy solo; I like the feel and the tone. That's one of my favourite little bits that I did on that album.

The funny thing is, if I remember correctly, we recorded the basic tracks of those two albums generally at the same time. So when I think about them, they sort of smooshed together. We'd do like a couple weeks on *Goes to Hell*; then we'd do a couple weeks on *Lace and Whiskey*. Not sure why it was done that way, but I just seem to remember that we were doing both of them at the same time.

We knew they were for two different albums. At least I did. But I liked the idea of doing it that way, because it kept that continuity in the core band; the feel of the core band playing stayed pretty much the same. Even when there were some different players. I think Tony Levin and Jim Gordon played on a lot of things. So there was a variety of players but there was a continuity that had developed in doing the two albums like that. I hope I remember that correctly (laughs).

Bob Ezrin:

It probably felt like the same session because he was in my house band. We were working in that room all the time, and Alice came and did those sessions, and I think we probably segued into another project, and we probably didn't stop in between (laughs). So it might've felt to him like one big long recording session, but they were entirely separate.

I haven't thought about those albums in decades. What do I think about them? Not much right now, to tell you the truth (laughs). The challenge each time was trying to come up with something that could be played theatrically on the stage. Alice was primarily a great live act. But I'm not putting down our records—the records were very important—but his stage show was the most important component of his career.

So whenever we were making records, even all the way back to *Love It to Death*, we saw the show as we were making the record. You know, we talked about where you would be on stage and what props he would be using for this and that. We really did think in terms of show, then recorded what we thought the show would be.

So we got to *Lace and Whiskey*, I feel like that's the one record where we didn't have a coherent through-line, from a show point of view. We decided, at that time, we almost consciously said, let's just write a bunch of stuff that we like and then we'll string it all together in a way that makes sense, in terms of live presentation. So there's a little bit more economy for each of the songs, on *Lace and Whiskey*. They were just, "Wow, I was just listening to this, and boy, I'd like to do a song like this." And so we went with that. So yeah, it was less driven by a through-line than anything that had come before it.

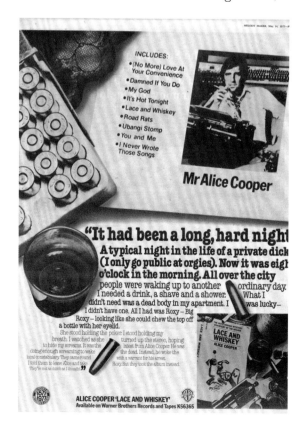

May 2, 1977. Alice Cooper band members Dennis Dunaway, Neal Smith and Michael Bruce form a band called Billion Dollar Babies, along with keyboardist Bob Dolin and guitarist/vocalist Mike Marconi. In 1977 they issue on Polydor, their lone album *Battle Axe*, which, despite a thrilling album cover, sold poorly. Comparisons were instantly cast with the self-titled album from Spiders from Mars issued the previous year and also a commercial flop. The band play a total of four shows.

All right, you guys, you'll like this album or get fitted for cement sneakers.

Neal Smith:
When we took the year off to do solo projects, Michael Bruce was the one who wanted to do the solo project. So that opened up the door for everyone else to do one, including Alice. Alice did *Nightmare*, which was the biggest one of all, I did *Platinum God* and Michael did *In My Own Way*. When I was working on *Platinum God*, I met a guitar player up in Rochester, New York, and his name was Mike Marconi. So he played all the tracks, Dennis played bass on the album and did a great job, so it was like a power trio thing. I always wanted to play with Dennis in a format like like BDS, Bouchard Dunaway Smith.

Mike Marconi was another great guy to work with. We spent a lot of time together, so it ended up when we finally weren't going to get back together as Alice Cooper, and Alice took the name. So we took the name of the biggest album we have ever done, which was *Billion Dollar Babies*. So there was Alice Cooper and there was Billion Dollar Babies. So for our band, we got Mike Marconi, continued, from the solo album, because I worked with him and liked him a lot. Mike Bruce liked him and of course we knew Bob Dolin really well. So that's how Mike Marconi and Bob Dolin got into the band.

Our producer, Lee DeCarlo, I don't know too much about Lee. I know he had done a lot of recording, and I forget the band he used to record. He was all right, but he wasn't as professional. He sure was no Bob Ezrin. It was a little bit disappointing, working with him. I don't think we really got the sound we were trying to get. Because if you go back to some of the original demos we'd done in my studio, I think some of the demos actually have a better feel than the final product for some crazy reason. I don't know why. I think the songs were great on the record. I love the songs, and the concept was great. But I guess in my opinion it just didn't get the big live sound I was hoping for. It sounds a little bit too studio.

I certainly wasn't disappointed in it, but it we had to do one remix because it was just mastered so hot for some crazy reason. Not a remix, but a remaster, and that was fine and it sounded a lot better. But a lot of the momentum had been broken when we had to pull it off the shelves and do the remaster. "Rock Me Slowly" is a great song on that album, and that was one I wanted a really big giant drum sound on. I think it came out very cool, but it was different. There was some experimenting on it but we had a lot of fun with it. I still think it's a great record and the concept was great, but we just couldn't get the album to chart enough to get the concert dates we were looking for.

I especially like the whole idea of the last suite of songs. With *Love It to Death*, what I particularly like is that the finale of the album, for like two or three songs together, it's almost like a mini opera. On *Killer* there were a couple of songs that were tied together. *School's Out*, almost the whole second half of the album is a mini album, but the end really worked together. That's what we were trying to achieve with "Ego Mania," "Battle Axe," "Sudden Death" and "Winner." We were trying to make a little mini opera of the album *Battle Axe*, which was like a futuristic crossing bloodsports with rock.

Dennis Dunaway:
I donated a lot of time to helping Neal with his *Platinum God* album. I retreated to my basement and wrote lots of songs in the spirit of proving that they couldn't take away my love of music. Thank my lucky stars, I had my wife Cindy to pull me through. As far as Alice was concerned, I was disillusioned and heartbroken, and I slid into a dark place that eventually drove my health into critical condition. Allowing that to happen was more my fault than anyone else's, but I just couldn't shake it.

Glen and I were getting together to play music, but he didn't want to have anything to do with the band. He kept saying they're taking it from us. I didn't believe him but he was right. We had a lot of fun nights jamming though.

Once it finally sunk in that Alice wasn't going to honour our agreement, Mike Marconi and Bob Dolin became official Billion Dollar Babies. It was a solid band, and they loved music as much as we did. If the rest of us hadn't been so snagged in dealing with overwhelming legalities concerning the Alice Cooper name, we would have been fine. Despite the blizzard of distractions, we managed to pull off four spectacular theatrical shows. But without the finances to support that massive stage production, in the end, we suffered extreme losses.

That album was written as the new Alice Cooper album and the new theatrical stage production. It had futuristic gladiators who fought to the death with axe-shaped guitars. Alice was to oversee the battle until one gladiator fell, and then he was to encourage the crowd to motion "thumbs down." Then he would use the plexi-glass battle axe with the jagged blade on its headstock to finish off the fallen warrior in a splatter of blood. Then the hydraulic boxing ring would slowly roll back into the dramatically lit fog.

But rehearsals proceeded without Alice. We tried to roll with the punches but as expenses mounted it slid into a matter of survival. Michael was forced to take on the lead vocals. Since we could no longer rely on Warner Bros., who had made fortunes off us, we had to scramble for management and a record deal. The Alice Cooper name, which we had invested our careers in building, was no longer working in our favour. It was working hard against us. So we had to decide if we should sue our best friend.

The overwhelming situation did affect the quality of the recordings. Nevertheless, I was very disappointed in our fans for quietly allowing us to be swept under the rug like that. I was bitter about our artistic vision becoming a money-generating machine.

There are rumours of threats of lawsuits for using the name Billion Dollar Babies. How can we take that part seriously, since the group was named Alice Cooper and he was able to move on with that being his name, and into solo success? There were all kinds of legal threats coming at us from many directions, and some of them made no sense other than to scare us out of suing. Anyway, we didn't have the funds to support such an elaborate show out of pocket. Without Alice and our manager and our record company, it was a financial disaster.

That would have turned out to be a great Alice Cooper group album, even though some of the songs went in a different direction. Because once we got to the point where we knew Alice wasn't going to show up… you can't get somebody to show up if you keep trying to call them and they won't put you through. But once we realised that, then we decided that we would go with some of the other types of songs that Michael Bruce wanted to record, himself, like "Rock Me Slowly," which I think is a great song. But I don't think the Alice Cooper group per se would have done that song. But ironically, we wouldn't have done a song like that, and then Alice put out "Only Women Bleed." I thought that was ironic (laughs).

The Alice Cooper group had already invented the most elaborate shows ever. We were destined to do even greater shows. We had the hair before the '80s hair bands, we had the glam before any of them. We had the punk attitude and we had plenty of creative ammunition for making competitively entertaining videos. But after all that promise it collapsed. For the next while, Cindy had a fashion store that I helped run and then I became the general manager of a mom and pop chain of video stores. I needed the health insurance because I had Crohn's Disease.

Michael Bruce:
Alice was getting into theatrics and I remember him talking to us about the *Nightmare* show and about his dream and the dancing spiders. And at the time, he refers to this as the time where we only wanted to wear blue jeans and that wasn't quite the case. If that was really his understanding of it or if that was merely a convenient thing to say when you're not with the band anymore, fine, but we had done *Battle Axe* which was quite an extensive show with costumes. It was probably as complicated if not more than any of the things he's ever done.

But we being the band and him being the namesake, we just weren't in a position to make it happen like we could with him. But I think it was just a case of him building up excitement and interest in what he was

doing and trying to explain the past. He got it partly right but it certainly wasn't... I think maybe at the time we weren't too interested in doing the stage show because we had just done *Muscle of Love*.

Mike Marconi:
While working on Neal's *Platinum God* album, Michael Bruce was also working on a solo album in Phoenix at that time. I really can't tell you what prompted this whole thing, but I think both Michael and Neal decided to put their side-projects aside and came up with this thought of, "Look, since we're on hiatus here, Neal, you've got some songs that you've written, and Michael you've got some songs you've written, why don't we get together and form a band—Billion Dollar Babies—and see what happens?"

It was at that point, that Michael Bruce got involved in this. It was like a whole change, of dropping those projects. Or culminating them—because I know that "Rock n' Roll Radio," Neal wrote that song and that wound up on the *Battle Axe* album. Michael and I, there's a few songs that we worked on together. God bless Michael, he worked his hiney off; he went for singing lessons religiously. He practiced with the tapes; he worked really, really hard. But sure, we missed that individual out in front. The image of the Alice Cooper band was so powerful, that without the Alice thing there, people just aren't going to buy in to it.

But it was an experience. Bob Dolin—great keyboard player! I don't know what Bobby did afterwards, but Bobby would've been the world's best studio musician, because first of all he's brilliant on the keyboard, he's got perfect pitch, but also he's not the guy that wants to be in front, in the spotlight. He's very happy just to do his thing. He added a lot to the melody parts, playing it on the keyboards with Michael, working out melodies. All of them were self-motivated; there wasn't anybody cracking the whip. But there was a lot of anxiety, because there was a lot of money invested into this, a lot of time, reputations were at stake and they had some big shoes to fill.

May 15, 1977. With old buddies Flo and Eddie as catcher and batter, Alice throws the ceremonial first pitch at an Angels game. It serves as subtle promotion for the big package show coming up the following month.

June 14, 1977. In a case that would grind on for years, Cindy Lang sues, essentially, for half of what Alice Cooper is worth, claiming that there was an understanding that they would marry one day, and that she had been there through his rise to the top. The suit was settled out of court in 1982.

June 19, 1977. Alice performs at Anaheim Stadium, in California, along with The Tubes, Nazareth, Sha Na Na and The Kinks. The show is issued, on video as *Alice Cooper & Friends*. The show kicks off an intensive run of dates in support of the *Lace and Whiskey* album, closing out August 30 at McNichols Sports Arena in Denver. Support comes from the likes of Atlanta Rhythm Section, Trooper, Derringer, Clover, Burton Cummings, Dr. Hook, Mama's Pride and Styx.

August 19, 20, 1977. Alice performs at the Aladdin Theatre in Las Vegas, the recordings of which would be source material for Alice's first live album.

Mid-October 1977. Alice is checked into the Cornell Medical Center in Westchester County, NY to deal with his alcoholism. Shep says that visiting Alice was so emotionally distressing, he'd stop at a bar and get drunk to get up the courage to see him. He says that he wasn't much of a drinker and this is the most he ever got loaded. He'd be with Joe Gannon for these trips, who conversely was a heavy drinker so he'd have no problem doing the same. But part of Shep's distress was guilt for putting Alice there and also the fact that the various wild mental states of the inmates unnerved him.

Alice is there for about six weeks. He had been throwing up blood and hiding it from Sheryl, but she knew and talked to Shep about it, Gordon springing into action, with Alice saying that he didn't put up a fight. As Sheryl puts it as well, Alice's mood had definitely changed as the drinking had started earlier and earlier in the day, with Cooper sitting in front of the TV more and more and withdrawing.

The first three days of withdrawal for Alice were torture, made tolerable only by the drinking of gallons of Coke, designed to manage the sugar imbalance from years of whiskey in his system. He was also put on lithium. He had to be in bed by nine every night, make his bed (pretty much a cot) in the morning, show up on a schedule for meals (when he went in, he hadn't eaten for a week), and worst of all there was only one TV.

A paranoiac female at the place had already smashed up the only stereo, and at one point she made a run at the TV and Alice had to stick out his arm, which she ran into and hit the deck, after which she was given a Thorazine shot and taken away for some alone time. On the other hand the grounds were impressively upscale and there was a small nine-hole golf course. The experience would provide the inspiration for his next album, *From the Inside*. Once Alice was done at the asylum, he flew home on his own and just walked into the house to greet Sheryl, who was pleased to see the same ol' Alice, just a sharper, clearer, more energetic version of him.

Alice Cooper:
I was drinking like a bottle of VO a day, Canadian Club, a day. When I went into the hospital, I couldn't sign my name, my hands were shaking so bad. I had what Ozzy had, tremors. But it was embarrassing. I was in for about two months. The alcohol was as prevalent with me as cancer was. You could look at it and say, this is the biggest alcoholic you've ever met.

It was one of these. I drank beer all day, and okay, nobody gets to be an alcoholic from beer, you know, thought I. Of course, I was. When alcohol becomes medicine, that's when you become an alcoholic. In other words, a beer was great with the boys, jump in the airplane, have a beer, get off the airplane have a beer, go to rehearsal, have a beer, drink beer all day, it's okay. I can take it or leave it. When it was, you've got three interviews today. I go in the room, okay, I better have a beer. Then you have a show that night, okay, I better have a beer. All of a sudden that beer became medicine. Anything I had to do was fortified by beer.

Then, it got even more to the point, okay, at 10 o'clock I'll start drinking whiskey. At nine o'clock I'll start drinking whiskey. Pretty soon it was, I'd wake up in the morning, first thing I'd do is pour myself a glass of whiskey and Coca-Cola. Then I couldn't even drink beer. Then it was nothing but whiskey all day. Being a totally functional alcoholic, it was one of those things where, nobody saw any problem, because I never missed a show, never missed an interview, I'd never stumbled, I never slurred a word. I was just always on my game. I never drank enough where I wasn't totally functional.

October 28, 1977. The Sex Pistols issue their landmark lone album, *Never Mind the Bollocks, Here's the Sex Pistols*. All the punkers were supposed to hate the old guard, but Johnny Rotten has never hid his love of Alice Cooper, indeed, in the Alice Cooper box writing, "*Killer* is the best rock album ever made."

Alice Cooper:
I guess I'm the only person in the world that he doesn't hate. But I've always found that he really understood the punk movement, because he had the sense of humour to go with it. He's very funny. Remember that he's playing a character, too—John Lydon was playing Johnny Rotten, whereas I play a character named Alice Cooper—and they're very funny, scary, theatrical characters.

Mid-November 1977. On a strict two-day leave from the hospital. Alice does some filming for his part as Father Sun in the *Sgt. Pepper's Lonely Hearts Club Band* movie, working sober for the first time.

November 29, 1977. Alice Cooper issues his first live album, *The Alice Cooper Show*, which enters the charts at No.156, rising to a paltry No.131 before working its way off the chart.

Steve Hunter:
We recorded that two nights at the Aladdin and just moved on. It was done the same way we did the Lou Reed live album, *Rock n Roll Animal*. It was two shows and they picked the best of both shows. Just did the show like we always did it, regular crowd, no cameras, just set up the recording mics and there was a truck outside.

December 11, 1977. Alice is out in public again after his rehab stay, attending the *Rock Music Awards*. Shortly thereafter, he tempts fate by throwing a raucous party celebrating his freedom, at which his celebrity guests drink freely while he sips water. Later in the month, Alice attends a wrap-up party for the *Sgt. Pepper* film.

December 16, 1977. The Billion Dollar Babies band play one of the only four shows ever performed in their short career, in Tampa, Florida.

Neal Smith:
It was a great stage show. Cost us a fortune, to produce it, and we only did a short tour. The only footage that I know was ever shot of it was actually, if you look at the album cover, it is like a futuristic warrior with big protective armour on, body armour, and the weapon was a guitar that was turned around and has one big sharp edge on it like an axe, on his guitar. Dennis has an actual instrument in his possession—he still has it—and at the top of the head, where the tuning pegs are, there was also a really sharp wicked-looking blade. That thing could kill you.

So it was held up like an axe, and Mike Marconi and Mike Bruce… actually an official-sized boxing ring came out from under my drum riser. It was very difficult to learn and master but once we had it, it was great. So while we actually played that on stage, the boxing ring would come out from under the drum riser, and then the turnbuckles, pulleys lifted them up until they were actually right in front of the drums. The lighting was on both sides of the ring. There would be like "$2 million, $3 million, $4 million." So the more you would score, the more money you would make. It would go up like a game show. Then at the end, if you kill the person, it was actually a fight to the death, you would win $1 billion. Which, in those days was probably a bit of a reach, but these days (laughs), with what the sports guys are getting paid these days.

Anyway, that was the concept. Then I think right before that, because that was the finale of the show, my drum riser actually went up on a 45° angle. This is before anybody ever did this stuff. My drums and myself were strapped in. This was before Mötley Crüe had the drum riser that floated out over the audience. There were a lot of cool things. Everybody who saw the show thought it had gone farther than anything Alice Cooper had ever done before as a band. That was one of the coolest things technically we had ever done. This was like a natural progression for us, a whole new level.

Mike Marconi:
The actual show itself was pretty spectacular, actually. The whole "Battle Axe" sequence, which we all choreographed ourselves, with Michael and I, we had a whole arena, a ring that would come up, it was very elaborate. But we only did a few shows. It would've been very expensive to tour like that. It just seemed to me that with all that staging that we couldn't be a warm-up act; we had to be the headliner. And without a hit record in the charts, getting a promoter to make you the headliner was difficult. But that live show was very, very exciting. Everyone put their heart and soul into that project, they really did. It was all put together with the lighting and the costuming, and the theatrics was really well done. It deserved more promotion and more hype, certainly.

In the end, we couldn't get a tour, there was a management problem, he got fired, I remember they got rid of him, and in the process of looking for another manager other things were going on between them and Alice. I think there was always this hope that they were going to get back together. The end was just really casual. "Here's the state of affairs. This is happening, this is happening, Polydor isn't going to re-up, the management is crumbling, we can't get any dates, it's not looking good." And realising that, I accepted an offer from some friends of mine to play in Buffalo, and that was with Talas. So that's when I left there and moved to Buffalo.

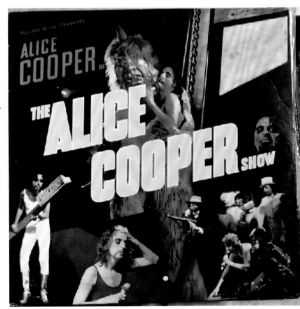

1978

A year of sobriety and then relapse, 1978 finds Alice showing up in two movies, *Sextette* and *Sgt. Pepper's Lonely Hearts Club Band*, touring clean, and then falling hard off the wagon by the fall of '78. So by the time his sobriety album hits the shelves, Alice is drinking and snorting, making the press rounds with his new pal, Bernie Taupin.

From the Inside will be forever regarded as Alice's most "easy listening" album, although somewhat of a trio in that sense with the previous two. Produced by David Foster the album is provisionally saved from total rejection by "How You Gonna See Me Now," Alice's ballads issued as singles getting progressively maudlin and housewifey of melody each and every time. Also, Keith Moon dies.

March 2, 1978. The Ken Hughes-directed musical comedy *Sextette*, starring Mae West, is released to theatres. Alice says that West, 85 at the time, came on to him and every male star on the set, including Ringo Starr, Keith Moon and Timothy Dalton, trying to get them to visit her in her trailer. Nonetheless Alice was proud to chalk up another celluloid experience, doing a musical number with a legend, despite finding the song itself horrible. Meanwhile, Alice and his regular band of Hollywood Vampires welcome to the fold whoever happens to blow through town, Cooper recalling drinking at the time with Bruce Springsteen as well as John Belushi and members of Emerson, Lake and Palmer and The Faces.

Alice Cooper:

There were basically three clubs. In London there was Tramp, in New York there was Max's Kansas City, and in Los Angeles it was the Rainbow. That was just sort of where all the rock guys ended up at night, and everybody would drink. I think the most important thing was that none of us ever talked about music. Because that's all we did. We were all at the top of our game at that point. Either you're recording or you're touring, and so when you got to the Rainbow, that's the last thing you wanted to talk about was music (laughs).

So you'd sit there with Harry Nilsson and John Lennon and Keith Moon. If you could imagine, if John got political, the more you'd drink, how ridiculous it got. Because once you get these arguments started, they just got hysterically funny. I would tell John, "John, I'm not political at all." I said, "I'm here to entertain the country, not to change it."

He was very cynical and funny and that was just him. Then there were nights where all you talked about was other stupid things. But the great thing was, we would sit there, and we would wait to see what Keith Moon was going to wear. One night he would show up and he would be the Queen of England and then he would be Hitler and then he would be a French maid. We had to keep reminding each other, he's the best drummer in the world.

April 27 – September 2, 1978. Alice mounts what is called the *School's Out for Summer Tour.*

June 14, 1978. Alice's PR firm Solters & Roskin summon the press to El Privado, Carlos and Charlies on Sunset Blvd. to find out why Alice has decided to call himself Alice Coper for the next couple of months. At the press conference, Alice pledges $1000 from each of an ensuing bunch of shows to help rebuild the Hollywood sign in Los Angeles. In September, he turns over a cheque for $27,777.

July 21, 1978. *Sgt. Pepper's Lonely Hearts Club Band* hits theatres. Alice is part of the cast, playing Father Sun. The featured stars of the film are Peter Frampton and The Bee Gees. Alice, with Sheryl, attends an advance premier on the 18th at the Palladium in New York.

July 23, 1978. Release date for the two-LP *Sgt. Pepper's Lonely Hearts Club Band* soundtrack album. Although the record technically went multi-platinum it was considered a commercial flop due to massive returns of the shipped records and the huge costs to produce the record. Alice Cooper is featured on only one track, covering "Because" with The Bee Gees.

September 7, 1978. Alice Cooper loses his friend—and fellow Hollywood Vampire—Keith Moon, deceased on this day from the demon drug and drink. Coinciding, Alice was about to fall off the wagon. A year since his so far successful stint in rehab, Alice, Sheryl and Brian Nelson are driving in Alice's Rolls Royce to a rehearsal in Reno, Nevada. At a restaurant in Truckee, just north of Lake Tahoe, Alice has a sip of Sheryl's white wine and as he puts it, by that night at the house at Lake Tahoe he had three bottles of whiskey stashed, and was drinking again, albeit slowly and hiding it.

Alice Cooper:
All the guys that tried to be their image onstage and off stage died. They all died early, if you think of it. Jim Morrison, Jimi Hendrix, Janis Joplin, Keith Moon, look down the list. If you can make it past 27 you might have a chance of living, but every single person that I knew that was living their life to the fullest to the point where they were like, I can't just be Janis Joplin onstage, I gotta be Janis Joplin all the time, it's going to kill you.

    I saw that and they were like my big brothers and sisters, and I watched them die off and went, okay, I've got a character that's even more severe than these characters. How am I going to deal with this? I'm going to have to draw a line where Alice lives here and when I get done with the show, I walk away from him and I can be myself now and I don't have to be this monster—but I can't wait to play him again the next night.

October 3, 1978. "How You Gonna See Me Now," backed with "No Tricks," is issued as the first single from *From the Inside*. The song reaches No.12 on the UK charts and although it was a success commercial and was played regularly on the ensuing tour, it hasn't been part of Alice's set list since 1980. The song was written for Sheryl, who at the end of 1977 had to deal with an Alice she'd never known, a sober Alice, upon his release from rehab.

October 16, 1978. Elton John issues his 12th album, *A Single Man*. Notably absent is lyricist Bernie Taupin who has struck up a working relationship with Alice Cooper. To come up with the songs that would fill out the forthcoming *From the Inside*, Bernie would go to Alice's mansion in Benedict Canyon and around the pool, the pool table and the TV; the two would discuss the staff and the inmates Alice met at Cornell. Bernie would write a character sketch in lyric form and Alice would write one and they'd cut-and-paste these into songs, sometimes with Dick Wagner in attendance. Bernie recalls that it would get quite competitive and even heated, given that both he and Alice normally didn't really collaborate when it came to lyrics.

November 28, 1978. Alice Cooper issues his fourth solo album, the David Foster-produced *From the Inside*, which Alice frames as a confessional. The irony of the situation is that when the album comes out,

not only is Alice drinking again but his cocaine use is ramping up, to match that of all of his friends in the midst of what he calls a cocaine blizzard, which blows through Hollywood strong through the rest of the '70s and much of the early '80s. Soon Alice, and, as he says, everybody he knew except Shep, was smoking it, because at the beginning it was felt that cocaine wasn't addictive if you smoked it. In a return to the novelty packaging of the original band years, *From the Inside* is presented as a special die-cut gatefold. All the lyrics on the record find Alice in collaboration with Bernie Taupin. Alice is pleased to get David Foster to produce, both because he was in great demand and as a result hard to get, and because he brought with him some of the top session guys from in and around LA, a class of players with which Alice was previously not acquainted.

Alice Cooper:

From the Inside was ten songs making up a concept album of all the characters I met in the insane asylum, when I went in for my alcohol, in New York; they put me in this really sort of rich sanatorium. I ended up realising I was the only one in there for alcohol. Everybody else was in there because they were so bloody rich and they had committed some crime and got committed here instead of going to jail. So all those characters were real characters. I just named them something else.

So I went in, I was in there because of alcohol, and everybody else was in there because they were criminally insane (laughs). So when I came out, I talked to Bernie Taupin, who was my best friend. I said to Bernie, "We're both lyricists; let's play a ping-pong match. You write a line and I'll write a line." So, that's what we did with that album. David Foster put it into musical form, and it ended up with a lot of people saying it's our best album, as far as just music goes.

Dick Wagner:

Goes to Hell album I like very much, *Lace and Whiskey* was okay, pretty good, but *From the Inside,* I love. Even though they're not all mine, I think there are some great songs on there. I'm partial to my songs. I sound a little egotistical but I like the stuff that I did with Alice, especially "Inmates." David Foster did a great job of producing as well.

1979

A curious year for Alice. Now on a quick descent, Alice mounts the notorious *Mad House Rock tour* (*Nightmare* x ten), but then burns it out before the spring is through. Illogically, he's touring an album that talks about what not to do, but then he's a wild man again. Alice stays on the airwaves, through *The Midnight Special* and *The Strange Case of Alice Cooper*, but there are grumbles among the real fans that the records are not backing up the swag, that he's gone soft and mainstream, and that even as heavy as *Welcome to My Nightmare* was, in retrospect now with four solo albums to look at, even that one's somehow missing the authenticity of the original band albums.

February 6, 1979. Alice appears on *The Midnight Special*, with more appearances to follow in the coming weeks. Bernie and Alice conduct a promotional tour of radio stations, mostly by helicopter.

February 11 – April 29, 1979. Alice conducts the *Mad House Rock tour*, in support of the *From the Inside* album. Opening on most shows is The Babys. Meanwhile, Neal Smith and his band Flying Tigers are playing small gigs around his home base in Connecticut.

Dennis Dunaway:
The Flying Tigers were a rowdy bar band featuring Neal and I and two singing guitar players from Chicago named Paul Roy and Dave Stackman. We did a demo with Jerry Wexler, and Ron Delsner considered
managing us, but we never recorded an album. We had quite a few rocking pop songs and a solid local following. That band has lots of stories about bar fights. Cindy even got into one. One night in the Bowery, a gunfight erupted. Ah, what we go through just to play some music.

May 1979. Alice cancels an additional 11 *Mad House Rock* dates claiming excitement at the writing process for his next album.

July 27, 1979. Alice loses some of his gold record awards when his dad's Indian arts store in Scottsdale, AZ is firebombed—they were in storage at the back of the store. Also destroyed was $200,000 in Indian art.

August 3, 1979. Stan Lee and Marvel Comics issue a comic book based on the *From the Inside* story line, minus the alcoholism.

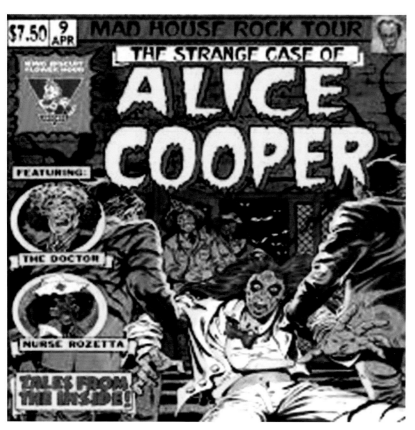

August 10, 1979. Concert film *The Strange Case of Alice Cooper* airs on Showtime.

Dick Wagner:
I love Alice Cooper. I think he's a great guy; funny, smart. He and I were really good friends, when we worked together. We really don't talk to each other very much anymore. A brilliant lyricist, very good sensibilities about what he wanted out of this business, what he wanted to become. This guy had balls. He went out there and he was really different at a time when people really didn't know anything about that stuff. Got chased out of town by cowboys, got beaten up. He went through the ringer but he stuck with it.

In the end, he was right because he was a tremendous influence on the entire business, really. He ushered in the age of glitter rock and everything else, and he definitely brought in theatrics to the forefront of the rock 'n' roll business. I love Alice Cooper. I think he's a great guy and he's got a great family, and I love all of them too. I wish we could spend more time with each other and see each other and do more work together. Because he and I writing together is magic. We always come up with great stuff.

1980s

As we enter the 1980s, I'm dispensing with the year by year intros and going blanket for the decades, given the relative historical importance of all that went on in the '70s, versus the ensuing years, as well as in deference to the importance of the original band.

Okay, so Alice is in rough shape for the first few years of the decade, descending into a manic state of booze and cocaine, progressing from snorting to freebasing. He stays busy however, issuing four albums that form a suite.

Experiencing these records at the time, I always looked at *Flush the Fashion* as the successful and worthy stand-alone (and apart) from the quirky, underground and summarily ignored *Special Forces*, *Zipper Catches Skin* and *DaDa*. But now, given what we know of Alice's mental state, one could also group the first three as a set, leaving *DaDa* apart 'cos at that point Alice was only boozing. The distinction is small however. All four records find Alice, if we may generalise, trying to sound modern and new wave, not post-punk in the English sense but all over various new wave ideas from his own country.

So even when songs seem to be fairly heavy and guitar-centric, they are recorded spare and jerky, as if Alice was trying to undermine any tendency toward bombast. Subsequently, they are all little and modest and deferential albums. Although, like I say, *Flush the Fashion* was a mild success. Some of that surely has to do with its strong Roy Thomas Baker production as well as a detectable enthusiasm for the Bowie-level direction change. Plus both "Clones (We're All)" and updated '60s garage cover "Talk Talk" actually got quite a bit of radio play at the time, at least here in Canada, where the record managed gold.

Touring is sporadic and Alice withers to a wren, followed by a dead reckoning. He is hospitalised at home in Phoenix near death, which promulgates a slow recovery of both his flesh and his marriage, phoenix-like. His creativity never faltered during the underground record years, but the rest of him almost gave out. Alice didn't suffer for his art (that's not his personality), but he suffered and kept making art.

After two years in the lab, Alice emerges in 1986 as the "give the people what they want" version of himself, a muscled-up caricature, mirrored by his enabling guitarist Kane Roberts. *Constrictor* and *Raise Your Fist and Yell* are heavy but primary-coloured records thrown on the hair metal fire and Alice is participating in the world again, although wholly without irony. Before the decade is out, he would happily sell right out, he and his LA boardroom issuing *Trash*. The album sells platinum, achieved the old Alice way, off the back of one hit single. "Poison" could have been phoned in by Aerosmith or Bon Jovi or Heart but fortunately for Alice, it's cooked up for him. "Bed of Nails" and "House of Fire" don't do as much damage, but it is of no matter, one is all it takes.

Alice leaves the decade successfully taking back what's his. Along with the likes of Kiss, Aerosmith, Heart and Cheap Trick, Alice Cooper built the foundation for the insane rush of commercial success that was to shower down upon the hair metal bands of the Sunset Strip. Smartly, Alice and Shep made sure they got their vig, when a number of bands kinda missed it. UFO, Black Sabbath, Blue Öyster Cult, Judas Priest, Scorpions, AC/DC… most of these bands experienced some of their greatest success in the '80s, but this was mostly early to mid. By the late '80s, they were floundering.

Alice, on the other hand, when metal was initially monster, first with the New Wave of British Heavy Metal and then the first flush of bands from California, essentially tripped and let the cocaine write the records. Then once back, it was a slow burn back to the top. *Constrictor* and *Raise Your Fist and Yell* remain uncertified in the US, but *Trash*, as noted above, is proudly platinum, Alice's first of that colour since *Welcome to My Nightmare*. As career arcs go, against the wheel of rock's trending, Alice's renewed success would be short-lived as he would be kicked to the curb with the rest of them once folks woke to the ridiculousness and materialism and corporatism of song doctors, insane video budgets and records produced with what they called "cocaine ears," no expense spared, but at the expense of relevance.

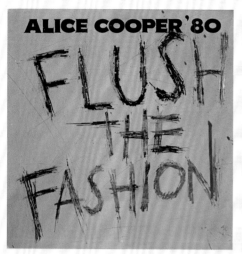

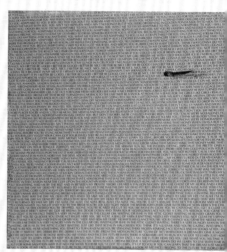

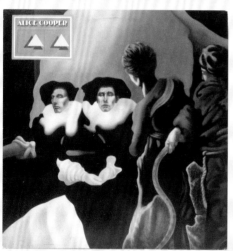
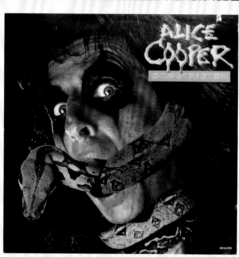

1980

February – March 1980. Alice and band work at Cherokee Studios on tracks for what will be Alice's first record of the '80s.

April 29, 1980. "Clones"/"Model Citizen" is issued as a single from Alice's forthcoming album, *Flush the Fashion*. The angular Cars-like rocker reaches No.40 on the singles chart.

Alice Cooper:

"Clones" was sort of like us… yeah, okay, we'll use a synthesizer even though I'm kicking and dragging my feet into that. But for that song it was perfect because it was about sci-fi. It was about a guy who had twelve of himself. I'm number three, I'm number five, number six. Number six is having a problem relating to his clone status. It was very mechanical and sort of a Gary Numan-type of thing.

May 6, 1980. Alice Cooper issues his fifth solo album, the Roy Thomas Baker-produced *Flush the Fashion*. Most of the record is penned by Alice along with Elton John guitarist Davey Johnstone and session keyboardist Fred Mandel. The album would reach No.44 on the Billboard charts.

Alice Cooper:

We had already done seven albums with Bob Ezrin and they were all gold and platinum albums. But he was working with Pink Floyd then, so Roy Thomas Baker stepped in and he produced that album, *Flush the Fashion*, which had a couple of big hits on it. But it was different; it moved in a different way. Now The Cars and The Knack and these guys were out. There were a few songs that you'd hear on the radio that made you go, oh wow, somebody's got it. "My Sharona," people make fun of that song, but that's one of the greatest hooks I've heard in my life. It's impossible not to like. First time I heard that I went, that's great, that's really good. First time I heard "Turning Japanese," I went man, that's great. There were certain bands that were starting to crank out good records.

You're still in this business going, okay, the sound is now moving that way. I'm not going to give up Alice Cooper but we can make that creepy too. We can turn around and make this sound just as creepy as what I was doing. We were still a guitar rock band. By that time I wasn't with the original band. I was on my own, and so I really could stretch in every direction, which was neat. So I thought okay, I'll go in this direction this time. Next album I might go in a totally different direction. But the rest of that album was all guitar rock. But every album was a different part of your life, so *Flush the Fashion* represents that '70s into '80s thing.

June 4 – August 19, 1980. Alice conducts his *Flush the Fashion* tour, the third album cycle in a row that would not include European dates. Main support comes from post-Motors band Bram Tchaikovsky, like Alice now, a traditional rock band with a new wave edge.

June 13, 1980. Rock 'n' roll movie *Roadie*, starring Meat Loaf, hits theatres. Alice and his band are in it (or more accurately, a band that is half Alice, half Utopia).

July 13, 1980. Alice Cooper jumps onto one date of the notorious Black 'n' Blue tour, a co-headlining campaign featuring Black Sabbath and Blue Öyster Cult. Also on the bill was Alice's support act, Bram Tchaikovsky as well as regular Black 'n' Blue supports, Riot and Shakin' Street. Because of the 101-degree heat on the day, half the forecasted crowd of 30,000 stays home.

August 19, 1980. Scheduled to play the CNE in Toronto, Alice cancelled at the last minute due to illness. A riot ensued causing $175,000 in damage.

Mike Pinera:

I'll never forget, one of the big shows that we did that summer was at that stadium in Toronto, and Alice was drawing a much tougher crowd now. They weren't quite so wannabes. Teenagers with black mascara and stuff done to look like Alice. The people that came to the stadium that night reminded me of soccer fans. There was no fooling around—they were there to rock.

Alice got really sick and he couldn't go on, so he asked me to make the announcement to the audience. I said, "Why me, man?" He says, "Because I know the promoter's just going to go out there and say it really cold and he's going to be matter of fact and he's going to piss the people off and there could be a riot, but I know you can smooth it out." I went, oh, okay.

So the show was already running thirty minutes late while the doctor was trying to figure out whether Alice could play or not. He says, "No, you're burning up with fever; you can't go out there." So the crowd was already on edge and then I come up and I grab the mic and go, "Hey, it's Mike Pinera from the Alice Cooper band." They went, yeah, big roar. I said, "Listen, I'm really sorry but Alice is not going to be able to play tonight. He's not feeling well. The doctor just said that he couldn't come on. But we just want to tell you we'd love to make up the date and we're going to talk to the promoter here and find out the soonest we can do it and we'll come back and we'll rock it out."

They were neutral, a little disappointed. But then the promoter takes the mic and says, "No, there's not going to be any makeup date. You had your chance, you didn't play and you lost it, and the people are not getting any refunds. That's it. This is the end of the night." I went oh my god. There was a big riot. They set police cars on fire, the whole place was like crazy. It was called the Alice Cooper Riot. When we got back to our rooms about a half-hour after I made that announcement, every channel was covering it and showing the sports stadium burning and police cars upside down. It was a full-scale riot. Then they showed some footage of me making the announcement. It was a wild time.

December 8, 1980. John Lennon is gunned down dead by a deranged fan in New York City. Alice loses a second friend, after Keith Moon who died in 1978, of his coterie of drinking and snorting pals nicknamed the Hollywood Vampires. Bernie Taupin, who is introduced to freebasing by Alice in Alice's rec room at the house, quickly pulls back and decides that's not for him. Fighting his own battles with coke and drink, Bernie withdraws from Alice for the sake of his own health, something for which he bore enormous guilt.

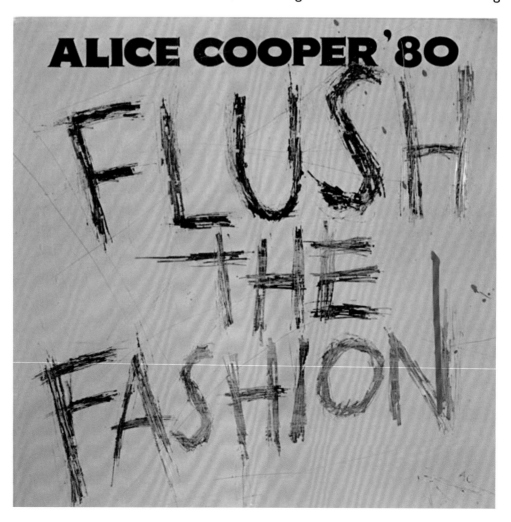

1981

May 20, 1981. Calico Cooper is born. Devoted to his daughter, Alice might just finally have found a reason to clean up for good. Long beyond the eventual full recovery, Calico will join the cast of the never-ending Alice Cooper revue. Also on the personal side of things, in 1981, Neal goes through a divorce.

June 20 – November 28, 1981. Alice Cooper conducts dates in support of the forthcoming *Special Forces*. Delays in getting the record finished result in only two songs being played from it at the outset, "Who Do You Think We Are" and Love cover "Seven and Seven Is." Support comes from the likes of Phil Seymour, Spider, The Rockets, The Joe Perry Project and Joan Jett & The Blackhearts.

July 1, 1981. "Who Do You Think We Are"/"You Want It You Got It" is issued as a non-picture sleeve single, and it fails to chart. France, however issued the song, as a picture sleeve in both 7" and 12" formats.

September 1981. Alice releases the *Special Forces* album. Alice's writing is influenced by the fact that he was reading a lot of magazines like *Soldier of Fortune*, resulting in a record that evoked the horror of what is everyday reality in other parts of the world. Musically, Alice wanted songs that sounded halting and militant-like, choppy, with lots of sixteenth notes.

Mike Pinera:
So Alice calls me and says, "You remember all those good times we used to have back then? You used to give me sandwiches, you used to share your food with me." I said yeah. He said, "Well I want you to form a band for me, a new band, an Alice Cooper band, and get whatever guys you want and let's go out and make some music and let's do some touring. So I joined Alice Cooper and did the *Special Forces* album and *Zipper Catches Skin* and did world tours.

Alice was a recovering alcoholic and he was really doing his best. He wouldn't touch a drop of whiskey or anything any more, and so he wanted guys around him who were of the same mindset. So I formed a band with guys that didn't necessarily have to get drunk and take a bottle of Jack Daniels onstage and stuff, so we had a good band.

But the problem was this. Alice would always collaborate with people in his band, and the way he collaborated with us is he would come to me and say, "Look, Mike, let me tell you what I like. I like what KROQ is playing in LA, which is like a punk alternative sound." He said, "You know, when everybody was playing normal, I was playing weird. Now, a lot of people are playing weird so I gotta get weirder." So I said, "Oh, okay, so you don't want any predictable stuff?" He says, "No, give me some outside stuff, man, really out there." We would sit there and put some songs together. He'd come over to my house and we'd write. He'd go, "No, that's too normal. Get further out, more dissonance, more this…" And one day he said, "Mike, give me terrible or give me great, but don't give me mediocre." I said, "You got it Alice."

So one of the first songs I wrote for him on the Special Forces album was called "Vicious Rumors," and it's pretty far-out. It's dark, it's got a lot of drive to it, we got the right guitar sounds this time, and we recorded some of it in London at Air Studios with Elvis Costello sitting in and watching us and talking with us and stuff. And we had a good album there, but the problem was Warner Bros. didn't like it at all. They said, "This is too weird; there's nothing commercial here. We're not even going to promote it."

Alice didn't care; he had just bought the Bank of Beverly Hills. He also owned a couple of big restaurants and night clubs on Sunset Blvd., so Alice didn't really care. He said, "Man, I don't care if they promote it or not, we're going to go out there and we're going to play this music. This is great stuff." Then he brought in Arthur Lee, and Love. He liked them a lot because they were psychedelic and stuff and he brought one of their tunes in.

Richie Polodor produced *Special Forces*. He's a great guy, he did Iron Butterfly and he did The Blues Image, and somehow he got his way in there and I just think that Richie was spiralling out. Ritchie's real strength was, with Three Dog Night and Steppenwolf, he would go out and find them songs by hit writers; "Jeremiah was a bullfrog," "Joy to the World" and stuff like that. None of that was written by the band. That all came from outside writers like Randy Newman and people who had hit after hit after hit.

Polodor was great at that. He could match the song to the band. But as far as his chops in the studio, he was more of a lighter approach, like The Turtles or the Grass Roots and Three Dog Night. Steppenwolf he got away with, I think, because they were just so heavy that there was no way of stopping them.

September 12, 1981. *Billboard* nominates Shep Gordon for a Manager of the Year award. For the previous five or six years, Shep had dedicated a lot of hours to acts other than Alice Cooper, including Teddy Pendergrass, Blondie and Rick James, as well as working with his film company, having done *The Duellists* in 1977.

October 10, 1981. *Special Forces* is at No.125 on the *Billboard* charts, its highest placement. In the UK the album does slightly better, reaching No.95.

November 7, 1981. Ozzy Osbourne issues his second solo album, *Diary of a Madman*. Arguably, Ozzy is at his shock rock peak, through this record, the subsequent tour and through the subsequent *Bark at the Moon* album and touring cycle. With Alice off the radar, Ozzy is unmistakably this year's model, selling tons of records and garnering lurid headlines.

Gavin Baddeley:
There are a lot of parallels between the careers of Ozzy Osbourne and Alice Cooper. The most obvious one is two vocal performers with rather unusual vocal styles who become very popular and successful, concentrating on material that focuses on the macabre, and sink vast buckets of alcohol in the process. With Ozzy Osbourne, from the start, the idea of this being a persona, the wild man stuff, that has a lot to do with the alcohol.

A lot to do with the pressures of touring. For an outsider you think, oh, the pressures of touring, I'd do that job in a day. It looks great. But it gets tiring over a period of years. There's a lot of stress, and people tend to do stupid things just to pass the time, especially if you stir in a lot of intoxicants and so forth.

Ozzy Osbourne, although he's not become this evangelising Christian in the same way Alice Cooper has, he's repeatedly said that he doesn't regard his music as being occultist and that the people who misunderstood Black Sabbath, misunderstood the Ozzy solo material as well. It's a character. He's gone as far as saying people can go and watch *The Omen* and *The Exorcist*, and they know they're actors. Once the camera's off, they'll go down and have a cup of coffee and whatever else. They're not really the Devil's son or whatever.

1982

January 14, 1982. The performance and conceptual 17-song, 46-minute *Alice Cooper a Paris* (*a.k.a. Alice in Paris*) is aired in France. Filming locations included a butchery and an auto scrapyard.

Mike Pinera:
If you want to see something really, really original, there's a DVD called *Alice Cooper in Paris* that we did together with *Special Forces*. We got to produce a one-hour special for French television. Alice and I got to dream up the locations and what we were going to do, and we just got further and further out. We were underground in abandoned subway stations. But the peak of it has to be, Martin, when Alice says to me, "I got it. Here's what we're going to shoot tonight. We're going to Notre Dame, we're going to get on the steps of the cathedral, you guys are going to dress up as nuns, you're going to put the black makeup under your eyes. I'm coming out with a sword, it's a full moon out there, we're going to have smoke machines going, and you guys dressed as nuns weaving from left to right in sync together, and I will sing 'You can go to Hell.'" I said, "Alice, you're barking up a wrong tree there, bro." He says, "No, I'm saying exactly what the priest says at mass; that if you're bad you can go to Hell." I said, "No, I understand, I know where you're coming from. But people seeing us out there going that, they're going to think we're mocking or something." As it turns out Notre Dame would not let us do it there so we went to another cathedral that night called (Momant?), another big cathedral, almost as big as Notre Dame, and we were there on the stairs with a full moon behind us, smoke machines, him hitting us with a whip and us dressed as nuns. That's one of the songs on the DVD for *Alice Cooper in Paris*.

January 26 – February 27, 1982. Long neglected, Europe gets Alice Cooper and his band for quite a few dates, although all of them are either in France or the UK. These would mark Alice's last shows until late 1986. The last date of the French leg is February 9th, with February 11th being a show in Brighton, England, supported by Big Country, who were quickly tossed off the UK leg to be replaced by Shaphire.

Early 1982. Blue Öyster Cult guitarist and vocalist Buck Dharma issues a solo album called *Flat Out*.

Neal Smith:
Donald "Buck Dharma" Roeser was a very good friend of ours. We played some shows in the 70s where BÖC had opened for us. We got along pretty well. So when Buck did the solo album he had asked Dennis and I to play on some of the tracks for him. I co-wrote the song "Born To Rock" and it became the single from the album, and the video that was on MTV. Dennis and I played on that song as well and I also played on "That Summer Night." The next year I co-wrote a song with Joe Bouchard for the *Revolution by Night* album called "Shadows Of California." Buck and his family are very good friends of ours. Even though they don't live in the state anymore we still keep in touch.

April 1982. Alice quickly puts together a thank you for the British fans, prompted by how much he enjoyed the crowds in the UK on the *Special Forces* tour. *For Britain Only* contains three tracks live from the Glasgow date on February 19th, plus the exclusive studio track "For Britain Only," recorded at AIR Studios and produced and mixed by Steve Churchyard. The item was issued as a picture sleeve single in both 7" and 12" formats.

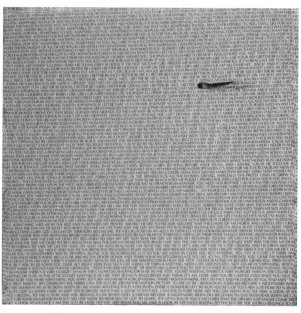

August 25, 1982. Alice Cooper issues *Zipper Catches Skin*, his 14th studio album, including the band albums in that count. What Alice calls a minimalist sound for the band continues. Although he rues perhaps the new wave direction and the lack of melody, he stands by his lyrics penned during the cocaine years, impressed still by their cleverness and the sheer volume of material he had to pick from.

Dick Wagner had been called back after a few years away and he was horrified at how skinny and old Alice looked, recalling him crafting pipes in his basement totally under the spell of crack. Dick recalls many trips writing for the record with Alice in the back of his Rolls Royce, on the way to the studio, the two of the both smoking crack, the long descent to this point beginning all the way back at the initial writing sessions for *From the Inside*, which were fuelled by regular cocaine use but not crack. Once at the studio, Alice performed his vocals behind a black curtain, beside a stool that had his crack and his Bunsen burner on it. Between takes, the band would be invited behind the curtain for regular hits.

Alice Cooper:
"I'm Alive (That Was the Day My Dead Pet Returned to Save My Life"—that whole album, I took a *Weekly World News* and I just found headlines. Like every single song title was from a headline from the *Weekly World News* and the funny thing about those is that once you create the headline, there's a rhythm to it. It actually created the song. It creates the rhythm of the song and whatever it was, I was stuck with that (laughs).

Mike Pinera:
Between *Special Forces* and *Zipper Catches Skin*, well, the first one still had a bit of the flow of the albums that had been out shortly before, like *Welcome to My Nightmare* and *From the Inside*. We had some tunes that were still one foot in there. But we were definitely on our way out. So when it got a year later, when we went to do *Zipper Catches Skin*, by that time Alice wanted the throttle full-bore. He said, "Man, I want to be the weirdest. I want everyone to say Cooper has just completely lost his mind, and he's playing the most bizarre stuff we've ever heard. That's the stuff I want you to bring me."

So we started writing even further out. I think Alice, because he had been off alcohol for a year or so, a couple years, was really white-knuckling it. Some guys, you see them go to meetings and you see them hang out with other musicians and they talk and share, but Alice was a loner. He would stay in that tour bus and we'd drive all night and he'd go in his hotel room. When his kids would come and his wife would come he was a great father, always playing catch with his kids and taking them on tours of the cities we were in. He was a great guy.

But if I could have advised him, I would have said you should maybe go to some meetings or something and share your feelings because you're sitting here trying to do this on your own, and from what I understand that doesn't work. So that was the problem, I think. He had a lot of rage going on. But he wanted it weird and so we made it weird. So *Special Forces* and *Zipper Catches Skin* are something that I believe any good Alice Cooper fan probably didn't even know those albums were out because they didn't get any push.

But Alice was very private. He would go into the back of the tour bus and lock the door, and he'd say, "Look, I'm going to sleep" or "I'm going to write" or whatever. Nobody would bother him. When we'd get to our next destination and get out of the tour bus and go right to his room, we wouldn't see him until shortly just a few minutes before the set.

As for drugs, there was always all kinds of rumours that he was possessed by a spirit called Alice Cooper. I can only tell you what I saw with my own eyes, and what I saw was a great guy who really took a lot of care and a lot of concern for his music and always had concern for his friends and for his fans. People would stop him in the middle of the street, he'd stop and sign an autograph and stuff.

John Nitzinger (touring guitarist):
Man, we were going nowhere. This is one of those deals where I try to think, should I tell the truth or should I tell you what you want to hear. It's like writing a book and then going to the people and have them pay me not to put them in the book. It's that deal. It was a bad scene. I've been all over the world and I've been around and done some things, but I ain't never seen nothing like that.

It was... I was going to try to raise the Titanic and write some songs for Alice, because that genre, I can fit right in there and get crazy. I love it. love the makeup, and Alice even came to me and told me to cut down on the makeup, because I was upstaging him (laughs). But the whole tour revolved around cocaine. That is not my deal. Well, now it's not! I've been clean and sober for ten years now, but that's what that tour was all about, to amazing extremes. You wouldn't believe some of the stuff that went down because of that.

As for what that record is, when you're in that

condition—and we all were—you can't tell what is what. You can't say that you did anything... because you can't, you're under the beast like that and that dictates everything. So it was just ridiculous, the whole process. I would write songs and he would take the words off and put his on and say that other people got writers royalties and stuff when they didn't write anything. It was just totally fogged-out. I can't even begin to say what it was, but I suppose that is Alice (laughs). Then. He's straightened up now.

September 18, 1982. Twisted Sister issue their debut album, *Under the Blade*. Visually, the band are pioneering a sort of garish femininity last seen with Alice Cooper and now somewhat practiced by Mötley Crüe on the other coast. Dee Snider says as well, that he transitioned vocally from a Robert Plant-type singer to something like a new version of Alice, with the sneer and the spoken work style, somewhat prompted by the change in his voice, but also inspired by his love for Alice.

Jay Jay French:
Twisted Sister started out as a glam/Bowie band, and then me taking the lead vocals, we became a Mott the Hoople/Lou Reed-type band. When Dee joined, he was very much influenced by Alice Cooper and Black Sabbath. So we became a glam band again, but not a pretty glam band like the original version. We became a more theatrical band, not gross—that's probably not the best way to put it—but theatrical. The original band was a real attempt at female impersonation, but when Dee came in, it was a very theatrical glam look.

Alice Cooper:
Twisted Sister were nothing but fun. These guys went up there and it's like, oh who are these guys? Half way through the thing I'm smiling and going, this is really fun. They're not the Beatles, they're not the Rolling Stones, but what they're playing is simple, and this guy up here, Dee Snider, is really good at what he does, because he's making me believe and eat all of this. I went great, it's a new show biz.

Late 1982. Alice's relapse into alcohol and regular cocaine and then "base" has him holed up in his Beverly Hills mansion with an unpaid-for baseball-sized rock of crack cocaine and a gun, the outside world kept out by Sheryl's dresses put up around the windows. Sheryl goes to live with her parents, Shep won't talk to him and even Bernie Taupin had retreated from Alice's paranoid world. After a three-day binge and an episode in front of the mirror where he says he swore that his eyes were bleeding, he flushes the rock down the toilet. With the Myers's 151 proof handy that he would use with a Q-Tip to light his pipe, Alice falls into a deep sleep, broken by slugs of the rum and more sleep. After a few days of this, Alice says that was it for the crack, although now he was heavily back on booze.

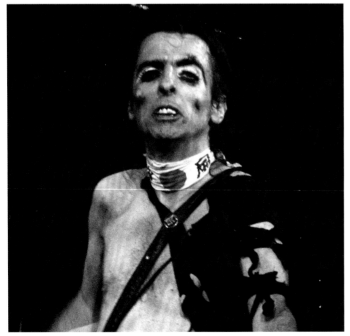
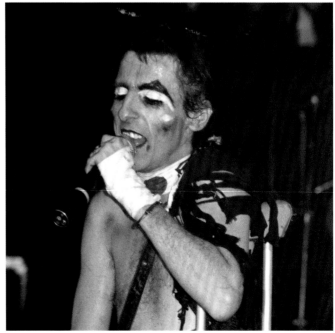

1983

1983. Michael Bruce issues his second solo album, a short odds 'n' sods record called *Rock Rolls On*. As with his first record, featured are Bob Dolin and Mick Mashbir.

Early 1983. "I Am the Future" from *Zipper Catches Skin* is issued as a single in the UK and mainland Europe. The track is used as the theme song to low-budget punk movie, *Class of 1984*.

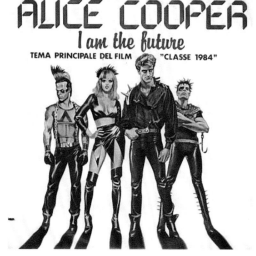

Mid-1983. Alice and band are in a studio on Buttonville, Ontario working on the tracks that will comprise *Dada*. The core team is Alice, Bob Ezrin (returning for the first time in six years) and Dick Wagner, along with Prakash John on bass and Richard Kolinka on drums. Alice by this point is off crack or any form of cocaine but still drinking, although he figures not really any more heavily than he had been during the *Welcome to My Nightmare* period, leading to what he deems conscious participation in the process, close collaboration with Bob Ezrin.

At first, a compromise is struck. Alice wants to make the record in Phoenix and Bob, in Toronto. Bob sends Dick to write with Alice in Phoenix and then they would record in Toronto. Alice won't—or can't—write. Dick says Alice is somewhat withdrawn, plus he's worried about his financial situation relating to some tax problems. Shep saves the day with a cheque apparently in the amount of around $90,000 and Alice feels he can now leave home. Wagner and Cooper end up writing the record in a massive two-bedroom hotel suite in Toronto, drinking vodka every day, but, recalls Dick, not doing any drugs. They would write in the hotel room and then be down in the lounge at night into the early morning, Dick at the grand piano, Alice singing, sometimes rehearsing the songs that they'd written upstairs in the room. Sessions were casual, broken up by three-hour lunches, by Bob going home in the evening and turning the production over to Dick, whose work the next day as often as not, would get over-ruled.

Graham Shaw:

I met Ezrin through Bernie Fiedler, and he and I had been around the music scene. I actually went to work with him on a Jeff Beck project that didn't really get off the ground in England, so he asked me to come and co-write and play on this project. It started out at ESP Studios and then we moved over to Phase One. But at the beginning, it was just me and Bob and a wonderful man named John Jones who was the wrangler for the Fairlight.

We did a lot of preproduction in Bob's basement; he had a bomb shelter thing down there. We didn't record per se; we programmed some Fairlight stuff, but I don't even remember it was sequenced at that point. I think it might've been. So we did some preproduction in Bob's basement and we took that to ESP. The Fairlight is as big as a footlocker at the end of a bed. It's a large homely thing. So we did that preproduction, and that's mostly Bob and I. Dick Wagner showed up pretty well around there. But yeah, Bob and I would go there every day.

I did a lot of synths, some guitar, lyrics, background vocals, some of the Fairlight—that was my contribution on most of the tunes. Some are credited and some aren't. The credits are a little fast and loose here but they're pretty close. I see in the credits Bob says that he's the only guy who played Fairlight. I'm not going to knock anybody around here, but he and I predominantly played the Fairlight. Actually me probably a lot more than him, but yes, he did too. In terms of playing, "Dyslexia," I definitely am on that. "No Man's Land," not sure. "I Love America;" yeah, sure, I wrote a lot of that tune. "Fresh Blood;" I would've programmed on that.

I played acoustic piano on "Pass the Gun Around," but I don't know if that made the final mix. Really it's only "Former Lee Warmer" that I should have got a writing credit on that I didn't.

ESP went south for a number of reasons. I'm not entirely sure. I know we did a lot of writing at ESP. I think Ringo walked out, drove away in a fit of rage at one point, and was gone for bit. Ringo was Bob's sidekick and engineer. He's been involved with Bob for quite a long time. Bob being a bit mercurial let us say, pissed Ringo off, and I think Ringo hightailed. I remember that, because Earl Torno was the engineer on a lot of the cuts for a while, and then he was in the chair at Phase One. I would say most of the album got tracked at Phase One, actually. But I know that Ringo left in a huff. By the time I was on the way to the studio, I saw Ringo driving the other way, like a bat out of hell, in a Volkswagen, right?

So when we started out at ESP, Cooper was there, me, Ezrin, Dick Wagner, John the Fairlight guy and that was it. We were just writing tunes and roughing them out. So not a lot of stuff really went to tape there. We just demoed stuff. The lion's share was done at Phase One, and we were there about a month.

Dee Long (ESP Studios co-owner):
I didn't have much to do with the album. I showed up for work, they started on the album, we did a bunch of modifications in the studio to prepare for them, and Ezrin was there, and his sidekick Ringo was there, and we were setting up stuff and Ringo said, "Could you do this for me?" I started changing the setting on the console and Ezrin just flipped out on me, started screaming at me. So I just said, okay, fine, I'm out of here. So all I did was demonstrate the Fairlight to them when they arrived.

But I walked out of the sessions. I hung out and played pinball when they were working. Sometimes I'd hear them arguing. That did a lot of yelling. It was mostly over publishing, who wrote what. I remember hearing a few tracks through the wall. I also remember that Alice and some of the guys from the Toronto Maple Leafs hockey team would sit and play cards in the front all day long, well the rest of the guys were out back making the album.

Late Summer 1983. Frail and close to death from years of drinking, somewhat deliberately in place to replace crack, Alice enters a hospital in Phoenix where he is stabilised over a two-and-a-half week period (mostly to replace all the potassium he had lost, which took three days of shots), his most serious ailment being cirrhosis of the liver. To help him rally, his old high school coach Emmet Smith pays him a visit. He's in hospital for four months, a needle-phobe, getting a needle every four hours along with a blood test every day. Alice does in fact rally, quitting everything cold turkey, and stays out of the spotlight, mostly in Phoenix, for the next three years.

Alice Cooper:
When I came out, I was totally, absolutely, totally sober. I could not have been more sober. The insane thing about it is, that comment, you know, people talk about how miracles don't happen anymore. Well, yes, they do. I come from a real Christian family. My father was a pastor, my grandfather was a pastor, my wife's father is a pastor. I was the prodigal son, who did come back to Christianity. But the thing about it was, at that point, I certainly wasn't a Christian.

I haven't had a drink since. I never went to an AA meeting. Never saw a doctor. Never had a guy who was calling me up and saying, "How are you doing today?" None of that. None of that ever happened. I came out and I was totally sober. In every situation, in the most high stress situation, I never thought, it never occurred to me to take a drink. So that was the total healing, I call it.

September 1983. Sheryl, with Calico, moves out on Alice and fly back to live with Sheryl's parents in Chicago. But first she, along with her parents who had come to Phoenix for the task, and with the help of Alice's parents, put Alice in the hospital. She sets in motion an arbitration process for a legal separation, mid-November. Sheryl says that it never got as far as actual divorce proceedings. They are apart for ten months.

September 20, 1983. Kiss remove the makeup and go hair metal with considerable success, issuing *Lick It Up*. The band's non-makeup era would find them staples of MTV all through the '80s. The album is their first platinum certification in the last three tries. Meanwhile Alice is still loosely exploring a new wave direction, but would soon join his shock rock brethren in Kiss in finding a second life through straight unapologetic heavy metal of a hair variety.

September 28, 1983. Alice Cooper issues *Dada*. The cover art is based on a painting by Alice pal, Salvador Dali. The album is never toured and none of its songs are ever performed live.

Alice Cooper:
Now you're talking about the blackout albums. Those are albums that were written in a blackout. To be honest with you, I don't remember writing them, I don't remember recording them, I don't remember touring with them. If there was a time in my life that I was on automatic pilot, that was it.

I listen to those songs now and I go, "Wow, these are good songs (laughs). I wish I would have been there for this session, I would've done a better version of it." In fact, I always toyed with the idea of taking twelve songs from that era and going in and rerecording them as just a unique album, *Songs from the Blackout*. Redoing them and really doing them right and seeing what they would sound like. I would love to repeat some of those.

But I was just in a total state of, okay, do an album, write an album, do an album, go on tour. Right, now do an album, go on tour. That was so automatic pilot that I didn't even think about it. "*Zipper Catches Skin*, we'll do that. All right, let's go. All right, after *Zipper Catches Skin,* let's see, it's *DaDa*, okay, let's go." Those are some of the quirkiest lyrics I've ever written. I will not sit down and say that when you're out of your mind that you don't… that it doesn't help you write great stuff. I wrote some of my best stuff when I was loaded. The real Alice fans' four favourite albums are the four blackout albums. The ones that I wrote totally subconsciously and I go back now and listen to them and go, "For somebody who doesn't remember writing that song, recording or touring it, that's a pretty cool song!" (laughs).

Graham Shaw:
Alice was doing okay. He'd wake up and be drinking. He was civil and coherent, but I wouldn't call him energetic or motivated. Then he left for a little lapse for about ten days. He just went back to Los Angeles, then he came back and they finished it up. But he was pleasant guy. I liked him. We got along fine. But you could tell, he was mildly embalmed from sunup to sundown. Dick was delightful throughout the whole thing. I quite liked him. I respect his talents and consideration as well. I remember him fondly.

But after Alice came back he looked a lot better. He was fine. He's a pleasant guy. Alice did his thing, and Bob was doing his wrangling and there wasn't a lot of fights. Bob has to be the biggest swinging dick there, right? So nobody really fights about that much. He does have the final word. I wasn't artistically committed to the point where I would get in a big fight about it.

As for a mission or an overview, well, there was some mention. It was almost like fulfilling a responsibility for one last album for Warner Bros. So there was a sideways disrespect to "Former Lee Warmer," who is formerly Warner, so the reference is there. The snide aspect of the music should be largely apparent if you can read halfway between the lines. So yes, that was a mission statement to an extent (laughs).

Dick Wagner:
I think it's an excellent album, very experimental yet very musical. It's interesting, though, that people would think it's weak. I just think that musically it's very good, but it may not be hit songs. But then again, it wasn't pushed by Warner so there couldn't be hit songs. The musicality and imagery, especially "Former Lee Warmer," it's really about leaving Warner Bros. It was the last album for Warner Bros. All the imagery there was about Warner Bros, like the evil old man in the attic, and leaving Warner Bros. But there are a lot of spooky, cool songs on that album.

November 1983. *Dada* cops up one single release, but only in the UK, for "I Love America."

Graham Shaw:
We tried to make some good music. In "I Love America," we've got a sample of a stampede of horses riding back and forth and we had the sound of sabres rattling and things like that. It was fun. For Bob and myself, that record represents some of the baby steps of working with samples to that extent. I just got the zeitgeist of the record and the project, and I started writing that way. Also the Fairlight, because I started writing on that keyboard, that would evince different kinds of music. Also this was the first time I was writing to a drum machine. That causes you to write differently too.

1984

February 28, 1984. *The Nightmare*, Alice's conceptual rendering of *Welcome to My Nightmare* from 1975, is up for a Grammy award in the Best Long Form Music Video category now that it has just been issued on VHS and Betamax. It doesn't win. But a healthy-looking Alice is at the gala, taking place at Radio City Music Hall in New York, presenting an award with Grace Jones.

March 1984. Alice severs ties with Warner Bros. When he returns, he will be with MCA.

March – April 1984. Alice is in Spain, where he is filming his parts for his starring role in camp horror film *Monster Dog*. In part, Alice uses the project as a test to make sure he can work sober.

Alice Cooper:
I get ten scripts a week from people that want me to do movies, and I got this one that was going to be three months in Spain, and about a million-dollar budget. I said great, because I didn't want to do a heavy budget movie. I said if I do one of these I want to make sure it's sleazy. I want it to be really cheap. I said, "How many people do we get to kill in this? (laughs)." Yeah, I wipe out everybody. But it was totally for fun. They told me it would never get released in the movie houses, and I said, "Great. It should just be one of those movies you can rent at the video place." They said that's what it would be, so I did it. I got a lot of money for it (laughs). I think I was the biggest part of the budget.

May 10, 1984. Twisted Sister issue their smash hit *Stay Hungry* album, featuring "We're Not Gonna Take it" and "I Wanna Rock," both with iconic MTV hair metal videos featuring the band's pre-meditated yet fully juvenile twist on and Alice Cooper-style glam ten years in the making.

Summer 1984. Sheryl and Alice reconcile, remaining one of rock 'n' roll's model couples to this day. Sheryl's chief ultimatum to Alice is that they start going to church together, along with telling Alice he needs to set up Christian-based counselling for himself, and that she might attend. Shortly after they agree to toss out their legal proceedings, they move to Chicago (staying in the Lakepoint Towers, paying $2000 a month rent). Sheryl goes back to college as well as works with a local dance company. Alice fulfils his promise to Sheryl and works on himself under the ministry of Sheryl's pastor father.

August 17, 1984. Blackie Lawless and W.A.S.P., issue their self-titled debut album. The band is quickly associated with Mötley Crüe as part of a dark, decadent strain of hair metal, although Blackie pulls generously from Alice Cooper's bag of tricks.

1985

Mid-1985. Rumours persist that Alice is working with Andy McCoy of Hanoi Rocks. Cooper also managed some writing with Joe Perry. As well, Alice strikes up a relationship with guitarist Kane Roberts, a Berklee College of Music grad, and the two start writing songs. Bob Ezrin finds Kane, in Albany, New York, after Roberts was recommended by a music publisher friend. Bob meets Roberts in New York City and then, recalls Ezrin, the first meeting between Alice and Kane takes place at his house in Toronto (Kane remembers it differently, as indicated below). Alice has an instant connection with Roberts, through love of comedy and slasher movies.

Kane Roberts:
We were playing in New York strip clubs in New York, and different clubs that had a rock night, just to keep the creative juices flowing. We weren't necessarily doing it for money. If I wanted to make money, I had to do other things. I used to deal cards at this illegal blackjack game in Manhattan. They'd rent a hotel room every weekend, so after playing, we'd get our $20 each, because you were just playing for the door or whatever. Then I would go there and deal cards 'til eight in the morning and hopefully there's more than 20 bucks.

But we would do originals and covers and stuff like that. It was just the average kid trying to become a big rock star. I knew early on how much I loved music. I was such a little kid. I had no choice, I had to do it. So when I started playing with my band around New York, we got a phone call—because we would open for bands like Joan Jett, Molly Hatchet, bands like that—and then we got a phone call that Alice Cooper needed an opening band. I never met him or anything, and I remember just looking at him, freaked out, so we didn't talk to him or anything. We did the show.

So it was strange years later to go down to their office in Manhattan and meet with Shep Gordon and Danny Markus and Bob Ezrin and Alice Cooper all in the same room. I had to act really confident, like I'm not nervous. But it was funny, Alice and I immediately became friends. It had nothing to do with the music. Just as soon as we met each other we became very tight and we ended up hanging out all day. But the first thing that we were writing for, actually, was sort of a metal/dark version of that *Sgt. Pepper* movie, and it was going to have Def Leppard and Twisted Sister and Alice and all these bands in it, but none of that panned out. Then we moved on to *Constrictor*.

Essentially my tape landed in the hands of Bob Ezrin and he suggested I hook up with Alice to begin writing and see what gives. Ezrin is one of the most innovative and insightful people to walk the earth. I was very lucky to have caught his attention. In terms of guitarist in the original band, I wasn't a fan of any individual player, necessarily. I always seemed to judge that band as a collective energy type of thing. I've met some of them, and they're really great guys and I know they still make great music. It's not my nature to feel apprehensive about stuff like that. I can admire/respect someone's work without feeling pressure to match or surpass their effort. An artist's standard of creative output has to come from within. I was excited to be working with such an amazing artist as Alice and hooking up with manager/mentor Shep Gordon.

June 28, 1985. Alice, Sheryl and Calico welcome a baby boy, Dashiel, to the family, while they are still in Chicago. They are on their own, doing domestic things together, changing nappies, getting groceries together and going to the zoo on their Honda compact. Meanwhile, Alice is flying back and forth to LA to write with Kane Roberts, Sheryl recalling that even the 45-minute grind of back and forth from the apartment to O'Hare airport was a slice of domesticity that was helping Alice heal.

Summer 1985. *Metal Edge* magazine debuts, championing the glam scene clear through to 2009, when it and heavier sister publication *Metal Maniacs,* ceased publishing. Also by this point, *Circus* magazine goes near relentlessly hair metal. The newly reconfigured Alice Cooper will soon benefit from the likes of such publications.

November 9, 1985. Heir to Alice, Dee Snider—until Alice returns and Dee is nowhere to be seen— has Alice Cooper perform a cameo on "Be Chrool to Your Scuel" from the band's fourth album *Come Out and Play,* issued on this date. Alice appears in the video for the song in his trademark makeup. Recalls Dee Snider, Cooper was hesitant, but Snider talked him into it. The video, therefore, essentially marks the debut of the new (old) Alice, months before he would debut the *Constrictor* show live.

1986

Mid-1986. As the Cooper family moves back to Phoenix (never to relocate again), Alice and his new band begin recording sessions for his comeback album on MCA, finishing up in the summer. The family move back to Phoenix because soon Calico was about to start kindergarten and Sheryl didn't want her moving schools. They move back into the small bungalow they retained ownership of when they went to Chicago. Sheryl says that they were in Chicago "almost two years," although in Alice's telling, they weren't there very long because it was too cold.

A big part of Alice's healing process during this time was his new addiction, golf, which, granted, he'd regularly played throughout the years. Alice says that once he took to golf with a renewed sense of obsession, he played 36 holes of golf for a year—18 holes with Jim Mooney and 18 holes with Craig Yahiro at the Pima Golf Resort in Scottsdale, Arizona—and wound up a single digit handicap.

July 28, 1986. "He's Back (The Man Behind the Mask)" is issued as an advance single from the forthcoming *Constrictor* album.

Alice Cooper:
I had to take some time off. We'd been working forever. Also it was a time when they weren't really playing heavy metal music. There wasn't the new popularity of metal or glam or whatever you're gonna call it. But now that's in, it's big now. My kinda music is back in.

Constrictor is a pretty straight-ahead rock 'n' roll album. When we put the ballads out, it was only at the time when disco was so big and that was the only way we could more or less keep in the game, in the realm of being on the radio. But if you'll look at the time period for that, there's been a lot of bands kinda dropped away. Aerosmith did. Alice Cooper did. We all just did the honourable thing and got out while disco was big (laughs). So now everybody's back with a vengeance. Aerosmith's back out playing and Iggy's back out and Alice.

For the cover I played around with a lot of image changes, and then I decided that what I wanted—and pretty much what my fans wanted—was the Alice Cooper from the *Nightmare* era. So that's pretty much what we did. I went back to that character. But picking favourites is like picking a child. You can't pick out what you're favourite kid is, 'cause they all mean different periods of your life. I loved *School's Out* and I loved all of those albums in the '70s, but I think by the far the highest energy album is *Constrictor.*

Dani Filth: (Cradle of Filth):
I got into Alice Cooper, and I think it's because my mom, when she had been young, had listened to a bit of Alice Cooper. So I decided to buy her a copy of *Constrictor,* and it had a slew of big '80s hits on it, although I wasn't into hair metal, but it

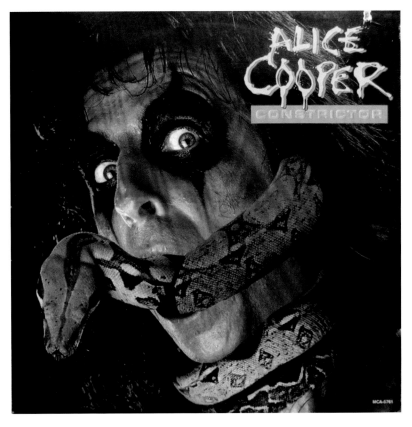

was something that I could actually listen to safely in the house (laughs). Now he's playing golf with ex-presidents and stuff—hardly shocking. Now it's about nostalgia. Alice Cooper, to be fair, always has really nice things to say about Cradle of Filth. I have a lot of profound respect for someone who is genuinely nice (laughs).

Gavin Baddeley:
You can split Alice's career into component parts quite easily. You have the early albums, the sort of experimental stuff leading through to what I'd call the classic stuff of the '70s. That sort of reaches a crescendo with *Welcome to My Nightmare* and appearing on *The Muppet Show* and all this stuff. Suddenly he's the biggest show in town. There's a crazy film noir album with him dressed as a private detective and a black and white photograph on the cover.

 Then things start to fall apart in his private life. He starts to struggle to cope with all of this, and these increasingly crazy albums start coming out. *Special Forces, DaDa,* you almost get the impression that as much as he's aware of what he's doing—he's tried to become artistic—that he's trying to work out where to go.

 Then he cleans up, reinvents himself and decides to cash in on this legacy of all these kids who've grown up worshipping the Alice Cooper show. But I think what happens in the late '80s is it becomes by numbers, very much generic. This is when, for me, Alice Cooper becomes shocking (laughs). As an Alice Cooper fan, you have this guy who used to be a real loose cannon, this crazy-looking guy with a big nose wandering around in a leotard waving a sword about. You know, he's really fascinating to watch. But *Trash?* That's the only album I've actually given away after I'd listened to it once.

August 1, 1986. *Friday the 13th Part VI: Jason Lives* hits theatres. Its theme song is "He's Back (The Man Behind the Mask)" which is heard repeatedly in the film. Two other songs are featured as well, "Teenage Frankenstein," also from *Constrictor,* and the non-LP "Hard Rock Summer."

September 22, 1986. Alice Cooper returns from a three-year retirement, after having done three weird, new wave style albums high on crack cocaine, and then one while still drinking. He comes back clean and sober, as a no-nonsense hair metal shock rocker with *Constrictor.* He is on a new label, MCA. Most of the album is a co-write with metal guitarist Kane Roberts, who is also in the band as Alice's right-hand man

and soon has Alice pumping iron a couple hours a day until Alice is in pretty impressive shape. What's more, Kane didn't drink and the two continued bonding while watching horror movies and cracking jokes. The front cover of *Constrictor* features Alice in makeup with his snake wrapped around his neck and face.

Alice Cooper:
I did not want to come out with anything with the soft underbelly to it. I wanted Alice to come out there and punch the lights out. I saw all these bands. I knew who Kiss was; we helped invent Kiss. We told them where to buy their makeup. They were no shock to me. And I said, I need to blow these guys off the map. To me, attitude-wise and show-wise, we did. Kiss were a different thing from us. Kiss were comic book, where Alice was still the master of theatre. I was the master of surprise. This was much darker than anybody in Kiss.

 The one thing about *Constrictor* is that I took metal, and to me, made it a little smarter. The arrangements, the guitar playing of Kane Roberts… he is the most underrated guitar player of all time. The fact that he looked like Schwarzenegger really detracted from his guitar playing, people did not listen to him. They'd listen to the album and say, "Who played the guitar on this? It's incredible! Is it Eddie Van Halen? Is it Steve Vai?" "No, that's Kane Roberts." He was a genius guitar player, on both those albums. If you listen to those albums, there's a lot of early Alice melody lines. I learned my lessons from Bob Ezrin. I never wrote songs that didn't have great melody lines. It's just now I was attacking it differently. I was attacking it with a much more aggressive guitar, bass and drums.

Beau Hill:

Alice didn't really have a band. He had a co-writer, Kane Roberts. They spent a great deal of time writing this record, and Alice got a new deal on MCA, and that's how they got me in. I introduced Alice to Kip Winger, and Kip played bass on the album, and then subsequently Alice hired Kip to go out and tour that particular album.

Alice was so easy to work with. He was such a gentleman and such a riot. He was really open. It was like, "Okay, how about we try this?" "That's great; let's do it." I was an Alice fan when I was a kid and so this was a real privilege for me. He had already come back from the edge of all of his various abuses that he was so notorious for. The weirdest thing that he did is that he'd like to fall asleep on the couch and watch what he referred to as splatter movies, stuff like *Halloween* and *Friday the 13th*, all that stuff. He was a very gracious person to be around, and any time we were out walking on the street, he would stop and sign autographs.

But don't forget, he had Roberts with him, and these guys had written most of the record, and it certainly reflected in the writing what was going on musically at the time anyway. So by the time I inherited the project, they were very comfortable with the direction and very comfortable with the approach, and they liked the work that I had done. Obviously they had heard it, so they thought, okay, we can blend Beau's production approach with the material we're writing, and we think we're going to do something really good with it.

Michael Wagener:

Constrictor was recorded with drum machines, and the programming of that drum machine was pretty crazy. I don't know who did the original programming, but whoever it was was a drummer that wanted to program all the stuff that he ever wanted to play. Then I worked mostly with Kane Roberts on it. Kane was the initial contact to Alice, and we replaced a lot of the drum patterns. You can imagine, it's hard to do. We're talking 1986. The media was just invented, and there was no digital workstations or anything like that. It was a hard job. But yeah, by the time I got the record we just started replacing stuff, played a couple of solos and then we mixed it.

Kane Roberts:

Beau was cool and he suggested Kip and some of the other players. Ultimately, we took the tapes to Michael Wagener where we re-recorded a lot of the tracks. Wagener is off the hook when it comes to an overall understanding of the production and engineering process. We still work together and he always wants to punch me in the face and then eat sushi. That record's production comes from the initial elements being incorrect on the first go-round as I mentioned. We were looking for a somewhat bare-boned approach so what you're feeling is intentional, although we wanted you to like it! A real drummer is very often better but there were budget and time constraints. Oh well.

Neal Smith:

I've been in residential real estate since 1985. When we had the success of *School's Out*, I started investing in real estate. Mike Bruce did it and so did Alice. Back in the early '70s it was called a tax shelter and we invested in real estate as a group too. I was interested in it in the early stages of my musical career. But your art and your passion always stay number one in your life. I've got hundreds of drums around the house and I'm excited about getting my next set with 25 pieces in it. I still love monster drum sets. It's still a passion for me and it will be till the day I die.

I was really happy to see Alice come back after all the hell he had been through. He called me in 1985, after he'd been through all the rehab stuff, and said he was doing great and that Kane and he were going to use computerised bass and computerised drums on their next album, but they wanted to work it out with a real band. So, he came back here to my house in Connecticut to see Dennis and me before the *Constrictor* album. I've always left the door open for Alice or anybody if they need help because I have a studio and I'd be happy to work. He said he wanted to do pre-production with Dennis and me just like we used to do for two weeks. So, Alice and Kane stayed in a hotel and we worked every day for two weeks and totally worked it out. We did some recordings and then they took them with them and recorded the whole album, but there's no indication of any of that collaboration on the record.

The fact was that it was just great to get together. Dennis, Alice and I played together for the pre-production of the *Constrictor* album and we worked out the arrangements that were used on the record and he went ahead and recorded it. It was the beginning of the second phase of his solo career. He had passed his *Zipper Catches Skin* thing and came back with a solid rock album. Then four years later when he had "Poison," there was nobody happier than me. I just thought that was great. It was a great song.

October 20, 1986. Alice plays a warm-up show in advance of his *Constrictor* tour proper. It is his first show since 1982. A few more low-key shows take place before the official Halloween kick-off.

Alice Cooper:
The thing about *Constrictor* was that I had just sobered up. I had never been Alice Cooper on stage sober. What do you think that first gig was like? Me putting on all of the gear, getting ready to go onstage and realising, what if Alice doesn't show up? I'm going to be out there in front of these people, without the alcohol. What if Alice just doesn't show up?

Well, the first night we played, Guns N' Roses opened for us and I had this new band with Kane Roberts and Ken Mary and Kip Winger on bass—a great band. What I wanted to do was come out with an album that had no ballads on it. It was just pure heavy Alice. It was heavy metal, but I called it heavy Alice. It wasn't really metal like Metallica or Megadeth, but I had this new sound and I had the new image.

If I look at Alice now, back in the *Billion Dollar Babies* or *School's Out* days, I see a character that was a whipping boy. I look at his posture and he's humped over. I look at the fact that he gets his head cut off and he gets hung. He was always society's whipping boy, and that's the way alcohol made me feel. He appealed to the outcasts of the world.

Now Alice was this incredibly vicious villain, who stood straight up, who wore all black leather, and he was now this character that was an arrogant Captain Hook. He looked at the audience with disdain, as if, "You are the great unwashed and I am of course Hannibal Lecter" (laughs). It was a new way of me performing Alice. I didn't feel beat up anymore. I needed to prove to the audience that there was a new generation Alice here.

Kane Roberts:
Alice and I set out to layer some different colours on the older material. Quite a daunting task as those songs, too many, are sacred ground. Alice still has a rebellious side and he wanted to upset the apple cart a little, so we added some different influences to the classic songs. Some of the ideas worked better than others, but it was an overall success to both of us.

October 31, 1986 – April 1, 1987. Alice Cooper makes his triumphant return, sober, healthy, putting in a massive North American tour called *The Nightmare Returns* in support of his *Constrictor* album. Support for part of the campaign in early '87 comes from Megadeth, followed by Tesla into March. The first show is at Joe Louis Arena, but even this Halloween Night fright-fest is preceded by more soft launching: the October 31st gig sold out in three hours, so a second show was added for the night *before*. The Halloween show is filmed and aired as *The Nightmare Returns,* on MTV. Support on this show and a couple previous is Vinnie Vincent Invasion.

Alice Cooper:

This new show is absolutely diabolical. It's like *Nightmare* Part II. There are some special effects that I can't really talk about. But we're doing the guillotine again. Only it's much more vivid this time. A lot more blood. We have a couple of guys that worked with us on this who did some of the costuming on *Aliens* and *The Fly*.

So it's gonna be a full-blown Alice Cooper production. I've got a band that's just a real heavy street band. They're not studio guys; they're just killers. Kane Roberts and Kip Winger. When you see Kane, you're not gonna believe him. He's bigger than Stallone. He's a body-builder. Yeah, they're great! They're rock! They're animals! They're bloodthirsty! They're frightening! And they're snappy dressers too.

I think the most important thing about it is that there's nothing mellow about it. Alice is back totally, totally, to be more Alice than he ever was, you know? There are parts of the show that are just… every time I get home from rehearsal I have to go and clean the blood off myself. It's great.

But I think there was more violence with punk music than there is with heavy metal, the slam dancing and stuff like that. Heavy metal is much more of a show thing. With my show we have very few problems in our audience because the audience is riveted to the stage. If they look away they're gonna miss something.

As far as Alice's violence, Alice is a character that lashes out at three main things. There's three things that Alice totally makes fun of, and that's sex, death, and money. Those are the three things that he finds to be the most spiritual things with people (laughs). Not religion or politic—those things he doesn't touch—he only talks about sex, death, and money 'cause those are the three things that affect more people. They've killed Alice on stage more times than they've killed Jason in the *Friday the 13th* movies.

But there's nothing to do with any Satanism or anything like that. Then you're talking about religion, something we 're not involved in. I don't even think that those Satan bands—whoever they are—even know what they're talkin' about. I think it's just sad more than anything else.

Chris Poland (Megadeth):

We toured with Alice Cooper, who I feel broke the band. Actually, Janie Hoffman, who worked with MCA, she was a big part in getting us that tour. If we didn't do that tour, I think things would've been a lot slower. Because we faced full houses every night, playing with Alice Cooper.

I'll tell you a story on the tour, that you'd probably be able to figure out, eventually. He brings us on his bus, he sits us down and he says, "Hey guys, I'm really happy you're on tour with us. Is there anything I can do for you that…" whatever. And we're all like, "No, we just want to thank you for having us." We were being on our best behaviour, and right before we leave, he says, "Listen guys, you gotta be really careful out here. I know what you guys are up to and I'm just telling you that." I can't remember exactly what he said, but we all just knew exactly what he was saying. Because he was sober. He was like, you guys are fucking crazy and you guys need to get your shit together (laughs). So that was a cool moment. Luckily we did.

Dave Mustaine: (Megadeth):

I know that that's the stuff I needed when I first started. Alice Cooper tried to talk to me when I went out with him in the beginning—Alice is my godfather. He sat me down on his bus one night. He was sitting there with eyeliner on and I'm just out of my mind. I'm going like, "Cool, Alice Cooper—we are going to get wasted." I didn't know he had stopped drinking at the time. He goes, "You know what? You really gotta cool it." It really put a damper on things. But you know what? There's a way that you can be out there and try to help people in a way that you don't discourage them, but you can also show them that there are some good things to do and there are some not so good things to do. The choice is yours. If you have any problems, call me. I will always be here for you.

Dave Ellefson: (Megadeth):

Alice Cooper took us on tour with him. That didn't mean we were a shock rock gore band. We weren't going to start wearing makeup and cutting heads off babies. But Alice Cooper was kind enough to entré nous us into the mainstream, even though we were really there to establish our own identity."

November 23 – December 5, 1986. The UK leg of *The Nightmare Returns* features support from Alien Sex Fiend.

1987

March 29, 1987. Alice makes an appearance at *Wrestlemania III* in Detroit.

May – June 1987. Alice and his band conduct the recording sessions for what will become *Raise Your Fist and Yell*.

Michael Wagener:
Oh, the band was brilliant. I think that was the best band he ever had. It was Kane Roberts on guitar, who is still a very, very good friend of mine, Kip Winger on bass, Paul Taylor on keyboards and Ken Mary on drums. It was just an amazing band; very, very high quality. Alice was in a great state of mind. He had all the abusive stuff left behind and really was just working hard on the record, trying to get the best record together. Never, ever any problems with him. I don't know if you've ever met him, but Alice is an extremely funny guy and also an extremely smart guy.

In terms of that heavy metal style, there was no plan as such. It was just the songs that came out between the collaboration of Alice and all the guys he was working with. Obviously there were those influences at the time, but it wasn't planned that we were going to say okay, now we're going to do a record like this. It just came out. I remember Kane told me a story that him and Alice were writing in Maui, in Hawaii, and they just had to leave because it was too relaxed. He goes, this is not a place you can write a rock record (laughs).

But the big difference for me from *Constrictor* is that *Raise Your Fist and Yell* was a whole production from the bottom up. I was involved from the first note on. So that was the big difference for me. *Raise Your Fist and Yell* was all real drums. Those were really good budgets in those days. A normal rock record, even to this day, takes me about 60 days to do it right, a couple of months to do it right and to get the right vibe and all that going.

Funny anecdote, we were in the studio and we had recorded the song "Gail." Really dark, dark song and Alice had just sung the last words when the power went out. There was a lightning storm outside and the studio was right next to the gas company. So everybody was standing there, fearing for their lives. Alice took that as a sign that we might not want to put that song on the album. But we ended up doing it anyway.

July 21, 1987. Guns N' Roses issue *Appetite for Destruction*, which goes on to sell 28 million copies worldwide. Everybody, including Alice, is now operating in their slipstream.

August 30, 1987. Alice plays the 25th anniversary of Reading festival, where in the press tent he personally doles out advance cassettes of his new *Raise Your Fist and Yell* album.

Kane Roberts:

I've always said that you have a bass player, you have a drummer, you've got all those guys, but the most important member—it sounds sappy or maybe too idealistic—but the most important thing is what you're creating, the energy you are generating with the fans. It's a very strange thing. The audience is there and they're listening to music and you're playing, and so it's so different from being in a studio or playing alone. There's not much of a difference between playing for one person or, you know, I've played for 90,000 people. Other than having to project differently, the energy that is out there will create the energy on the stage, to a great degree. It's a back and forth.

September 5, 1987. Alice Cooper issues his second corporate hair metal kiddie rock album in *Raise Your Fist and Yell*. Again, the album is co-written with Kane Roberts. The relationship for a spell gets rocky with Kane on account of his steroid use and its effect on his personality. At one point, at one of the writing trips to Kan's home in Van Nuys, CA, Alice knocks on his bedroom door with a suitcase in hand and says "I'm leaving you." They have a laugh about it, but they indeed take a two-week break from each other, Kane cleans up and the partnership is back on.

September 21, 1987. Alice Cooper guitarist Kane Roberts issues a self-titled debut solo album. The song "Full Pull" is a co-write with Alice.

Kane Roberts:

"The funniest album cover in history" is the most distinctive element of that album. I found the next Cooper album, *Raise Your Fist and Yell,* a lot more satisfying as a heavy metal fan. But that was always my push. Alice and the management were always really good about, you know, whatever you want to do. It was a real decision for them to heavy the sound up and to change it for that period of time, so Alice and I decided to do a certain thing.

And in the process of doing that, management and everything goes, they wanted me to do my own records, so I started with that first record. My main focus was always my own career, but at that point everything was focused on Alice but they let me branch off and do other stuff. I felt totally supported that way. So when I stepped into that, I met Michael Wagener, who did the Dokken album, and I thought that was a great sounding record. I decided to work with him and I brought some of the guys from New York to come in and record. So yeah, it was a good experience.

Alice and I are both obsessive about everything we do. The weightlifting caught me and I went a little crazy with it. I stopped when I realised that the smaller my legs got, the bigger my dick looked. We came off the road and hit the ground running. Wagener was my idea and an easy sell because he's so good at what he does. Alice and I wanted to capture the energy from playing live and we also wanted to make the CD more of a theatrical effort. "Prince of Darkness" to "Roses on White Lace" is to be viewed as a serial killer's descent into dementia.

October 15, 1987 – February 29, 1988. Alice conducts a tour called *Live in the Flesh*, in support of his *Raise Your Fist and Yell* album. Early support comes from Ace Frehley and Faster Pussycat. Guns N' Roses support in December 1987. January and February 1988 find Motörhead supporting.

Kane Roberts:

At this point, it's mostly a *gigantic* feeling. Alice and I stayed together in the back of the bus and watched movies etc. I'm glad we were such good friends because the bunks were way too small for me. I do remember us selling out Wembley in Great Britain. On that night, I pointed my guitar—which shot flames at the end of my featured solo—at Alice and a fireball exploded from the muzzle and rocketed 40 feet across the stage and hit Alice. Uh, not intentional! We laughed about that later but the crowd loved it!

October 23, 1987. John Carpenter horror film *Prince of Darkness* hits theatres. Alice Cooper song "Prince of Darkness," from *Raise Your Fist and Yell* is briefly heard and Alice has an equally brief cameo.

October 26, 1987. "Freedom," backed with "Time to Kill," is issued as a single from *Raise Your Fist and Yell*.

December 13, 1987. Alice loses his delightful and dynamic father, Ether Furnier, who dies in Phoenix, hometown now for all the Furniers and Coopers.

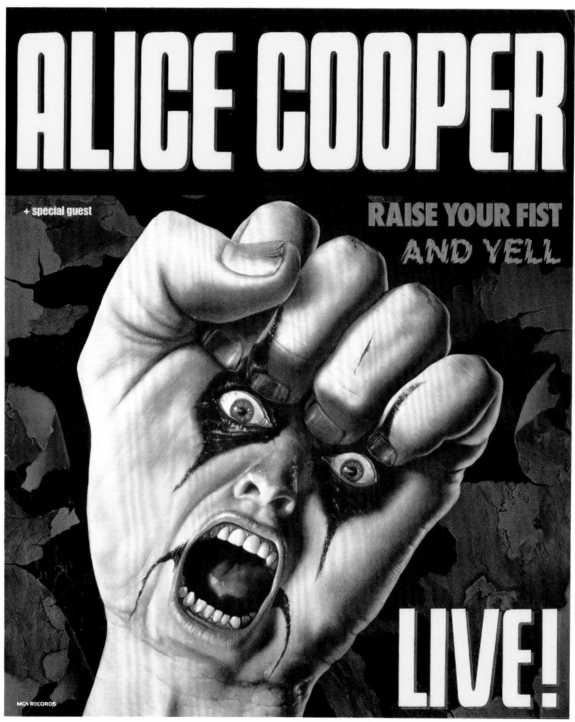

1988

February 1988. Alice breaks ties with MCA after two albums. Although both *Constrictor* and *Raise Your Fist and Yell* sold acceptably, and both were certified gold in Canada, neither reached certification levels in the US, and this while gold, platinum and multi-platinum albums were happening for similar sorts of bands all up and down the Sunset Strip. As for the charts, *Constrictor* had reached No.59 on *Billboard,* with *Raise Your Fist and Yell* peaking at No.73.

April 1 – April 12, 1988. Alice tours, the UK, supported by British pop metal act Chrome Molly.

April 15 – May 6, 1988. Alice takes his *Live in the Flesh* tour over to mainland Europe.

June 17, 1988. *The Decline of Western Civilization Part II: The Metal Years* is released, placing glam in a morally bankrupt, vacuous, dim light. Although Alice is included, the highlight is an interview with W.A.S.P.'s Chris Holmes, lounging in his swimming pool, guzzling vodka, his mom watching on from poolside. Also

appearing in the film are Vixen, London, Odin and Poison. Opening track to the soundtrack album is Alice performing "Under My Wheels" with Axl, Slash and Izzy from Guns N' Roses guesting. Half the rest of the album is by bands who recently supported Alice on tour.

August 10, 1988. Winger issue their self-titled debut album. The band is led by Alice Cooper bassist Kip Winger and is produced by Beau Hill, who previously had produced *Constrictor.* The album sells platinum. After two records with Alice, Winger leaves the fold, as does Kane Roberts. Neither would be on board for Alice's next album, which sells platinum. But Winger does pretty well himself, with his 1990 album *In The Heart of the Young* certifying platinum as well. After Kane produces his two solo albums, he would quit music for a spell.

Kane Roberts:
I think what happened was, I played with Alice, I did the *Saints and Sinners* record, and there was just a moment where I looked around and said, I'm going to stop. I'm not going to do this for a while. It was just such a natural decision. I was talking to Bob Ezrin about it, because I went on to do other creative stuff, and he said, "No matter what you do, it's always the same creative person." But he said, "Watch out, you'll come around again to playing music." And that's where I am right now.

But the music industry itself, the business, is really strange, because it stands between the artist and fans of music. You get these real knuckleheads making decisions about how a record comes out or what it sounds like. Some great records never make it to the public, you know? So I got sick of that. But it was more like, I'm just gonna do something else. I didn't put my guitar away. I played all the time and I did little gigs with friends and stuff like that, but I definitely did turn off that light switch for a while.

It seems like a really basic thing, but as we go through our lives, there are so many moments that we wonder what to do. Even the loudest moments on stage, there's a really quiet voice that directs you and point you towards the right decisions, to feel and experience the moment in a real way. I think that's the thing, everyone's yelling at you what to do but you have to listen to yourself.

November 11, 1988. *Iron Eagle II* hits theatres. Alice Cooper's cover of "I Got a Line on You," produced by Richie Zito, appears on the soundtrack album.

December 1988. Alice and song doctor Desmond Child do some songwriting in Woodstock, NY for Alice's proposed third comeback album.

1989

1989. Dennis, Neal and Blue Öyster Cult's Joe Bouchard team up for the first of many times for the album *Electrocution of the Heart,* operating under the band name Deadringer. Rounding out the band is Jay Jesse Johnson on guitar and Charlie Huhn, notably for his stint with Ted Nugent, on lead vocals.

Dennis Dunaway:
I liked and respected all of the musicians a lot but there wasn't much of me in that album. I liked the music but it just wasn't my style. The only time all of the musicians were together at once was for a photo session. An album needs togetherness to have a heart.

Neal Smith:
I think Charlie's an incredible singer, and we were lucky to have him. That was released on Grudge Records. The guitar player, Jay, was a guy who I'd been working with and writing songs with in Connecticut for the last ten years. He was really the focal point of the band as far as the music goes; he'd written a lot of the songs, and helped to co-write some of the others with me that were on the record. It was a great record, and we had a lot of fun recording it. I do wish we had had more time in the studio.

February 22, 1989. Graphically exposing idiocy in the Grammy award process, Jethro Tull notoriously beats out Metallica for a hard rock/heavy metal Grammy. Reading the unfortunate news off the envelope on the night is none other than Alice Cooper.

May – June 1989. Alice works on both coasts (in a series of studios, befitting the excessive times) on tracks that will comprise his next album, *Trash.*

July 7, 1989. Power ballad "Poison," backed with "Trash," is issued as the first single from the forthcoming *Trash* album. The song is an enormous hit for Alice, peaking at No.7 on the *Billboard* charts.

Alice Cooper:
We took three days writing that song. Now usually I say a hit is written in five minutes. So maybe the basics of "Poison" was written in a half-hour. But when you're working with Desmond Child, he is a song doctor, he is a surgeon. He spent two days just on the background vocals. He really, really made that song work.

The basics were written in maybe an hour. But he really sat down at the piano and worked out every one of those background vocals, which is something I never would be able to do. Desmond was good, because Desmond came from a whole different place and he did push me. He wasn't satisfied with, "That's a good song." He would sit there and go, "Yeah, it's good. It's not great." He would just work on that song until it was great. That's why *Trash* sold three, four million copies, because there was somebody at the helm that really, really was working there but also making sure the album was great.

Michael Bruce:
He had a hit with "Poison" and I thought it was really, really done well. I listened to it and it's got some really neat stuff on it. I don't really listen to his stuff and go, "I could have played that." I more or less listen to it and think, "Wow, I couldn't have played that" (laughs). Because it's a different guitar. It's a different attitude. It's more of your LA hired guns where they got the whammy bars white hot from use and everything's over the edge.

July 12, 1989. Alice Cooper issues *Trash*, the biggest hit of his three hair metal albums (of, arguably, four total), and his first in a new deal with Epic Records. There are four videos from it. Rote and synthetic power ballad "Poison" is by far the biggest hit, but the other singles/videos were "Bed of Nails," "House on Fire" and "Only My Heart Talkin'." Jon Bon Jovi and Steven Tyler guest star. Nine of ten songs are co-writes with producer Desmond Child.

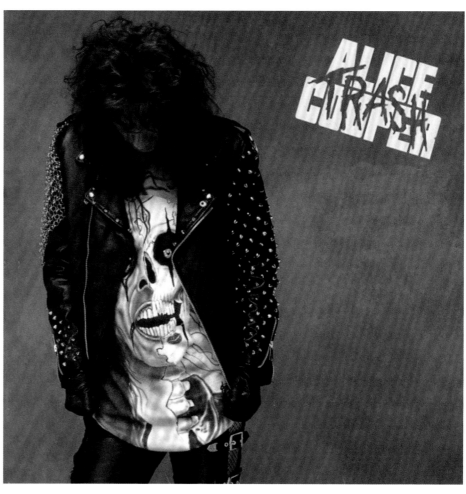

Alice Cooper:
It's less red, more bed. I didn't want to paint myself into a corner with blood, 'cause I think if I would have done another album like that, people would have said, "Well, that's all Alice can do anymore—just horror." I wanted to show a different side; that Alice can also write about this, and you know, in some cases, sex is more dangerous than horror.

The only other two really commercial albums I made were *School's Out* and *Billion Dollar Babies*, and this album was actually written to be more like those albums. With these songs, we sort of followed the trend back towards the '70s, with Guns N' Roses and The Cult and Aerosmith happening again. Alice and Aerosmith were like the two American hard rock bands of the '70s. Plus I didn't want to write lyrics to riffs like we did on *Constrictor* and *Raise Your Fist and Yell*. I really wanted to write songs, like we did on *Billion Dollar Babies*. Desmond is such a great songwriter that it was very easy. We wrote twenty-two songs and had to narrow it down to ten.

July 17, 1989. "Poison" is issued as a single in the UK, where it vaults to No.2 on the charts. It is an advance single, as the record would not come out there until the following month.

Alice Cooper:
Desmond Child suddenly emerged, with Aerosmith and Bon Jovi. Aerosmith suddenly went from being a blues rock band from, well "Walk This Way" is good, and all of a sudden there was this "Janie's Got a Gun" and it was classy. People were laughing at Bon Jovi for the hair and all this—listen to those records. Holy crap, they're great records, and I even worked with Desmond. I got him on the *Trash* album, and that's where "Poison" came from.

I look around now at this whole new scene from Sunset Boulevard where all these great street bands like Mötley Crüe and Faster Pussycat and all these bands came along, and they weren't just bands. They were good and they did a show. They weren't kidding around; they did lighting and sound. Poison was a good band and Warrant and Ratt were good bands. I think we forgot that those bands live were really good. It was a new era. Even though they were doing old Alice Cooper, because it was very much like our stage show, but it was new and fresh and I really liked it.

August 27, 1989. *Trash* is released in the UK, home of Alice's most loyal fan base.

September 25, 1989. "Bed of Nails," backed with "I'm Your Gun," is issued as the second single from Trash, but only in Europe and the UK, where it managed a No.38 ranking.

October 27, 1989. Wes Craven horror film *Shocker* hits theatres. Kane Roberts appears in the film as does Alice Cooper music. On the soundtrack album, Megadeth cover "No More Mr. Nice Guy." Alice is in on the writing of "Love Transfusion" and Desmond Child's fingerprints are everywhere. Alice attends the Hollywood launch party for the film.

Kane Roberts:
Big Wes Craven fan. Heard he was making a movie and tried out for a role. Unbelievably, he gave me a bigger part! I met Paul Stanley during the soundtrack recording for the movie. Bob Ezrin had me come in and write with Paul and it was a joy. His success comes from a massive dose of talent and is not an accident. He and Gene are so over-the-top intense about their work. Paul was real easy to work with and we wrote and played at the studio and his house in Hollywood. Of course, Bob Ezrin had a masterful hand in all of it as well.

October 31, 1989. Alice plays a warm-up gig to kick off his tour in support of *Trash*, at the Cathouse, in LA.

November 1989. "House of Fire" is issued as a single, reaching No.56 on the *Billboard* charts, and managing a No.65 placement in the UK.

November 21 – December 23, 1989. *The Alice Cooper Trashes the World* tour hits Europe. Great White and Britny Fox support on almost all the shows, making this a heady hair metal fest.

December 29 – January 20, 1989. Alice mounts an exclusively Canadian tour in support of *Trash,* East Coast, West Coast and all points in between. Support comes from Great White.

1990s

Alas and alack, Alice gets jerked by history like every other hair metal band in the '90s, but emerges from the decade having capitalised like the winner he more often than not is, due mostly to his personal capabilities, efficiencies and all-round enthusiasm for life and people.

The decade begins with more trips around the touring cycle for 1989's hit *Trash* album—that's what you do; you pack a lunch and go to work. Always, always, you strike while the iron is hot. Come time for a follow-up, Alice does the logical and delivers in *Hey Stoopid, Trash* part 2, featuring more song doctors and more guest stars and another big name producer in Peter Collins. Then the mob shows up with pitchforks and torches, and rather than feeding Alice's Frankenstein, it's back to the original storyline: the monster must be destroyed.

First Nirvana and Pearl Jam ignite the imaginations of rock fans, who flock to this new music called grunge, percolating in Seattle since about 1988. Soundgarden and Alice in Chains soon see success as well and then an alternative metal wave spreads, proposing acts like Smashing Pumpkins, Jane's Addiction, Faith No More, Nine Inch Nails and White Zombie, the latter, the Alice Cooper of the mid-'90s, en route to Marilyn Manson.

Cooper responds, again, like many '70s and '80s acts did, picking one of two directions available, not grunge (dabbled with by many), but a sort of mature, regular rock. *The Last Temptation* becomes one of Alice's most highly regarded albums, an artistic album, a record by a grown-up, which one would never ascribe to his previous four. *Hey Stoopid*, still in the wake, goes gold, but *The Last Temptation* remains uncertified. You can only fool the kids for so long: rock 'n' roll will always be a young man's game, and only a handful of institutions cross over to ubiquity.

But that's records. Alice, again, showing his eye for career, for sensible decision-making and good business sense, spends the rest of the decade cementing his legacy and not particularly trying to compete head-on with a new generation of writers and musicians. Ergo, there he goes, touring hard, while also making the rounds of all manner of celebrity golf tournament. He's a remembered part of smash movie *Wayne's World*, he issues an (ignored) live album called *A Fistful of Alice* along with, at the end of the decade, a somewhat noted and quite special and well-appointed box set called *The Life and Crimes of Alice Cooper*.

On the dark side, October 19, 1997 marks the passing of original Alice Cooper guitarist Glen Buxton, his death containing a silver lining, in that it slowly brings the guys back together, as history would reveal, never for anything terribly significant, but nonetheless promulgating a rebuilding of friendships.

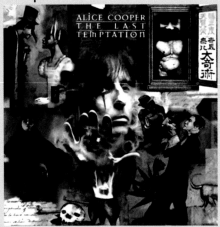

1990

January 22, 1990. Alice and band perform "House of Fire" on the American Music Awards. After this event, drummer Jonathan Mover is replaced by Eric Singer.

Eric Singer:
I was in Badlands and we had a falling out, so basically I got fired. I started going through my phonebook, calling every musician I knew and said I'm looking for a gig. I called Doug Goldstein, who used to be a security guard for Black Sabbath when I played with them in 1986 on the *Seventh Star* tour. He was now managing Guns N' Roses and also Great White who were the support band for Alice Cooper.

    He said Alice Cooper needs a drummer and he'd tell him about me. He did and a week later they came to LA to do the *American Music Awards* and the next day I auditioned and got the gig and that was it. So I was out of work for maybe one or one-and-a-half weeks, ten days or something like this. Everything happens for a reason in life. I know we don't always want to admit this and sometimes we don't understand why things don't work out, or when they go bad we don't understand it. We say "Why me?" or "Why is this not happening?" In the big picture, I think everything is for a reason, so this worked out good.

February 23 – April 12, 1990. Alice conducts the US dates of his tour in support of *Trash*. Support comes from Danger Danger and The Front.

Derek Sherinian:
I worked with Alice on and off until 2006. It was a very exciting time in my life. One week I was struggling in LA and sleeping on someone's floor and the next week I was in the Alice Cooper band, making MTV videos and playing Wembley Arena. Alice was a great gig. As a fan, he was before my time, but I knew who he was. He's iconic and that *Trash* record was big. To this date, I haven't done a tour that has had as much excitement around it as the *Trash* tour because he had a Top Ten single with "Poison." There's big difference going out on tour supporting a Top Ten single and just going out to play the old catalogue. One tour later in '91 or '92, it just fucking died because Nirvana and all these bands came out and just stole the thunder.

March 1990. "Only My Heart Talkin'" is issued as a single from *Trash*.

April 19 – 28, 1990. Alice conducts a short Australian and New Zealand tour.

July 1 – 22, 1990. Alice tours mainland Europe.

Alice Cooper:
Europe is a madhouse! I'll see the same faces in the front row for 25 shows. These guys save up all year and quit their jobs so that they can go on the road and attend all my shows, like an Alice quest. I see them everywhere. They stay in the same hotels, eat in the same restaurants and they take pictures every day. They wear the makeup at all times. It's really weird. I get to the point that I start missing them if they're not there. I think what they've ultimately found is a spokesman for them, someone who can say the things that they're not allowed to say. They're so steeped in it that they believe in it. They know me better than I know me. They know lines in the songs which I've forgotten. It's scary, but it's great.

August 18 – 30, 1990. Very surprisingly, Alice Cooper tours Japan for the first time.

October 1990. Alice begins writing for a new album.

1991

March 5, 1991. Kane Roberts issues *Saints and Sinners*, a second solo album. Producing and writing on every track is Desmond Child, who previously had collaborated with Alice on *Trash*.

Kane Roberts:
I was signed by A&R legend Michael Alago, who signed Metallica and White Zombie, and the hook-up with Desmond was a natural. I believe Shep Gordon suggested him. Desmond is truly prolific and has a work ethic that's astounding. He's still knocking out hits! The important part about making music is focusing and making sure it's close to your heart. I remember when I was working with Desmond, he said to me, you should never let anything out that you wouldn't go to a store and buy yourself. So those are the things that I will be looking back at as I record in the future. But back then, I was hitting my stride in a lot of areas, and was very excited about the future recordings. I didn't tour the album, but I did a promotional tour and was very pleased to see the single was No.1 in a lot of cities, like Cincinnati, Boston etc. MTV resisted for some reason, but it was a total blast meeting so many people.

June 1991. The title track is issued as the first single from *Hey Stoopid*. The song reaches No.78 on the *Billboard* charts, but No.21 in the UK. Supporting the theme of famous guest stars on the album, this track has Slash and Joe Satriani doing the guitar work while Ozzy Osbourne chimes in on backup vocals.

Alice Cooper:
I wasn't out to write another "School's Out" anthem for the summer, but I think that I naturally write that way with big sing-along choruses. I think we got that with "Hey Stoopid"—everybody likes to sing that chorus, and at the same time everybody thinks it applies to someone else (laughs). They go, "I know who he's talking about." The great thing about it is that I got to write a monster hit-sounding record, and it had a message to it. You know, there are "street smarts" and "street stupids," and teenage suicide is street stupid. It's so stupid it deserved its own spelling: STOOPID!

I would hate anyone to think that Alice is preaching. That's why the line, "This ain't your daddy talkin'" is in there. I've seen it all, but I ain't your parents and I ain't here to preach to you, but let me just tell you how I see it. Kids look up to Alice like they did for the Fonz—someone who's anti-establishment but still has common sense and is cool for it. Hopefully Alice saying that suicide is stupid will get across to kids—"Alice says suicide is stupid." Great, now we don't have to do that.

We did videos both for songs and for our shows when there were no places to play them. I felt then that shows like *Welcome to My Nightmare* should be recorded for all time. We thought that the stuff we were doing then was so natural to be on film that it was so important to at least have a visual record of it. The fun part with videos now is trying to come up with something new. The video for "Hey Stoopid" was a six-day shoot. The idea behind it was to take the audience on a rollercoaster ride through Alice's psyche. It was a really fun video to do.

July 2, 1991. Alice Cooper issues the last of his big budget corporate rock kiddie metal hair albums, the Peter Collins-produced *Hey Stoopid*. Song doctors are everywhere, as are guest stars, namely Slash, Joe Satriani, Steve Vai, Nikki Sixx, Mick Mars and Ozzy Osbourne. Despite the flash and considerable promo push, the album fails to reach gold status. Chart-wise, the album reaches No.47, with the record doing strong in the UK, reaching No.4 and certifying sliver, but also selling platinum in Canada.

Alice Cooper:
Without the Desmond influence, it's a heavier album. This time I really wanted it to be an Alice record. Trash

did great, selling three million copies, with 1.5 million in the US, and 1.5 million elsewhere, and I've got nothing against it. In fact, it's still selling steadily. There are songs on it, like "Poison" that I think are real Alice songs, that I really like, but I don't think that "House of Fire" and "Bed of Nails" are really Alice. But, once you get into the studio, you don't really hear that until the production is out. It wasn't until later on that I saw that some of the songs weren't really quite me. It would have been perfect if we'd written more of the unique things, like "This Maniac's in Love With You," but I think it got a little overbearingly Desmond on some of the songs. I'll be honest with you—I didn't catch it until some time after the album was done.

I was lucky about one thing. "Poison" was very uncorporate for a hit single. It was very out there. That was the main hit off that record, and I'm glad it was 'cause it was one that was really unique-sounding. It kinda paved the way for me to write the things for this album. *Trash*, though, really surprised me. I thought it was going to go platinum, but it just went crazy. I feel this album is going to do better than Trash. It's got a lot more texture and is heavier—a lot more Alice. *Trash* had pretty much only one attitude of Alice, whereas *Hey Stoopid* has a lot more of Alice's attitudes. It's a nastier album.

It's much heavier. I've always been a hard rocker. If there's anything you're going to want to hear on an Alice record it's my attitude, my voice and hard rock. So when "Feed My Frankenstein" and "Snakebite" came along I went "Yes!" I can't wait to play them onstage 'cause they're pure Alice. When I did them in the studio I was thinking about how great these songs are going to look onstage. And that's how I usually gauge a good song for me.

I think that my record company saw what had happened with Aerosmith. We were both perfectly parallel in what happened to our careers. At a certain time we were both huge, and we almost killed ourselves with excess during an era when nobody was playing our records. Now we've come back at the same time and are doing well on the charts, probably better than we did then. I don't think my music, or music in general, has changed that much since '70s. When I listen to Guns N' Roses or Skid Row or Jane's Addiction I hear '70s-influenced bands. They've got it down—'70s rock was very experimental and guitar-oriented. I'm a guitar freak, and it's my record; that's why there's monster players like Satriani, Vai, Slash, Vinnie Moore and Mick Mars on this record.

When I get together in the studio with a song, I can tell if it's dated-sounding or doesn't belong. I just have an instinct about it that's right for now, and that goes for the show too. So I don't sit around and think too hard about it. We wrote fifty songs, but there were thirty-eight songs that didn't belong on this album. They might be on an album later on, and some of them might even be better than these songs. I don't psychoanalyse it too much. I just go with the feel. The trick is to choose the right songs and make them fit together. I narrowed it down to fifteen songs, and had to pick twelve for the album, and I ended up going, "This song, this song, this song," quite fast. The first order I picked them in was the one that ended up on the album. So instinctively I was right on the money this time (laughs).

I know more what to expect in the studio but I'm always just as excited about doing any record, maybe more with this one, as I was when I was doing *School's Out* or any of them. I'm not jaded to them at all. Every time I go in I say to myself, "I can't wait to see what happens today." So I'm not in the least bit bored with it. Every single album you do reflects a period in your brain. From the Inside was done when I'd just gotten out of the mental institute for drinking, and that's where I was right then. When *Welcome to My Nightmare* was done, I was into this creepy mood. With *Trash* I must have been going through some sort of sexual thing (laughs). So now with *Hey Stoopid*, I feel there's a lot of fun on this album. It sounds like a good, fun summer album to me. I'm in a good mood at this point. Even the nasty songs have got a nice sense of black humour to them.

Stef Burns:

I was into jazz, blues, soul records of my parents. My dad played a little guitar and I picked it up around seven years old. Then I became more influenced by the great guitarists like Jimi Hendrix, Jeff Beck, B.B. King, Allman Bros, then later by Larry Carlton, Robben Ford, Mike Stern, Scofield, Pat Metheny. Sax players, singers and drummers all were very influential too. Big records for me were Hendrix - *Are You Experienced*, Jeff Beck - *Blow by Blow*, Allman Bros., the live one at the Fillmore East, *Montrose*, Deep Purple - *Machine Head*, all the Led Zeppelin and Beatles.

I was recommended to Alice by Joe Satriani, who I know from the Bay Area, and I sent Alice a tape, got hired to do the *Hey Stoopid* album, then to tour. Then I recorded *The Last Temptation*, which I felt more involved in creating sonically. Songwriting-wise, I really didn't have anything prepared that was in the Alice Cooper style, unfortunately. *Hey Stoopid* was fun though, with all the guest stars. I was only present during the Mötley stuff. Oh yeah, and Slash too. He was super cool, a little bit drunk, but... And then the next one, I guess that was Alice's choice to make it more of a band sound. Some of my favourite songs there are "Stolen Prayer," "Cleansed by Fire" and "You're My Temptation."

Then I toured a lot with Alice from '91 to '95 and again in the end of '98. It was always fun. Alice is a breeze to work with. Very easy on stage and rehearsal. Great poker games on the bus. Haven't talked to him in a while though we sent messages to each other through mutual friends.

July 9 – August 19, 1991. Alice Cooper headlines a North American tour called *Operation Rock & Roll.* On the bill are Judas Priest, Motörhead, Dangerous Toys and Metal Church, like Alice, all Epic/Sony acts. The name is in tribute to the US troops involved in *Operation Desert Storm.* Alice's touring band for the campaign is Vinnie Moore and Stef Burns on guitars, Greg Smith on bass, Derek Sherinian on keyboards and Eric Singer on drums.

Alice Cooper:

I think this tour is great. It's good for the audience as they're going to get to see us and Judas Priest do our entire hour-and-15 minute sets each with all our special effects. They're seeing two headliners in one show and nobody's suffering for it. I think the other three bands are going to go up there and kick ass too for forty minutes each. It's almost a festival thing, which to me is really fun. Judas Priest and I are alternating headline position from night to night. Rob and I are really good friends, so there's no ego thing going on. When the record company came to us, they asked us timidly what we thought of it, and we said, "Great! Good idea!" They were shocked that we were so easy to deal with. What's it matter? We're both going to get up there and slay the audience. I think it's more fun now to work like this.

The most important thing is that I'm more focused now than ever before. Alice was more of a victim years ago because I was an alcoholic. Alice acted like a victim onstage—a little sucker—because I was sick myself. Alice is physically better in shape, more than I was when I was 25. The Alice character onstage now is more dangerous than before because of this. He's more vicious. Before, he knew whatever he did the audience was going to love it, but now he goes out and works for it. This tour, we're doing "Generation Landslide" just to prove that I can do that song live 'cause before I couldn't do it 'cause I couldn't remember the lyrics 'cause of booze.

It wouldn't be an Alice show if there wasn't a certain tinge of redness to it. We were doing Gwar before Gwar, not to their extreme, but in principle. What I like about the show now is that we just rock the first eight tunes, then I go off stage, put on the makeup, and give them this middle section that's dark, where I turn into the real evil Alice. On this tour we're doing "Feed My Frankenstein," "Cold Ethyl," "Sick Things," "Only Women Bleed" and some other songs during that part. The theatrics will be really heavy. Then, we rock it into a big finale.

I can get away with doing the show I do 'cause the world public has given Alice sort of a license to do what he wants. When we first started, we could only do what we could afford to build. We created our own guillotines and gallows. But now we're more advanced than that. On this show I dissolve into a film, shown up on a screen and then re-appear onto the stage. All these great illusions take a month of rehearsals, but now we can do them 'cause we have the money and the technology. My philosophy has always been music first—80% of the time is music, and the other 20% is the stage stuff. If the music doesn't back it up then it shouldn't be onstage.

I think that people can come to an Alice show, or buy and Alice record, and they know they're going to get their money's worth. We've always made it like that for the last 20 years. Even when we didn't have a hit record, we could still sell anywhere 'cause people were coming out knowing they're going to see a great show. Now I'm making music that when a fan buys my record, they can relate to it too. I believe that's why so many people are getting into bands that either are from the '70s like myself or Aerosmith, or that have that '70s groove like Jane's Addiction or Faith No More. People know that they're getting a complete package. A lot of bands can been seen on MTV and they look great and sound great on record, but when you go see them you go, "Geez, this sucks!" I think people are really going more for quality. I hate to use that word for Alice Cooper (laughs), but that's the bottom line. You have to be quality through and through, and people are now supporting it.

This tour and album has all of the energy, if not more energy than Alice has had ever before. I can't even think about the thought of retiring. It doesn't even enter my mind. I go out and run three miles a night at 7:10 per mile, and I think that as long as I can do that I can still get onstage. I'm saying to the guys in my band that they'd better be in shape or else I'm gonna blow them off the stage (laughs). The thing is that I still love rock music. I still love hearing what's going on and new things that are getting accepted. When I first heard Faith No More, I thought, "Great record! This deserves to be a hit." And when I saw them live, I thought, "Great! These guys are out of their minds." And because they did make it, it encourages me.

Derek Sherninian:
You'd have to ask him why he's a born rock star. I guess it's just the spirit, you know? You either love and live for the art form or you don't. I also live the lifestyle as much as I can (laughs). But Alice is great. A total gentleman. A class act. Very easygoing guy. One of the very easiest people I ever had to work for. He knows if it sounds good or if it sounds wrong or whatever.

August 19, 1991. The *Operation Rock & Roll* tour swings round to Toronto, where Judas Priest's lead singer Rob Halford hits his head when making his entrance on his motorcycle, unleashing a chain of events that finds him tearing on out of the band, not to return for over a decade.

August 27, 1991. Alice is inducted into LA's Rock Walk. Meanwhile, same day, Seattle's Pearl Jam issue their debut, *Ten*, an instant phenomenon of a new type of hard rock. The record eventually sells 13 x platinum in the US.

September 3 - 13, 1991. With the *Operation Rock & Roll* tag put aside for the name *Nightmare on Your Street* (prompted by the implosion of *Operation Rock & Roll* co-headliner Judas Priest), Pete "Freezin'" Friesen replaces Vinnie Moore as Alice Cooper's touring guitarist while the band conduct a short campaign playing radio stations, parking lots and other "street" locations.

September 17, 1991. Guns N' Roses issue their *Use Your Illusion I* and *Use Your Illusion II* albums on the same day. The first one includes a song called "The Garden" featuring a vocal duet between Axl Rose and Alice Cooper. Slash got the idea to bring Alice in because he thought Axl's vocal style on the song bore a similarity to Cooper's singing style.

September 23, 1991. "Love's a Loaded Gun" is issued as a single in Europe. The B-side is a cover of Jimi Hendrix's "Fire." It manages a No.38 showing on the British charts.

September 24, 1991. Nirvana issues their second album, *Nevermind*. Grunge explodes and the record eventually certifies diamond in the US, representing sales of ten million copies. Any of the hair metal bands, whether it's the ones from the '80s or the ones from the '70s giving it a whirl, have about 12 months dwindling shelf life left. Bands that started in the '90s might have their major label unenthusiastically put their second album on the shelves, but then they too would be kicked to the curb.

September 28 – November 9, 1991. Alice conducts an extensive European tour leg in support of *Hey Stoopid*, main support coming from Wolfsbane and The Almighty.

1992

February 1992. "Feed My Frankenstein" is issued as a single from *Hey Stoopid*.

Alice Cooper:
They're friends to begin with, and Satriani was Vai's teacher. When I got down "Feed My Frankenstein," I sent them a tape of it, told them Nikki Sixx was playing bass on it and said I'd love to hear you guys play on the same track. I thought it'd be semi-historical. I wanted this song to be a Frankenstein, so I wanted the two best monster guitarists on it. They agreed and they had real fun with it.

I worked with Nikki Sixx on a few songs and with Rachel Bolan on one. That one didn't make the album, but I had fun working with him. I worked with a lot of different people, including Zodiac Mindwarp, Jim Vallance, Mick Mars and Desmond Child. The first thing that these people have to do is to get past nervousness of working with me. If I was going to write with someone who I emulated, I'd be nervous too. It got to a point where we had to get past that so that we could really get down to business. I'd go to these parties and award ceremonies and I'd bump into these guys and say, "Let's get together and write something someday," so I took people up on it. I'd call and say, "I'll be at your house at three," and they'd be like, "What?!" It was fun.

The most fun though was working with Jack Ponti because he really understood early Alice Cooper music. Songs like "Love's a Loaded Gun," "Snakebite," "Little by Little" and "Hey Stoopid" are pure Alice. I got to write with a lot of different writers on this album. I got to work with producer Peter Collins because I didn't want to work with a songwriter/producer—I wanted a sonic producer. I spent from last August to January writing this album—50 songs in total—and what I've come to understand from my career is that the most important thing to an album is the quality of the songs, not the length of time you spend in the studio.

February 14, 1992. Smash hit heavy metal comedy *Wayne's World* hits theatres and becomes a pop culture phenomenon. Alice cameos in a memorable scene and he's included on the double platinum soundtrack album as well, with "Feed My Frankenstein" from *Hey Stoopid*. Mike Myers had wanted to use "I'm Eighteen" and "School's Out" in the film, but manager Shep Gordon steers him toward the brand-new song.

Alice Cooper:
That was a whole new audience right there. In fact, I told Mike Myers and Dana Carvey, "You stuck me with this for the rest of my life! From now on this is me!" I went to a Suns basketball game in Phoenix and I got up to get an ice cream and half of the section got up and bowed, "I'm not worthy, I'm not worthy" (laughs).

December 14, 1992. Alice and Sheryl welcome a third child to the family, daughter Sonora Rose.

1993

1993. Alice works for much of the year on what would be one of the most ambitious albums of his career. Cooper collaborates on author Neil Gaiman on the concept as well as an attendant comic book that tells the story.

Alice Cooper:
"If you were going to write a story that tells everything, you'd have to write a total opera where everything had to be said in the lyrics of the song, and that's too grueling," he states. "Plus you can't take a song off the album and let it stand on its own as it sounds out of place. So what I wanted to do was write the story first, and then write the songs into the story. That way when you read the comic book you can see where the songs fit in. Then you can take the songs off and they'll stand on their own."

1994

January 15, 1994. Harry Nilsson dies, and Alice loses another friend form his notorious cocaine and alcohol days at a so-called Hollywood Vampire in the late '70s. Cause of death is a heart attack; he was 52.

Alice Cooper:
The first time I ever smoked a joint was with Jimi Hendrix. He turned me on to marijuana. When I was 19 or 20 years old. I was in awe of Jimi Hendrix. We were sort of a little high school band trying to make it, and here we are with Jimi Hendrix. Jim Morrison took us on a tour for a while. The Doors took us out to open for them. So they were like our big brothers. You don't sit down and try to out-drink Jim Morrison or Janis Joplin, because they were professionals (laughs).

The crazy thing was, if you look at the guys that were the next generation, the Steven Tylers and the Alice Coopers and the Ozzy Osbournes and Iggy Pops, we are all still here. I think that's because we watched our big brothers die, and learned that there is an expiration date. Each generation learns from the last generation. You come to that crossroads where you're either gonna stop drinking or you're going to keep drinking and die and join your friends. I got to that point. I just went, okay, I'm ready to stop. You know, throwing up blood in the morning is not fun. I'm sure Steven Tyler had the same thing, and Joe Perry and all these guys got to that point of just, you have to make a decision. You're gonna live or die.

When you're Christian, it does take the sting out of death. If you have faith and it's what you believe. I don't know with these guys, what their belief system is. I know that it was weird that the Jimi Hendrixes and the John Lennons and the Janis Joplins, Brian Jones and people like that, you never really felt they were going to get to 30.

At that time, it was like you lived every day as much as you could, because your career could be over

next week, or your life could be over next week. So we watched. I certainly didn't have any death wish but I think Jim Morrison did. If you really look at the lyrics, he was pretty much predicting his death.

It's how everybody takes it. Some people think that they're going to come back as a butterfly or that's it, once you're gone, you just rot away. I don't believe that. I believe in the biblical version of it. Because at least I can refer to the Scripture and go, well, at least I have 2000 years of this Scripture to fall back on that I can't find any fault with. So I'm putting my faith in that, rather than, well, whatever happens, happens. You know what I mean? I call it fire insurance.

May 14, 1994. In the midst of a European promo tour (doing what Alice does better than anybody), he video for "Lost in America" debuts on MTV. Two days later, the single is launched in the UK.

July 6, 1994. Alice Cooper issues *The Last Temptation*, his 20th album in 25 years. The story is told in a series of three comic books, the first of which comes with purchase of the album. Soundgarden vocalist Chris Cornell guests on two tracks, "Unholy War" and "Stolen Prayer." Once more, Alice works with a number of song doctors as well as keyboard player Derek Sherinian, who will soon leave and find considerable success with Dream Theatre.

Alice Cooper:
It's a very strong concept album, a real morality play. It has a protagonist, a hero, a victim; it has a reason and a conclusion. The only way I could get that across doing ten songs was to put a comic book with it. I didn't want to do ten videos because then the videos are limited as little pieces. Besides, the comic makes it more fun. Since albums disappeared, Alice hasn't been able to have any fun with the packaging. This way they get the CD and the full-sized comic book.

There's three comic books to tell the story. We worked with Neil Gaiman, who is the writer of *Sandman* and another character, Death. It's very well done. I especially picked him out because I really liked his personality, and I liked the way he wrote. I just didn't want to do another album of just songs. I think Alice is, at this point, pretty good at getting a story across or doing something theatrical with an album, and I just felt that I hadn't done that in a long time. I wanted to do another *Welcome to My Nightmare* and this was the perfect vehicle for it."

The things that I used to make fun of are real now. I realise that I'm not going to be able to write a song that will get to a kid that is growing up now, especially in the inner city. I grew up with the problems of my generation, but I don't have the problems of Generation X. Everything that they're bombarded with is based on death. Sex didn't used to be deadly—now it is. I never had to worry about going to school with everyone carrying guns and being in gangs. There were gangs in my day, but it was good fun—but now it's almost science fiction! The bottom line of this album is to say that life isn't cheap. Life seems to be really cheap right now. There's a real defeatist attitude out there today. Alice never promoted anything defeatist. Alice always made fun of death, sex, and money. But I never promoted it; I never said this is the way to get out of this life. I've always been very pro-life.

But the characters on the album, every time I do the Showman character, he's half speaking it, half singing it, because that's his character. I went back to the old Alice and said let's dig that up. When he speaks we should definitely know it's him. Those signature songs. Some of the most fun stuff on the album was "Nothing's Free" and "Bad Place Alone." Those are real *Love It to Death* Alice.

Chris Cornell is on here and Chris is great. It was an interesting thing how he came to write with me. We had all the songs written, and Bob Pfeiffer from Epic, who was working with me on the album, told me that Chris Cornell had some songs that he wanted me to hear. Two of the songs, one in particular, "Holy War," really fit into the concept with just a little surgery. "Stolen Prayer," the other song that he wrote, wasn't quite a song yet, and we sat down for six or seven hours working on it. That song ended up being one of my favourites.

If I'm going to work with someone, I can't trust them to write an Alice Cooper song on their own, because Alice has a certain way, a certain perspective in looking at things. When I look at a song that someone else has wrote, I'll read it and I'll say, "That's not Alice. Alice wouldn't say that." So I make changes. Or if I'm writing with somebody they'll come up with a great bit and I'll say, "That's really good, but I can't see Alice thinking that way." So we have to write for him as a person, a character. It's funny because they never had to do that before. They figure everything is pretty generic, anybody can sing anything, and it's like, "Anybody can, but Alice can't."

July 11, 1994. "It's Me" is issued as a single from *The Last Temptation*. The song finds Alice collaborating with Tommy Shaw from Styx and Jack Blades from Night Ranger, both also from Damn Yankees.

September 10, 1994. Amidst a flurry of worldwide press duties, including in-store appearances and the odd appearance with Neil Gaiman, Alice receives a lifetime achievement award from the Foundations Forum.

Alice Cooper:
Alice brought theatre to rock 'n' roll, and we brought attitude to rock 'n' roll. Now, lyrically, I'd like to get some things across. I probably won't be making twenty-five more albums, but at this point, while I have the energy, I'd like to say something. I've left this thing open for *The Last Temptation*, part two. You never know! At this point, if it sells a million, great. If it sells three, I still had fun making it. I know the die-hard Alice fans will like it. Alice Cooper has been around for a long time and people are expecting this to be an Alice album and it will be. As long as I keep making albums that I'm not embarrassed by, that I really like, I think I can do it for pretty much as long as I want to do it. I'm in better physical shape now than I was twenty years ago. Actually it's the least of my worries. I'd actually like to see some of these new bands try and do an Alice Cooper show—they'd be dead! They wouldn't be able to do it.

1995

February 1995. Alice has now left Epic/Sony and signed with Hollywood Records. Nothing will come of the union.

September 2 – 9, 1995. Alice Cooper performs his first dates in four years, playing four shows in South America.

Alice Cooper:
Alice has never been a wimp. Every time he goes out onstage, he goes out with total vengeance—he wants to burn the audience for the entire show. He's never walked onstage humble at all. That's just the way Alice is—it's not the way I am; it's him. At the end of the show I want the audience as tired as I am. Usually at the end of the show, I'm doing jumping jacks saying, "Hey look, I'm still going and you guys are tired!" That's just Alice—he's an arrogant, egotistical, sadistic character, but you'd hate him if he wasn't like that. People need Alice to be like that. If I were a kid in the audience, Alice would be my favourite rocker because he is like that. That's how I judge Alice, and when I can't make Alice like that, then I shouldn't be him.

November 26, 1995. David Briggs, producer of *Easy Action*, passes away at 51 from lung cancer. He is best known for producing many Neil Young records as well as his work with Nils Lofgren.

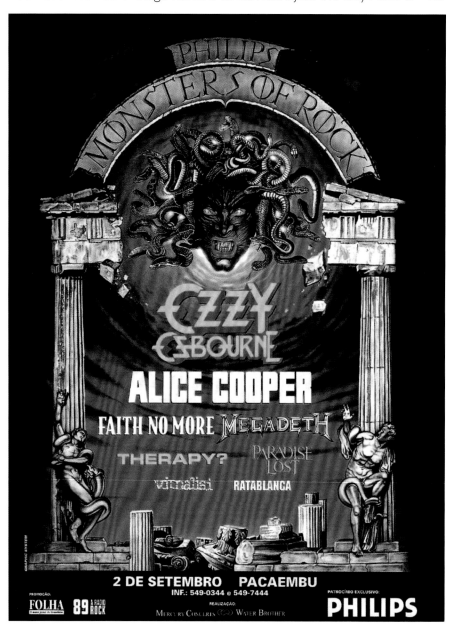

1996

January 28, 1996. On Super Bowl Sunday, Alice collaborates with Rob Zombie on a song called "Hands of Death."

Rob Zombie:

Alice took everything to a new level. He was first and best at everything. There were very few people before him who were doing anything, especially with a dark vibe; he was the first one to do that. He's like the Beatles for this type of music. What was happening onstage before Alice? I don't know, everything seemed so boring. When he started, we'd go back and watch some old footage of him and it just made no sense. Opening for the Doors? What must that crowd have thought?

I feel bad for Alice sometimes, too, because I don't feel he gets the credit he deserves for everything he does, for some reason. The thing with Alice that's great is he's so smart. So a lot of times people do visual stuff and it's embarrassing and it's stupid, but he was so smart that it always was not obvious what he was doing. Especially in the early days because they had such a weird… it was very Hollywood, and I mean that in a good way. It was that weird sort of Vaudeville way he was doing things that really was amazing.

To me Kiss always seemed like, "Hey, if one Alice Cooper worked, let's have four." That's what it seemed like. But I'm trying to think as a kid, they both hit me almost within the same time. I was into Alice first and then Kiss second, but I think Kiss just seemed more rock 'n' roll. Alice was so theatrical and especially once you get to *Welcome to My Nightmare* it was very story-oriented, which was amazing. But Kiss was more a straight-up rock band. Kiss is funny sometimes, too, because when I watch them and you hear a song like "Beth," it's so bizarre. There's a guy in cat makeup holding roses singing this ballad?! Like I would hate this song if he wasn't in makeup, but somehow as a kid you were fine with it. It's weird.

But in a weird way Alice seemed more scary. Kiss never seemed scary. Alice seemed like Jack the Ripper and Kiss always seemed like superheroes, like they were the fantastic four. They were definitely more accessible. Alice was shocking and repulsive to people at first. When you see his early stuff, they seem like degenerate drunks tearing everything up. Whereas Kiss always seemed in a weird way wholesome. It was weird and over-the-top but it never seemed dangerous. I'm not saying that as an insult, but it always seemed like a big fun show, where Alice seemed like a deranged lunatic back in the day.

March 26, 1996. "Hands of Death" surfaces, on soundtrack album *The X Files/Songs in the Key of X.* The following year, it receives a Grammy nomination for Best Metal Performance.

June 2, 1996. Alice plays Sammy Hagar's Cabo Wabo in Cabo San Lucas, Mexico, with the show being released as *A Fistful of Alice*. Guesting on the night are Slash, Rob Zombie and bartender Sammy Hagar.

June 6 – August 17, 1996. Alice performs an intensive amount of North American dates on what he calls the *School's Out Summer Tour*, playing a set studded with hits in a co-headling configuration with Scorpions.

October 1, 1996. Michael Bruce, co-writing with Billy James, issues his autobiography, *No More Mr. Nice Guy: The Inside Story of the Alice Cooper Group.* This coincides with a move to Houston, Texas.

Mike Marconi:
Michael Bruce is the type of individual who will hear a riff—and there was so many times, because Michael moved and lived with us, right in the same house, and we had a recording studio in the downstairs area— I'd be playing something and Michael would come running downstairs and he'll stop me and go, "Is that original? Is that your own? You didn't steal that idea, did you?" I'd go, "No, that's my own riff!" (laughs) Michael would either pick up his guitar or go to the keyboard, and I'd play it, he'd learn it, and the next thing I know, now Michael's got a change going into it, then another change, and the next thing I know he's got a melody. It just would amaze me. I learned so much from him on arranging, the bridge, the length of a song; it was a great experience.

October 8, 1996. Marilyn Manson hits his peak with *Antichrist Superstar*. Many parallels with Alice Cooper exist, but one interesting one is that despite the massive fame and notoriety, neither act sold a commensurate amount of records.

Gavin Baddeley:
Marilyn Manson upped the ante in a number of ways, and one of the ways is that he's noted that Alice Cooper quickly developed the idea that Alice Cooper was a character—it was makeup he could take off at the end of the show. Marilyn Manson's gone on record criticising him for that, saying that's short-changing the kids. Once Brian Warner became Marilyn Manson, he became Marilyn Manson. Brian Warner wasn't waiting in a cupboard somewhere to come back. Brian Warner was dead; it was Marilyn Manson or nothing.

He also upped the ante by including a vast amount of dense content in his music, so you could read a lot in there, which was threatening to some critics because there are all these deviant philosophers. There's Nietzsche in there, Crowley, all these dangerous ideas which he's packaged on a CD that your 12-year-old son can buy, and that's far more threatening than thinking your son might have his head turned by Kiss and "God of Thunder."

I think he's sincere. He says that what he really wants the kids to do is to think. He says that if you think I'm influencing these kids to be evil, that's nothing to do with me. That's your job as parents to bring your kids up, and if you're bringing your kids up right, then they can read as many Crowley and Nietzsche books as they like and it won't do them any harm at all.

Kiss and Alice just wanted people to buy. They were far more all-American. That's the all-American aspect of it, and I think to a certain extent why they didn't cause the same level of hostility. Marilyn Manson was operating under death threats. He was getting daily communications of various kinds that people were going to shoot him. That upped the ante as well because as I understand it, that's something Alice Cooper or Kiss never really encountered.

December 28 – 31, 1996. Alice follows up a fall full of celebrity golf tournaments, small projects and appearances at events with three "New Years Rotten Eve" shows with Ted Nugent, with the last gig being a Detroit's Joe Louis Arena.

1997

February 20 – 23, 1997. Alice puts on the First Annual Alice Cooper Celebrity-AM Tournament and Celebrity Shoot-out in Arizona, amidst participating in other golf tournaments to kick off 1997.

June 20 – July 24, 1997. Alice takes his *School's Out Summer Tour* to Europe.

July 29, 1997. *A Fistful of Alice* is released in the US.

July 30 – August 31, 1997. Alice Cooper capitalises on the hair metal package tour trend of the late '90s with something he calls the *Rock 'n' Roll Carnival* tour. Support for the shed tour comes from Dokken, Slaughter and Warrant.

Alice Cooper:
It's like some warped carnival. To me the scariest thing in the world was those carnival guys. You know, you walk in there and you go, "Where do they find these people?" So that's what this show is, only it includes all of the hits, and everybody's involved in the show. If you're anywhere near the stage, you're in the show.

September 5 – 11, 1997. Alice Cooper plays a series of dates in Australia.

October 12, 1997. Michael Bruce, Glen Buxton, Neal Smith and Richie Scarlet perform a show at Area 51 in Houston. It will be Glen Buxton's last performance.

October 19, 1997. Glenn Buxton passes away, age 49, in Clarion, Iowa due to complications from pneumonia. He is buried on October 24th.

Dennis Dunaway:
A week before I heard the sad news, I had a lengthy phone conversation with Glen. He was excited about the show he did with Michael and Neal out in Texas. He wanted to do some more shows but with me included. He had written a new song that he wanted to play for me over the phone. He kept asking me what I thought of his playing. I told him that my only criticism was that he needed to get control of his feedbacks, otherwise he was as unique as any guitar player I had ever heard. I complimented his ability to play by feel, which was something that he always said was the most important thing. He once asked me what I thought he should play on "Drive Me Nervous" and I said, that's easy, play nervous! You'll never find a more nervous guitar break anywhere. But Glen was extremely funny, with a very unusual sarcastic sense of humour.

As for Michael, the late '90s and on, Michael Bruce went through some serious issues, to the point he wasn't allowed backstage, from what I'm told, at Alice Cooper concerts. Michael and I have always had occasional phone calls and we see each other every year or so. I haven't heard anything about him not being allowed backstage lately. He was backstage in Phoenix, LA and New York. He's got a great sense of humour. Recently, after the original group finished a lengthy pose for fans who were taking way too many photos, I said I

...aster. Michael asked if I was a cubist.
...ways the rock star. I think it was on
...where around there, Glen was
...and we were listening to it in the
...ot believe all the racket. Bob Ezrin
...whatever happened to that recording
...acelets and everything that he had on.
...n strip down (laughs). He was like Harpo
...nore stuff. You would look at the pile of stuff
and the ... in his pockets and everything and go, "Whoa,
how did he get ... ch stuff in his pockets?" The craziest stuff he
would come up with too; there was always a switchblade and stuff like
that but there would be stuff where you'd wonder, "Why does he have
that? Why is he carrying that around?" He used to have chicken claws
hanging from a necklace and those would get caught in his strings.

With Glen's personality, he had always been against authority.
He always rebelled, he resented people who would tell him how to
conduct himself and he wouldn't do it no matter what it was. In the
early days of the band it was us rebelling against the world and then all
of a sudden as it became more of a business with more people
standing around telling us what to do—that made it unappealing to
him. The less he would be inspired the more people would try to
make him inspired and as things moved forward he just didn't find it
fun anymore. There's also something that bugs me about that. People
always point the finger at him for that behaviour when Alice was
drinking just as much as him. Alice was forgetting the words,
singing off-key and falling down onstage but nobody points that same
finger at him. That was rock 'n' roll. That was the lifestyle. It gets the
best of some people while others survive."

Glen always had respiratory problems and he had several
physical problems that he had dealt with even way back when I first
met him. I may be guessing but I think that might be why his family
moved to Arizona. A lot of families did because Arizona was a place
where you could get away from pollen. Unfortunately so many people
moved there and tried to grow lawns that it defeated the purpose.
Glen was a night owl and an insomniac. He would stay up all night and
sleep all day whenever he got the chance but as we got rolling, if you
got to bed before four or five in the morning you were lucky. Then
you'd have an 8:00 AM call for the flight and not everybody can handle
that. I could sleep on the plane so I had my way to handle it but that
didn't work with his insomnia; he couldn't sleep and it was tough on
him.

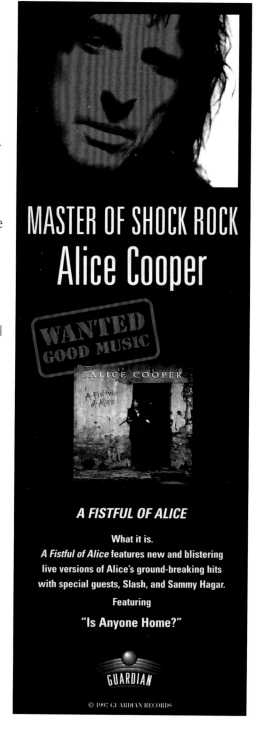

MASTER OF SHOCK ROCK
Alice Cooper

A FISTFUL OF ALICE

What it is.
A Fistful of Alice features new and blistering
live versions of Alice's ground-breaking hits
with special guests, Slash, and Sammy Hagar.

Featuring

"Is Anyone Home?"

GUARDIAN

© 1997 GUARDIAN RECORDS

Alice Cooper:

What was the character's name in *Catcher in the Rye*?" Holden Caulfield. Glen was like that, the true juvenile
delinquent. Glen was right out of *West Side Story*. He was a Bowery Boy. And always, couldn't help, from always carrying something illegal of some sort with him. That was just his nature to do that. He was the guy
who smoked, he was the guy who drank, he was the guy who did everything that was... he was like our Keith
Richards. He couldn't help... honestly, even in the most dire situation, we would be crossing the border, and I
would say, "Guys, this is 1972, we can't have a seed or an open beer container or anything, to cross the border."
It would take four hours to cross the border; they were being so strict with us. We never did have anything
with us. But Glen would always smuggle, like a switchblade. That was his nature. That's what made Glen great.
Because he was truly that greaser.

December 29 – 31, 1997. Like the previous year, Alice performs three of what essentially are New
Year's Eve shows, again, closing out in Detroit. At the State Theatre in Detroit, Alice
debuted a rendition of "Jailhouse Rock" where he vamped as Elvis.

1998

March 27, 1998. Alice participates in a groundbreaking ceremony for his Cooperstown—common usage is Cooperstown, but formally it's Cooper'stown—location in hometown Phoenix. Two days later he's at an Arizona Diamondbacks game helping a few other local rock stars sing the national anthem.

May 25 – June 7, 1998. Alice plays a series of European dates, opened by the likes of Backyard Babies, Glitterbox and Skew Siskin.

June 19 – December 31, 1998. Alice plays US dates, and into December, peppers them with other activities, including golf tournaments and the opening of Cooperstown in Phoenix, where he performs with Michael and Neal. And then closing out the year, he does his usual trio of more casual New Years Eve Shows.

1999

Spring 1999. Alice plays a series of celebrity golf tournaments.

April 20, 1999. Rhino issues a plush four-CD box set called *The Life and Crimes of Alice Cooper*. Stuffed with rarities, the well-regarded career retrospective is almost five hours long. Unfortunately, the release date is also the day of the Columbine High School massacre.

May 2, 1999. *A Behind the Music* documentary on Alice Cooper airs.

May 19 – June 29, 1999. Alice does a promo tour of Europe.

August 28, 1999. Alice and band play an unannounced tour warm-up show at Alice's Cooperstown restaurant in Phoenix.

September 1 – October 16, 1999. Alice and the band hit the road for US dates. At this point, Alice has with him Ryan Roxie and Pete Friesen on guitars, Greg Smith on bass, Eric Singer on drums and Lindsay Vannoy on keyboards. Supporting are the likes of Chlorine, New Meanies and Jessie Camp.

Eric Singer:
With Alice Cooper, look at how many people have been in his band. Now he's considered more like a solo artist, but originally Alice Cooper was the name of the band—it was a band, those original guys. Eventually he became the solo artist, and he was able to do it on his own. He still can go out and tour every year. No disrespect to anybody in Alice's band, because I was one of those guys in that band for many tours. Alice loves having guys that are really good players, are good musicians and guys that are name guys from other bands and all that.
But at the end of the day, people go to see Alice Cooper. Not saying that some of them don't enjoy or are fans of some of the members of the band, but they don't care who is playing drums. They might say, "It's really cool, because Eric from Kiss is playing drums" when I was playing with them, but I think most of them really don't care.

October 3, 1999. At a tour stop in Atlantic City, Michael Bruce joins Alice on stage for "Under My Wheels," marking the first time Alice had played with an original band member since 1974.

October 23, 1999. The Alice Cooper band reunite for the first time, at the second Glen Buxton Memorial Weekend, playing Cooperstown in Phoenix. On stage for a six-song set is Alice, Michael, Neal, Dennis and Rockin' Reggie Vincent.

2000s

After a decade of reflection, Alice Cooper stormed back in the 2000s as a creative force, issuing an impressive five albums over ten years, and touring hard in the cracks. But given the legacy carefully built, Alice wasn't exactly in the cracks. Cooper and his team thoughtfully built bands of bounding babies, highly professional players seasoned but still enthusiastic, resumes uncommonly stuffed for such young folks. They raised Alice's game, and the fitness and seriousness of Alice in terms of rocking hard his audience in turn inspired his rotating army of band mates, who were also spurred on to sparkling performances by the opportunity to work with a legend, and one who was clearly still into it.

As well, the regular touring in the '90s was quietly showing dividends, as Alice was now firmly in the camp of classic rock bands with huge built-in audiences. Also, given the youth in his band and the continued adherence to keeping the show big, dads brought their boys and the crowds represented a wide range of ages. This was both intentional and a natural by-product of Alice's personality. Alice was deeply a man of Christian faith, he was just a good all 'round family kinda guy and as a result the show was kept wholesome enough—still loud and heavy metal and scary, but Halloween scary.

Back to the records, Alice opened the decade with his two-part tale of fire and brimstone—*Brutal Planet* and *Dragontown*—set to a sort of depressing industrial metal beat. Now on a mid-sized label, attention was limited, but the dour Sabbatherian melodies along with the warmed-over White Zombie music had fans for the most part, thrusting thumbs down.

By 2003 and already on the way to a third record of the decade, Alice changed tack. Part Alice being Alice, part Alice being Bowie (he would bristle at that), part "this techno sound is done like dinner, let's move on," the man's new sound was a return to regular lunch bucket hard rock. Alice might call it "Detroit" rock, which wouldn't be inaccurate. Fully 2003's *The Eyes of Alice Cooper,* 2005's *Dirty Diamonds* and 2008's *Along Came a Spider* (concept album notwithstanding), are of a set, part garage rock, a wee part psych, a snatch from the Kane-brained '80s, but mostly the type of music the original Alice Cooper band might have been making together from 1974 to 1979, say, but down a pronounced guitar-charged road.

Now, see, Alice Cooper was giving the fans what they want, very much what any Alice Cooper fanatic would specifically request from the guy. But this rarely works decades down the line when it comes to actual record sales, and Alice Cooper remained in the category of classic rock bands that was fully legendary and known, could put bums in seats, but sold no records. Fair enough. Fact is, an act is always more legitimate if they put their boots on and get out and make records rather that rest on their hits played live. In the 2000s, this was Alice, and his dedicated fans appreciated him for it.

2000

February 23 – March 11, 2000. Alice is part of the cast for the Austrian tour leg of British *Rock Symphony: A Musical Tribute to The Rolling Stones, The Beatles, The Who, Led Zeppelin and Others....*

April 2000. GlamNation, a glam covers band, usually relegated to gigs in and around LA, conducts a short Scandinavian tour. The band is essentially Alice's backing band, forming in 1999 with Eric Dover, Ryan Roxie, Eric Singer, Derek Sherinian and bassist Steven Adika. In 2000, Derek Sherninian would be replaced by Teddy Zigzag, both keyboard players having served with Alice at various points.

Eric Dover:
I started with Alice in late 1999. We had this band called GlamNation which was a sort of send-up revue of '70s rock. As far as touring, we played Gothenburg, Stockholm and Malmo. Those were some great shows. Then I joined Alice in 1999 and toured with him for a while. Alice with myself and Ryan Roxie, we wrote *The Eyes of Alice Cooper* and we toured for what, five or six years, I think, in total. Then one day I had enough and I had to just take a break.

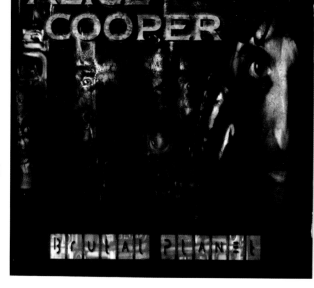

June 6, 2000. Alice issues the Bob Marlette-produced *Brutal Planet* album, through his new deal with Spitfire Records. Personnel for the album is Alice plus Ryan Roxie on guitar, Bob Marlette on bass and keyboards and Eric Singer on drums. The Japanese bonus studio track is called "Can't Sleep, Clowns Will Eat Me."

Alice Cooper:
I wanted to write something that was very apocalyptic. I wanted to write something that we all know is coming, but we don't want to say it. It is fiction, but maybe not so much fiction. Maybe a lot of it is based on what everybody thinks eventually is going to happen but even a song like "Blow Me a Kiss" is an exaggeration of what happened at Columbine, but maybe not so much of an exaggeration. I don't want to say it is about Columbine though. But the guy is saying, "Are you going to blow me away just because I'm black, that I'm gay, that I don't know you, because I'm happy? It doesn't matter to you. No matter what I am, you're going to blow me away."

So a lot of it is very current. "Pick Up the Bones" was written basically about, I was watching CNN, while I was doing an interview and I'm literally sitting here watching a guy, with the sound down. He's got a pillowcase and he's going through all these ruins and he's picking up ribcages, skulls, and he was basically coming back to his village and collecting his family. I just went, "That is the most horrific thing I've ever seen in my life."

This is my uncle, this is my brother, and I had to write a song about it called "Pick Up the Bones." To me that is future horror. This guy is going through the rubble of the destruction, literally collecting his family so he can put them all to rest. He's going to put them into a big pile, set them on fire and let the smoke go up to heaven. We don't say how he got there, how they got there. It's just said that there were men with guns that marched through this place, which is actually going on now, soldiers leaving nothing but dead bodies and bones, for no apparent reason.

The last thing that I had written was *The Last Temptation*, which again was very novelistic, almost

Something Wicked This Way Comes. Before that period, I've always tried to write in concepts. I've never really written anything science fiction, and I wanted this one to be in the form of a futuristic novel. So *Brutal Planet,* I think that's what this planet is going to turn into.

I have to go by not what I feel. I'm very optimistic. Alice is very pessimistic. I have to write the way Alice would think. He thinks we're flying toward a brick wall at 100 miles per hour. He would like to be there and see what happens at the end. This is Alice's state of the world address, a future state of the world address. But I like the fact that a lot of these things he sees are things that are going on now. One of the songs called "Eat Some More" is about the way we are just eating ourselves right off the planet. It's just gluttony for the sake of

gluttony. There's something real poetic about that (laughs) and I don't know what it is, just the fact that we can be this gluttonous. It's very destructive. Every one of these songs point to destruction. Our attitude is very destructive.

Personally, for me there is hope, but I'm not going to let on that there is. Personally for me this album should not point to any hope at all. It should point to the fact that again, we've already fallen off the cliff, we just haven't hit yet. It's a much more dramatic album. It's a mighty long drop, and it's not the drop that kills you, it's the sudden stop.

I think that is one of the important things about Alice is that I write mini novels. Any one of my albums can be written into a movie or a story. I almost write my albums as soundtracks for the story. You could write a comic book on almost every single album I've ever done because they definitely all lead towards storylines. So I tend to try to write some sort of cohesive work every single time. I really don't like writing twelve songs that don't connect. I like them all to connect.

In fact, I like them to connect to other albums, sort of like a Vonnegut thing where certain characters keep coming back. I think with this one, one thing that does connect back with other albums is the Alice voice. I use voices that I've used on different albums. You hear these voices and you go, "Wait a minute, that is the voice he used back on *Welcome to My Nightmare,* and that voice is used on *Temptation,* and wait a minute, that one he used on *Hey Stoopid,* you know what I mean? So I have three or four different voices that are used for different characters. Steven keeps showing up everywhere, even though we don't know who Steven is. I don't even know who Steven is. He's been on four or five albums; he's my Kilgore Trout.

Eric Singer:
The *Brutal Planet* record was done very quickly on my part. I came in and replaced drum machine parts with "real" drums in just over two days. I liked the heavier approach but did not have a lot of time to absorb the music or think about my drumming other than to play what I felt or was directed by the producer. But I loved working with Alice and my time with Alice goes back a long way. I auditioned for Coop in January 1990 to replace Jonathan Mover on the *Trash* tour and have worked on and off with Alice since then, doing twelve tours, three albums and have been on two live concert long-form videos. *Billion Dollar Babies* is a classic record and one of my fave all-time records. In fact, all the early stuff is great and enjoy playing anything from that era. But I never saw the band live in the early years—my mom would not let me go to the *Billion Dollar Babies* tour in 1973!

June 10 - July 29, 2000. Alice tours Europe in support of his *Brutal Planet* album, although he arrives there two weeks in advance to perform his typically well-orchestrated press duties. Alice's touring band for the campaign consists of guitarists Ryan Roxie and Pete Friesen, plus bassist Greg Smith, drummer Eric Singer and keyboard player Teddy Zigzag. Songs from the new album played live are "Brutal Planet," "Blow Me a Kiss," "Pick Up the Bones," "Gimme," "Take It Like a Woman," "Wicked Young Man" and "It's the Little Things."

Alice Cooper:

"Brutal Planet" is the opening track, and it's actually a conversation between the survivors of the planet and they are talking about look where we are. Then when the girl's voice comes in, that is coming from what I call the angel's view. The angels are looking down on the planet and saying, "What a beautiful place; isn't it gorgeous? Isn't this just the most beautiful planet?" Then it gets back to the survivors going, "You know, it's not so pretty down here! It's hell down here!" (laughs) They're going, "Yeah but from up here, it looks wonderful." So it's a little mini opera there, a conversation going on between two entities.

The story starts right where we are—it's the future. I think it's pretty obvious that we're picking up right here. It's the future and it's a mystery how we got here. All we know is that we are here, and we don't know how we got here, but everything is destroyed.

"Wicked Young Man," he's the character that is the young guy that basically has grown out of this whole planet. He's the worst of the worst. It even says in the lyrics that he is so violent that the different Aryan sects—I don't say Aryan—but the different brotherhoods won't even take him. He is more violent than anything that they have ever done. He is a total product of violence. He is not happy unless something violent is happening. That definitely comes along with the lyrics.

What I'm doing is I have portrayed him, not necessarily as myself, but the song is saying I am a wicked young man. "It's not the games that I play, the movies I see, the music I dig, I'm just a wicked young man." It dispels the fact that these people who do all these horrible things get it from the arts. I'm just saying that some people are just wicked. Some people are just vicious, born psychopathic, born sociopathic. So that's who this guy is. The problem is, there are a lot of them. And in the story, I think that violence is more the product—it's what is left. That the only way to survive on Brutal Planet is to be like this guy.

Now, "It's the Little Things," that one is a personal thing to me. It's basically about taking the little things and blowing them up. Road rage is basically a small thing. Somebody beeps at you, do you shoot them? You know, that's where we are at. It used to be that somebody beeps you, you might flip them off or something. But you didn't pull a gun out and shoot him. Now we're like that. Now we're at the point where we're all on a hair trigger. It's the smallest things that trip us off. I'm not worried about the big things, but it's the little things that make people snap.

I've been in movie theatres where people talk all through the movie, where I was ready to turn around, and I didn't care if I was going to jail or not, I'm just going to break this chair over this guy's head. I would feel totally vindicated if I did go to jail for doing it. Just so I could say it's just because they needed to talk through the movie. It's just the little things that drive you absolutely out of your mind. "Alice, how did you get your name?" (snide voice). After all this time, that is the one thing that puts an ice cube up my spine.

Finally, "Take It Like a Woman" is definitely the "Only Women Bleed" of the next millennium. "Take It Like a Woman" is probably going to be the hit single. It is the quote power ballad, the song that radio will probably catch onto. That one is talking about how things just didn't turn out the way she planned it. Everything was just running along and she figures she was going to get out of school and get out there. At the end you realise that she's already dead. But she took it like a woman, much to her credit. She was bruised, she was this and that. People always say, hey, take it like a man. Well, she was even better than that—she took it like a woman. It praises womankind. You have to give her credit. She was a victim and she did everything she could to survive, but she just didn't survive.

August 2000. "Gimme" is launched as a single from *Brutal Planet*, but only in the UK, where it reaches No.103. A video was created for the track as well.

Alice Cooper:

Right, "Gimme this, gimme that" that's definitely my take on future Satan. He is saying, "Everything is okay, you're fine, in fact, you're the best thing that ever happened, and your just wonderful, don't you deserve everything?! I'll give it to you." Of course, man goes, "Gimme this, gimme that, gimme everything," so there is a definite theme of greed. Is there a spiritual dimension? I think there always is. I don't think you have to look for it, I think it's always there. I think there is always a moral level to everything. No matter what it is, there is morality; whether it's *Frankenstein, Dracula*, there is always a moral, good and evil. And I think this evil here is just m*an.*

September 1 – October 31, 2000. Alice takes his *Live from the Brutal Planet* tour around the US. Main support comes from Tidewater Grain, and to a lesser extent, Dope.

Alice Cooper:
I think my music will always be hard rock. I'm never going to go techno or country. My roots are in The Yardbirds. We used to listen to everything from The Yardbirds to Stockhausen. You may hear electronica in there right now, but it will always be a very 4/4 beat, it will always be right on the money, with driving drums. I don't pretend to be anything other than a hard rock writer, because I think that's what I'm best at. I do get to weave strange little stories around that writing though, and I do try to get it as quirky as possible. But if you really strip it down to what it is, it's bass, drums and guitar-driving hard rock. Some people might call that heavy metal, but it's just good riff rock is what it is. I think this is the only music that is going to survive. Look at the bands you hear today from 30 years ago. Every one of them is a hard rock band, from Aerosmith to the Rolling Stones to us to Kiss; basically hard rock bands. It's one of the things where all the derivatives will run their course and be gone. Grunge rock is gone. It had it's time. Alternative rock in its different forms is basically not what is going on now. Punk rock is gone. But what is the basis for all that rock? Hard rock. It's garage bands, and we're just a really good garage band.

November 15 – November 20, 2000. Alice tours again with the British Rock Symphony, this time in South America.

December 5, 2000. Eagle Records issues the *Brutally Live* DVD, documenting a show Alice did at the Hammersmith in London, July 19, 2000. Included is the band's cover of The Who's "My Generation." In 2003, the package was reissued with a bonus, slightly shorter audio CD.

Alice Cooper:
For me, technology takes the heart out of everything. Any time you make life easier for man, it suddenly takes the heart out of it. When I hear techno music, I hear music that is basically a machine's idea of music. I hear pulse but no heart. So it's an artificial pulse coming from an artificial place. In other words, when you hear a real drummer play, he makes mistakes. He has timing mistakes. I would personally rather hear that than a perfectly controlled machine that doesn't know how to make mistakes. So I think all techno basically takes the humanity out of us. That is basically the one thing I have against technology. I think it makes us less human.

Now when I say I don't like the hi-tech stuff, and I'm missing a lot of the heart in that stuff, I do like what Rob Zombie is doing, because he injects himself into it. Suddenly then it has a sense of humour. It has a sense of humanity. He wraps himself inside of the package, insides of that sound and it works, because I hear all kinds of stuff that comes right from his personality.

What I hate is when I hear an album that literally sounds like it could just be a computer writing an album. The person doesn't even really need to be there. But I do like what Rob Zombie has done. I'm never going to get away from the fact that, an album to me, if you notice, every one of the Brutal Planet songs pays off in the chorus. It pays off with a melody line all the way through. I am never going to avoid melody lines.

Because I think to write a song, if you take every one of these songs, and took all of the heaviness out and all the crap out and just played them on piano, they're good songs. I think that is what we strive to do. We said let's get to the energy of Rage Against the Machine but let's pay it off with a great song. So it's a combination of, sure, tapping into that sound but never losing Alice's melodic sense or his sense of humour. Even while this album is so pessimistic, it's got a great sense of humour to it. All of my albums I can listen to, and I would say that's because 80% of them have a lot of humour to them.

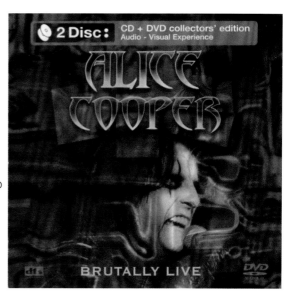

2001

2001. Warner Archives/Rhino issues the US-only *Mascara & Monsters: The Best of Alice Cooper*, 22 tracks on one CD. The slightly altered international version is called *The Definitive Alice Cooper*.

April 13 – 21, 2001. Alice's second leg of his *Brutal Planet* tour first finds him in Australia. Jimmy DeGrasso is drumming for these dates, but Eric Singer, on break from Kiss, rejoins Alice for the European dates. Also guitarist Eric Dover replaces Pete Friesen.

April 26 – May 21, 2001. Alice conducts a rare Scandinavian tour, in support of *Brutal Planet*. Also on the bill are Dio and Ratt. Dates in Germany and France follow, with a half dozen shows in the UK closing out the leg, these supported by Dio and local doom heroes Orange Goblin. Guesting at the May 18th show at Wembley is Brian May.

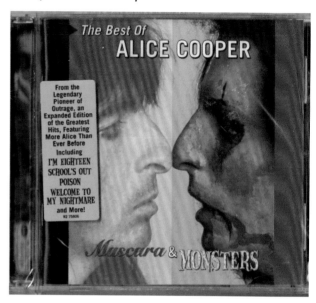

Alice Cooper:
I honestly think I have lasted because I do a good show.
I think it's because I make really good records and I'm not fat and bald (laughs). I've maintained my artistic energy and my physical energy for all these years. I can still go on stage and blow any young band off the stage. That is my objective. I've never gone up there with the attitude of like, "Well, here we are, a bunch of old guys, just want to do our hits." I've always gone up there with the attitude that these songs are still viable, and not only that, but here are a bunch of new things to digest. I like to give them the old stuff, but then I like to hit them with new stuff and say, "Guys, let's not live in the past—we also have this."

May 2001. Bouchard Dunaway Smith, otherwise known as BDS, issue an album called *Back from Hell*.

Dennis Dunaway:
Blue Öyster Cult opened for the Alice Cooper group in '72 so that's how long Neal and I have known Joe and

the guys. The three of us had done a lot of various demos together, even a trio of original Christmas songs and so we finally decided to make a CD. We played lots of shows in the US and Europe. Some BOC songs are tricky to play properly. Joe says the same thing about our Coop tunes.

May 30, 2001. Alice plays an intimate show to open his Cooperstown in Denver, Colorado. Along with seven of his own, he plays covers of The Kinks' "You Really Got Me," Beastie Boys' "Fight for Your Right (to Party)," and Cheap Trick's "I Want You to Want Me."

September 11, 2001. 9/11.

September 18, 2001. Alice Cooper issues his 22nd album, *Dragontown*, again working closely with Bob Marlette, which creeps onto the bottom rungs of the Billboard charts at No.197. The personnel for the album is Alice along with Ryan Roxie on guitar, Greg Smith on bass and Kenny Aronoff on drums. Bob Marlette, co-writer of every track with Alice, adds guitar, bass and keyboards. The album is considered a sequel to *Brutal Planet* with Alice delivering another fire and brimstone sermon indicative of his strengthening Christianity.

Alice Cooper:

This one's got a bit more colour, a bit more texture, and it's character-driven. I think I have more characters actually on this album. The first one, *Brutal Planet*, was sort of explaining what *Brutal Planet* was and why it was there and that you weren't going to get off (laughs). This one is a lot of the characters that are there. Basically, they're asking all the same questions. They're all asking how did I get here? How am I going to get out? Some of the questions are also, hey, I'm a nice guy, I shouldn't be here, and this is saying that a lot of nice guys are in Hell.

My general purpose on this thing is to just establish that there is a Hell. Let's say you're not religious at all; let's say you don't believe in anything, let's just say that you die and you're worm food. This is like saying okay, let's pretend that there is a Hell, let's pretend that there's a *Dragontown,* okay? Let's pretend that, well, after all is said and done, you do have to pay for your transgressions. Let's say you do have to answer for your bad moral choices.

Well, then that's where we are here, but we're just pretending. What it does is it throws a scare. I don't care who you are; you're lying in bed at night and you may be an atheist, you may be anything, and there's that possibility. For other people, maybe for the Jewish or Muslims, they have their own idea of what it is. For Christians, and for me, it's salvation through Christ. That's my belief. But what I'm proposing here is that for all of those who don't believe that there is any afterlife or any payment, this is to propose that, this is what's happening here. This is where you find out, "Oh oh, I was wrong—there is a price to pay." You have all these people saying, "I was a nice guy and I did more good things than bad things and I'm going to Hell?!"

So Alice is the narrator; Alice is the tour guide of this place. Of course, it's a place that he would know about. I think he includes himself in all of this. But I think the biggest misconception of this album is that it's political. It's not about politics. Politics is secondary. It's about morals, which is something that everybody has to deal with. Politics, I hate. I don't even deal with politics in my life. If I have to, I do. But morals, I have to deal with every day. So this is a matter of, when I say welcome to my nightmare, we all have to deal with nightmares. That's something where you don't have a choice. You go to sleep and you have a nightmare and you can't do anything about it. Well, somebody in China is having a nightmare too, someone in India is, someone in Pakistan is. It's a worldwide universal human thing—same thing with morals.

But I haven't let Alice understand it. Alice is the prophet of doom here. All he's doing here is he's telling you about the place. He's not explaining how to get in or out. Again, I come from a Christian attitude on this thing. If you were to say to me, as an author, how do you think you get in there? I would say well, by my beliefs, you *don't* go to Hell by accepting Christ. That's how you stay away from being there. So I believe that.

Now, if you're asking me as Alice, I would say, "Gee, I don't know. All I know is that once you're there, you don't get out (laughs)." So Alice is the prophet of doom. He's the one who's going, "Here we are, now what are we going to do? We're screwed, you know, we're really screwed. Now let me show you some of the people who are here with us. We are in trouble." I like the idea that it poses the question, "Well, now what?!" "I don't know. Let's figure it out. As far as I can see, there's no way out." I like the idea that there's no way out. I like the idea that when I write about scaring people, I usually write about something that's under your bed, or something that's in the closet or something that's in your psyche. This is saying, we're dealing with eternity here—that's even scarier. Eternal damnation of way scarier than what's under your bed (laughs)."

As far as constructing the album sonically, I leave a lot of that up to Bob Marlette. I'll write the song with him but when you hire a producer, you hire him for all the right reasons. You hire him because you believe in him, right? I don't go into a studio pretending like I know more than the producer. I hired Bob Marlette because he knew this music. I knew how to write it, he knew how to write it, and I said now, when it comes to putting this on tape and getting this onto a CD: your job.

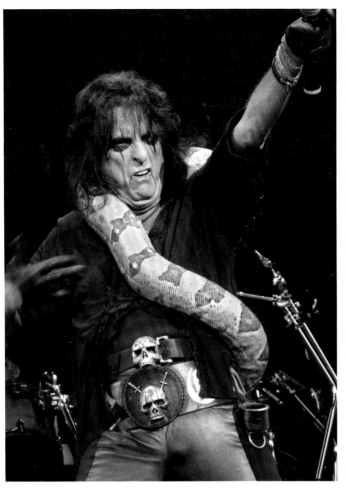

So I would say, let's have this guy play drums on this one, this and this, and he would say, "We'll do whatever you want to do, but you have to give me the last say on if it works or not." Same as Ezrin. Ezrin would say, "Alice, you have to give me the last say. If this drummer doesn't work, we have to re-cut it." I would say, "Okay, I'm with you on that." I would say let's try this guy, this guy, this guy.

So, you know, Ryan Roxie and Eric Dover or somebody would come in and play something and we would say, "Okay, they played on these five songs. These three really worked. These two, we need this guy because he is a little bit more authentic rockabilly on say "Disgraceland." Or this guy has more of an authentic metal sound. Or this guy plays a little bit more right on top of it on the drums on this thing.

So that's how you have to go into that. You can't just say, well, this guy plays on everything, because that doesn't make for a great record. I'm at a point now where I don't have to use the band that I'm using live. I say, use the best guys that you can use. Now when my guys get this onstage, they play it better than anybody could. Like right now, some of the guys who play it on the record, they could never touch my guys onstage. So I say, use the best guys for what they're great at.

In the end, Bob Ezrin was the third ear. Bob Marlette and I, we finished *Brutal Planet* and I said, "Boy, that sounds good. I really like this album; good, we're all happy." Then I started writing the next album and I kept writing the same album and I said obviously I haven't finished with this album. So I said, "Bob, with *Dragontown*, let's take it deeper." First of all, nobody's ever done a two-part concept album, staying on the same subject; nobody has ever really taken it anyplace different.

So I said, let's keep writing this. Let's go to *Dragontown* now, the worst part of Brutal Planet and see who is there and first of all, we haven't let anybody off of *Brutal Planet*. On *Welcome to My Nightmare,* I woke everybody up and on Alice Cooper *Goes to Hell,* I get out and on From the Inside, everybody escapes. But *Brutal Planet,* everybody's still there. In *Dragontown*, I haven't let anybody up, so there might be a third part.

September 29 – November 9, 2001. Alice conducts the first leg of his *Descent into Dragontown* tour. Although *Brutal Planet* tracks are down to three, one new selection is "Sanctuary." Songs played from *Dragontown* are "Triggerman," " Dragontown," Fantasy Man," "Sex, Death and Money" and "Every Woman Has a Name."

October 4, 2001. Next to his Cooperstown restaurant in Phoenix, Alice opens for business Alice Cooper's Nightmare, a haunted house that scares the locals through to November 3rd. Proceeds from opening night go to September 11th terrorist attack relief efforts.

2002

2002. Michael Bruce issues a live (in Iceland) album of Alice Cooper hits called *Halo of Ice.*

April 3, 2002. As the Denver Cooperstown closes, one opens up on Cleveland.

September 1 – November 2, 2002. Alice conducts a second tour leg in support of *Dragontown,* again, almost all the dates being American, with the odd Canadian date thrown in. His band consists of Pete Friesen and Eric Dover on guitar, Chuck Wright on bass, Eric Singer on drums and Teddy "Zigzag" Andreadis on keyboards. On opening night in Cheap Trick's hometown of Rockford, IL, Rick Nielsen guests On "Under My Wheels" and "School's Out." Support comes from the likes of Gilby Clarke and Clockwise. With Jimi Hendrix' "Fire" being put aside after the first leg, early shows include a cover of Guns N' Roses' "Welcome to the Jungle."

Alice Cooper:
I've got Eric Dover and Pete Friesen is back. Ryan is in LA starting a little family, so we gave him a leave of absence, which is great. He wanted to be there when his baby was born. Pete was with me all through the Trash era and it's great to have him back. Teddy Zigzag, who I've had on keyboards for the last three or four years from Guns N' Roses. Eric Singer on drums, and a new bass player called Chuck Wright, who was with Quiet Riot and a few bands like that, just a really good strong bass player.

As a little surprise, we do a little "Nurse Rozetta" in there, and I'm trying to think of a few other ones, a little "Steven" where it wasn't before, and "Dead Babies." Yeah, every once in a while a song will pop up there where people go, "What?! I haven't heard that in a long time." That's always fun to do. I always like to go back and find one really obscure little song that people just thought they would never hear.

We're always changing the show. If you see this show tonight and then you see it three months from now, you'll be seeing a marked difference in everything. Because the show changes every single night. There'll be little subtleties; somebody will say after the show, you know, it would be great to use a sound bite right here on this bit. Wouldn't it be a great idea to move this bit right here, take that out and shorten this, but we'll add this little piece.

So every night we probably change three things in the show, and I think that's great because I like the band to be part of it. I like the band to have ideas, and these are very creative guys. Even lighting guys will come up to me and say, "Hey, you know what would be really cool is that when Alice first comes up, that the backlighting is really heavy up-light. Right now we're using sidelights." I'm like, "Well, let's try it. Show me what it looks like." I like the fact that the show is in the works; it's always changing and it's not so set in stone that you can't have fun with it. There are some nights where I might go, "No ballads tonight." They go, "What?!" I go, "This crowd is not a ballad crowd. It's an outdoor monster crowd and they really don't want the ballads."

September 24, 2002. Spitfire issues a special edition of *Dragontown*, limited to 7,500 copies, adding a bonus EP consisting of "Can't Sleep, Clowns Will Eat Me," "Go to Hell" (live), "Ballad of Dwight Fry" (live) and "Brutal Planet" (remix).

Alice Cooper:
After living with Alice for 30 years now, he's actually taken a position on certain things, which he never did before: Interesting although still very apolitical. It probably began with *The Last Temptation,* and then moved on to the three-part thing, *Brutal Planet, Dragontown,* and the part three that's coming up. He never really had much interesting to say before but just to be cynical, then all of a sudden more things got caught in his craw. They were maybe things that people were not expecting him to say, like what this whole planet needs is a shot of morality (laughs). You never expected him to say that, but you have to agree with him! Then the way he says it is through how it all works. He's going, "Well, look around. Tell me we don't need a shot of morality."

    The next part is going to be really interesting, and I just got it the other day. You know how you let ideas just swirl? All of a sudden it hit me what the next one is. The storyline... I would actually love to see this movie. I think it's going to be called *Meet the Chill-dren.* It's "chill-dren," and it's all of the kids that died, all of the abortions, all of the abused kids, all of the kidnapped, murdered kids, they're all there. Any time one of these people dies, they've got to go up and meet the children and it's really scary (laughs).

November 2, 2002. An Alice Cooper convention called Sickcon 1, put on by the highly professional and information-packed SickthingsUK website and Jerkin' Crocus Promotions, takes place at The Limelight Club, Hightown, Crewe, Cheshire, UK. Guesting are Joe Bouchard, Michael Smith, Dennis Dunaway and Neal Smith. Bouchard Dunaway Smith—BDS—play for two-and-a-half hours.

November 5 – December 14, 2002. Alice plays an intensive amount of dates all over Europe, in support of *Dragontown.* The UK dates are billed as Monsters of Rock shows. Support comes from the likes of Dogs D'Amour, Thunder and Quireboys.

Alice Cooper:
I love part three-type album idea to go with *Brutal Planet* and *Dragontown,* that's probably still a great short story. I still think that's a wonderful idea. *Spirits Rebellious* was actually going to be the name of that. We ended up writing a song called *Spirits Rebellious,* but when I finished *Dragontown,* I realised that the point I was trying to make, was once you're here, you don't get out. There's no penance, there's no amount of time you can do. The thing that is the hell of it, is that you cannot get out. There's no way out. You have made your bed, you're going to sleep in it. It's not like God is going to come along and say, okay, well, I think you've done... you learned your lesson. This is it! You're there.

    So there's a certain claustrophobia about that, and I got to writing the third part, and I started going, I just can't finish this because there's no finish to it. I've already put the people in Dragontown, in Hell, and there's no way out. So that's it, you're there. So then I decided, well, what do I really want to do? I started listening to bands like The Vines, The White Stripes, The Strokes, groups like that, Star Spangles, and I said, why do I feel so comfortable liking this music? It's because it's us. It's us when we were 19, 20 years old. So I feel totally at home doing this music.

2003

Early 2003. Alice fills his Spring of 2003 with golf tournaments, signing sessions, low-key and one-off performances and the developing of a relationship with the auto racing world.

June 12 – 21, 2003. Alice and band (guitarists Ryan Roxie and Eric Dover, keyboard player Teddy "Zigzag" Andreadis, bassist Chuck Garric and drummer Eric Singer) adopt the mandate of trying to record an album quickly, which they manage, laying down the tracks for *The Eyes of Alice Cooper* in a couple of weeks at Mates Studios in North Hollywood, CA.

Alice Cooper:

It's sort of a return to garage rock for Alice, which is fun. We went out of our way to not produce it. We did all the tracks live in the studio and we took twelve new songs. I wrote everything with Eric and Ryan. I said, I want to do a band album. I don't want to go outside for anything. In other words, let's write everything in-house and when we come to record this thing, let's record it… let's rehearse the song for the day, have a dinner break, record it, put it to bed. But you're not allowed to go back in and change the guitar. You're not allowed to go back in and change the drums, no overdubbing. You might be able to add something, maybe, if it's desperately needed. But I would rather keep it to what the band plays is what it is. So when you hear those songs, that's exactly what they're going to sound like onstage (laughs).

So we actually took a room. We were rehearsing at Mates, where there were five other bands there at the same time. Mudrock came in and he listened to it and he said, "You really gotta record this stuff live." I said, I absolutely agree. I would really like to not worry about overdubbing. I would really like to just do it live and let the band be the band. So we went into this other room and said, if we set this room up, if we just put an amp there, drums there, mics right there, we can do everything right here. I came back in three days and it was now a studio. Which was great, because it was just like recording in somebody's garage.

Eric Singer:

Great record, in my opinion, and it was fun making that record. We had a real band vibe with Mudrock as the producer, who encouraged us to play live in the studio together as a band with no click tracks. He had a real vision and direction, which was a much-needed fresher approach from the previous record I had recorded with Alice, *Brutal Planet*.

July 3 – August 9, 2003. Alice Cooper executes his *Bare Bones* tour, a mainly American jaunt (featuring a preponderance of country fairs), with a few European dates thrown in. The band as it appears on the album is the one that delivers the shows, save for the absence of Teddy Zigzag. Alice's daughter Calico provides backing vocals and plays the part of the nurse character on stage. Select late July and early August are with Ted Nugent, who is name-checked in *The Eyes of Alice Cooper* song "Detroit City," along with many other rock legends from that town. The setlist for the two warm-up dates in January and February are all old hits plus covers, including the Beatles' "Back in the USSR," The Who's "My Generation," Elton John's "Saturday Night's Alright for Fighting" and "Brown Sugar"

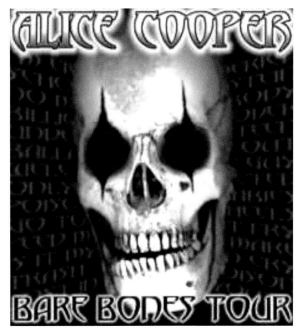

and Honky Tonk Woman" by the Rolling Stones. Once the tour starts, the covers are dropped and it's still all old hits, save for "Gimme" and "It's the Little Things" from Brutal Planet and "Detroit City" from *The Eyes of Alice Cooper.*

July 21, 2003. Neal's legendary *Platinum God* album, started back in 1975, sees release, featuring mostly original recordings plus additional work. All over the album are the likes of Dennis Dunaway, Mike Marconi and Michael Bruce.

August 1 – 3, 2003. The Glen Buxton Memorial Weekend features performances by Bouchard Dunaway Smith and Michael Bruce.

August 2, 2003. Bouchard Dunaway Smith issue *Live in Paris.* Joe, Dennis and Neal play a combination of band originals, Blue Öyster Cult songs and Alice Cooper selections, namely "School's Out," "Caught in a Dream," "Black Juju" and "Under My Wheels."

September 24, 2003. Alice and band appear on *The Late Late Show with Craig Kilborn* serving up new song "Man of the Year" and oldie "No More Mr. Nice Guy."

Alice Cooper:
It's interesting with these guys because both Eric Dover and Ryan Roxie played with Slash. I always liked Slash because Slash was just a great lead guitar player. He wasn't Eddie Van Halen, he wasn't Steve Vai, he was more of a Joe Perry/Keith Richards guitar player, and to me that's always been my guitar player.

So these two guitar guys, when they came in and a played, neither one of them over-plays; they keep it right there in the chord, they're right there in the middle, nobody's hammering (laughs), nobody's doing all that stuff. I said, they're keeping it right exactly where I want it. They're both in a band called Glamnation, which they do when they aren't playing with me. Eric Singer and these two guys and another bass player do nothing but glam songs which is, you know, exactly what I wanted on this thing. I said, I want to take glam, I want to take Alice, mix it all up, put it in a garage and play, and it's going to come out so cool.

Eric Dover is a little bit funkier. Eric Dover is a bit more Rolling Stones. A song like "Bye Bye, Baby", which is real Stonesy. A song like "What Do You Want From Me? ", which is much more of an early Stones type thing. Whereas "Between High School & Old School", that's Ryan Roxie, a little bit more pop-oriented. Ryan is going to be a little bit more pop than Eric is. "Backyard Brawl" though, came out of Ryan, which is a little bit more Sex Pistols. I'm So Angry is a combination of both of them. But I think they both came from both those schools of music. You know, in some of these songs, we absolutely tip the hat to certain people. "Bye Bye, Baby" was a tip of the hat to the Stones. "Man Of The Year" was certainly Sex Pistols.

September 26 – November 1, 2003. Alice plays the US, along with one Canadian date, Toronto, in support of *The Eyes of Alice Cooper*. The personnel for Alice's band remains unchanged. Main support comes from Silvertide. Songs from the new album are "Between High School and Old School," "What Do You Want From Me?," "Backyard Brawl," "Novocaine" and "Man of the Year." An interesting inclusion is "Who Do You Think We Are?" from *Special Forces*. As well, "Brutal Planet" and "Wicked Young Man" persist from *Brutal Planet* and there are no songs from *Dragontown*.

September 30, 2003. Alice Cooper issues the Mudrock-produced *The Eyes of Alice Cooper*, a raucous and raw garagey rock 'n' roll album that reverses the jets on the doomy, dystopian and industrial tones of the *Brutal Planet/Dragontown* suite. MC5 guitarists Wayne Kramer guests on "Detroit City." The album is issued in four versions, with Alice's eyes either red, blue, green or purple. The album peaks at No.184 on the Billboard charts.

Alice Cooper:
I thought, if there's going to be anything that holds this album together lyrically, it's going to be the fact that every song is just a little ironic slice of life. One guy is living in a haunted house with his girlfriend because he figures, well, if she's dead, I can still live with her, until I die, then we can both be ghosts. But right now, what's wrong with living together in the haunted house? Okay, that's an odd little Edgar Allan Poe-ish way of looking at it, but it makes for a great song (laughs).

"What Do You Want From Me?," there's a white trash guy and the deal with him is he thinks he can buy this girl with a LoJack for a Pontiac; it's a total Jerry Springer moment and to me, that's funny. The guy isn't offering her diamonds or anything; he wants to take her to Target for her birthday. I found that there was much more humour in this album than any of the other albums. I haven't had real fun with an album for quite awhile.

The guys played so well. I let Ryan be a little country on "Novocaine." I said play it the way you think it should be. He played it and it really was way too country. I said yeah, that fits that song. It's *Sticky Fingers* but no, I need a little more angst in it, so when he played it the next time, he played with a bit more of an "Eighteen" sound to it. But that's the most natural song on the album.

That and the ballad. In fact, all three ballads were written in probably ten, fifteen minutes. They were those songs that just came out. I said, I want to write a song about a guy who lives in a haunted house, da-da-da, and Eric starts playing that riff, and I said okay, I like that, that's good. But the song's one take, lyrically; just went all the way through it and started writing sort of flow of consciousness and I said okay, here's the song. I went back to try to rewrite the lyrics and I couldn't because they were exactly right the first time. That doesn't happen very often.

"The Song That Didn't Rhyme" probably gets the most attention of any song. I don't know why. It's just one of those songs that was a joke and it ended up having a life of its own. Yeah, as I say in the lyric, the melody blows, the drummer can't keep time and the singer can't sing it. The song will not die. It just will not die. It's like the thing that would die. Nobody likes the song, yet it has its own life. I did 45 interviews in Europe and every single one of then mentioned that

song first. Isn't that weird? I said, oh please, don't let this be the hit.

"Spirits Rebellious" is just total rebellion. It was just a kid who said, no matter what you say, I will not do it. It's almost a celebration of the most obstinate kid on the block, him just saying, even if it's right, even if I know it's right, I'm not going to do it. I was born with a chip on my shoulder and it's just who I am. I met people like that. Rebelling just for the sake of rebellion, right? So I decided to write a song about that particular type of human being. I was never like that but I did know people like that. Glen Buxton was like that. Glen would go out of his way to rebel, even if he didn't enjoy it. He just enjoyed the fact that he was rebelling.

Eric Dover:

I'm very proud of it. I haven't listened to the record really since I left the band and that's not because... I guess it's just because you play it so much you know how it goes. I'm happy with it. We were trying to go back to the roots. *Brutal Planet* and *Dragontown* are great records but we just were like let's not do metal for a bit. Let's go for a more classic direction and I'm glad we did. It almost came off more garage rock, like MC5, Stooges; we were really trying to go for some of that.

We had a wonderful time. We had Mudrock to produce it and he was a blast to work with. We did it near our rehearsal place where Mike Clink, I think, produced Guns N' Roses. He had a studio there and I think we used his studio to do the tracking. It wasn't a state-of-the-art studio by any means. It was sound acoustically but no frills, just get in there and play. We played live. We tracked that live which, for whatever reason, seems to be unheard of now. It was really cool. It takes a lot to track a band live. It takes a lot of studio equipment, a lot of studio time that you may not be able to afford. Digital is cool because it does allow you to do some things, but for that record it was a great experience because playing live together is something you don't get to do a lot. It's usually piecemealed together.

After Alice Cooper I made a decision for myself which was just to pursue my art and pursue what I like to do and damn the torpedoes. I'm not somebody who likes to be out on the road six months out of the year; I'm not made of that material. At the end of the day I'm very comfortable being in the studio and just writing music. It could be anything really. I write a lot of stuff that really you can't classify very easily. That's what life is about to me—freedom and liberty. I feel very fortunate and lucky to be doing what I'm doing.

December 2, 2003. Alice is awarded a star on the Hollywood Walk of Fame, a far greater and more establishment honour than his hands-in-cement induction into the Rock Walk. In and around this honour, Alice does a bunch of radio, guesting and on his own, with the announcement that he will soon be doing his own regular radio show.

2004

January 26, 2004. Alice's new radio show, *Nights with Alice Cooper*, begins airing.

April 3, 2004. After a February and March full of golf tournaments, Alice in on hand at the Juno Awards in Edmonton, Alberta to induct Bob Ezrin into the Canadian Music Hall of Fame.

June 4 – 27, 2004. Alice takes his tour in support of *The Eyes of Alice Cooper* over to Europe. Replacing drummer Eric Singer is Detroit's finest, Tommy Clufetos.

Tommy Clufetos:
I first saw Alice when I was 12. He came around to Detroit and I remember going, "This is so cool, dude." He had long hair, boots, this is rock 'n' roll. The next two years went by

and I said to myself, "I'm going to play in that band one day." So when I finally got the gig, it was a great time and I've been lucky that all the guys I've worked for have great iconic songs. They are not just big time musicians;

they are legends, living legends! All these guys have survived the trends in music and are still doing it. That, to me, is the biggest form of success. I hope I'll be doing this in forty years as well, because that's what it's all about—survival.

July 9 – October 31, 2004. Alice tours *The Eyes of Alice Cooper* in the US, as well as logging a substantial amount of Canadian dates, early ones with Foghat and Edgar Winter, later ones with Supagroup.

August 15, 2004. At a show in Saginaw, MI, Dick Wagner sits in, performing on "School's Out." This is the first time Dick had performed with Alice is approximately twenty-five years. In and around many of these summer dates, softball games are arranged, with the band team being called the Nightmares.

2005

January 24, 2005. In conjunction with the showing of *Rock School*, Alice guests, performing "School's Out."

March 22, 2005. Alice and his band, recording with producer Steve Lindsay, complete work on the tracks that will comprise the forthcoming *Dirty Diamonds* album, his first release on New West Records.

Cameron Strang (New West Records):
A friend and business partner of mine Steve Lindsey was producing Alice's album. We have a studio here in our building so Alice was around a lot recording. Everyone liked him; he charmed all the girls that work here. Some of us have been fans since way back. Steve introduced me to Shep Gordon, Alice's manager, and it seemed like a mutual decision for New West to put out the record.

One difference for us is that Alice is an international star. The demands on his time are greater than some of our artists because he tours all over the world. Some of the specific publications, stations etc. are different but we can deal with that. Alice also has a big loyal fan base which makes marketing the records fun. There are lots of people who want to know what Alice is up to. We are pretty open-minded to artists of different styles if the act and timing is right and there are some fans of those acts at the label.

I was an Alice fan. I remember my older brothers listening to *School's Out* and *Billion Dollar Babies* in the mid-'70s. *School's Out* had to make an impression on every kid who heard it. It made you cool by association. Alice was larger than life to me then. I certainly didn't think I would ever meet him. Alice to me is one of the great characters in rock; there have been many imitators. He is also a nice guy to work with.

Alice Cooper:
This is definitely part two. Not officially, but it's the same theory on this one, which is write the song, record the song, put the song to bed. I'm a very big advocate, if you're going to do an album like this, the first thing you're getting from the band is going to be the best thing you get. Let the band be the band. When you hear the record, don't let it be a slick, overly produced version of the band.

This band is so good live, that I say we write the song, let them record the song live, in the studio, take twenty takes, take the best take. On *The Eyes of Alice Cooper*, I wouldn't let anybody go in and do any overdubs, but on this one I'm saying, okay, we can add a guitar, or we can add this or that, but, we're not going to change the basic tracks. Because I want to hear a band feel through everything. So I put all the pressure on the writing and on the performance rather than production. That way, you get twelve great songs, other than nine songs and three fillers that you have to work on to make them into songs. I hear that a lot; I hear records where you go, okay, here's half of the song and they decided, well, we like the chorus on that song, so let's just keep adding stuff until the verse sounds okay (laughs).

June 21 – July 5, 2005. Alice Cooper begins his campaign for *Dirty Diamonds* with an extensive tour of Australia, supported by local legend Billy Thorpe. An interesting set list wrinkle is *From the Inside's* "Wish I Were Born in Beverly Hills." From the new album are "Dirty Diamonds" and "Woman of Mass Distraction."

July 4, 2005. Alice Cooper issues his 24th album, *Dirty Diamonds,* in the UK and mainland Europe. Personnel on the album is Alice along with guitarists Ryan Roxie and Damon Johnson, bassist Chuck Garric and drummer Tommy Clufetos (although Eric Singer is pictured in the booklet). Rapper Xzibit guests on "Stand," designated a bonus track but available on all issues of the album. The album reaches No.71 on the UK charts.

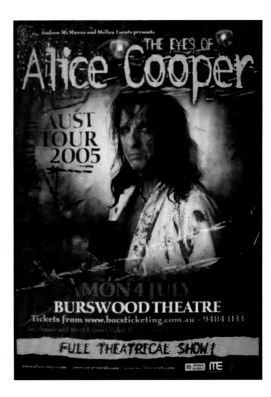

Alice Cooper:
In all honesty, I could put every one of the songs in a hat, pick one out and say, that's the single. Any one of them could be a song I would pick as the song to be on the radio. It's definitely eccentric and eclectic, as far as you can almost take each song and pick an old Alice album and put it on that album. I think that's great. If anything, I've captured Alice on this album (laughs).

It's called *Dirty Diamonds* because that's what they are. All of them are little gems that have been left unpolished. If Bob Ezrin was going to produce this album, we would have been in the studio for three months and we would have really been working hard on each section of each bit and it would've been a different album. It would have sounded like *Billion Dollar Babies* or *School's Out* or something like that. I would've went, okay, that's great, that's not what I want to do right now. Right now I'd rather take the songs, and make it sound like a really good garage band. Because basically every good hard rock band is a garage band. I think the Stones were a great garage band. I think AC/DC, Guns N' Roses, Aerosmith, every guitar band that is out there making it was probably a great garage band. Jet is a great garage band.

As for highlights lyrically, well, "The Saga of Jesse Jane" is great, because, it was one of those songs that was borne out of working on a song, or two songs, all day. Then somebody comes up with a country western riff, and somebody just starting off singing it, "I was born in a Texas town," like Johnny Cash. Pretty soon it ended up being Jesse Jane, the play on words, Jesse James into Jesse Jane. All of a sudden it was what it was, and it became one of the classic Alice songs on the album. We just kept writing and going, "No no, more country, go more Johnny Cash on this. Steel guitar, let's put a steel guitar on it." I like having at least one novelty song. On *Eyes of Alice Cooper* it was "Song That Didn't Rhyme," and the funny thing is, almost every time, when I go to Europe, this is the first song they'll mention.

Then "Steal That Car," well, I'm just an absolute car addict. I think I've gone through ten cars in the last year or two years. I'm driving an Aston Martin DB7 V8, which I'll never get rid of, because it's the best car I've ever had. I'm building a '66 GTO right now. A friend of mine and my son and I have got a company together where we build old cars and then sell them at the big auctions. It's just a great hobby. I like to build them, drive them, then sell them. It's just something I really enjoy doing. My son and I are really... it keeps us close.

But at the same time, we love finding old cars and saying, "Okay, this one's doable; let's do this one." It doesn't matter what it is, as long as it's a '60s muscle car or '70s muscle car. My other cars right now, let's see, there's a little runaround Porsche there that I use every day. A '69 Shelby Mustang, Grabber Orange. Problem is, at this time of year it just overheats like crazy. So I drive that in the wintertime. But of course, that's one of my prizes there. Anything that's a '60s classic is something that I go for. My son's got a Mustang Mach 1. So "Steal That Car" is just borne out of that. I go to these big auctions and I'm sitting there looking at the Ferraris stuff, and I'm going, "Okay, I'm going to steal that car" (laughs). And then that song was okay, let's just do that. Let's do a hard rock rockabilly (sings it). That's such a great riveting guitar riff, and on stage it's unbelievable. We put that right next to "Under My Wheels," so they really connect up nicely.

The title track, "Dirty Diamonds," that's pure Alice. When I think of how Alice connects up, the cinematography and the song, I tried to make that sound like a soundtrack for a movie that has not been written yet. If there was a movie like *Lock, Stock and Two Smoking Barrels*, and it was called *Dirty Diamonds*, this would be the soundtrack for it. We wanted it to sound like either a heist movie or a little bit of James Bond in there and on stage it just really roars. It's just got the real Alice theme to it. There is no movie called *Dirty Diamonds,* but there should be.

As singles go, well, right now we only do two songs off the album; "Woman of Mass Distraction" and "Dirty Diamonds." I have a feeling it'll be "Woman of Mass Distraction" although Europe is leaning towards "Dirty Diamonds" and I bet that America picks "Perfect." "You Make Me Wanna" definitely has that snotty glam thing to it, but "Perfect" is one of those songs that every good songwriter I know, wants to at least, once in their

life, write a song that reminds them of early Beatles. That's what "Perfect" reminds me of. When we started doing the verse on it, some songs fall into a category; you can't help it. I always say, when you start singing the song, let the song go where it has to go. It's like water rolling down a hill. It's going to follow its own path. So, when we started doing this song and we got to that chorus, "She's so perfect," I said, we've got to go total Lennon/McCartney here. Because that's what it wants to do. The song really wants to go there. So let's do that. There's not one band on this planet that wasn't influenced by Lennon/McCartney. So, let's make this an early Beatles song. Even though the guitar is more T. Rex. I would love to have one Beatles song under my belt. In fact, I'm going to send this one to McCartney and say, "This is a tribute to you and John."

In the end this album reminds me of *Killer*. *Killer* had a lot of those songs like "Long Way to Go," stuff like that. Although certain songs on *Love It to Death* remind me of things like "Sunset Babies," which is another one that could be a single. You know, "Sunset babies all have rabies." That song was just truly borne out of the fact that every picture I see of every little Hollywood starlet, they've got one of these little Chihuahuas in their hands. So there's that secondary thought that they're all capable of biting you and giving you a disease (laughs).

At the same time, on stage, we gave Britney a break this year. She's pregnant; she has her own problems. You know, you always attack somebody when they're on top. When they can fight back. Britney can't fight back right now. But Paris Hilton, Paris just walked right into the crossfire, and so Calico this year, instead of Britney she's doing Paris. We do "Wish I Was Born in Beverly Hills" and of course the Chihuahua does rip her throat out, much to everybody's delight.

Damon Johnson:
Dirty Diamonds was incredible. When I went through that experience, I just assumed we'll make more records in this way. The next one will be like that and the one after that. The timing of it was in that I had left Alice's band to work on my country project, Whiskey Falls, as he was putting *Along Came a Spider* together. There's actually one or two songs in that record that I had a co-write on, with some ideas, that Chuck and I worked on, that made its way. He's always collaborating outside of the band. But we never really committed much time on the road to songwriting. When you're in a band like that where everybody lives in different cities, you're not gonna write off the road. It makes it tough to write, when you're off the road, because you want to be with your family. You've got other obligations.

So the only way this really happened was that all of us, Scott, Michael, even Brian and Darren, man, we were writing songs on the road, on the bus, in the dressing room. All of them, Alice even commented, wow, we've never done this before. Well, come to think of it, neither have I. But this is the only way we're going to be able to do this album. That's even tougher, because everybody goes to London, Dublin, Southern California, Alabama, yeah, it's hard (laughs). To write on a bus together. So it's really gratifying, for lack of a better word, to just sit down and reflect on the last year of activity, and how it all came together.

For *Dirty Diamonds*, Alice wanted to make a dirty garage record, a dirty rock 'n' roll record, and he definitely had the right band to do that with. Particularly, with Ryan and I in the band. Ryan is really a top songwriter—really great melodies, really great arrangements—and then we had Tommy Clufetos on the drums and he's just a basher. So it made a lot of sense, and it was just fun, because Cooper was in the mindset than that that was what he wanted to do. So again, we all got really busy and brought in tons of ideas. I'm really proud of how that record came out, and the mix is almost purposely trashy. I had somebody say it sounds like you made that mix in about four days, and, well that was on purpose (laughs). We wanted it to sound like that.

July 9 – August 13, 2005. Alice conducts an extensive campaign in Europe, in support of *Dirty Diamonds*.

August 2, 2005. *Dirty Diamonds* is issued in the US. The album peaks at No.169 on the main *Billboard* chart, the *Billboard* 200, and at No.17 on the Top Independent Albums chart.

August 20 – October 31, 2005. The third leg of Alice's *Dirty Diamonds* tour finds the band on home turf, playing the US and Canada. Cheap Trick co-headline on a number of early dates, with Supagroup, Still Standing and Wednesday 13 supporting as the tour grinds on. Two additional *Dirty Diamonds* songs not played on the first leg are "Steal That Car" and "Sunset Babies (All Got Rabies)."

Damon Johnson:
Come on, bro, the original Alice Cooper band?! That's an iconic group right there. That's when I have to put my fan's hat on and go, you know, it's amazing to be in Cooper's band, with those songs, to be part of the show and the production and all of that. But I think Alice knows—as well as us and the majority of the fans—they know that that was just a special moment in rock history, when the original band were together. They not only broke a lot of rules, they made a lot of rules that are here to stay.

So I think if you were to talk to Cooper, he would say, hey man, I was just really lucky. I was lucky I was able to parlay it into a solo thing and have all these different bands through the years, and great line-ups. You can't say the guy's afraid of hard work, because he would turn up everywhere. For me, he's a role model in that respect. There's no question that he loves music as much as you and I do, and that has never wavered. I think that's really true of a lot of the legendary guys out there doing it, like the Stones or Aerosmith. I don't think they have to do it; they want to do it, they love it, it's still fulfilling.

But one of the reasons I eventually moved on from the Alice Cooper band... and I love Alice—he is my brother and we are bonded for life. But Alice never really needed a songwriter to be with the band. He just needed a guitar player that plays great. We toured and I can certainly do that, but I have never been any less passionate about songwriting than I am of playing guitar. So I've always longed to be involved in something that I can write again.

September 16, 2005. Michael Bruce issues *The Second Coming of Michael Bruce: Alive and Re-Cooperated*. The album features three studio tracks plus additional selections from the live show documented on *Halo of Ice*.

November 2 – November 17, 2005. Alice delivers his show to the ever-faithful fans of the UK, with Twisted Sister supporting. On the last night, Dee Joins Alice for "Under My Wheels."

December 17, 2005. After Alice's annual Christmas Pudding Show in hometown Phoenix (this year with Dick Wagner guesting), Alice spends Christmas and New Years in Hawaii.

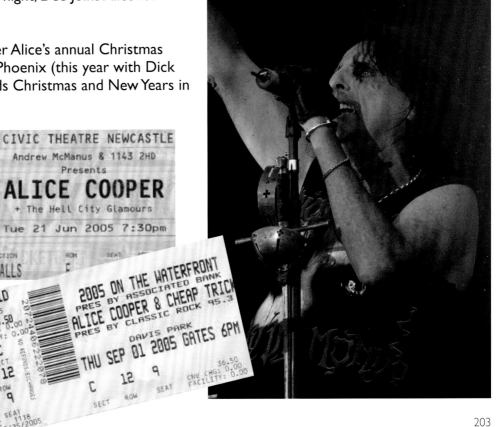

2006

February 6 – 18, 2006. Alice and band play shows in Germany with Deep Purple.

May 2006. Eagle Vision issues one of their *Live at Montreux* DVD series featuring Alice Cooper from his performance at the *Montreux Jazz Festival* on July 12, 2005.

May 1 – May 17, 2006. Alice and band mount a Canadian tour, support coming mostly from Crash Kelly and Helix. By this point, the only songs from the new album played are the title track and "Woman of Mass Distraction."

May 27 – June 17, 2006. Alice Cooper plays a grab bag of European dates, a few at the end once more with Deep Purple.

July 30 – October 31, 2006. The band are back for more US and Canadian dates, support coming from the likes of Wicked Wisdom, The Vacation, Fireball Ministry Crash Kelly and Wednesday 13.

Alice Cooper:
When I look at old stage footage, I go "That was pure Alice," but that was a different Alice to the Alice we have now. That was the outrageous society's whipping boy Alice who was drunk all the time and was stooped over and half there. Every kid that was an outsider totally related to him. They were outsiders too; they weren't with

the pack. I totally got that. But when I got sober, I immediately went, "That Alice doesn't work anymore." I need an Alice now that is a dominatrix. I need an Alice now that is the arch-criminal, the Moriarty, the smarter than society villain. That's the character I play now. I kinda made him arrogant. There were two very definite Alices, the alcohol Alice and the non-alcohol Alice.

September 2006. Dennis Dunaway Project issues *Bones from the Yard.*

Dennis Dunaway:
That group was me helping Rick Tedesco get the bugs out of his brand new studio in exchange for getting some demos recorded there. We brought in Russ Wilson on drums and Ed Burns on Keys and vocals. We got the bugs out of the studio and were pleased that the quality of the recordings was more like an album than a demo. The band had great chemistry so we decided to make an album, which Ian Hunter participated in. Ian played piano, sang backgrounds, helped with the writing, and was our all-around musical guru. We were halfway through a second album when the chemistry disintegrated. Rick used some of those songs on his solo record, *Light in the Attic.* We're still trying to figure out what went sour.

November 6, 2006. At the Classic Rock Awards, Alice receives Living Legend accolades, the award presented to him by Brian May. Two days later, Alice is back at home, supporting the Rolling Stones at Cardinals Stadium.

December 16, 2006. At the annual Christmas Pudding show at Dodge Theatre in hometown Phoenix, Alice welcomes a pile of rock stars, but also plays a six-song set with Damon Johnson, Dennis Dunaway, Neal Smith and Michael Bruce. Shortly thereafter, Alice is off to Hawaii for Christmas again, just like the previous year.

Alice Cooper:
We're doing our Christmas show in Phoenix, the *Alice Cooper Christmas Pudding Show* at The Dodge Theatre. Every year I get a bunch of guys together. Last year, it was Ted Nugent and Cheap Trick and The Tubes. It's a five-hour variety show and the money goes to the Solid Rock foundation, for inner city kids. This year I called Neal, Dennis and Mike and said, "Why don't you guys come in and we'll do the original band for half an hour? We'll do "Nice Guy" and "Under My Wheels" and "Eighteen" and "School's Out" and all the hits and they said, "Yeah sure."

There never was any animosity between the band when the break-up happened. It was more like everybody was just bushed. We were tired. One guy wanted to do his own album. Another guy wanted to do his own album. I think they were burned-out on the theatre, whereas I was thinking, "No, no, let's take it further." I was thinking *Welcome to My Nightmare* and they were thinking, "Let's just do an album and not the theatre." We were on totally different tracks and that's really what it was.

But our Solid Rock foundation, it's up and running right now. We have 30,000 square feet and, in fact, my daughter is teaching dance there. We have guitar lessons, bass lessons... The whole idea is to give kids a chance to do something that they don't know they can do. You have kids out there selling drugs on the streets, robbing stores and stuff. That same kid may be the best guitar player in Arizona except he's never had a guitar in his hand. So come on in, we'll give you the guitar, we'll give you the lessons and all you have to do is show up and learn. That's it—it's so simple.

I do this because I grew up in Phoenix. I went to elementary school, high school and college here. When people say, "So you're a Christian now," well, that doesn't mean sitting around on your knees praying all day. What do you do as a Christian that can help a kid out? I'm not beating them over the head with a Bible. I'm saying, "How about me investing some time in you and making your life better?" The only thing it's costing me is time. So, what? I have tons of time and it's the same thing with Sheryl. She said, "I'll go in and teach." So, to me, the whole idea is investing time with kids who probably don't have parents that are giving them any time.

A lot of these kids have no idea who Alice Cooper is. Some of them do, but a lot of the Spanish kids

that come in... Sheryl had 400 girls come in the first night for dance and you know what they were fascinated by? Ballet. They'd seen street dancing and they can all street dance, but when they saw ballet; they were fascinated by it. They had never seen ballet before and to them, it was unbelievable. When you introduce something to kids who think they've seen everything and they get knocked out by it enough that they want to keep coming back and learning about it, then you've won half the war.

This is the prototype and we've already had six or seven other cities call us and say, "Build one here." As far as we're concerned if they come up with the finances to do it, we will build it and show them how to do it. The only trick about this is that there is no catch to it. A kid is coming in purely to learn and that's it. If it's an Islamic kid, a Jewish kid... it doesn't matter to us. We're giving them an alternative to something that will probably kill them or put them in jail.

2007

May 1, 2007. Alice Cooper debuts a new autobiography, called *Alice Cooper, Golf Monster: A Rock 'n' Roller's Life and 12 Steps to Becoming a Golf Addict.*

June 10 – July 21, 2007. Alice's *Psycho Drama* tour plays South America, Europe and Australia. Alice's band features Keri Kelli and Jason Hook on guitars, Chuck Garric on bass and Eric Singer on drums. At a July 1st festival date in Bucharest, Romania, Marilyn Manson guests on "Eighteen" and Alice returns the favour, guesting on "Sweet Dreams."

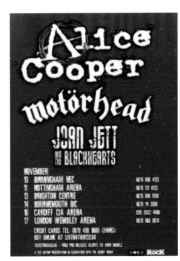

Keri Kelli:

I had known all those cats from about five, six years back and Brian Nelson just called me up one day when they needed someone. I gotta tell you, it's really fantastic. I attribute it to the top-notch organisation that is Alice Cooper. He has a totally pro team on every level, so it makes those long months of not being home very bearable and enjoyable. As a fan, I knew the big songs from the '70s, as my parents were rock music fans. I also saw Coop myself in '86 or '87 at Long Beach Arena and it was killer!

    I remember when I was a kid watching him on a USA network show called *Night Flight*. They would show the new video by whoever and then they'd show that old Alice Cooper psychedelic video for "I'm Eighteen" and I'd be like, "Who the hell is this guy?" I was intrigued and then I started getting the records. My parents were always into music like The Rolling Stones and stuff like that. They were into me exploring music. I'd go to the record store and buy all the Coop records, all the Thin Lizzy records, all the Led Zeppelin records and, of course, my parents already had all the Stones records.

    I definitely grew up with Alice and I thought his stuff was awesome. The greatest thing about Cooper, for a guitar player, is that he always, even to this day, knew when a great song was a great song. The songs were very broad. He'd have a nice loving ballad, then he'd have a heavier song like "Black Widow" and then he'd have more of a pop song like "No More Mr. Nice Guy" or whatever. But what's cool for a guitar player is that he always had that "riff." He always had that legendary guitar lick, vocal hook and even legendary little intro parts like on *Welcome to My Nightmare*. It was cool, man, and I'm happy to be here.

    Doing this compared to other bands I've been in, it just seems to run a little smoother. Everybody from the band to the crew are all brothers out here. Everybody looks out and helps each other, so it feels like a family. A family of 25! I really try to make the best of every project I find myself in and really have never had any "nightmarish" situations... Well, there was that one time, but... ah, forget it!

August 10 - October 31, 2007. Alice's *Psycho Drama* tour rolls around North America, with many of the middle dates being played with Heaven & Hell and Queensryche.

November 6 – December 2, 2007. Alice goes to Europe, playing predominantly Eastern Europe and the UK. Support comes from the likes of Motörhead, Joan Jett and the Blackhearts and Uriah Heep.

Keri Kelli:

The writing is going great. We have something like 15 things together at the moment and are working up more. The tunes have a wide range of vibes, fast, slow, heavy, soft, major and minor sounding pieces. Obviously at this point there's no telling what will actually be on the CD, but we've got a great start. Cutting

the CD is gonna be awesome, really. I think what's going to make it such a great experience and CD is we all are friends and have a great time playing together. That alone will make the process flow nicely. No friction, just working together to bring the best CD we can.

Eric Singer:
I'd like to do the song "Yeah, Yeah, Yeah" and I'd always love to do anything off *Billion Dollar Babies,* like "Mary Ann." I like that whole record. We're now doing "Raped and Freezin'." We don't always do it. Some nights we play it, some night we take it out, we switch it around a little bit. I always wanted to do "Generation Landslide," which we did do once a long time ago, but it didn't stay in the set long.

Sometimes the problem is—and this is the same problem that happens with Kiss as well—sometimes the song that you think is really great and all the diehard fans want to hear, when they play it live there's like five people going, "Yeah, this is great." You look around the audience and most people are going, "I never even heard this song—what is this?" So this is unfortunately the predicament that many bands find themselves in where even they like the old songs, they'd love to do these obscure songs, but they realise they want to get a reaction from the crowd; they want to appeal to the whole audience and not just a handful.

I honestly am surprised we don't do more from *Trash* or *Hey Stoopid.* On one tour we did "Teenage Frankenstein" and then we have done "He's Back (The Man Behind the Mask)." We haven't done that one in a while. We used to play it every time we played in Sweden because the only place where that song was popular was in Sweden.

2008

February 14, 2008. Neal Smith issues his second solo album, *Sexual Savior,* under the band label Killsmith.

Neal Smith:
At the time of writing, in the late '90s and early 2000s, I was experiencing a lot of the European heavy metal, amazing bands and huge, like Rammstein from Germany. So I wrote *Sexual Savior* influenced by that and it came out great; I was trying to get some of that shock value of the Alice Cooper group, lyrically, whatever. I can have a pretty foul mouth when I want to, and I don't want anything to censor my thoughts or what I wanted to write or say on the album. So if you're under 18, you probably shouldn't listen to it without doing so secretly.

March 19 – 25, 2008. Alice tours Australia and Japan, with a New Zealand date including Kiss on a festival bill. *Along Came a Spider* songs "Vengeance Is Mine" and "(In Touch with Your) Feminine Side" are introduced into the set.

Eric Singer:
Keri's a great player. Unfortunately—because I've been through similar circumstances before—when you play in a lot of bands, people start thinking you're just a hired gun.
Well, you know, we are hired guns, but that's how you make a living. Somebody calls you up to work and you're available, you're going to go work. I knew who Keri was for years, but I never really worked with him and I would have to say he's an excellent player. He's very professional. When he comes in he's very prepared with the material. He made it very easy for us when he joined the band last year—super easy.

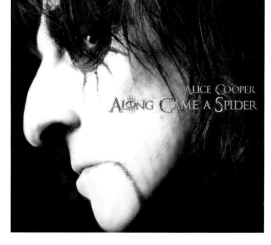

You have to remember Alice Cooper is a solo artist, it's not a band. When the tour ends, everybody goes their separate ways. Alice would love to keep everybody in the band all the time, but he understands that everybody has other outside interests and sometimes they're trying to pursue their own band, like in the case of Damon Johnson. Damon has a band called Whiskey Falls. They came out with their record this year and Damon was writing and recording this record while he was in the band last year. He was juggling his schedule, like I do back and forth with Kiss. Eventually he realised he had to devote all his time to Whiskey Falls because they had a record deal, a lot of promotion, a lot of money put into this band. They're really great; I saw them when they did their record release party in Los Angeles. So in a case like Damon, he had another outside project he was pursuing and this is what happens.

Like Ryan Roxie; he moved to Sweden two years ago with his family, so he decided to stay home because he wanted to be with his children that are very young. You make a lot of sacrifices to be a musician and to be in a band; you sacrifice a lot of relationships, a lot of family and friends. It's very difficult—a lot of people forget about this.

May 27, 2008. Alice's book, *Golf Monster,* from a year previous, is issued in paperback.

July 6 – 25, 2008. Alice conducts a short leg of his *Psycho Drama* tour in Europe.

July 29, 2008. Alice issues his 25th album, the conceptual *Along Came a Spider*, through his new deal with

Germany's Steamhammer/SPV label. Ozzy Osbourne guests on "Wake the Dead" and Slash guests on "Vengeance is Mine." As for personnel on the record, Alice, Eric Singer and Chuck Garric are joined by Danny Saber and Greg Hampton, who not only provide guitars and keyboards, but also receive the production credit on the album. The album is the most successful record for Alice since the major label deal days, reaching No.53 on *Billboard* and No.26 in the UK.

Alice Cooper:
Evil should get punished. It should never win. And that, to me, is what's most satisfying. I may love Darth Vader when I watch *Star Wars*, but I feel relief when he finally gets what's coming to him. Every album I've ever done has been guitar-driven rock 'n' roll. Danny Saber and Greg Hampton are both guitar players. They know all the classic Alice music and began referencing favourite moments before we even started to record. That's when I first realised this could become a really special Alice album. I know my fans are going to love it.

Eric Singer:
The recording of drums happened very quickly. I played what I felt for the songs even though the vocals were not done yet, which makes the approach sometimes harder. I like to play off the lead vocal melodies whenever possible to be more musical/melodic. Essentially I "write" my drum parts, which is sometimes overlooked by most people. Drummers contribute a lot when it comes to arrangements and vibe to songs. Last time I looked out into the crowd during a show, the people pump their fists in the air to what? The beat, the rhythm.

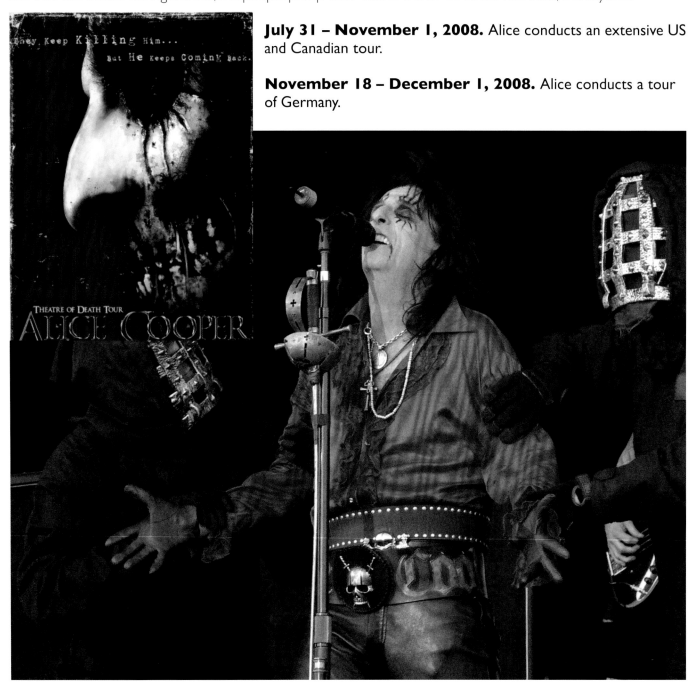

July 31 – November 1, 2008. Alice conducts an extensive US and Canadian tour.

November 18 – December 1, 2008. Alice conducts a tour of Germany.

2009

March 13 – 15, 2009. The *Monstermania* horror convention in Cherry Hill, NJ has as guests, Alice Cooper, Neal Smith, Dennis Dunaway and Michael Bruce.

April 26, 2009. Alice and Ace Frehley play together at a star-studded charitable event, the *Second Annual Rock & Roll Supergroup Benefit Concert.* Around this time, Alice appears at events in support of a variety of social causes, in fact joined by his son Dash at an event for the National Center for Missing and Exploited Children.

May 13, 2009. At the Arizona State University commencement ceremony, at which President Barack Obama spoke, Alice performs "School's Out" to a crowd of 63,000.

June 12, 2009. Alice's capable personal assistant for 28 years, Brian "Renfield" Nelson, passes away.

June 14 – 28, 2009. Alice plays a series of dates in Russia with Scorpions, The Rasmus and Kingdom Come.

July 31 – August 13, 2009. Alice conducts a short US leg of something he calls the *Theatre of Death Tour.* From the new album, only "Vengeance Is Mine" is played.

August 18 – September 4, 2009. Alice plays Australia and New Zealand.

September 17 – October 31, 2009. Alice conducts an extensive leg of his *Theatre of Death Tour* in the US.

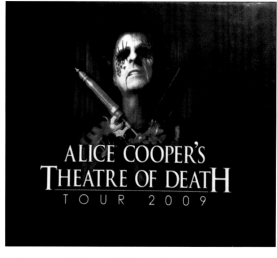

Gavin Baddeley:
I think it's changed a lot. I'm sure the sales figures and a lot of fans will go right against this—but I think it's a classic case of where what is good for the artist is not necessarily good for the art. So a lot of the stuff from the early period that established him, I'm not sure he knew where it was coming from. It was very stream of consciousness, with a lot of stuff coming from TV and the mass media and so forth

Whereas today, I think he's very much a businessman. He's reinvented himself. When he's been criticising artists like Marilyn Manson, he's always said, whenever we sort of dipped our toes in the realm of decadence and darkness, we were warning against it. Which rather begs the question, just how urgent was it to warn America about the risks of necrophilia? So I think he's reinvented himself. There are at least two and probably several more different Alice Coopers. His modern stuff is very by-the-numbers. I think if he could make his living as a golf pro, I'm sure he would.

Again, looking back at the show, when Alice Cooper came on in his half-assed cross-dressing, I don't think they really appreciated quite the reaction they were going to get, with this drawing attention to yourself. But inevitably over time, people do become more professional and skilled at manipulating any aspect of what they're doing. Today's so-called shock rockers have learned by the successes and failures of preceding acts. It's become more professional now and become more difficult. The obvious spaces have been taken.

October 30, 2009. Dick Wagner issues a rarities CD called *Full Meltdown*.

November 18 – December 11, 2009. Alice tours in Europe, hitting Eastern Europe, the UK and Scandinavia. Support comes from Man Raze, featuring Simon Laffy from Girl, Phil Collen from Girl and Def Leppard and Paul　　　　　Cook from the Sex Pistols.

2010s

Is it time for another victory of lap of sorts? I think so, and the world responds with much-deserved cheers. Okay, a lot has happened over the 2010s for our man with the plan, Alice Cooper, despite this not being an era stuffed with new material like the preceding productive ten-year span.

The decade begins with a guest slot on Slash's record along with tour dates with Alice 2.0, Rob Zombie. There's a big live DVD, Dennis and Albert Bouchard kick off what will be a prolific band situation in Blue Coupe, and before 2010 is out, it is announced that the original Alice Cooper band will be inducted into the Rock and Roll Hall of Fame.

Into the spring of 2011, the band is indeed inducted with much fanfare, including a band reunion on stage, kicking off a series of such happy circumstances since. In September of 2011, Alice hires on a female guitarist in Michael Jackson flashback Orianthi and the same month, a special album is hatched. *Welcome 2 My Nightmare* includes a partial original band reunion and is produced by Bob Ezrin, but the assembly is somewhat haphazard and piecemeal and the event doesn't quite have the effect it could have. In this writer's opinion, *Welcome to My Nightmare* is hallowed ground, and arguably, only a close and even solemn reassembly of the original band, working on directly related material, would have been more suitable.

As the decade progresses, there are subtext victory laps taking place. Publishing their memoires are no less than Dick Wagner, Dennis Dunaway and Shep Gordon. Keeping visible, Neal is finally issuing lots of music and there's also more from Blue Coupe. Alice does a symphony tour of Europe, bringing along Orianthi, while Alice also acts as himself in Johnny Depp's *Dark Shadows*. Both along the victory lap theme, Alice tours on Mötley Crüe's never-ending farewell tour and Banger Films issues *Super Duper Alice Cooper*, a doc on Alice's career through to *Constrictor* that upholds the company's proven high standards (disclosure—I work there!).

Finally, mid-decade but late in our tale, Alice appears with Johnny Depp and Joe Perry in supergroup Hollywood Vampires, issuing an album of covers and originals and playing some dates as well. But our story ends with the arrival of Alice's 27th album and one that is arguably among his very best. *Paranormal* features a bevy of guest stars, but they don't detract from the sturdy songsmithing. This is vintage, prime, mature, gorgeously written and well-appointed Alice Cooper of the highest order. Jewels of songs emerge through perfect sequencing and the entire, confident pageant of tales holds together steadfast, representing Alice's fully fifty years of experience. If, indeed, this is to be Alice's last record, he has left us and his whirlwind of a career on an impressive high.

2010

March 31, 2010. Slash issues a self-titled solo album. It is issued in many configurations, one being a version for the UK only that contains a song called "Baby Can't Drive," which is co-written by Slash with Alice and Nicole Scherzinger from The Pussycat Dolls. Nicole and Alice also sing on this bonus track. Rhythm section on the session is Flea and Steven Adler.

April 16 – 18, 2010. *The Chiller Theatre Expo* welcomes as guests, Alice, Neal, Michael and Dennis.

April 20, 2010. The 5th Avenue Vampires, featuring Dennis Dunaway, issue an album called *Drawing Blood*.

Dennis Dunaway:
The 5th Avenue Vampires began with me agreeing to play bass on a recording that Richie Scarlet was involved in. But their drummer didn't show, so I called in Russ Wilson on the fly. The instrumental track came out great and that would have been the extent of it, except Dennis Dunaway Project hit a landmine, so Russ and I finished recording an album. The singer was Joe Von T and the songs were hard rock and spooky vampire ditties. We played a bunch of shows including opening for Alice five times.
     We had started recording our second album when the announcement of the Alice Cooper group's nomination for the Rock and Roll Hall of Fame hit with months of total chaos. It was too overwhelming for me to continue working on so many projects, including Blue Coupe and a blues rock thing that I was enjoying with Cactus singer Jimmy Kunes and the original Alice Cooper group had plans to play shows in several major cities.

April 26 – May 22, 2010. Alice Cooper and Rob Zombie conduct their *Gruesome Twosome Tour.*

Alice Cooper:
Rob Zombie, at the end of their show they used CO2 and pillows, and I go, "Where have I seen that before, Rob?" He goes, "You weren't using it!" I said, "That's fine, go ahead. But don't be surprised if at my next show there's fire. Rob's whole show is fire."

May 26, 2010. *American Idol* features as guests Alice and Keri Kelli who help with a contestant's rendition of "School's Out." Future Alice guitarist Orianthi is also part of the show.

June 19 – 26, 2010. Alice conducts a short European leg of his *Theatre of Death tour.*

July 9 – 25, 2010. Alice plays a handful of North American dates, including two large Canadian festivals, *Rock the Park,* London, Ontario, July 23, and *Heavy MTL* in Montreal, July 24.

July 30 – August 14, 2010. Alice plays a series of festival dates in Europe, followed by select US dates into early September.

September 28, 2010. Alice Cooper issues a double CD and DVD package called *Theatre of Death: Live at Hammersmith 2009.*

Keri Kelli:
The DVD is awesome, man. The last record we did a couple of years ago, *Along Came a Spider,* was very cool and I played on four of the songs, three that I helped write. The record is cool. It's Alice Cooper and it is what it is and I was very proud of being on that record. But having the DVD where it's the whole show performance and we're out there doing our thing… you see it, you feel it. It's showing us playing all those great songs. It's an honour, it really is—it's awesome. We've been watching it on the bus for the last little bit and we get ourselves all excited. To be playing with Coop every night is a honour and I'm being honest with you.

The quality of the package has everything to do with Alice and his long-time manager, Shep. This was set up last year and we filmed it in December. They got the HD cameras. They really captured the sound properly and then Bob Ezrin mixed the sound. So, they really did it the right way and we're excited because it does sound great. Having Bob involved is a really great thing and it's awesome. I know they've recorded with a lot of the guys from the past history and I hope that we, the new band members, are involved in the recording process of the new record. That would be great for us new guys.

Working with Bob would be great. He's a very musical guy. I've met him at the few shows he's come out to. He's always been very nice to me. I've sent him tracks that I've been working on and it's pretty cool to hear him say, "I like that" or to make suggestions because he's such legend. I don't know what's going to develop as far as the new Alice Cooper album, but as far as my songs go, maybe he'll like one enough to bring to one of his other projects. Who knows? But he's a great guy to know.

I'm definitely here for Alice. I've played guitar my whole life and as a hired gun it's always a battle to stay afloat and there's nothing else I would do but play guitar. So, I'm here for Alice and I'm here until he decides to hang it up. But I don't see that happening anytime soon. Certainly not with the great reunion that is taking place with Bob, the new record, the new DVD, etc. I like to do things in between, but only on Alice's down time because as soon as they start putting the Alice machine together, I'm ready to go.

September 30 – October 24, 2010. Alice plays dates in America, which he calls the *Halloween Hootenanny Tour.* Rob Zombie is part of the package.

October 5, 2010. Evangeline Records out of San Francisco issued the two-CD *Be Your Lover: Michael Bruce Anthology.*

October 31 – November 1, 2010. Alice chooses to spend Halloween in the UK, playing two dates at the Roundhouse in London. By this point, Alice and Bob Ezrin had written 13 songs for Alice's next album as well as having recorded three of them with original band members Dennis, Neal and Michael.

November 4 – 29, 2010. Alice plays solidly through November, playing Germany, Switzerland, Italy, France and Spain.

November 9, 2010. Blue Coupe issue their debut album, *Tornado on the Tracks.* The band consists of Joe Bouchard and Albert Bouchard, both ex-Blue Öyster Cult, plus Dennis Dunaway.

Dennis Dunaway:
Blue Coupe are more willing to get down in the trenches and travel than BDS was. Scrapping up decent gigs has gotten even bleaker since then. We all work very hard on every aspect of music and we always have fun with it. As brothers, Joe and Albert's voices blend well. Then we often have sisters Tish and Snooky of Manic Panic and The Sic Fucks singing high harmonies, which sounds majestic at times. I handed Alice a copy of our CD, *Tornado on the Tracks,* and he said that Robby Krieger had already given him one with a big enthusiastic hype. Robby played on the BÖC *Imaginos* album with Albert so they're long time friends as well.

Like some songs on the Dennis Dunaway Project *Bones from the Yard* album—"Man Is a Beast" and "Home Sweet Home"—some songs on *Tornado* came from a concept album that I had originally written for the Alice Cooper group. "God, I Need You Tonight" was intended as the mental breakdown of the Alice character in a futuristic cityscape where street gangs and corporations battle for power. The Alice character gets caught in a crossfire because he is trying to do both.

As for comparing Albert with Neal, they both favour percussive styles with lots of floor toms and heavy kicks, which is right up my alley. Neal has a more natural swing feel but Albert has swing in his arsenal. He's a music teacher in New York City. Joe teaches music too. Neal and Albert are both seasoned pros and I'm a lucky bassist.

December 15, 2010. It is announced that Alice Cooper will be inducted into the Rock and Roll Hall of Fame.

December 16, 2010. The Alice Cooper band conduct a second reunion of sorts, this time adding Steve Hunter to the fold. They play the Dodge Theatre in Phoenix.

December 31, 2010. In a benefit for the Maui Food bank, Alice performs on stage in Hawaii with James Hetfield, Mick Fleetwood, Patrick Simmons from The Doobie Brothers and Mike Kroeger from Nickelback.

2011

February 2011. Alice announces on his radio show, *Nights with Alice Cooper,* that he's finished work on his next album.

March 10, 2011. Alice plays the Tucson Convention Centre, as part of a benefit concert in aid of Tucson shooting victims.

March 14, 2011. A reunited Alice Cooper Group play as part of their Rock and Roll Hall of Fame induction ceremony. The band perform "I'm Eighteen," "Under My Wheels," and "School's Out." Inducted are the members of the original band. Rob Zombie conducts the induction speech.

Dennis Dunaway:
It's a true honour and it's great to get an award for being crazy. Now our fans have proven to the world that it's okay for them to be crazy too. They are what the Hall of Fame induction is all about, really. They are why we dedicate our lives to doing what we do. To be acknowledged as Alice Cooper, the group, is fitting and proper. I just wish Glen had been there to accept the honour. We tipped a few toasts to him in the Waldorf Astoria bar. They couldn't kick us out 'til the wee hours.

Neal Smith:
I always tell everybody that it is certainly not about any of us individually. This was a labour of love and starvation and blood and sweat and tears. It was a shame that Glen couldn't be there. I really was good friends with him and Michael Bruce. I happened to be living with them at the time when their drummer quit in 1967. There is a lot of stuff that happened. It goes back to the days before there was Frank Zappa or before there was Joe Greenberg or Shep Gordon, our managers. There were a lot of emotions tied up in that.

As far as I'm concerned, when so many people laughed at us and told us that we could never do it… there were five of us against the whole wide world. That was a hard uphill battle all the way. Music was so different from what we were doing. We hooked up with Bob Ezrin and he actually was one of the first people to really understand what we were doing. He turned what a lot of people thought was uncommercial into a commercial monster. We became the No.1 band in the world with *Billion Dollar Babies.* It was almost like what we projected on *Love It to Death* in the song "Caught in a Dream." We looked into the future and saw what we wanted to be. The song "Billion Dollar Babies" got us there.

We just said fuck you to anyone who ever doubted us. There was nobody in the band for a second who doubted what we were doing. It is not an "I told you so." It is even worse than that. It is, "Go fuck yourself and anyone else who ever criticised us." We didn't care. Once we opened that door... we didn't open it, we blew it open with a nuclear bomb. Once it was open, then everyone saw you could go onstage and have theatrics and wear makeup and be a commercial success. You can be a freak. It opened the whole thing. To this day we look back at the bands that followed us and some of them are in the Hall of Fame now. There was a lot of pride going into the Hall, but there was sadness because Glen was not there. He was the nucleus and the heart

of the band. Dennis will say the same thing. Michael and Alice will say that as well. He put us over the top with his influence in the song "School's Out." That is what made us a household name. It was Glen that did it. Our reputation was built, but we didn't have that monster hit yet. "School's Out" did it. Glen had the attitude. It was a shame he could not be there.

We got in the first time we were nominated. We looked at who got in on their first nomination and it was Led Zeppelin, The Beatles, The Rolling Stones, the Who and us. I am always grateful for every single second the original band can get up and play. I love every guy in the band and I get very emotional. When we got into the Hall, we were all able to hug each other. We were able to just give them a hell of a show like we always did and that is what we did.

Dick Wagner:
I was very happy to see that happen and I think they deserve it. I understand they have a section in the Hall Of Fame for sidemen, so maybe I'll get a chance someday. But the original band created such a movement in music. They lead to David Bowie, Lou Reed, Kiss and Marilyn Manson. It all started with Alice.

April 20, 2011. A reunited Alice Cooper group play Club Nokia in Los Angeles, as part of the *Revolver Golden God Awards.*

May 11, 2011. The reunited Alice Cooper group plays London's Battersea Power Station for the *Jagermeister Ice Cold 4D* webcast.

May 12 – December 14, 2011. Alice Cooper conducts a worldwide campaign called the *No More Mr. Nice Guy* tour, playing pretty much every country they've ever played, and then some, except for, oddly, Japan. His band for the campaign consists of Damon Johnson, Tommy Henriksen and Steve Hunter on guitars, Chuck Garric on bass and Glen Sobel on drums. "Clones" from *Flush the Fashion* is added to the set list, as is *Welcome 2 My Nightmare* track "I'll Bite Your Face Off." Late October, the band is supported in the UK by the New York Dolls.

Steve Hunter:
We did a seven-month run. Pretty hard tour. It was pretty brutal, a lot of travelling, I think we went around the world twice or something. But it was fun getting on stage and looking over and seeing my old buddy Alice on stage. We were on stage again after 35 years—it was awesome. The thing that's wonderful about him is he knows that character so well, that he can get into that character as soon as the lights go down. He's still got a marvellous, wonderful sense of humour and he's all the vibe that he had back in *Nightmare*. The only difference is we were a little younger then, so it's a different angst, if you will. There's a little bit different angst. But being on stage with him, when I looked over at him, we were little bit older but the vibe and the energy was still there.

Damon Johnson:
This Alice tour is going on and it's my favourite one ever. It's been such an honour to play in a band with Steve Hunter. Steve is a hero of mine from when I was a kid. I've sat down and learned so many of his guitar solos from the records, so to be in a band with him now is such an honour. The other new guys, Tommy Henriksen on guitar and Glen Sobel on drums, we've gone to such detail to get back to the original recordings. We wanted to revisit all those parts and make sure we had them down as close to the original as possible. I believe this band is delivering that in a way that I don't know any Alice Cooper band has.

June 26, 2011. Alice plays play his first ever UK club gig in 30 years at the tiny 100 Club in London's Oxford Street. Tickets sold out in seconds. Stripped of his usual stage theatrics this was an Alice Cooper show which had a garage days revisited vibe about it. He opens with The Yardbirds "Train Kept-A-Rollin'."

August 29, 2011. Ex-Michael Jackson guitarist Orianthi is announced as Alice's new guitarist. She replaces Damon Johnson, now busy with Thin Lizzy and Black Star Riders.

September 9, 2011. Orianthi debuts as guitarist for Alice Cooper in a performance on *The Tonight Show* with Jay Leno.

September 13, 2011. Alice Cooper issues his 26th album, *Welcome 2 My Nightmare,* which at No.22 on the *Billboard* charts, represents Alice's highest charting album since Trash. Notwithstanding a writing and performance credit situation that is both hugely complicated and populous, the core band on the record is Alice along with guitarist Tommy Henriksen and bassist Chuck Garric.

Alice Cooper:

When we work together it's like Tim Burton and Johnny Depp. We know each other upside down and backwards. I can go in with Bob Ezrin and say, "Here's the idea of the story. Let's not do part two of *Welcome to My Nightmare.* Let's just give Alice a new nightmare. You have a different nightmare every night. You dream totally different stuff every night. Let's give Alice an entirely new nightmare. What would be a nightmare for him in 2011?"

Well, technology would be a nightmare for him. Disco would still be a nightmare for him. We just started writing down things or ideas. Things that would really bother Alice. A nine-to-five job would really bother Alice. Then when we decided who's going to play the devil. Not a scary devil, but a provocative sensual devil. So we got Ke$ha and I said, "I don't want you to be scary. I want you to be a temptress, which is still a trait of the devil."

So, we approached that one differently. I said, "Let's do a disco song because Alice still hates disco." We challenged ourselves on a lot of these songs. "Bloodbath Boogie Disco Fever" had every cliché you could think of and ended up being a really good disco song. Definitely a slap in the face to disco.

This album would never have happened if Bob had said, "I don't really want to do part two or *Welcome 2 My Nightmare.*" We never would have done the album because his input means that much. I would have gone and done another idea for another album, but this idea was too good. It was the 30th anniversary and I said, "Let's go back and visit it. Let's even pull some of the hooks from *Nightmare* and let them creep around."

Every once in a while, in the new songs, you'll hear little section of "Steven" or "Welcome to My Night-mare" just to connect it back to the first one. There's no such thing as "We can't do that" when working with Bob. We'd be laughing and saying, "We can do this and this and this." So, I'd look at him and say, "Well, why don't we do a disco song? Let's sit down and lay down a disco track except make it scary." When he goes to the disco, he lines 'em up against the wall and shoots them with a machine gun and then buries them, but they just keep coming back to life. That would be an Alice nightmare disco song, so it's "Disco Blood Bath Boogie Fever."

"Last Man on Earth," he's on a train that crashes and he's the last man on earth. He wakes up and looks around and as soon as he's finished that song there's a pause. He turns around and there's the congregation and he has to deal with them. I love the way each song moves the story around.

When we did the Hall of Fame show, Neal, Dennis, and Mike were there and I told them I want you guys to each write a song with us. So, Dennis wrote "Runaway Train" which was something he had on one of his albums. I said, "Let's take "Subway" and re-work it. I want Alice to be on a runaway train where he can't get off and is chained to it. It's going to crash and he can't do anything about it."

Neal had a section of a song which we pulled out and we said, "Let's make this a tribute to the Rolling Stones." "I'll Bite Your Face Off" is a pure 1965 Rolling Stones song. So, we put the handclapping in there and anything the Rolling Stones did in the '60s. Michael came in with "When Hell Comes Home" about an abusive father. On that one, I told the guys, "I want you to play this one live in the studio." The reason was that it was the type of song that would have been on *Love It to Death* or *Killer*. I wanted to recapture what we sounded like in that era and the only way to do that was to play it live in the studio."

I didn't have to tell them to "stylize" it as a '70s song because that's just the way they play. Bob and I never had to give them one bit of direction. They just started to play and Dennis had his signature bass, Mike played it exactly how he would have played it in the '70s and Neal played it with all the same exact fills that he would have done in the '70s. I kept looking at Bob and going, "We don't have to say anything. Just let them play."

Damon Johnson:
Bob Ezrin had to produce the album while the touring band was on the road and a Bob Ezrin record is a pretty significant commitment, so logistically it just wasn't feasible to use the touring band on the record. There's a couple of tracks that we're on, but as you can see from the credits there's a whole potpourri of guys that are playing on the album.

As for the original band being on here, I was a fan of those guys when I was a kid. There's so much heritage and legend associated with the original band. If there ever was a great year to be in the Alice

Cooper band, it's 2011 because of the Hall of Fame induction. Alice Cooper is everywhere right now and it's been an amazing experience to be a part of it.

I just think that the new record is so good and, of course, the old record is legendary. It would be an amazing experience for the audience to see some mesh of the two records live and surround those with some of the other hits. That's a tip of the hat to the creativity and specialness that is Bob Ezrin and Alice Cooper as a team. It's no accident that those guys have had so much success with their early records and I'm as excited as any other fan that Bob is involved with this record.

Dick Wagner:
It's been difficult but I'm on the mend. I had a heart attack in 2007 with a stroke at the same time. I woke up from my heart attack with a totally paralyzed left arm. It's taken me four years to get back to playing relatively well. I'm certainly not back to where I was, but I'm certainly trying to get there. Hopefully, I will someday, but I just don't know when. I still know the guitar, but I just can't get there. I've done physical therapy and I'm on medication, but a year ago I got stricken with water on the brain, a condition known as hydrocephalus. I started falling down flat on my face and I had to have brain surgery. I've been a lot better since the surgery, but it's tough. My days have not been as good as they used to be, but I'm working on playing a couple of live dates in Michigan in September. These will be my first lives dates in over four-and-a-half years. I hope people will come out and see me."

As for *Welcome 2 My Nightmare*, I said, "It's about time." I've wanted him to do that for years. I've always thought we should. Just like I've always thought we should take the *Welcome to My Nightmare* band back on the road. I know he's got Steve back. It would have been great if it could have been Hunter and myself, but I'm just not playing well enough to do it. That's just a matter of fact, but hope springs eternal.

Right now, I'm good enough to have played on the album. I played guitar on "The Underture" and I think I did a pretty damn good job. When I got that piece of music, I was like, "Wow, that's beautiful." That was my first recording session in four-and-a-half years, so I see that I can do recording sessions. I know I can play on the records, but as far as live appearances go I just don't know when. I'm doing these lives gigs in Michigan and I'm proving to myself that I can do two hours of live music, and if I can do that, then of course, I can play an

Alice Cooper show. There's no doubt about it.

Also on the album is "Something to Remember Me By," which I wrote. Bob had called me and said, "I need another 'Only Women Bleed.'" So, I made a demo of a song that I knew Alice loved and I sent it down to him. They loved it and changed a few little words in it for Alice. I've had it for maybe ten years and Alice has always wanted to record it. This became the right moment to do it and I think it's a potential hit. It's one of those Alice Cooper/Dick Wagner ballads. When we hit into a ballad, it somehow translates to radio. Alice has never been a big radio guy, but it just seems that every time that we write a ballad, it's an immediate radio song. I can't explain it. It's just the way it is. We have a couple of ballads waiting in the wings that I think we should do.

To do my parts, I was here in Arizona. I didn't go to Nashville to do the recording. They sent me the stems and I put the guitar parts on them, so I was never part of that camaraderie. I wanted to be, but physically I wasn't quite ready for it. I haven't heard the album yet, but Alice told me that Bob is at his peak, and when he's at his peak putting an album together, you just know it's going to be brilliant on some level or another.

Jimmy DeGrasso:

I'm on a couple of tracks and God only know what ones. I have credit for something. Unfortunately, that record was done without the band. The band was on tour (laughs). So I guess session guys played on that. It's impossible to make a record when you're on tour, and we were on tour almost a whole year, so we thought we were going to be doing the bulk of the record and then when the tour was over we found out oh, the record is done. Oh, okay, thanks for telling us.

So it's a bunch of session guys. I'm sure they did a good job, I've heard blurbs of it but I haven't heard the whole thing. But there were different people on it, so no, it's not a band. There's other Alice records that were a band and you can tell it sounds like that one band. But you know, it is what it is. It's economic. The band's on tour nine months. You can't fly the band back from Europe for five days of sessions because it's so costly and plus it's just not practical. You can only do one or the other; you can tour or make a record—you can't do both at the same time.

Neal Smith:

"I'll Bite Your Face Off" is a rewrite of a song off of my new album, *Killsmith Two*, called "Evil Voodoo Moon." We've been throwing songs back and forth for fifteen years. I'll send songs to Alice and I'll play him a bunch of my new stuff. So this time he and Bob rewrote "Evil Voodoo Moon" into "I'll Bite Your Face Off." Michael Bruce had a song called "Hell Hole No.9" on one of his demo tapes which is pretty much the same song Alice has as "When Hell Comes Home," but with new lyrics. It's the same arrangement. The other songs were changed a little bit, but Michael's song is almost identical.

Just to have the four of us together is wonderful. We had talked, after the Hall of Fame, about doing a handful of shows on the East Coast, West Coast and Canada. Alice talked about it and we talked about, but I knew at the same time that he was booking his tour for 2011. Unfortunately, I knew it was never going to happen.

If there's enough interest from the songs we just recorded on this album and we go in to record an album with just the four of us, then it might be a possibility. But c'mon, you get into the Rock and Roll Hall of Fame and you can't do a couple of dates around the country? I know I was swamped with emails. Dennis was swamped. People were disappointed.

The current tour is called *No More Mr. Nice Guy*—that's Michael's song. All the appearances were there that something was going to be happening with the original band, but it didn't happen. You can never say no. I never thought we'd get nominated much less get into the Rock and Roll Hall of Fame, so that's great and it's a tribute to the original band. I said in my acceptance speech that it was all about the fans because they've really been there for us. Without that band, Alice, none of us would have been doing anything. I think that's a great testimonial to the music. It's 2011 and they're still playing "School's Out." I would have never guessed that. Then again I never would have guessed that I would have lived into the 2000s because drummers had a very short shelf life, if you recall.

October 28, 2011. Neal Smith issues a third solo album, and second of the Killsmith concept, *Killsmith Two.*

Neal Smith:
That was a little more radio-friendly, but still very heavy metal, maybe a little more commercial from the standpoint of a couple of the hooks on some the songs.

2012

February 11, 2012. Steve Hunter announces he's leaving the Alice Cooper band.

February 18, 2012. Alice Cooper Bobblehead Night at the Phoenix Coyotes hockey game. First 10,000 through the doors get one.

March 27, 2012. A storage facility that contains the Alice Cooper archives is broken into and a number of items are stolen.

April 11, 2012. Alice and Slash perform "School's Out" at the Golden Gods awards. Three days later, Alice and Sheryl are off to the Rock and Roll Hall of Fame ceremonies (the band were inducted the previous year).

May 11, 2012. Alice appears as himself in Tim Burton's feature film adaptation of well-regarded horror soap opera TV series *Dark Shadows*. The movie stars Johnny Depp who will soon be in a band with Alice.

Alice Cooper:
I keep telling them I'd rather play the priest, I'd rather play the school teacher, I'd rather play the nerdy father. I had fun playing Freddie's father in *Freddy's Dead: The Final Nightmare*. In Suck, I got to play a bartender that was really a bad-ass vampire. There was a lot of dialogue to learn and to me that was acting. It wasn't playing Alice. It was real acting.

But in *Dark Shadows*, Alice was the perfect character. Johnny Depp's character is coming back to life in 1972 and to make it realistic the teenage girl says, "I want to have a party." The only way to make it a cool party is to have Alice Cooper at the party. So, he says, "Fine. Get this Alice person." He kept referring to me as "that Alice woman." It's the funniest joke in the whole bit.

They connected that up to the girl's story, being in the straight jacket. Tim is a huge fan of "The Ballad of Dwight Fry" and both Johnny and Tim said we gotta do Dwight Fry, and Tim weaved the story around that song. So, it tells the story about how they put her in an insane asylum, in a straight jacket, with the, "I gotta get out of here, I gotta get out of here, I gotta get out of here." He did a magnificent job of weaving those two things together.

May 22, 2012. Shout! Factory re-releases on DVD The *Strange Case of Alice Cooper*, a concert film documenting a show from April 9, 1979 originally released on videotape in September of '79.

Alice Cooper:
I sat and watched it for the first time in thirty years because they wanted me to do comments. So I'm picking it apart because I forgot all about the show and I'm laughing my head off going, "That's funny. That's a great bit. What's going on here?" I forgot about the dancing bottles and all the insanity that was going on in that show. There are so many Alice Cooper shows. Every time we go out, we do a different version of the show. This is one that was coming out after *Nightmare* and *King of the Silver Screen*, '77 and '78. Alice was sober now. I'm looking at a whole different Alice. It's interesting to go back and look at that little section of your life.

There was a lot of, "What was I thinking?" I realise now that if I were to go back and do that show; I would do it with more finesse. I would do it a lot less chaotically and I would spend more time on the singing of the song rather than the performing of the song. When I did that I was not physically in the best shape. I was just out of the hospital and I just wanted to get back to work. I would love to go back and do that show now, in the shape I'm in now and in the voice I'm in now. It would be a much smoother show.

There's a point that I got to when I got sober that I said, I have to spend more time on the actual vocals of these songs. Yes, the theatrics come pretty easily, but let's make sure I sing these songs and really hit the notes. I really have to sing it like the album and let the theatrics come after that. In *The Strange Case of Alice Cooper*, it was getting back on stage after a year off and it looked like I wanted to put everything in and as fast as I could. That's okay. That was the attitude and fun part of that show. It was kinetic and chaotic, but I would do it differently now. When you stop drinking alcohol, you lose a lot of weight and then you want to put the weight back on. So, you start drinking Coca-Colas and then you have to lose that weight. I was like Robert De Niro for awhile, but I don't think I ever got over 160 pounds. That would have been heavy for me.

June 8 – July 21, 2012. The band conduct an intensive leg of the *No More Mr. Nice Guy* tour in the US and Canada. Guitarist Ryan Roxie has rejoined the band. Halfway through, drummer Glen Sobel is sidelined by a neck injury, to be replaced by Jonathan Mover. A number of the dates are in support of Iron Maiden and a handful are with Blue Coupe, featuring Dennis Dunaway. *Welcome 2 My Nightmare* is now represented by "I'll Bite Your Face Off" and "Caffeine."

Alice Cooper:

When you're the guest star on somebody else's tour... We'll be doing about an hour, so it'll be more of a sprint. We're going to do all the hits of course, but it'll be a very high-energy show. We're going to pack as much stuff as we can into one hour. This will have the guillotine and all that stuff. Then when we do our own headline shows... Iron Maiden only work two or three nights a week and we're used to working five or six nights a week. So, on what will be their night off, we'll be doing our own one hour and 40 minute show in other venues. We don't like too many nights off; that's just the way we are.

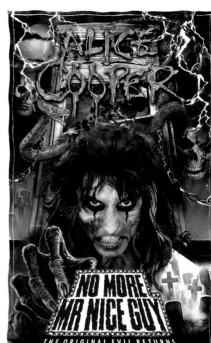

Typically we do a hundred shows/ hundred cities a year, which takes four or five months. We used to do 65 cities in 72 days when we we're doing *Nightmare*. That was ridiculous, but when you're twenty-seven years old, you're indestructible. I'm sixty-four now and I was twenty-seven during *Nightmare*. I have, by far, more energy in this show than I had then because that's back when I was drinking. It was focused and I never missed a show and you wouldn't know that I was drinking on stage. In fact, I never did drink on stage, just drinking in general, but you'll notice that this show now will be a lot higher energy than the *Nightmare* show was.

In the band we have Orianthi, who's a show unto herself. Ryan Roxie is his own show by himself. It ends up that Tommy Henriksen is my anchor, with Chuck Garric in the middle, and he ends up doing a show. It's just show guys up there and I have to tell them that when Alice is doing a theatrical bit to back off. When Alice drops back then go ahead and, by all means, be a rock star. If you're anything but that I will kick you in the butt! I need for "you guys" to be not in the least bit inhibited on stage. It's a great band all the way around. Glen Sobel, is one of the great drummers.

July 27 – August 12, 2012. The band conduct a short tour of Europe, closing out of the *Bloodstock Festival* in Derby, England, topping a considerably heavy bill, consisting of Paradise Lost, Anvil, Deicide, The Black Dahlia Murder, Nile and Corrosion of Conformity.

September 1, 2012. Dick Wagner issues his memoires, *Not Only Women Bleed: Vignettes from the Heart of a Rock Musician.*

October 24 – November 1, 2012. Alice conducts a UK leg of a tour he has deemed *Raise the Dead.* Support comes from Ugly Kid Joe and Duff McKagan side-band band Loaded. "Dirty Diamonds" is in the set, as is "He's Back (The Man Behind the Mask)." A third *Welcome 2 My Nightmare* track is on board, namely "The Congregation."

November 7 – December 1, 2012. Alice takes his *Raise the Dead tour* across the US and Western Canada—in Canada, Geoff Tate supports. On November 29th, at the Orpheum Theatre in LA, actor Johnny Depp joins him for several songs.

2013

February 15 – 18, 2013. Alice participates in an edition of the Rock and Roll Fantasy Camp. Also encouraging the aspiring rocker participants are Kip Winger, Kane Roberts and Teddy Zigzag.

April 30, 2013. Blue Coupe—Joe Bouchard, Albert Bouchard, Dennis Dunaway—issue their second album, *Million Miles More*. Alice guests on the song "Hallows Grave."

June 1 – July 20, 2013. Alice plays a combination of sheds and theatres across the US and Canada as part of a co-headlining tour with Marilyn Manson called *Masters of Madness*. Supporting is Picture Me Broken.

Alice Cooper:
When Marilyn came along it was back to getting the parents to hate you again. How do you do that? Alice already used a snake, he used this and this. I'll be a devil-worshipper and I'll be a drug addict. Marilyn did it really well, I have to admit. He even pissed me off a couple times. Tearing up the Bible, I'm a Christian and I went hey, you're stepping over the line a bit here, pal, and he and I talked about it. I said, "I'm not shocked that you're tearing the Bible up, but I certainly don't condone it." It's something I live by. I get it, why you're doing it, but I don't want to stand too close to you when lightning hits you on Judgment Day. But we know where each other stand on that. I would say theologically we're miles apart, but he was really good at what he did. I admit that. We're friends. We're not at odds any more, but certainly I had to tell him where I stood.

When I saw Marilyn, I looked at it and I said okay, that generation needs an Alice. That's who Marilyn was. Marilyn was that generation's Alice. Had all different things to piss off the parents, you know. A different set of things that he used. But I met Marilyn and we sat and talked about it. I told him the way to make this last is hit records. You have to have songs that people believe in. "Eighteen" they believe in, "School's Out" they believe in, "No More Mr. Nice Guy," they believe in those songs. I said you have to have those songs that are going to last thirty, forty years or it's going to be a short-lived career. I'm always encouraging these young bands to write quality songs. That's the whole trick.

Now image-wise, Marilyn took it and where I was snakes and androgyny and all this, his was Devil worship and blatant drugs. The videos, with Marilyn Manson, that was the scariest part. His videos were truly disturbing. The girl that did his videos was brilliant. I was shocked by the videos. I sat there and went wow, that is disturbing. That was powerful. Then Marilyn knew how to take it to the next level. Now the funny thing, the juxtaposition behind this that makes it really funny is that I became Christian, right? So Marilyn is like a pastor in the Church of Satan and I'm Christian and we are diametrically opposed when it comes to our theology.

Yet I see his show and I go, oh, I get it, I totally get it. I'm not going to do this (wags his finger) to him. I sat there and I go, so what are you doing? What's making you tic? I get it, okay. He understands though. At one point he said I really hate Alice now he's Christian. He starts tearing the Bible up onstage and eating it and doing all this stuff. I said that's not going to make the Bible go away.

August 1 – 8, 2013. Alice participates in festival season in Europe, highlight being *Wacken Open Air* in Wacken, Germany, where he plays on a bill with Deep Purple, Rammstein, Motörhead, Lamb of God, Nightwish, Anthrax and Arch Enemy.

September 7, 2013. The Mike Myers-directed *Supermensch: The Legend of Shep Gordon* premiers at the Toronto International Film Festival. Alice is in the documentary and he is also at the premiere. Also in Toronto, late August, Alice was a guest at Fan Expo and then on September 23rd, Alice is on hand to honour Bob Ezrin who receives a star on the Walk of Fame.

October 13 – November 27, 2013. Following two dates in Russia and one in Estonia, Alice plays a series of dates in the US and Canada.

2014

March 9 – April 5, 2014. Alice performs with his guitarist Orianthi, Primal Fear bassist Mat Sinner and the Bohemian Prague Symphony Orchestra on a campaign called *The Original Rock Meets Classic Tour*. Most of the dates are in Germany. The set list consists of "School's Out," "No More Mr. Nice Guy," "Welcome to My Nightmare," "Only Women Bleed," "House of Fire" and "Poison."

April 17, 2014. Banger Films' documentary *Super Duper Alice Cooper* premieres at the Tribeca Film Festival. The film is directed by Banger Films' co-bosses Sam Dunn and Scot McFadyen along with Reginald Harkema, three-time Genie Award nominee and Alice Cooper expert. In attendance are Alice, Neal and Dennis.

Michael Bruce:
We were supposed to go to Canada for Dennis' book signing thing—Neal, Dennis and I—and they were going to interview me for that film, and then that cancelled. When you live in the world like we have today, things are moving fast for a guy like Alice Cooper. You don't really have time to make any course corrections in the back, because you're already miles from there. But people were like, but isn't Michael Bruce dead? Aren't both guitar players dead? They're dead, aren't they? (laughs).

May 31 – June 8, 2014. Alice performs a short European leg on his *Raise the Dead* tour.

July 2 – November 28, 2014. Mötley Crue mount their *All Bad Things Must Come to an End* farewell North American tour, with Alice Cooper supporting (as well as The Ruskins).

July 29, 2014. Theory of a Deadman issue their fifth album, *Savages*. The title track features a guest performance from Alice Cooper.

July 30, 2014. Dick Wagner dies of respiratory failure, in Phoenix, Arizona.

August 29, 2014. Neal Smith issues his third Killsmith album, *Killsmith & the Greenfire Empire*.

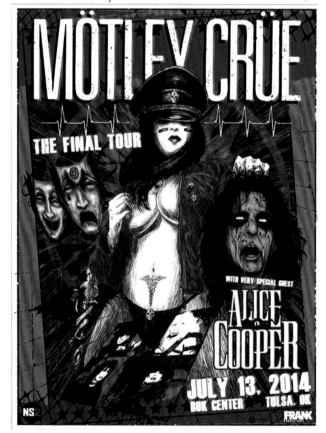

Neal Smith:
The newest one became a concept. Killsmith is a person, a mixture I would say between James Bond and Rambo. He's ex-military and that's all I'm really going to say. The Greenfire Empire is a big drug cartel from a warm climate in the southern hemisphere. It's a story of the reaction of him and this drug lord who invents a brand new drug that basically hooks the world. Killsmith has to stop it on his own, or try to. So there's like a movie theme to it. Although it's heavy metal from the beginning to the end, this time I have a little more dynamics in the music. Nothing as drastic as "Mary Ann," but there's a couple of big rock ballads and I even have a Christmas song in there.

October 20, 2014. UDR issues a DVD and CD package called *Raise the Dead: Live from Wacken*.

October 26, 2014. At a Mötley Crüe farewell date in Connecticut, Rob Zombie joins Alice on stage for "School's Out." The next day, a day off, Alice makes the best of it and attends a screening in New York City of *Super Duper Alice Cooper*, after which he is interviewed and conducts a Q&A. The following night is a show at Madison Square Garden.

December 16, 2014. It is announced that "School's Out" is on a list of songs that will be inducted into the Grammy Hall of Fame.

Neal Smith:
I loved the song "School's Out," but did I ever think that in 2016 I would still get royalties for it? Or be in the Grammy Hall of Fame for it? Hell no. If it would have been a Gold album, then we would have been successful. *School's Out* just skyrocketed. But that song, I didn't know it was a hit until it was out there. We released it just as school was really getting out. The album followed in the beginning of June, a few weeks later. The song opened the door for the album.

That element of timing and luck… if they don't happen, then we could have ended up with another *Pretties for You* or *Easy Action*. To be a fortune teller and say I knew it was going to happen—no. The only one that I heard and felt it might be a hit was *Love It to Death*. I remember lying on the floor half asleep and I put on the headphones and I heard the album through headphones and I went, "Holy fucking shit this is amazing."

But thank goodness "School's Out" was such a monster hit. Little kids these days may not know the name Alice Cooper, but they all know "School's Out." They will always and forever know "School's Out." It worked out on a magnitude that we could have never predicted.

One of the reasons we were out of the Rock and Roll Hall of Fame for so long was that we were not traditional. We were never mainstream, and that is what is so weird about the Grammy and the Hall of Fame. Everyone says Alice Cooper is mainstream. Give me a fucking break. Everybody used to shun us. But then "School's Out" was inducted into the Grammy Hall of Fame last year. It was the first time we'd ever been mentioned at the Grammys. Way back, the cover of the album for *School's Out* may have been nominated, but that was it.

2015

February 7 – 23, 2015. Alice conducts a handful of dates on his *Raise the Dead* tour, with the final shows, being part of the *Rock Legends Cruise*, Fort Lauderdale, Florida.

May 9 – 23, 2015. Alice Cooper continues to support Mötley Crüe on that band's farewell tour, hitting Australia and New Zealand.

June 9, 2015. Dennis Dunaway's excellent *Snakes! Guillotines! Electric Chairs!* memoir is issued, on Thomas Dunne/St. Martin's Press, marked by a book launch party at The Strand, famed bookstore in Manhattan. Same day, Alice is in London participating at a press conference announcing more Mötley Crüe dates. On the 10th, he's at the *Kerrang! Awards* collecting an accolade as Living Legend.

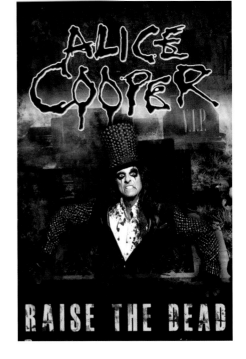

Dennis Dunaway:
I started it while I was in the hospital, when I was sick. My daughter was always telling me, "Dad, you're always complaining about this interview where somebody said something wrong and you're saying they are not telling the story right. Why not just shut up and write a book?" I was also not in very good shape in the hospital. Who can kick the bucket if they are writing a book? I had to finish it so I wouldn't die. It was a weird way of me setting a goal for myself so that I would have to pull out of that situation.

I wrote the book three times over. It is about the Alice Cooper group, and it mostly focuses on the early days, which to me is the real essence of the band. Again, I am really a conceptual artist who just happened to write a book. I wanted to get it right. I have Chris Hodenfield, who wrote for *Rolling Stone* magazine for ten years and he wrote the cover story for the Alice Cooper group in 1972, polishing it up with me, and it will be released on St. Martin's Press.

The book also has the stories of meeting Joe and Albert Bouchard. I met Joe and Albert in 1972. The Alice Cooper group had become headliners and our opening act wasn't working out. It was Dr. John, and three gigs into the tour Dr. John starts using a snake in his set. We were like, "Hey, we use a snake; you can't use a snake." He said, "I was using the snake a long time before you ever did." We were like, "You were not using a snake at the beginning of the tour. We have used the snake the whole tour. Stop using the snake." He kept using the snake. We said, "If you use the snake one more time then you're off the tour." He did, so we had to replace him.

We played this festival in North Carolina and it was a beautiful day. Alice and I… I think Neal was with us too. We were walking around the crowd and this band sets up with this giant backdrop with this symbol on it. They started playing, and I was like "Wow, these guys are good. We should let them open for us," and that is how we met. We did quite a few shows together on the *Billion Dollar Babies* tour. We became friends with the whole band. I managed to be more in touch with Joe and Albert because we lived in the tri-state area.

One day I was on the train to New York City and Joe is sitting there. We found out we only lived a couple of miles from each other. We would just get together and jam or go to each other's parties and just play music. One day we decided that we needed to put some of this music out as we were doing some good stuff and no one had ever heard it.

Albert had a gig and the guy wanted two sets, so Albert got the three of us together. Without rehearsals we played two sets and the owner begged us to play more. We didn't tell him that we hadn't rehearsed or even played together in front of people before that night. He offered a big chunk of money for us to do a third set. We even ended up doing Grateful Dead songs and the place went wild. We decided to make it official and make it a band.

June 19 – July 4, 2015. Alice, dependably, shows up for European festival season.

July 22 – December 22, 2015. Mötley Crüe's farewell tour returns to North America, Alice Cooper, again, supporting. November finds the two bands, squeezing in a European leg. Bottom support on these shows comes from The Cringe.

Chuck Garric:
I think that this is going to my thirteenth year. It's been a great experience and I hope for another thirteen more years. Seven different drummers, like eight different guitar players. The nice thing is it's cool having been in the band for so long and having so many different drummers, from Eric Singer, Brent Fitz and Tommy Clufetos to Glen Sobel and Jimmy DeGrasso. All these guys that come in and play and then there are the different guitar players.

And it's neat to just sit back and you get to experiment and experience so many cool different styles of music. Everybody brings in their own unique style and their own cool little vibe to it and I like that. I've always considered myself one of the luckiest bass players. I've had a chance to play with some of the best drummers in the business. Then I get to play with some of the best guitar players and it's a killer experience.

Then every once in a while, every other year, we'll go back and re-learn the stuff and make sure it's still fresh, and we're not getting lazy. It's fun, man. It's rock 'n' roll; it's got to have a little bit of sense of danger to it or else it's no fun. We always try to keep it fresh, we always try to keep it musical, we make sure that our parts are down. Everybody is always playing great, tones are great. That's just part of the job.

Nita Strauss:
I'm a guitar player and every guitar player out there knows the great history of musicians that Alice has had in his band. From Steve Hunter, Reb Beach and Al Pitrelli... he's had some of the greatest of the great guitar players come through his line-up. So it's just really been surreal for me. If I look at Wikipedia and I see this list of guitar players, I see my name right there next to Reb Beach. Even Ryan Roxie who I grew up with. I always had pictures of guitar players on my wall. I had a picture of Ryan Roxie on my wall, and now I look over and I see Ryan Roxie next to me on stage all the time and Tommy Henriksen, who is a phenomenal guitar player. I just feel very, very lucky to be a part of this band.

As for being a female, I think everyone else in the band wears more makeup than me—Ryan sure does. I have never felt any weird pressure or anything from the guys. I came right in and once they saw that I learned the parts and they didn't have to teach much; they've just accepted me right in as a little sister of the band. I feel really lucky to have my four big brothers around all the time.

Honestly I feel like the pressure came from the whole line of guitar players. Orianthi is absolutely a phenomenal player; I have a lot of respect for her. But if you look at the line of guitar players, with Al Pitrelli, Reb Beach the pressure comes from that and it comes from Alice. The pressure doesn't come from following another female guitar player. The pressure comes from just me. I love this music, I love being in this band. I wouldn't call it pressure, I would call it excitement rather than pressure.

Alice Cooper:
We've been on the road with them for two years. What I really like is having two bands that bring it every night. Last year there was Kiss and Def Leppard, and there was Aerosmith and Slash. Mötley Crüe and Alice Cooper. We're both bands who get up there and tear it up and bring it every single night. I don't care if it's 250 shows, there's not one show there that's a low-energy show. To me, that's what rock 'n' roll should be. That's giving the audience their money's worth.

September 11, 2015. Hollywood Vampires issue a self-titled debut, produced by Bob Ezrin, on Republic/UMe. The album features a pile of guest stars, but the core band consists of Alice Cooper, Joe Perry and Johnny Depp. The album—11 covers and three originals—reaches No. 43 on the *Billboard* chart, and notches a No. 30 placement in the UK. All proceeds from the album and concert appearances will go to the MusicCares charity.

Alice Cooper:
How we got together was an interesting thing We were doing *Dark Shadows,* the movie, in London. I was in that movie with Johnny Depp, and I'd just met him; first time we'd ever met. But I knew that he was a good guitar player. Because he came from Kentucky with his band to LA. I knew the story that he didn't come in as an actor, he came in as a guitar player. I've heard him play on different things with different people, so it didn't really surprise me when he came up and played on stage with us. He nailed it. But I was a little surprised at how tasty his guitar was. He really did know where to go on that guitar. He's not one of those flashy, Steve Vai-type of players. He's more of a Keith Richards-type of tasty blues rock player.

So he fits right in. We could do "Eighteen," he knows it, we can do "School's Out," he knows it. We could do "Brown Sugar" and he would know that. So you take his guitar playing, and then you take Joe Perry, who is another blues rock player, and Slash, who is a blues rock-type of player, and Joe Walsh, and we're all in the same world. None of these guys are Van Halen types. They're all much more in the mid, middle fretboard, not the real high up in the fretboard stuff. And that's my rock 'n' roll right there. That's where the gutsy rock 'n' roll is, is in the middle of the fretboard, not the higher or the low parts.

Now the flagship song on the album, the theme song, "My Dead Drunk Friends," the very first thing I was thinking about with that song was "Quarter to Three;" you know, "It's quarter to three, there's no one in the place but just you and me, so set 'em up, Joe." It was a lonely bar song. But in this place, it was Alice, let's say, at five o'clock in the morning at the Rainbow, when there's nobody there, and there's really nothing left there but ghosts. He's toasting them and it ends up going into a pretty much a pirate drinking song. "We puke and we fight and we drink and we fight and we puke and we fight (laughs)."

I wanted the album to end with a sense of humour. The very first song that we wrote, "Raise the Dead," we had this idea of getting a very recognisable voice, and Christopher Lee was the first person we thought of. If he could just read a page out of Bram Stoker's Dracula, and end up with, "Children of the night, what music they make." Then we go into the song "Raise the Dead" and it was the very last thing that he did. So that was a really cool to have. I've had Vincent Price on records. Now I've had Christopher Lee. I wish Karloff and Lugosi would've lasted a little longer (laughs).

But anyways, that song, "Raise the Dead," we've got to start this album out with a blazing rock 'n' roll song. Really tell the story, that the soul of rock, the heart of rock 'n' roll, is buried in a hole. But the creatures under there are coming up for air. In other words, we're not going to let them just die. We're going to raise the dead and we're going to play these songs that they played. We are even gonna make them harder and give them more life than they did, that the original ones did.

I like taking a song like "Jeepster" or "I'm a Boy" or any of these songs, "I Got a Line on You," and taking it up a gear. Rocking it out even more than they rocked it, because those songs were made for AM radio. I said, well, let's take them now and add that extra boost of guitar, and that extra ounce of energy and take a pop song and turn it into a rock song.

September 16, 2015. Hollywood Vampires perform at The Roxy in Hollywood.

September 24, 2015. Hollywood Vampires play *Rock in Rio* in Brazil; the show is streamed live.

October 6, 2015. The reunited Alice Cooper group conduct a surprise show in Dallas, TX, in conjunction with a signing even Dennis was conducting for his *Snakes! Guillotines! Electric Chairs!* memoir. The band consisted of Dennis, Alice, Michael Bruce, Neal Smith and guitarist Ryan Roxie. The following night at the American Airlines Center, Alice is joined on "School's Out" by Dennis, Neal and Michael.

November 2 – 18, 2015. After two UK headline shows at the end of October, Alice plays a series of European Mötley farewell tour dates.

Chuck Garric:
To be honest with you, it wasn't really that strange. We had Calico Cooper in the band before; she wasn't a musician but she was an entertainer. She was part of the show. So when I first joined the band, female band members, whether they were musicians or dancers or whatever, was part of the act.

So for me it wasn't, "There's a girl in the band?!" For me as a bass player, it was like, "Shit, now there's three guitar players. How do I fit the parts in there? How do we make this work?" For me it was musical, because I thought , Orianthi was a killer guitar player; she played great. Nita the same way. She comes in, she learned the parts, she was seamless. So to me it was professional; it was no big deal. The only thing, you deal with a little bit of the girly stuff every once in a while, but that's no big deal.

December 4 – 22, 2015. The Mötley farewell tour swings back to North America.

December 28, 2015. Ian Fraser "Lemmy" Kilmister dies after a brief battle with cancer. At the annual star-studded New Years Eve charity show at Shep's in Hawaii, the band play "Ace of Spades" in his honour.

2016

February 12, 2016. A deluxe digital edition of *Hollywood Vampires* is issued, adding The Who cover "I'm a Boy," Love cover "Seven and Seven Is" and an original called "As Bad as I Am."

February 15, 2016. Hollywood Vampires play the Grammy Awards, blasting through their original "As Bad as I Am" plus their cover of "Ace of Spades," in tribute to Lemmy.

April 6, 2016. Michael Bruce Force plays Asylum Records in Mesa, Arizona, commemorating Record Store Day.

April 29 – May 31, 2016. Alice conducts a tour called *Spend the Night with Alice Cooper,* all US dates with one casino show in Canada. The band consists of Ryan Roxie, Nita Strauss (ex-Iron Maidens) and Tommy Henriksen on guitars, Chuck Garric on bass and Glen Sobel on drums (of note, back on the Mötley tour, Sobel subbed for a good week in place of an injured Tommy Lee). The set list is greatest hits-themed, most recent selection being "Feed My Frankenstein" from 1991.

Nita Strauss:
It's a very carefully put-together immense wall of sound, is the way we think about it. Each piece of the wall is in its place. You have to be really mindful in a three-guitar line-up. No extra string noise, no notes ringing out, because if all three-guitar players are doing that, doing picks, grips and slides and that stuff, it's as mess.

We're very, very mindful of each other. Where our volumes are, where we are on the stage basically. You won't see us running into each other and you won't see us stepping all over each other's parts either. It's all about being mindful of what's going on.

Chuck Garric:

I think it was something that came about during the recording of the *Welcome to My Nightmare* record. Steve Hunter was such a big part of the sound of that record, and I think Steve wanted to get back and play with Alice again. With Steve playing and a little bit of Steve's disability with his eyes and stuff, we didn't want to put

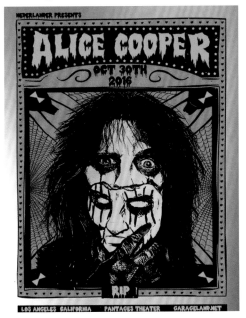

too much pressure on him to be so much a performer—we just wanted Steve's tone and Steve's playing. So it just made sense for Alice and Bob then to bring somebody else in; they wanted to just have a guy that could back up and play some rhythms and not really worry about being a soloist. So when they made that decision, they had Damon Johnson still in the band, and they got Tommy, who was a really good solid rhythm guitar player. Then you add Steve Hunter to the mix, which was great.

I think they wanted to get rid of the theatrical side, not get rid of it but maybe just replace it and start turning Alice into more of a guitar band. That all gave birth to the three guitars. It was unique and it was fun to have to go back and start from zero, and refigure out your guitar parts and the musical side of it and everything; and come up with these parts that were on the record. Steve has that history of playing with Alice since *Billion Dollar Babies*. So it was really great to get the perspective from him and realise, maybe those are some of the chords we were missing. So from a musical standpoint it was a lot of fun. Nita comes in and she learned from those parts that we had given her, and then she adds her own style to it and her own flair. Now it's become this really big monster.

May 6, 2016. Recording from the band's Columbus, Ohio performance on this day will be used as bonus material included with the next Alice Cooper album.

May 24 – June 6, 2016. Taking a break from *Spend the Night with Alice Cooper,* Alice performs a handful of dates with Hollywood Vampires, a warm-up show in New York followed by one show each in Portugal, Germany, Sweden, Denmark and Romania.

June 9 – June 24, 2016. *Spend the Night with Alice Cooper* transitions over to Europe.

July 1 – July 25, 2016. Hollywood Vampires mount a US tour.

August 6 – October 30, 2016. Alice and band perform another bank of North American *Spend the Night with Alice Cooper* shows.

Nita Strauss:

I learned the set from listening to the live recordings of the last band when Orianthi was in the band. So I hardly listened to the records at all. Getting ready for the tour, I only had a few weeks notice. So I just studied the live show. I learned a lot of the classic solos from listening to Orianthi play them. She's such a great blues player. She took the classic songs and really made them her own, made the solos her own. Did her own thing.

So Tommy took me aside the day of the first show—and keep in mind, I only had one rehearsal with the band—Tommy goes, "Strauss! You gotta learn the solo like it was on a record." I was like, "I thought I did." He goes, "No, you learned the other solo. You gotta learn like the record." He sat me down and he showed me some videos on YouTube of people playing it. He was, "You gotta do it like that tonight." So from just the very first show, everyone really put the idea on like, let's give the respect to the classic songs. Let's do the "Billion Dollar Babies" solo, a really iconic solo. Let's give them that respect and do them just like on the record, which has been great."

September 20, 2016. Shep Gordon issues an autobiography called *They Call Me Supermensch: A Backstage Pass to the Amazing World of Films, Food and Rock 'n' Roll.*

2017

January 3, 2017. Alice's long-time girlfriend, Cynthia Lang, with Cooper for his rise to fame In the early '70s, passes away at the age of 67.

April 21 – June 24, 2017. The *Spend the Night with Alice Cooper* tour continues, with more US dates.

June 9, 2017. "Paranoiac Personality" is issued as an advance single from *Paranormal*.

Alice Cooper:
If a guy is really paranoid, he thinks everybody's against him. Everybody's talking about him. He goes, "Can't you see that just feeds my paranoid personality?" So it was a total study on paranoia. The guy admits he's paranoid. "I have a paranoid personality. I'm gonna keep it, I like it. I like being paranoid." It doesn't sound depressing at all. It actually sounds up, you know? But a very unique song.

July 1 – August 6, 2017. The *Spend the Night with Alice Cooper* tour hits Europe for a second time.

July 28, 2017. Alice Cooper issues his 27th album, *Paranormal*, on earMUSIC. Producing is Bob Ezrin, Tommy Henriksen and Tommy Denander. The record features an army of players, including rock star guests Roger Glover and Billy Gibbons. Most notable however is that U2's Larry Mullen Jr. drums most of the album. If there can be said to be a core band, it is Tommy Denander and Tommy Henriksen, who on top of producing, play guitar on all tracks, with Henriksen adding keyboards and backing vocals.

Alice Cooper:
"Paranormal"... I did really want one song that was going to be Cooper-esque, in the same experience of "I Love the Dead" or "Sick Things" or something like that, and it's a love song, about a guy who's on the other side. He's dead. He comes to visit the girl but there's that curtain between them where he can't really touch her. She knows he's there and she feels the romance, but there's never a point where they can touch.

That's the conflict in the song. He says things like, that smell you're smelling is my cologne on your lace. He leaves things around that remind her of him. But there's never a point where they can ever touch each other and that's what I wanted. I wanted the idea of it being spooky, paranormal. If that phone rings at night, and there's nobody on it, that's me. If you feel a chill in the night, that's me. If something paranormal's going on in your house, don't be afraid, it's me. That's how he shows that he's there for her. It's a creepy song, and we really made it a little over-the-top creepy. I always want that one song on the album that really is signature Alice, that gives you a chill.

"Fireball" was a pure Dennis song. He brought that in, and he says, "I keep envisioning the idea of a guy seeing a fireball coming over, and destroying the city." I said, well, okay, what if we do a twist ending on it then, and make it so that the guy wakes up and says, "Oh, what a dream I had! The whole city was on fire, and the fireball was doing this." He gets up and goes over to the window to get a breath of fresh air, and he sees this fireball coming and for real this time. That was the whole trick ending on it. But it's a totally driving song. It's just got this freight train of a sound going through it. But again, it's Dennis on bass, Neal on drums. Great to have the original band play on those original songs.

"Holy Water", these two guys brought in. I said, "I love this song! But Alice wouldn't sing any of this. I have to rewrite the lyrics on it, if you don't mind." They said, "No, write it the way Alice would write it." I tried to describe Alice, black hat with a golden chain, top hat and a walking cane, all the stuff Alice uses on stage. Going to the river of love.

What he's saying is... it's almost like a New Orleans funeral, Dixieland thing. He's just going, hey, I'm laying my sins down. I'm going down to the water, I'm getting baptised, down in the river of love. It almost sounds like a Pentecostal thing. But it's so joyful. It's so much fun to listen to, this song is.

It's not rap. The parts in there they had, was rap. I said no, I'm gonna do it, but I'm not gonna make it sound like rap. I'm gonna make it sound like a Pentecostal preacher talking. You could call it rap, but it's not really rap. So we took a rap song and turned it into a rock song. But it's got such a joyful feel to it, that in the end, you just go, wow, it's like "When the Saints Go Marching In." Another totally different sound for Alice Cooper. Again, if there is a theme to this album, it's the fact that it's something you're not expecting from Alice.

"Fallen in Love" and I can't get up is a classic "No More Mr. Nice Guy" type of song. There's a commercial on TV where the old woman is laying on the ground and she goes, "I've fallen and I can't get up." From one of these little buzzers that you get her, and then somebody comes to the house and saves you. I went, "I've fallen in love and I can't get up" is a great rock 'n' roll title. Once we started writing it, it just fell into that ZZ Top type of flow, and that's why I just said, we gotta get Billy Gibbons to play on this. It was perfect. It's a true Alice Cooper pop song.

"Dynamite Road" is a place in Arizona. I've always wanted to write that song about racing with the devil, with your hot rod. In this case, he's talking about his buddies, his band, his guys, they're having the time of their life in the car, and they get run off the road. When he realises the devil was driving the car. The punch line for the whole thing is the fact that he wakes up, all the guys in the band are dead. He says, "Well, ma, the band is all in heaven, or more likely they're hell" (laughs). Knowing the nature of the band. In the end, he says, I can understand why you took the band. But did you have to wreck my car? That was my favourite thing in the world. I loved that car to death. That was the funny punch line of the whole thing. But it's a total driving song. It's one of those songs that when you're driving your car, all of a sudden you start speeding up.

"Dead Flies" was, I wanted to write "Generation Landslide" part two. "Generation Landslide" was one of those songs that lyrically, were one of the best lyrics I'd ever done. It portrayed what was going on in the world right then. Well now, forty-five years later, what's going on? I got to rant a little bit on false prophets, you know, cults, the idea that your phone knows more about you than your parents. That's an interesting point of view. So I used that song in order to get that point across. It's now Alice's overview of what's going on out there. "Dead Flies" says no matter what, we're all dead flies, you're just dead flies, we're just dead flies.

August 12 – September 10, 2017. Alice mounts a North American co-headlining tour with Deep Purple. The Edgar Winter Band is on as support.

Alice Cooper:
Like Kiss, same with Bowie, same with all the bands that this genera-
tion's grandparents would never let them see—now they're bringing the grandparents. You've got grandparents, fathers and sons, all loving the same music. The fathers are going, "Wow, if you think this Marilyn Manson is any good, you gotta see Alice Cooper." He brings his son to see Alice Cooper and the kid goes, "Wow, that's even more fun." So it's family entertainment. I always took the high road, though. I never used nudity onstage, I never used bad language ever. I had a boundary that I stayed within because I thought it was more creative for Alice to be specific, and I wouldn't let Alice do this over here. It's too easy to use the F word every five seconds. That's too easy. Nudity—too easy.

September 21 – 26, 2017. The band play three festival dates in Brazil, including *Rock in Rio*, where Joe Perry and none other than Arthur Brown join Alice for "School's Out" and a rendition of Arthur's 1969 hit "Fire."

November 7, 2017. It is announced that Alice is on the ballot for induction into the Songwriters Hall of Fame, along with the likes of Chrissie Hynde, Tom Waits and John Mellencamp. As well, on this day, *Welcome to My Nightmare*-era drummer Whitey Glan passes away, at the age of 71, from lung cancer.

Alice Cooper:
I picked Whitey Glan as the drummer for my *Welcome to My Nightmare* tour because he was simply the best drummer around, not knowing he could drink me under a table. He was just a great guy; everybody who's worked with him considered him one of their best friends. He was one of rock's premier drummers, but in my opinion he was very under-rated and under-publicised—he was certainly a drummer's drummer! Canada is less one world class musician. Rest in peace, Whitey.

November 11 – 16, 2017. Alice's UK tour includes a half-hour set with Neal, Dennis and Michael. The final icing on the cake, the exclamation mark on the career, would be a reunion band studio album.

Michael Bruce:
When we finally played the UK, I thought, man, it was like I had stepped out of a time machine in the future. When we started and lived in Michigan, we were driving around all over the Midwest in a nine-passenger station wagon. Then it was tour buses and then a private jet. This time now, we're in buses again (laughs). So the world's changed. But we had a great time and all the people in Alice's band and crew, they're great people and he's very lucky to have them.

March 16, 2018. This date marks fifty years since the first use of the name Alice Cooper for the long-haired heroes of our story. So we come full circle. From The Earwigs, through The Spiders and The Nazz, to Alice Cooper the band and Alice Cooper the man, Vincent Damon Furnier has been, for nearly every one of those fifty years, a highly entertaining and inspiring piece of the pop culture fabric. To reiterate, if *Paranormal* and the subsequent tour cycle—in which another form of full circle was achieved, reunion shows with the surviving members of the original band—then Alice has capped his career on a surprising creative high, once again, as he's done countless times before, bucking expectations. In that respect he is still shocking his public and those on the periphery, although through this act, insidiously, through subversion, through a seduction of the most sophisticated and demanding of Alice Cooper fans. Truly, the ramp-up to the fifty-year mark must be seen as a victory for all the long-time toilers involved—Alice, Bob, Dennis, Neal and Michael—and for that, we the fans must robustly thank the band at hand.

Michael Bruce:
I'm going to be 70. The clock is ticking. You know, if we're going to do something, we gotta do it now rather than later, because you never know. The world's a strange place. But sure, turn on the eight-track and let 'er roll (laughs). But every time we talk, Alice talks about getting the band back, and he goes, "Yeah, let's do an album like Killer." The next thing you know, he's getting songs from, ZZ Top, and all these other people. How can we do an album that's the band, when you got all this other stuff going on? You know what I mean? That's what you do when you feed the beast and you have a foundation and it takes off all over the planet, and you have three bands, the original band, his regular band and the one with Johnny Depp.

What's left of my little body here, is like, I've got arthritis in my knee and in my hand, and boy, when I get back to the East Coast, to the cold, I really, really notice it—I really do. But it's funny, I got on stage in England and we played... nothing; I was pain-free for half an hour. It's just amazing. The adrenaline rush. That whole tour, Alice came back after the Wembley show and said the reviews couldn't have been better if we had written them ourselves. He says, maybe we can do something in New York or Toronto.

So I still hope that he has this in his vision, to do this stuff. I was comfortable with doing the last half-an-hour, and we had our own little moment, our fifteen minutes of fame—again (laughs). It's a lot of fun playing with him. A record, that would be... God, that would be to die for. We'll make history. One of the members dies right in the studio. Bob Ezrin can capture that on tape. Yeah, we'll call it *Rigor Mortis*.

Studio Album Discography

Very simple discography for y'all. Big, long book so I didn't want to go too crazy with the dozen or so details one can pack into these things, nor solo career stuff from folks besides Alice. But I also realise that given the structure of the book, what follows is necessary or at least really, really handy, in terms of providing a tight roadmap of Alice's Herculean comings and goings, a sturdy frame upon which a hotrod of a life was built. And so here it is, the studio albums in order, with song titles.

A. Original Alice Cooper Band

Pretties for You
(June 1969)
Side 1: 1. Titanic Overture 2. 10 Minutes Before the Worm 3. Sing Low, Sweet Cherio 4. Today Mueller 5. Living 6. Fields of Regret
Side 2: 1. No Longer Umpire 2. Levity Ball 3. B.B. on Mars 4. Reflected 5. Apple Bush 6. Earwigs to Eternity 7. Changing Arranging

Easy Action
(March 1970)
Side 1: 1. Mr. & Misdemeanor 2. Shoe Salesman 3. Still No Air 4. Below Your Means
Side 2: 1. Return of the Spiders 2. Laughing at Me 3. Refrigerator Heaven 4. Beautiful Flyaway 5. Lay Down and Die, Goodbye

Love It to Death
(March 1971)
Side 1: 1. Caught in a Dream 2. I'm Eighteen 3. Long Way to Go 4. Black Juju
Side 2: 1. Is It My Body 2. Hallowed Be My Name 3. Second Coming 4. Ballad of Dwight Fry 5. Sun Arise

Killer
(November 1971)
Side 1: 1. Under My Wheels 2. Be My Lover 3. Halo of Flies 4. Desperado
Side 2. 1. You Drive Me Nervous 2. Yeah, Yeah, Yeah 3. Dead Babies 8. Killer

School's Out
(June 1972)
Side 1: 1. School's Out 2. Luney Tune 3. Gutter Cat vs. the Jets 4. Street Fight 5. Blue Turk
Side 2: 1. My Stars 2. Public Animal No.9 3. Alma Mater 4. Grande Finale

Billion Dollar Babies
(February 1973)
Side 1: 1. Hello Hooray 2. Raped and Freezin' 3. Elected 4. Billion Dollar Babies 5. Unfinished Sweet
Side 2. 1. No More Mr. Nice Guy 2. Generation Landslide 3. Sick Things 4. Mary Ann 5. I Love the Dead

Muscle of Love
(November 1973)
Side 1: 1. Big Apple Dreamin' (Hippo) 2. Never Been Sold Before 3. Hard Hearted Alice 4. Crazy Little Child
Side 2: 1. Working Up a Sweat 2. Muscle of Love 3. Man with the Golden Gun 4. Teenage Lament '74 5. Woman Machine

B. Alice as Solo Artist

Welcome to My Nightmare
(March 1975)
Side 1: 1. Welcome to My Nightmare 2. Devil's Food 3. The Black Widow 4. Some Folks 5. Only Women Bleed
Side 2: 1. Department of Youth 2. Cold Ethyl 3. Years Ago 4. Steven 5. The Awakening 6. Escape

Goes to Hell
(June 1976)
Side 1: 1. Go to Hell 2. You Gotta Dance 3. I'm the Coolest 4. Didn't We Meet 5. I Never Cry
Side 2: 1. Give the Kid a Break 2. Guilty 3. Wake Me Gently 4. Wish You Were Here 5. I'm Always Chasing Rainbows 6. Going Home

Lace and Whiskey
(April 1977)
Side 1: 1. It's Hot Tonight 2. Lace and Whiskey 3. Road Rats 4. Damned If You Do 5. You and Me
Side 2: 1. King of the Silver Screen 2. Ubangi Stomp 3. (No More) Love at Your Convenience 4. I Never Wrote Those Songs 5. My God

From the Inside
(November 1978)
Side 1: 1. From the Inside 2. Wish I Were Born in Beverly Hills 3. The Quiet Room 4. Nurse Rozetta 5. Millie and Billie
Side 2: 1. Serious 2. How You Gonna See Me Now 3. For Veronica's Sake 4. Jacknife Johnny 5. Inmates (We're All Crazy)

Flush the Fashion
(April 1980)
Side 1: 1. Talk Talk 2. Clones (We're All) 3. Pain 4. Leather Boots 5. Aspirin Damage
Side 2: 1. Nuclear Infected 2. Grim Facts 3. Model Citizen 4. Dance Yourself to Death 5. Headlines

Special Forces
(September 1981)
Side 1: 1. Who Do You Think We Are 2. Seven & Seven Is 3. Prettiest Cop on the Block 4. Don't Talk Old to Me 5. Generation Landslide '81 (live)
Side 2: 1. Skeletons in the Closet 2. You Want It, You Got It 3. You Look Good in Rags 4. You're a Movie 5. Vicious Rumours

Zipper Catches Skin
(August 1982)
Side 1: 1. Zorro's Ascent 2. Make That Money (Scrooge's Song) 3. I Am the Future 4. No Baloney Homosapiens
Side 2: 1. Adaptable (Anything for You) 2. I Like Girls 3. Remarkable Insincere 4. Tag, You're It 5. I Better Be Good 6. I'm Alive (That Was the Day My Dead Pet Returned to Save My Life)

DaDa
(September 1983)
Side 1: 1. Dada 2. Enough's Enough 3. Former Lee Warmer 4. No Man's Land 5. Dyslexia
Side 2: 1. Scarlet and Sheba 2. I Love America 3. Fresh Blood 4. Pass the Gun Around

Constrictor
(September 1986)
Side 1: 1. Teenage Frankenstein 2. Give It Up 3. Thrill My Gorilla 4. Life and Death of the Party 5. Simple Disobedience
Side 2: 1. The World Needs Guts 2. Trick Bag 3. Crawlin' 4. The Great American Success Story 5. He's Back (The Man Behind the Mask)

Raise Your Fist and Yell
(September 1987)
Side 1: 1. Freedon 2. Lock Me Up 3. Give the Radio Back 4. Step on You 5. Not That Love
Side 2: 1. Prince of Darkness 2. Time to Kill 3. Chop, Chop, Chop 4. Gail 5. Roses on White Lace

Trash
(July 1989)
Side 1: 1. Poison 2. Spark in the Dark 3. House of Fire 4. Why Trust You 5. Only My Heart Talkin'
Side 2: 1. Bed of Nails 2. This Maniac's in Love with You 3. Trash 4. Hell Is Living Without You 5. I'm Your Gun

Hey Stoopid
(July 1991)
1. Hey Stoopid 2. Love's a Loaded Gun 3. Snakebite 4. Burning Our Bed 5. Dangerous Tonight 6. Might as Well Be on Mars 7. Feed My Frankenstein 8. Hurricane Years 9. Little by Little 10. Die for You 11. Dirty Dreams 12. Wind-Up Toy

The Last Temptation
(July 1994)
1. Sideshow 2. Nothing's Free 3. Lost in America 4. Bad Place Alone 5. You're My Temptation 6. Stolen Prayer 7. Unholy War 8. Lullaby 9. It's Me 10. Cleansed by Fire

Brutal Planet
(June 2000)
1. Brutal Planet 2. Wicked Young Man 3. Sanctuary 4. Blow Me a Kiss 5. Eat Some More 6. Pick Up the Bones 7. Pessi-Mystic 8. Gimme 9. It's the Little Things 10. Take It Like a Woman 11. Cold Machines

Dragontown
(September 2001)
1. Triggerman 2. Deeper 3. Dragontown 4. Sex, Death and Money 5. Fantasy Man 6. Somewhere in the Jungle 7. Disgraceland 8. Sister Sara 9. Every Woman Has a Name 10. I Just Wanna Be God 11. It's Much Too Late 12. The Sentinel

The Eyes of Alice Cooper
(September 2003)
1. What Do You Want from Me? 2. Between High School & Old School 3. Man of the Year 4. Novocaine 5. Bye Bye, Baby 6. Be with You Awhile 7. Detroit City 8. Spirits Rebellious 9. This House is Haunted 10. Love Should Never Feel Like This 11. The Song That Didn't Rhyme 12. I'm So Angry 13. Backyard Brawl

Dirty Diamonds
(July 2005)
1. Woman of Mass Distraction 2. Perfect 3. You Make Me Wanna 4. Dirty Diamonds 5. The Saga of Jesse James 6. Sunset Babies (All Got Rabies) 7. Pretty Ballerina 8. Run Down the Devil 9. Steal That Car 10. Six Hours 11. Your Own Worst Enemy 12. Zombie Dance 13. Stand

Along Came a Spider
(July 2008)
1. Prologue/I Know Where You Live 2. Vengeance is Mine 3. Wake the Dead 4. Catch Me If You Can 5. (In Touch with) Your Feminine Side 6. Wrapped in Silk 7. Killed by Love 8. I'm Hungry 9. The One That Got Away 10. Salvation 11. I Am the Spider/Epilogue

Welcome 2 My Nightmare
(September 2011)
1. I Am Made of You 2. Caffeine 3. The Nightmare Returns 4. A Runaway Train 5. Last Man on Earth 6. The Congregation 7. I'll Bite Your Face Off 8. Disco Bloodbath Boogie Fever 9. Ghouls Gone Wild 10. Something to Remember Me By 11. When Hell Comes Home 12. What Baby Wants 13. I Gotta Get Outta Here 14. The Underture

Paranormal
(July 2017)
1. Paranormal 2. Dead Flies 3. Fireball 4. Paranoiac Personality 5. Fallen in Love 6. Dynamite Road 7. Private Public Breakdown 8. Holy Water 9. Rats 10. The Sound of A

Sources

Most of the interview footage used in this book has come from my own archive of interviews with these guys. Interviewed, many of these folks multiple times, including of course Alice Cooper for most of the records over the past twenty years, plus Gavin Baddeley, Johnny Bee, Ernie Cefalu, Jimmy DeGrasso, Jack Douglas, Dennis Dunaway, Bob Ezrin, Dani Filth, Kim Fowley, Bob Gruen, Beau Hill, Steve Hunter, Damon Johnson, King Diamond, K.J. Knight, Bob Livingstone, Dee Long, Allan MacMillan, Dave Mustaine, John Nitzinger, Mike Pinera, Chris Poland, James Randi, Graham Shaw, Derek Sherinian, John Sinclair, Neal Smith, Cameron Strang, Drew Struzan, Jaan Uhelski, Michael Wagener and Dick Wagner.

Additional quotes also by kind permission from Sam Dunn, Tim Henderson (bravewords.com), Kevin Julie, Mitch Lafon (check out Mitch's Youtube channel, One on One with Mitch Lafon), Drew Masters, MetalRules.com (as usual, it's Marko Syrjala who is on the case—thanks Marko!), Steve Newton (EarofNewt.com), Brian Rademacher (rockeyez.com) and Jeb Wright (classicrockrevisted.com).

I'd like to also acknowledge the excellent work of the SickthingsUK site, at sickthingsuk.co.uk for years at the top of the heap in terms of being a great info-packed fan site on any level, on anybody. Seriously, few sites on any band have ever been better. The timelines were a great reference as was the tour archive and press archive, although in terms of press directly referenced in this book, I stuck to my own stuff and the interviews of basically good buddies of mine, as cited above.

About the Author

At approximately 7900 (with over 7000 appearing in his books), Martin has unofficially written more record reviews than anybody in the history of music writing across all genres. Additionally, Martin has penned approximately 73 books on hard rock, heavy metal, punk, prog, classic rock and record collecting.
He was Editor In Chief of the now retired Brave Words & Bloody Knuckles, Canada's foremost metal publication for 14 years, and has also contributed to Revolver, Guitar World, Goldmine, Record Collector, bravewords.com, lollipop.com and hardradio.com, with many record label band bios and liner notes to his credit as well.
Additionally, Martin has been a regular contractor to Banger Films, having worked for two years as researcher on the award-wining documentary Rush: Beyond the Lighted Stage, on the writing and research team for the 11-episode Metal Evolution and on the ten-episode Rock Icons, both for VH1 Classic. Additionally, Martin is the writer of the original metal genre chart used in Metal: A Headbanger's Journey and throughout the Metal Evolution episodes. Martin currently resides in Toronto and can be reached through martinp@inforamp.net or www.martinpopoff.com.

Martin Popoff – A Complete Bibliography

Welcome to My Nightmare: Alice Cooper at 50 (2018)
Judus Priest: Decade of Domination (2018)
Pink Floyd: Album by Album (2018)
Popoff Archive – 6: American Power Metal (2018)
Popoff Archive – 5: European Power Metal (2018)
The Sun Goes Down: Thin Lizzy's Final Years (2018)
The Clash: All the Albums All the Songs (2018)
AC/DC: Album by Album (2017)
Lights Out: Surviving the '70s with UFO (2017)
Led Zeppelin: All the Albums All the Songs (2017)
Tornado of Souls: Thrash's Titanic Clash (2017)
Caught in a Mosh: The Golden Era of Thrash (2017)
Metal Collector: Gathered Tales from Headbangers (2017)
Rush: Album by Album (2017)
Beer Drinkers and Hell Raisers: The Rise of Motörhead (2017)
Hit the Lights: The Birth of Thrash (2017)
Popoff Archive – 4: Classic Rock (2017)
Popoff Archive – 3: Hair Metal (2017)
Popoff Archive – 2: Progressive Rock (2016)
Popoff Archive – 1: Doom Metal (2016)
Rock the Nation: Montrose, Gamma and Ronnie Redefined (2016)
Punk Tees: The Punk Revolution in 125 T-Shirts (2016)
Metal Heart: Aiming High with Accept (2016)
Ramones at 40 (2016)
Time and a Word: The Yes Story (2016)
Kickstart My Heart: A Mötley Crüe Day-by-Day (2015)
This Means War: The Sunset Years of the NWOBHM (2015)
Wheels of Steel: The Explosive Early Years of the NWOBHM (2015)
Swords and Tequila: Riot's Classic First Decade (2015)
Who Invented Heavy Metal? (2015)
Sail Away: Whitesnake's Fantastic Voyage (2015)
Live Magnetic Air: The Unlikely Saga of the Superlative Max Webster (2014)
Steal Away the Night: An Ozzy Osbourne Day-by-Day (2014)
The Big Book of Hair Metal (2014)
Sweating Bullets: The Deth and Rebirth of Megadeth (2014)
Smokin' Valves: A Headbanger's Guide to 900 NWOBHM Records (2014)
The Art of Metal (co-edit with Malcolm Dome; 2013)
2 Minutes to Midnight: An Iron Maiden Day-By-Day (2013)
Metallica: The Complete Illustrated History (2013); update and reissue (2016)
Rush: The Illustrated History (2013); update and reissue (2016)
Ye Olde Metal: 1979 (2013)
Scorpions: Top of the Bill (2013); updated and reissued as Wind of Change: The Scorpions Story (2016)
Epic Ted Nugent (2012); updated and reissued as Motor City Madhouse: Going Gonzo with Ted Nugent (2017)
Fade to Black: Hard Rock Cover Art of the Vinyl Age (2012)
It's Getting Dangerous: Thin Lizzy 81-12 (2012)
We Will Be Strong: Thin Lizzy 76-81 (2012)
Fighting My Way Back: Thin Lizzy 69-76 (2011); updated and reissued as From Dublin to Jailbreak: Thin Lizzy 1969-76 (2016)
The Deep Purple Royal Family: Chain of Events '80 – '11 (2011)
The Deep Purple Royal Family: Chain of Events Through '79 (2011); reissued as The Deep Purple Family Year by Year (to 1979) (2016)
Black Sabbath FAQ (2011)
The Collector's Guide to Heavy Metal: Volume 4: The '00s (2011; co-authored with David Perri)
Goldmine Standard Catalog of American Records 1948 – 1991, 7th Edition (2010)
Goldmine Record Album Price Guide, 6th Edition (2009)
Goldmine 45 RPM Price Guide, 7th Edition (2009)
A Castle Full of Rascals: Deep Purple '83 – '09 (2009)
Worlds Away: Voivod and the Art of Michel Langevin (2009)
Ye Olde Metal: 1978 (2009)
Gettin' Tighter: Deep Purple '68 – '76 (2008)
All Access: The Art of the Backstage Pass (2008)

Ye Olde Metal: 1977 (2008)
Ye Olde Metal: 1976 (2008)
Judas Priest: Heavy Metal Painkillers (2007)
Ye Olde Metal: 1973 to 1975 (2007)
The Collector's Guide to Heavy Metal: Volume 3: The Nineties (2007)
Ye Olde Metal: 1968 to 1972 (2007)
Run For Cover: The Art of Derek Riggs (2006)
Black Sabbath: Doom Let Loose (2006)
Dio: Light Beyond the Black (2006)
The Collector's Guide to Heavy Metal: Volume 2: The Eighties (2005)
Rainbow: English Castle Magic (2005)
UFO: Shoot Out the Lights (2005)
The New Wave of British Heavy Metal Singles (2005)
Blue Öyster Cult: Secrets Revealed! (2004); update and reissue (2009); updated and reissued as Agents of Fortune: The Blue Öyster Cult Story (2016)
Contents Under Pressure: 30 Years of Rush at Home & Away (2004)
The Top 500 Heavy Metal Albums of All Time (2004)
The Collector's Guide to Heavy Metal: Volume 1: The Seventies (2003)
The Top 500 Heavy Metal Songs of All Time (2003)
Southern Rock Review (2001)
Heavy Metal: 20th Century Rock and Roll (2000)
The Goldmine Price Guide to Heavy Metal Records (2000)
The Collector's Guide to Heavy Metal (1997)
Riff Kills Man! 25 Years of Recorded Hard Rock & Heavy Metal (1993)

See martinpopoff.com for complete details and ordering information.

Roll Of Honour

This page is dedicated to the kind souls who put their faith in this book ahead of publication. Wymer Publishing duly acknowledges you all for your support.